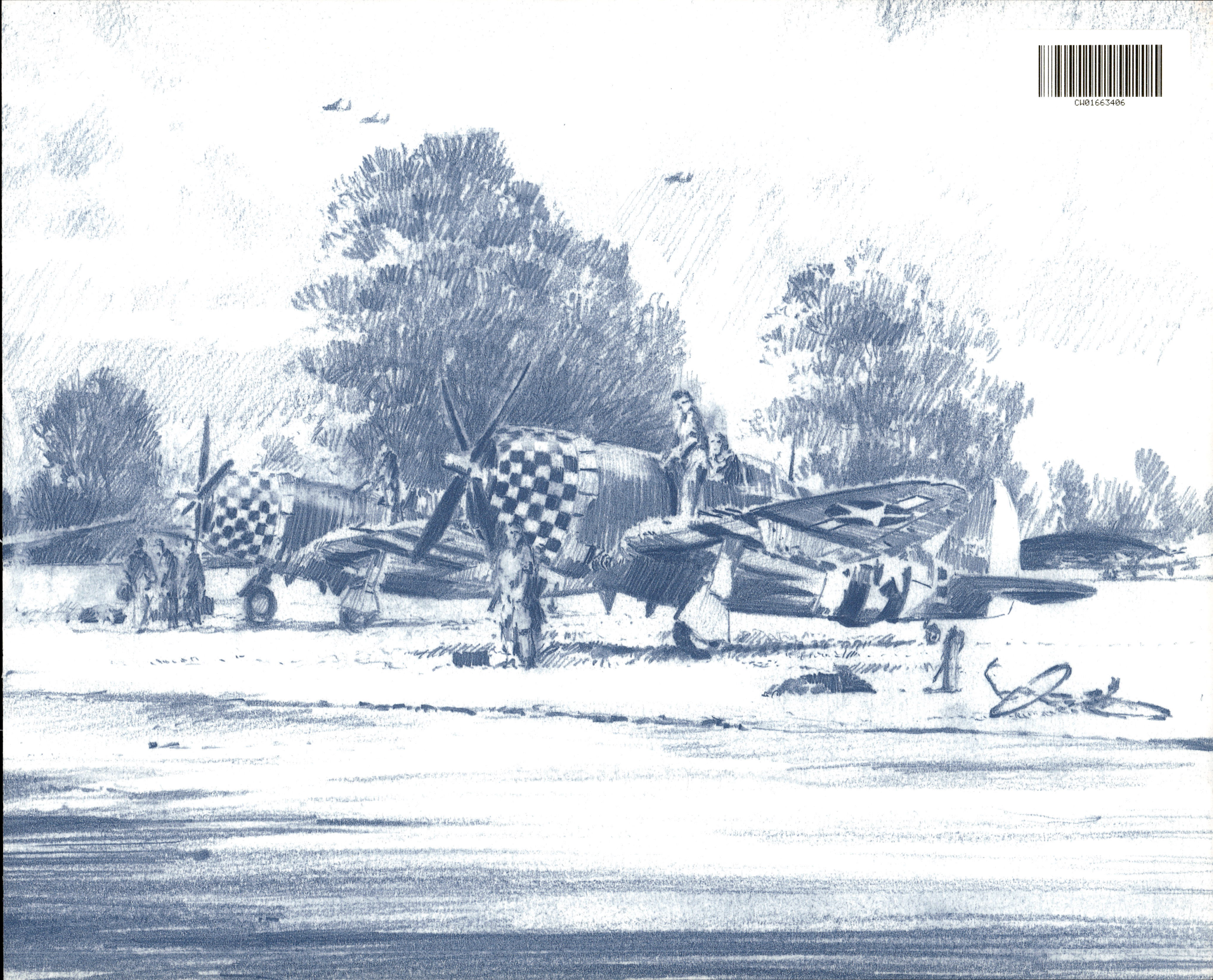

ROBERT TAYLOR

AIR COMBAT PAINTINGS VOLUME III

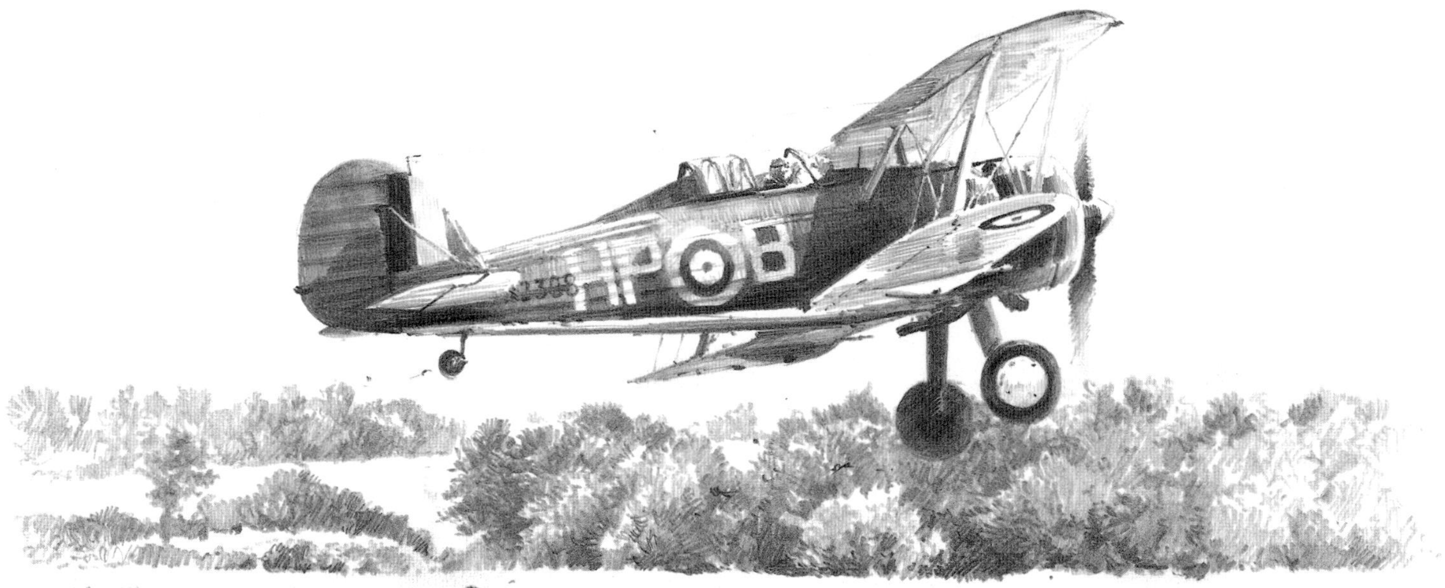

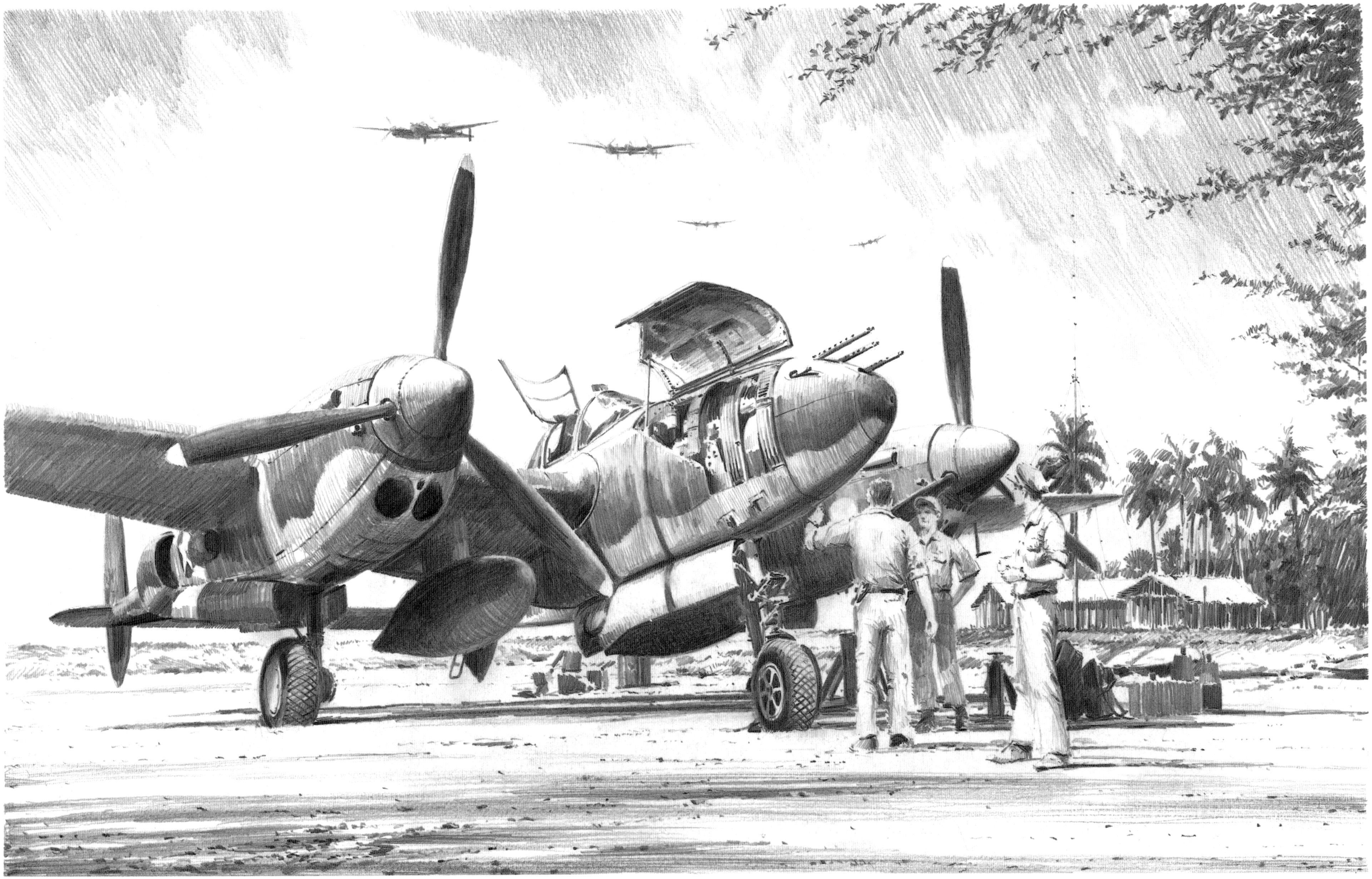

Maintenance crews make a P.38 Lightning ready for combat, Guadalcanal, 1943.

ROBERT TAYLOR
AIR COMBAT PAINTINGS VOLUME III

Charles Walker & Robert Taylor

FOREWORD BY

Wing Commander R. P. Beamont,
CBE, DSO, DFC, DL, FRAeS

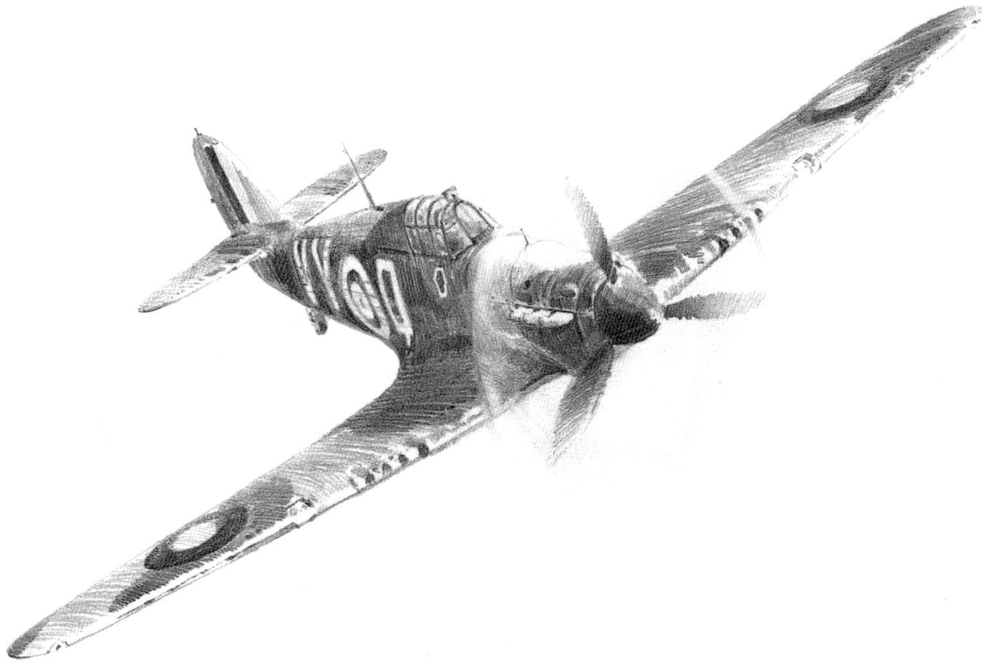

David & Charles

To Pat Barnard, and his superb team
at The Military Gallery

A DAVID & CHARLES BOOK

First published in the UK in 1996

A catalogue record for this book is available from the British Library.

ISBN 0 7153 0491 7

Printed in Singapore by C. S. Graphics Pte Ltd

for David & Charles
Brunel House   Newton Abbot   Devon

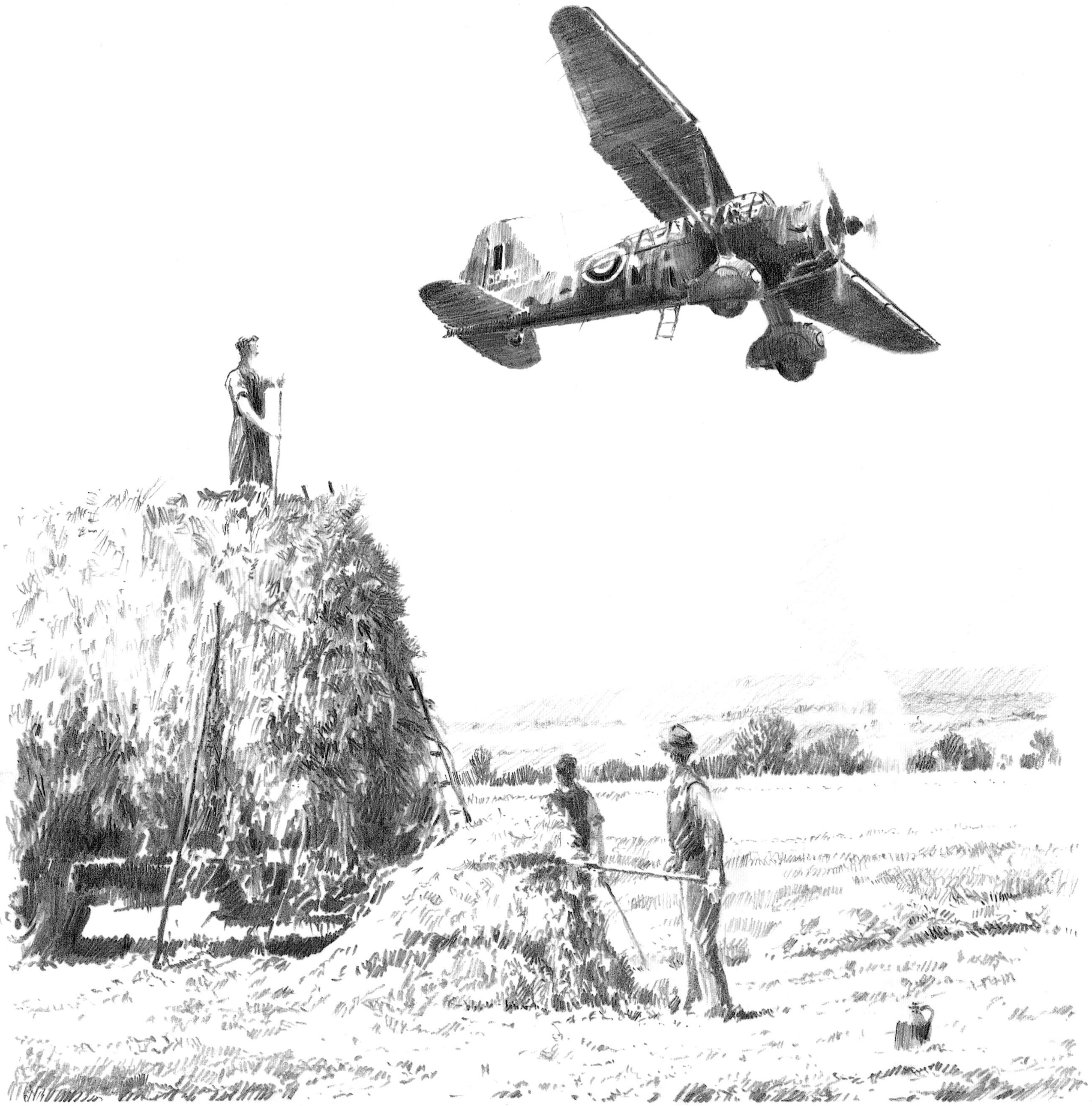

Publisher's Note

Despite the advances in metrication the world of aviation, and especially historical aviation, still reckons in feet, inches and miles. For those unfamiliar with this the following conversion factors may be useful. To convert feet to metres multiply by 0.3, inches to centimetres multiply by 2.54, and miles to kilometres multiply by 1.6.

CONTENTS

THE PAINTINGS

Introduced by the Artist

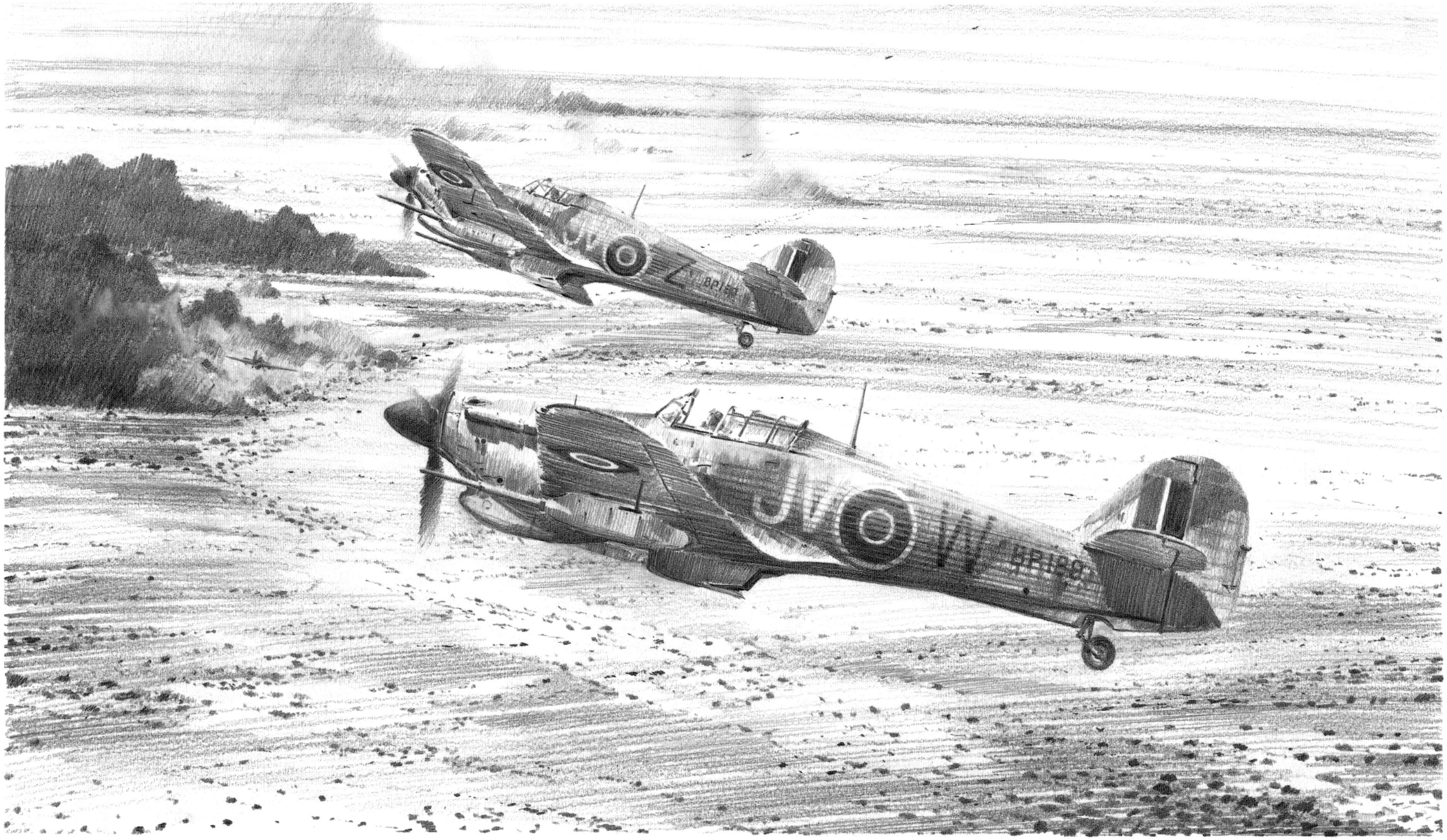

Tank Busters

Hurricane IIDs of 6 Squadron attacking German armour during the Battle of El Alamein. Oct 1942.

July 92. ©

FOREWORD

In the field of warfare, air combat is unique. Set against a stunning backdrop of glorious skies with clear clean air to the horizon in all directions, it has another unique quality - as often as not, it is all over in seconds!

In World War II fighter combat, sighting the enemy, judging the curve of pursuit into attacking position, the firing pass and then avoiding collision with the enemy could all take place in a head-on attack at closing speeds of 800 mph or more, and the total elapsed time from beginning to end could be measured in seconds. Seconds of intense concentration for the formation leader. How to attack - straight in, or with tactical manoeuvre round behind the enemy, or into the sun. Thoughts of the others in the formation and of how to ensure that the attack does not put them at unnecessary risk, and of course fleeting thoughts of self-preservation - how to make a good attack with a chance of fighting another day, so quickly check the sky behind!

Then the final concentration of aiming while fighting any turbulence or prop-wash from the enemy, ignoring any tracer fire from fighters or bombers which is probably not going to hit you if you can see it. This entire action can unfold in only 20 seconds from start to finish, yet all fighter pilots retain vivid memories like sharp still photographs of moments in these fleeting dramas.

Such moments present a huge challenge to the aviation artist, yet Robert Taylor rises supremely to that challenge. In 'Knights of the Eastern Front', for example, he has frozen brilliantly those seconds-in-time as JG52's Me109Gs slash head-on through a Yak 9 formation, in steel grey skies over Russia. An incident which mirrored for me an occasion in late 1944 over the Reichwald Forest, when effective radar controlling from both sides brought Fw190s into very high speed mutual head-on attack with my Tempests from Volkel - and lost one of their 190s in the process.

Such masterly skill is the hallmark of a great artist. In the first volume of his series of Air Combat Paintings, produced so successfully by Pat Barnard's Military Gallery, Robert set an exciting new standard in the world of aviation art; a standard which he repeated in his Volume II and which has never yet been excelled. Now in this new third volume he has exceeded all expectations.

Robert has an exceptional, and many would say, unique gift: not only to paint sky, land and seascapes of great beauty, but to put into them real aircraft in fluid, vibrant action.

To aviation people a picture of an aircraft with a slight fault in line or proportion can so easily detract from an otherwise beautiful painting; but Robert's infinitely painstaking preparation of his subjects establishes every significant factor in bringing out the character of his aircraft, together with prevailing weather, light levels, cloud formations and sea conditions, or when over land the subtly shifting colours of the seasons.

Few artists have succeeded in capturing so vividly the drama of air combat and the quiet bravery of some of the greatest names in aviation history.

This fascinating and lavishly illustrated volume is sure to delight his world-wide circle of admirers.

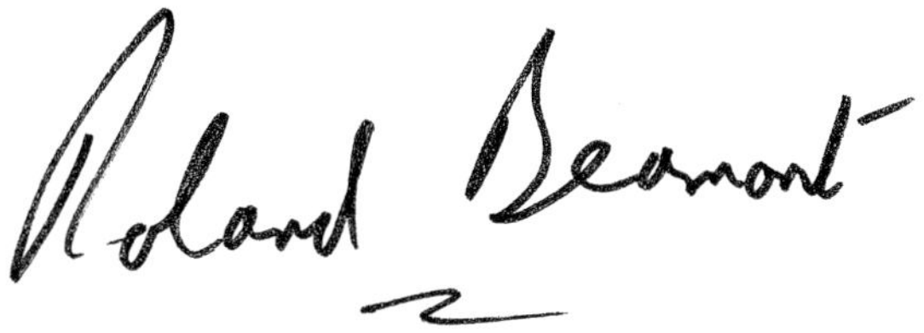

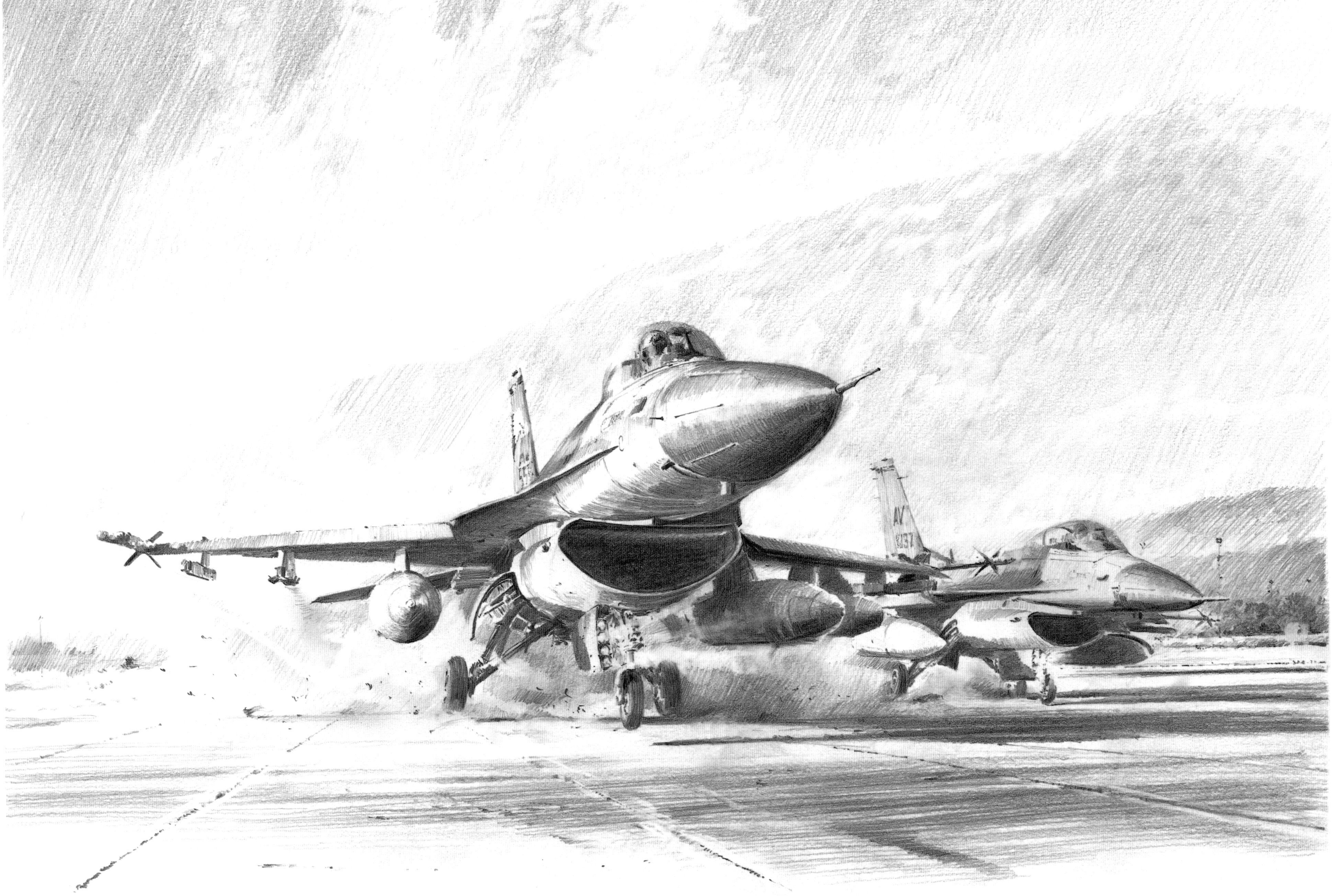

F16s of the 555th fighter squadron (Triple Nickel) begins to rotate from Aviano A.B. Northern Italy.
for a C.A.P. over Bosnia.

ROBERT TAYLOR

As a child, Robert Taylor was forever drawing. While other youngsters dreamed of becoming pilots, train drivers, soldiers and all manner of things small boys dream of, the young Robert Taylor had, from as early as he can remember, set his heart on becoming an artist. At school he had difficulty enthusing about any of his academic studies, his mind constantly wandering as he doodled designs of sailing ships and aircraft while others took copious notes on the subject in hand. Not that the young Robert Taylor was lacking in academic ability; it was simply that he was distracted by his all-consuming obsession. His ability to let his mind wander freely, such a vital attribute to the creative artist, was a natural instinct which was well developed at an early age, as any of his teachers would readily acknowledge.

Leaving school at the age of fifteen, he has never worked outside the world of art. After two years at the Bath School of Art he considered himself lucky to land a job as an apprentice picture framer at the oldest established gallery in the city. Framing the whole gamut of artistic expression – watercolours, miniatures, large oil paintings by professionals, even the humble efforts of the amateur – all gave him the opportunity to immerse himself in the world of art.

Soaking up every bit of information that came his way, he was soon completing watercolour paintings of his own, achieving a good enough standard to sell them in the gallery. His scenes of the famous Georgian city of Bath were popular with visiting tourists and, noticing the regularity with which the young Taylor's paintings were being purchased, the gallery owner moved his young picture framer into the restoration department where better use could be made of his talents. Now working with artists' brushes all day long, the young Robert Taylor at last felt he had taken an important step towards achieving his lifelong ambition of becoming a professional painter.

Picture restoration is an exacting art. It requires a deep understanding of the way each different artist has applied his paint, and the ability to emulate those techniques in such a way as to render the damaged area of the work undetectable. After a decade of diligence Robert Taylor was to become one of the most skilled picture restorers outside London, and today he attributes his great versatility to his years of painstaking work as a specialist in that field.

In the mid-seventies, after fifteen happy years at the gallery, Robert had the good fortune to meet Pat Barnard, a fine art print publisher whose business was coincidentally also located in the City of Bath. A mutual acquaintance had shown one of Robert's early oil paintings to Pat, who was impressed and invited Robert to bring him more examples of his work. The outcome of their meeting was a friendly business relationship that has lasted to this day, Pat's company, the Military Gallery, having published every print Robert has ever released. When offered the chance to become a full-time painter, Robert leapt at the opportunity, and within a few months of becoming a professional painter, he saw his first works in print.

Once he was painting full time, Robert noticed a rapid improvement in both his painting technique and the quality of his work. He was now painting only in oil, a difficult medium to master, but even at this early stage of his professional career, while still painting a wide variety of subjects, a noticeable style was beginning to emerge.

Greatly influenced by the colourful detail and accuracy of the Dutch maritime painters of the seventeenth century, much of Robert's early career was devoted to marine paintings. He exhibited regularly at the prestigious Royal Society of Marine Artists exhibitions in London, and his paintings came to the notice of, among others, Lord Louis Mountbatten, who became much enamoured with his work. This led to a number of commissions of naval subjects, including paintings for the Fleet Air Arm Museum, whose interest was naturally slanted towards aviation. Ironically, Robert's first aviation paintings were, as a result, commissioned for the Royal Navy!

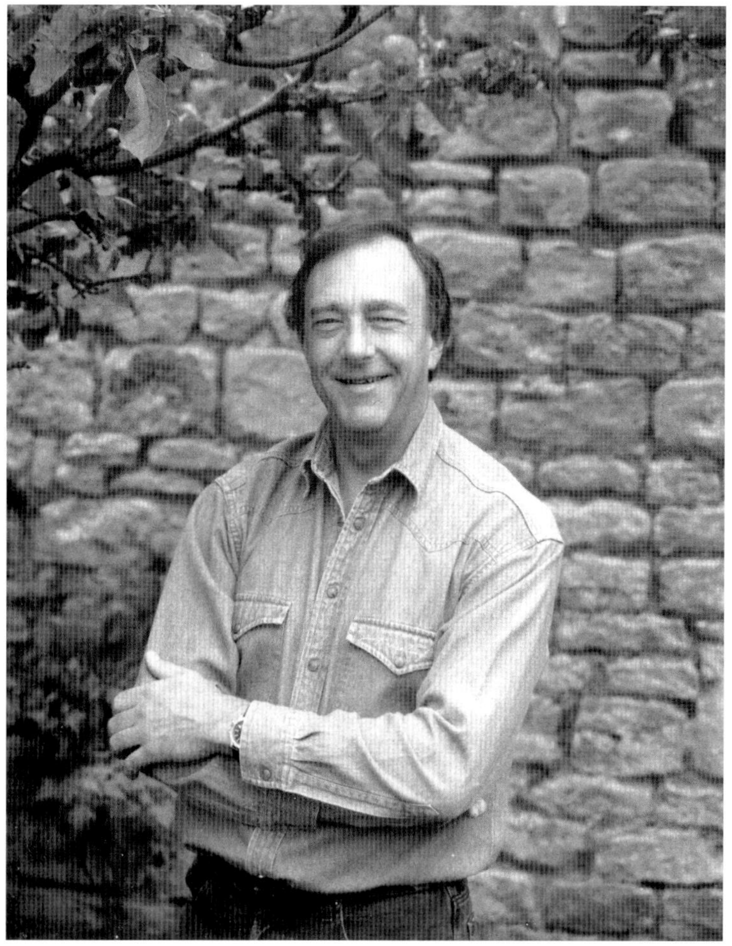

For the next decade and a half Robert Taylor was at the forefront of the emerging Aviation Art movement, gaining popularity literally all around the globe. His exhibitions included a one-man show at the Smithsonian's National Air and Space Museum in Washington DC, an art exhibition which to this day is quoted as the most popular ever staged at this prestigious museum.

In a professional career spanning almost two decades, Robert Taylor has continually pushed forwards the boundaries of aviation painting, while having much to do with its present-day recognition as an art genre. His integrity, creativity and inordinate talent have attracted legions of devoted admirers and collectors all around the world, making him one of the most successful painters alive today. But to me, one of his longest-standing fans, perhaps his most endearing quality is that he is much the same uncomplicated, friendly person I first met almost twenty years ago.

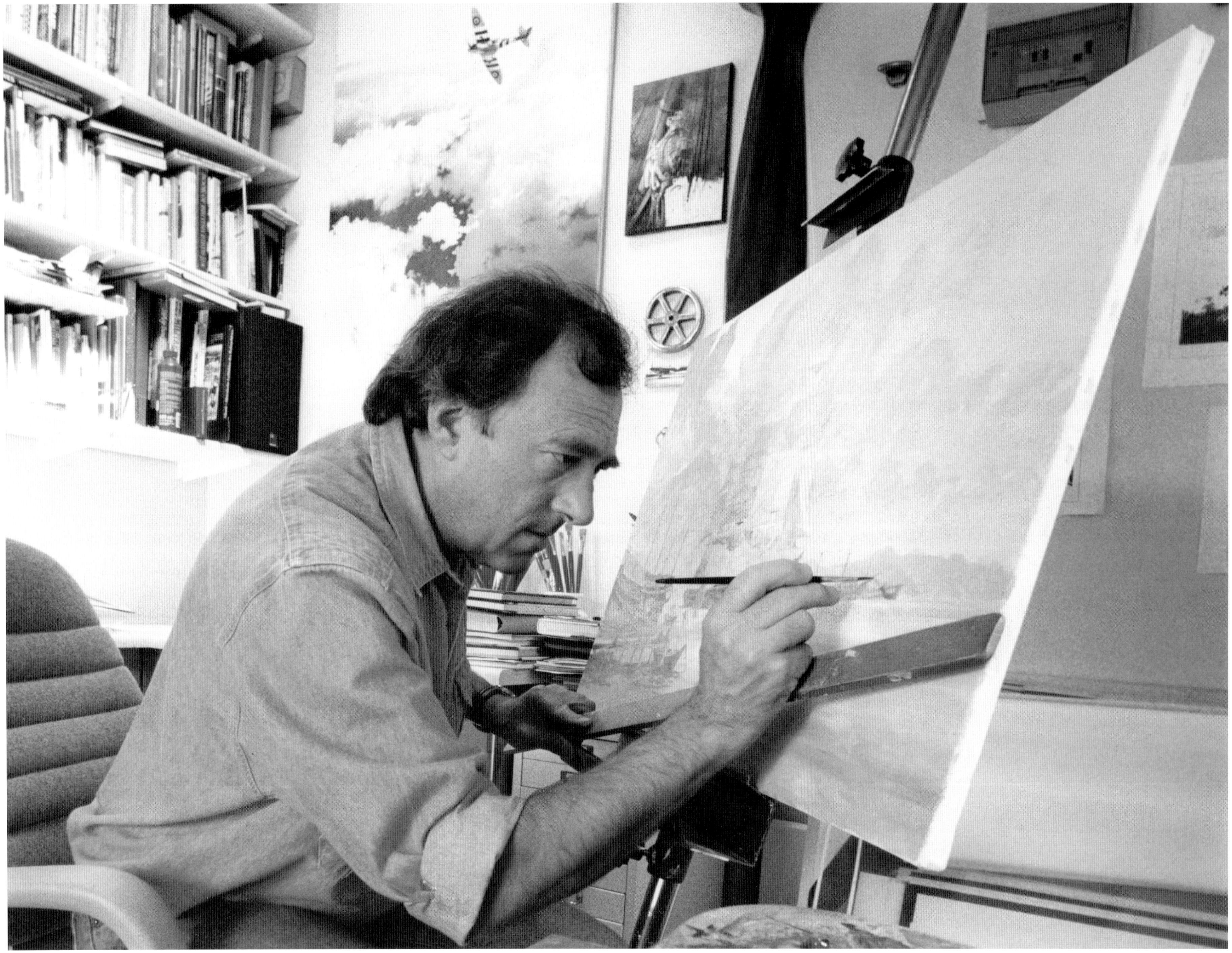

Photo: Tony Chandler

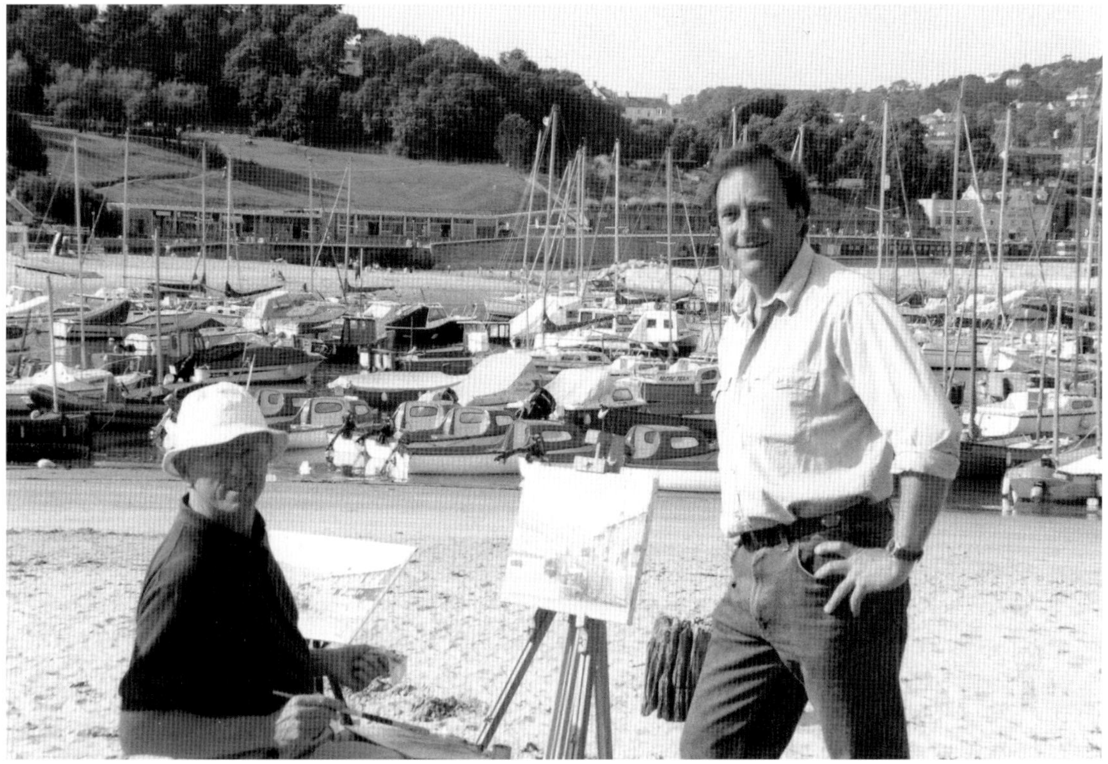

With marine artist John Stobart at Lyme Regis during filming of Stobart's Worldscape Series, *in which I briefly took part.*

INTRODUCTION

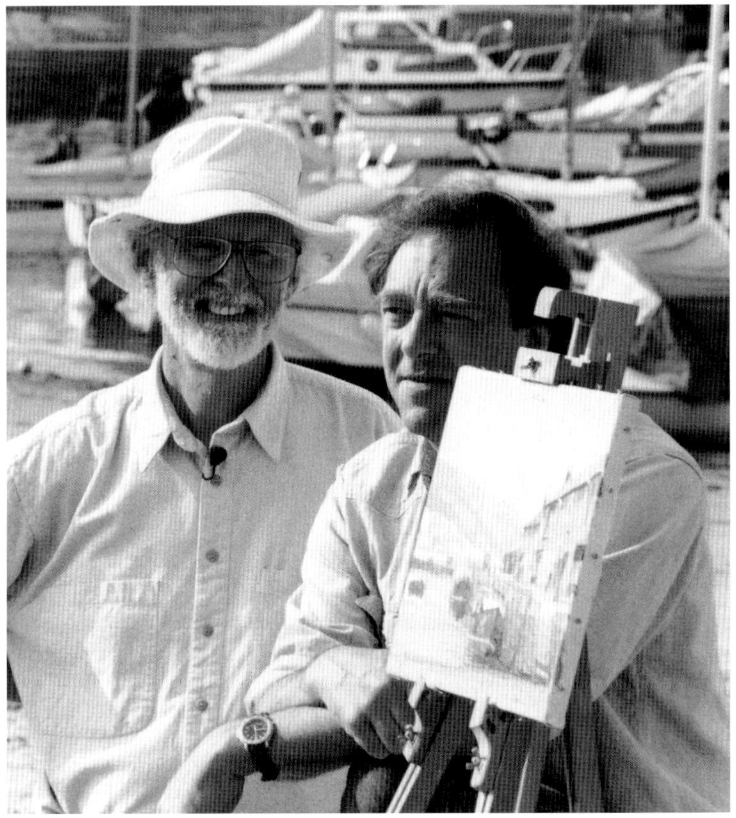

Discussing Stobart's plein air *painting with marine artist Bert Wright.*

When my publishers suggested to me that, since my biography has been written quite comprehensively in both my previous books of paintings, it should be somewhat shorter in this, the third volume, I immediately agreed. Little did I realise that they were going to suggest that I write a much longer Introduction instead! Being a painter and not a writer I tried to wriggle out of the onerous task, but when it was pointed out that the alternative was to give readers yet another long biographical section, I felt this should not be inflicted for a third time, and succumbed.

Not having a clue what I should write about, I enlisted the help of Charles Walker, who so expertly assists with my writing of the chapters about each painting. I put it to him that, as his task also involved writing the biographical section, he would now have more time on his hands, perhaps he could give me an idea or two?

'What are the questions people ask most?' he said. 'Well, mostly they want to know how I get inspiration for a painting, and how I get the initial idea onto the finished canvas,' I told him. 'Well, write about that,' he said. So here goes!

I have noticed that enthusiasts and art collectors are naturally inquisitive people. They have an insatiable thirst for knowledge about pieces of art they have collected, and this is both gratifying and flattering to an artist. When people express genuine curiosity and are appreciative of the subtleties of a piece of art, it makes the effort that has gone into its creation seem all the more worthwhile.

I am more often asked to describe the craft of making a painting rather than to talk about the actual image itself. How do I get started, how much paint do I put on the canvas, how much research is involved, whom do I talk to, how big are the original paintings, how long does it take to paint a canvas, do I paint every day or just when the mood takes me? Because I am aware of the interest in how a painting is developed, I have written about the most frequently asked topics in the chapters about the paintings. My musings here are of a more general and – according to Charles – rambling nature!

All artists have their own methods, routines and techniques, and I suspect that every one is slightly different from the next, but no artist will go anywhere until the *idea* comes. But how does one get ideas? Now there's a sixty-four thousand dollar question! In my case, every painting begins with a broad discussion with my publishers at the Military Gallery. Since virtually everything I paint is reproduced in print form I need to know the general direction in which we are all headed before contemplating anything else.

I get together with Pat Barnard, Michael Craig, Sean Whyte and other folk at the Military Gallery, and we chat about possible subjects in the most general of terms. Usually I will make a number of suggestions to set the ball rolling, and we sit around discussing scenarios, just broad ideas; we don't dwell on any of the details. From these informal discussions, which are always lively and good fun, come the general themes for paintings. We don't talk about anything visual at this point. I prefer to go away with just a broad concept in my mind so I can develop the image stage on my own.

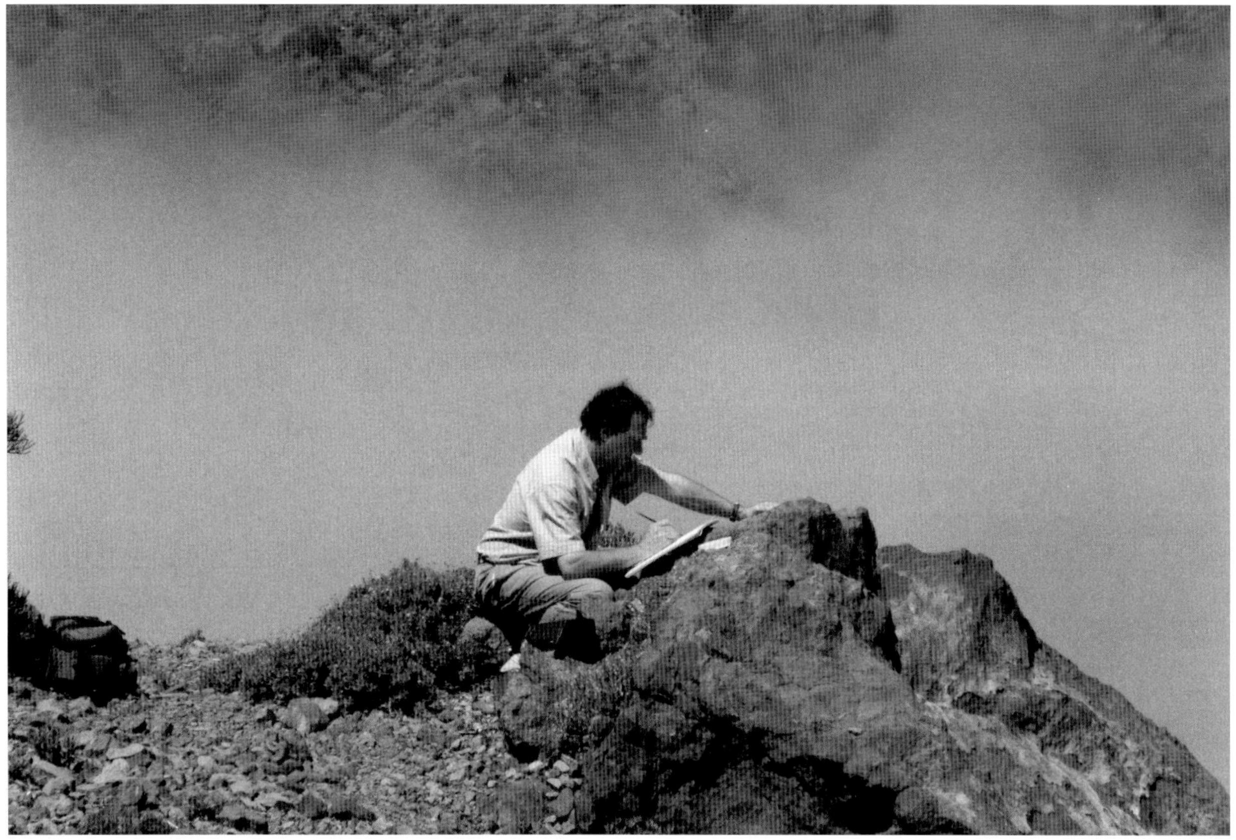

Making a watercolour sketch high in the mountains of Tenerife, an island off the coast of Africa.

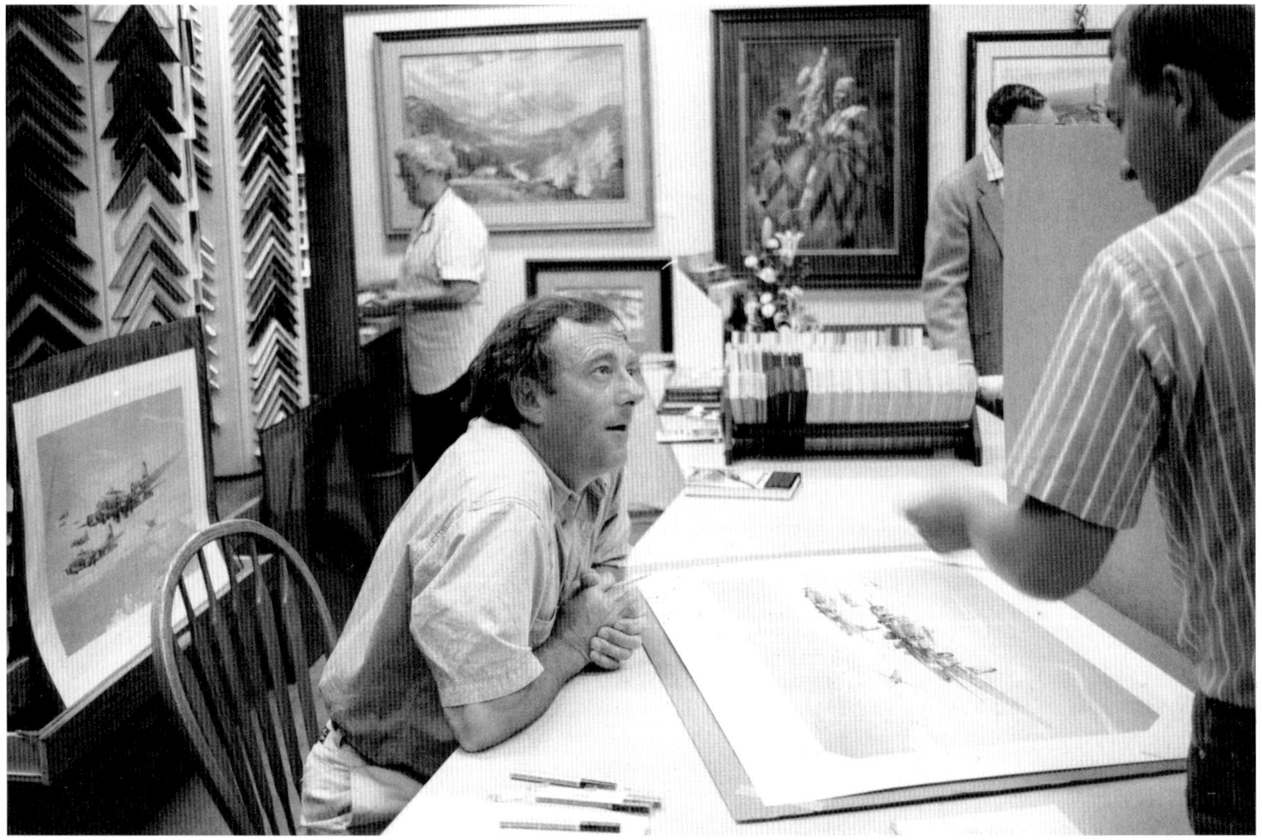

Signing prints and books for collectors at a gallery reception in California.

The process of coming up with an idea for a painting, for me anyway, is just a case of taking the subject generally, and letting the imagination wander. At this initial stage I don't discard any idea that comes to mind. I do lots of very rough sketches just trying out various compositions, and at this point I make no attempt to draw anything accurately. Sometimes the ideas will come quickly, but they require a lot of hard work.

I have a big collection of large-scale models of World War II aeroplanes which I find invaluable. When I know what aircraft type I am about to paint, one of the first things I do is study the model. Usually I play around with the fully painted replica under some strong lighting, sometimes in the studio, sometimes out in the sunlight; a glint of light off a wing, or catching a glimpse of an angle I had not previously thought about painting, will often stimulate the imagination.

There is no doubt that one of the best ways to come up with fresh ideas for paintings is to get out and about. Whenever I am travelling around I am looking for material for paintings, whether it may be some small item of interest or a complete landscape. I visit active air bases when the opportunity arises, and of course airshows are a great source of material for the aviation artist. I look constantly at the sky and the cloud formations, and above all, I watch the light. Visiting new places, and meeting and talking to others often produces a new perspective on old themes, or sparks a completely new idea.

Sketching outdoors is invaluable to the artist. For me it is also pleasurable, and even when I am on holiday I take all my drawing and painting paraphernalia with me. Sketching on location produces a spontaneity that is difficult to reproduce in the studio, but it is a wonderful way to record accurately little snippets which can later be incorporated into a painting. Though I paint only in oil, I make small watercolour sketches from time to time when out on location; these are visual notes for my own use, and not in any way finished pictures.

Some artists begin work on a new composition by putting paint directly onto the canvas without much preliminary work with the pencil; however, this isn't to say that they don't first put a great deal of work into the thought process. In my case I prefer to work with a lot of sketches before mixing any paint. This usually culminates in a fairly large finished drawing which, when I am satisfied with the composition, I transfer in outline onto the canvas. I do this using a number 12 filbert brush applying the paint fairly liberally, completely covering the canvas. When this is completed the painting will have taken on its basic form and is ready for the detailed work that follows.

The primary goal is always to feel enthusiastic about the composition and the subject of a painting. I believe an artist's mood, and the energy he puts into his work, comes through in the visual result, and it is this enthusiasm which brings a painting to life. Paintings are personal and to some extent idiosyncratic statements by the artist, and the significance of any art lies in its ability to communicate something of what the artist is thinking and trying to say. But before a painting can communicate anything, it must above all command attention, and it must attract, and hold an audience. If it is capable of doing this there is a chance that it may reveal the artist's message, and in so doing, entertain. That is the main goal.

It isn't hard to come up with ideas for paintings, but it is difficult to stay energised to the extent that one's paintings do not become predictable. When painting within the limitations of a single genre such as aviation art, particularly over a period as long as twenty years, it is important to keep experimenting in order to move forwards. All this certainly sharpens the thought process. As far as I am concerned, having completed hundreds of aviation paintings, there is an ever-increasing need to plumb the depths of the imagination to come up with fresh ideas, and ways to present them. But then, that is the challenge!

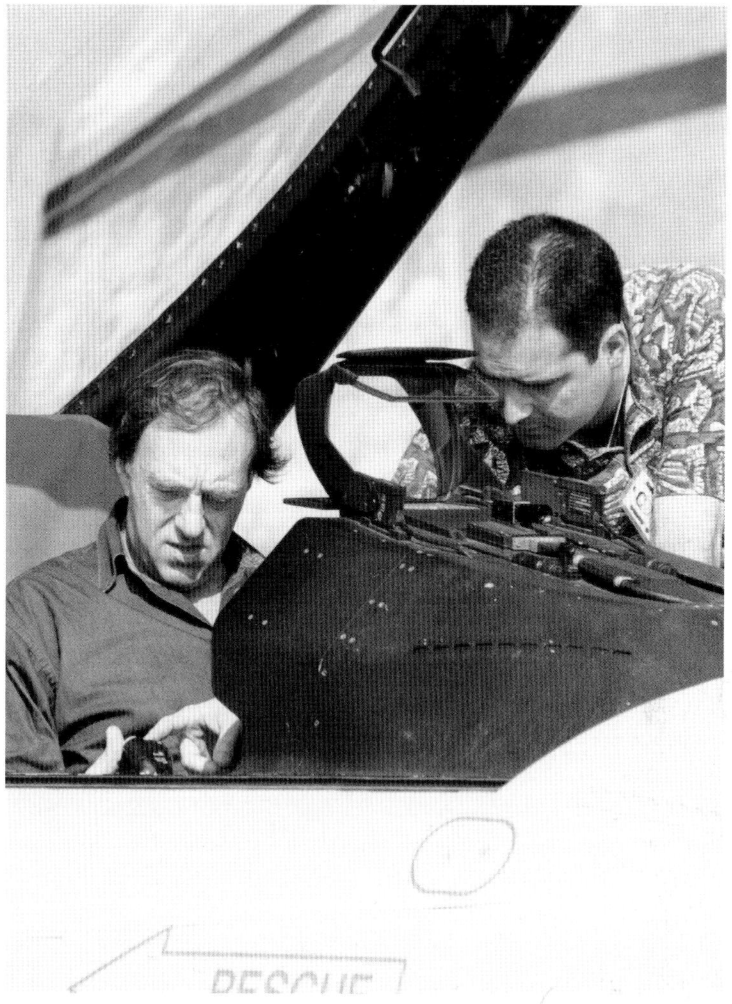

With Andy Uribe, a 555th Fighter Squadron F-16 pilot, at Aviano air base, northern Italy.

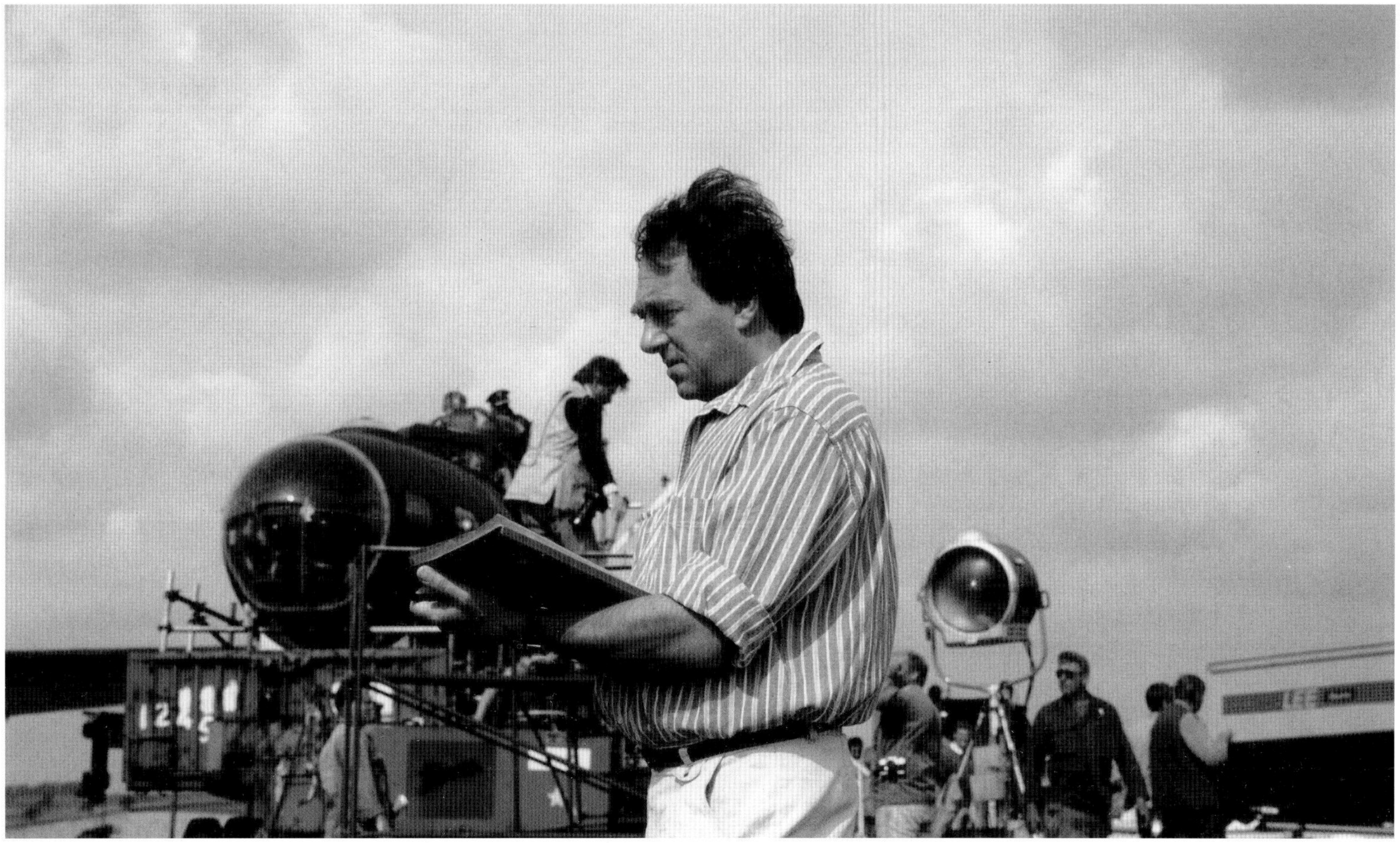

Sketching on the film set during the making of the Memphis Belle *at RAF Binbrook in Lincolnshire.*

At the beginning of my professional painting career I tended towards what today would be regarded as portraits of aircraft. But as time went by, my paintings became larger (most canvases measuring around 42 x 28in) and progressively more comprehensive in content. Then in 1986 I experimented with a picture featuring a Lancaster bomber on final approach to an airfield. Rather than painting the air base, I showed a rustic countryside location, making a feature of the haymaking scene in the foreground. Thus instead of the usual aerial portrait, this fairly comprehensively painted aviation picture showed the aircraft in an idyllic rural setting.

The response to that painting, *Early Morning Arrival,* more than to any other, influenced the approach and direction of my aviation art over the ensuing years. It appeared that there was, as I had hoped, a wider readiness to accept the more expansive type of aviation picture. Perhaps there might even be the possibility of trying to emulate in aviation art what the Old Masters had done for maritime art, with their complex and detailed paintings of ships and the sea back in the seventeenth and eighteenth centuries. It was a fascinating challenge and a course upon which I set sail.

I am asked a lot about the subject of research. Digging into the past can be fun, but more usually it is laborious, and often very frustrating. Because my paintings are attempts to recreate old battles or events from the past, there is an obvious and important need for information about them, and so careful research is an important part of the exercise. Research also helps with the creative process. The risk to the artist, however, is that the mass of detail which research turns up will invade and take over the painting, thereby destroying the creative input which is so vital to its energy.

Looking through the paintings chosen for this book, I am reminded of one of the most rewarding aspects of research: as I revisit each one I recall the happy conversations with many wonderful people – some no longer with us – whom through these paintings I have met and become friends with. I recall the enormous enjoyment each has given me during our conversations, and I am deeply appreciative of their friendship and encouragement. They are too many to name here, but they will not mind that. Their names are in any case etched into the history of aviation. Each and every one of them.

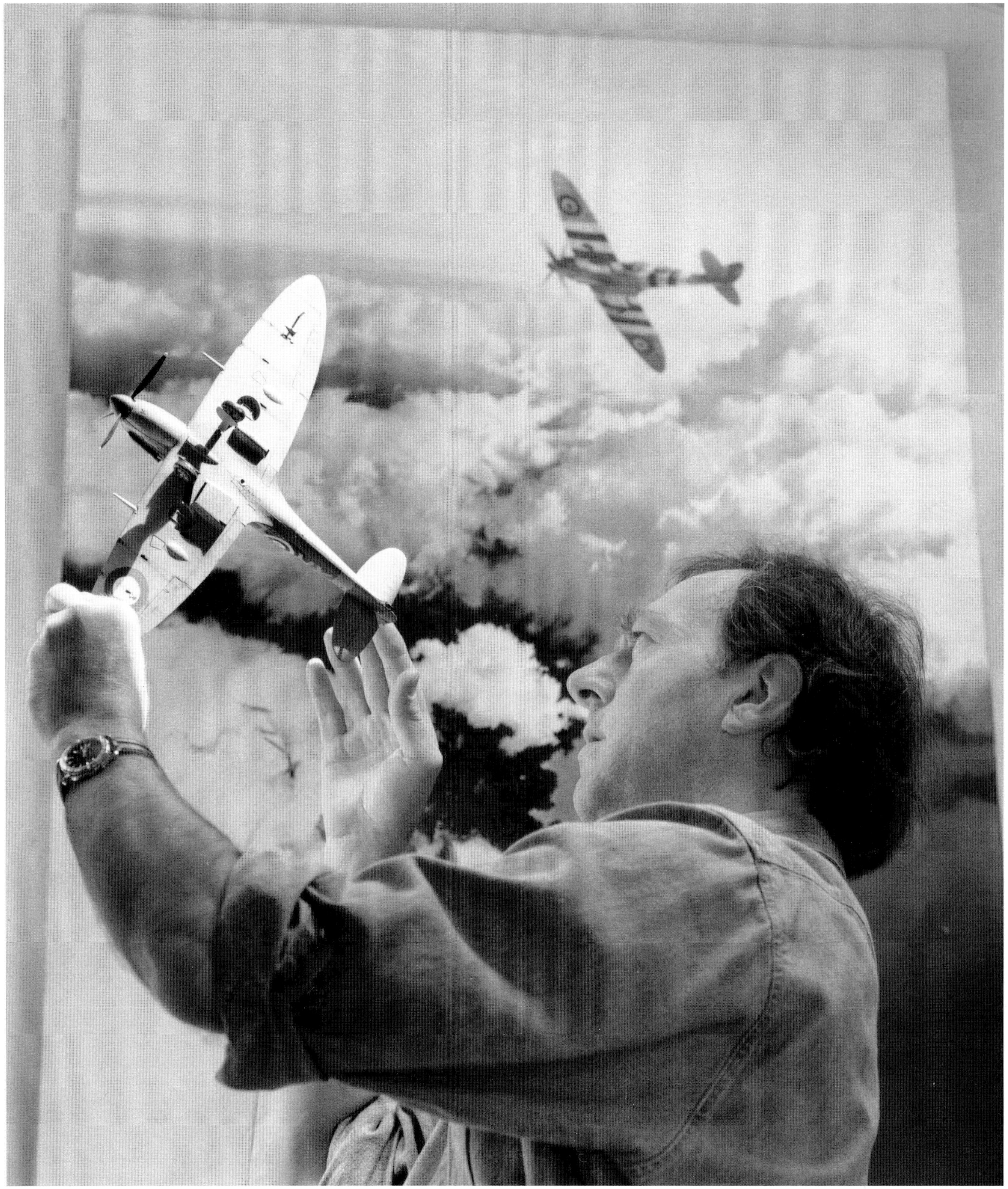

Photo: Tony Chandler

THE PAINTINGS

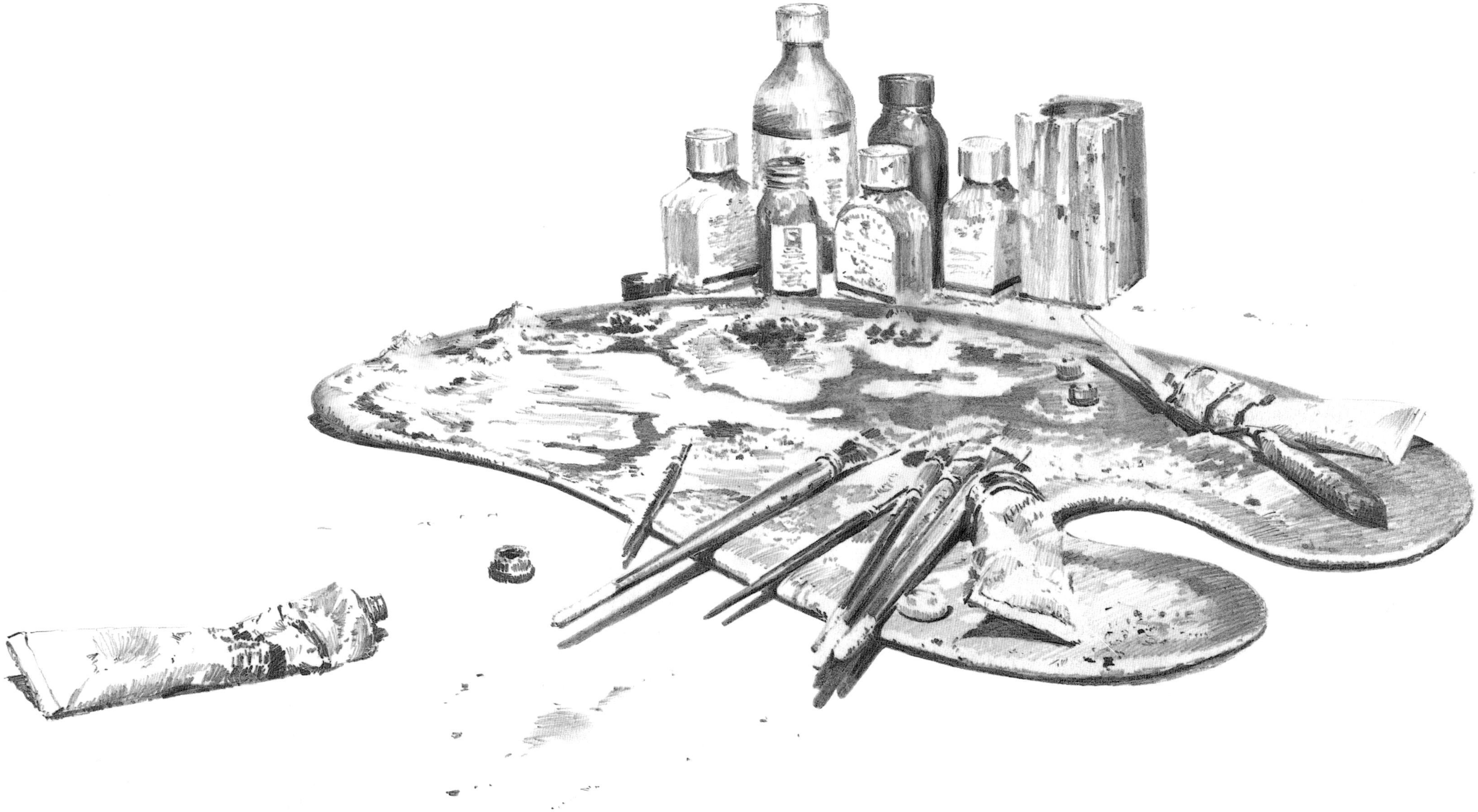

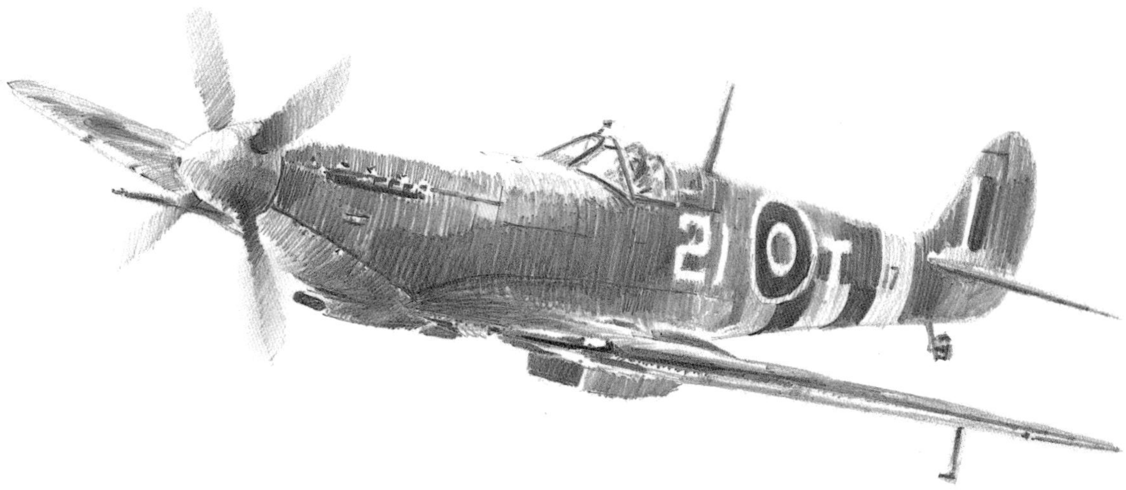

ESCORT FOR THE STRAGGLER

On 25 April 1945 the RAF despatched over 300 Lancasters to attack 'The Eagle's Nest', Hitler's private mountain-top castle at Berchtesgaden. It was a symbolic raid because the war was almost over, but it seemed appropriate that, after nearly six years of continual combat, crews of the RAF should be allowed this all but final gesture of the air war which had taken place in Europe.

After the Spitfires and Hurricanes of Hugh Dowding's Fighter Command had won the Battle of Britain and gained vital air supremacy, Arthur Harris's Bomber Forces were able to mount the systematic devastation of Germany's mighty war machine, which in turn paved the way for the D-Day invasion and the final liberation of Nazi-dominated Europe.

The Lancaster had become the mainstay of RAF Bomber Command, and its crews were typically representative of the men who had fought the six-year aerial campaign in Europe. Every one a volunteer, they came from Britain, Canada, Australia, New Zealand, South Africa, Rhodesia and many European countries under the threat of Nazi rule.

Magnificently brave, they endured overwhelming odds, frightening losses, and some of the worst flying conditions imaginable, never flinching in their task until victory was finally achieved. Their valiant efforts, together with the legendary exploits of the pilots of RAF Fighter Command, led the way towards victory in Europe.

Two aircraft, above all others, came to symbolise the deeds of the men and machines of the RAF: the Spitfire, magnificent in defence, lethal in attack; and the mighty Lancaster, the awesome heavy bomber that took the war to the heart of Nazi Germany.

It was against this background that I sat and considered how I should paint a picture that would in some way be representative of all these heroic deeds.

1995 saw the 50th anniversary of the end of World War II. Celebrations, parades, flypasts, official ceremonies and all manner of events were held in the cities and villages of the Allied nations which had participated; but above all it was a time of remembrance. My publisher commissioned a painting to mark the occasion, suggesting I produce a picture that would symbolise the men and machines of the Royal Air Force – leaving me to contemplate a task which, to begin with, I thought would be impossible.

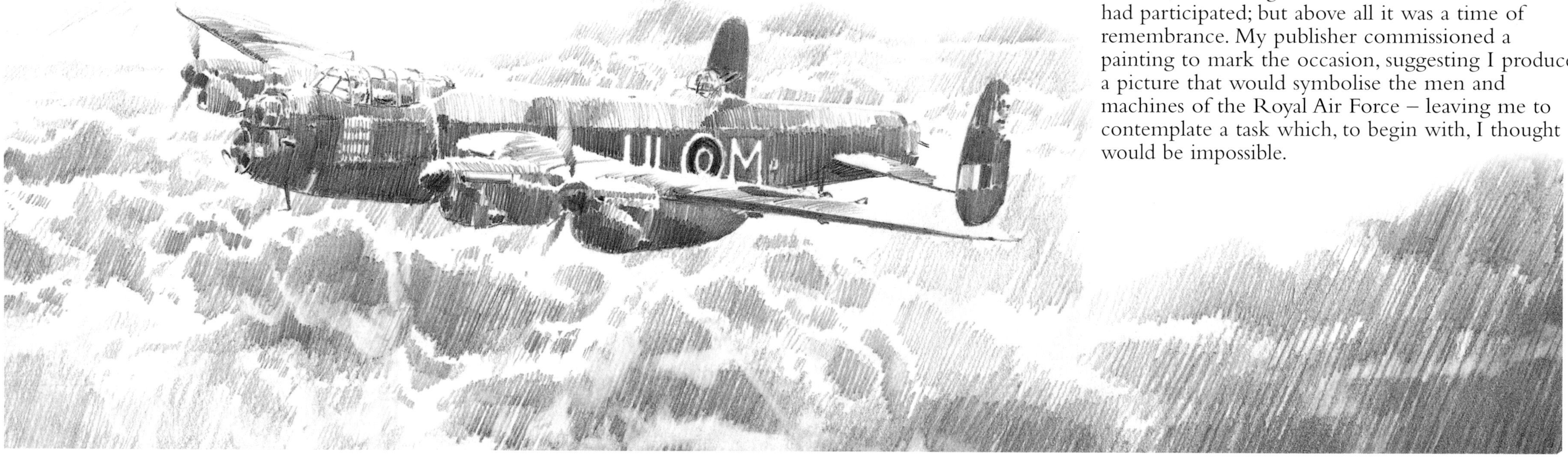

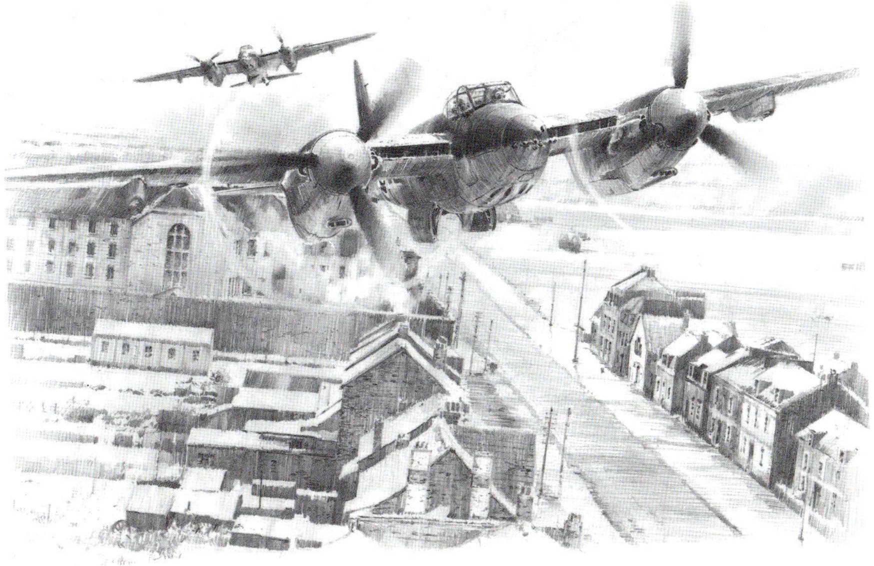

Ian McRitchie's Mosquito attacks the prison at Amiens, Feb 18, 1944.

Knowing I didn't want to paint one of those unrealistic, contrived pictures that contained almost every type of combat aircraft that ever flew, I had to come up with some other way of embracing all those magnificent men and their flying machines. Finally I concluded that it should be a real wartime scene, and that somehow I would need to inject into it both emotion and symbolism in such a way as to bring back fond memories for those who were there, and to remind those who were not of the dangers that the aircrews had faced throughout almost six years of continual conflict. *Escort for the Straggler* became that painting.

A group of Spitfires is seen escorting home a damaged Lancaster: UL-M2, flying with No 576 Squadron, has part of her rudder shot away and the mighty aircraft has fallen far behind the main force, an easy target for preying enemy fighters. Spitfires of No 504 Squadron have surrounded the struggling aircraft, providing protection and encouragement on the long journey home. Spirits revive as the friendly coast of England is crossed. Lancaster UL-M2, 'Mike Squared' to her crew, completed 140 operational sorties – more than any other Lancaster in RAF Bomber Command in World War II.

I painted this valiant group of aircraft as they flew majestically home in the early morning sun, fighter pilots and bomber crews together, emphasising the enduring bond of comradeship that in war proved itself to be invincible.

I made the first of two visits to Australia in 1995 in the month of February. I had painted two companion pieces to *Escort for the Straggler*, one depicting Mosquitos of No 464 Squadron (shown on this page) which had contained many pilots from the Royal Australian Air Force, the second portraying Halifax bombers from No 6 Royal Canadian Air Force Group. Both were reproduced as companion prints to *Escort*, and I was in Sydney to attend, among other things, the signing of these at a reception at a local gallery.

The aircraft depicted in my painting *Mosquito Mission* is that of Ian McRitchie who led the second flight of No 464 Squadron (Australian) in the famous attack on Amiens prison. I met Ian at a superb reception which John Rayner had organised in Melbourne on my later visit to Australia in November. John, who owns The Aviation Art Gallery, had somehow persuaded Rolls Royce to remove all their fabulous gleaming motor cars from the main showroom, except one, which stood in the centre of a massive exhibition of my paintings and prints. I can't speak for Ian McRitchie, but I was impressed.

MOSQUITO MISSION

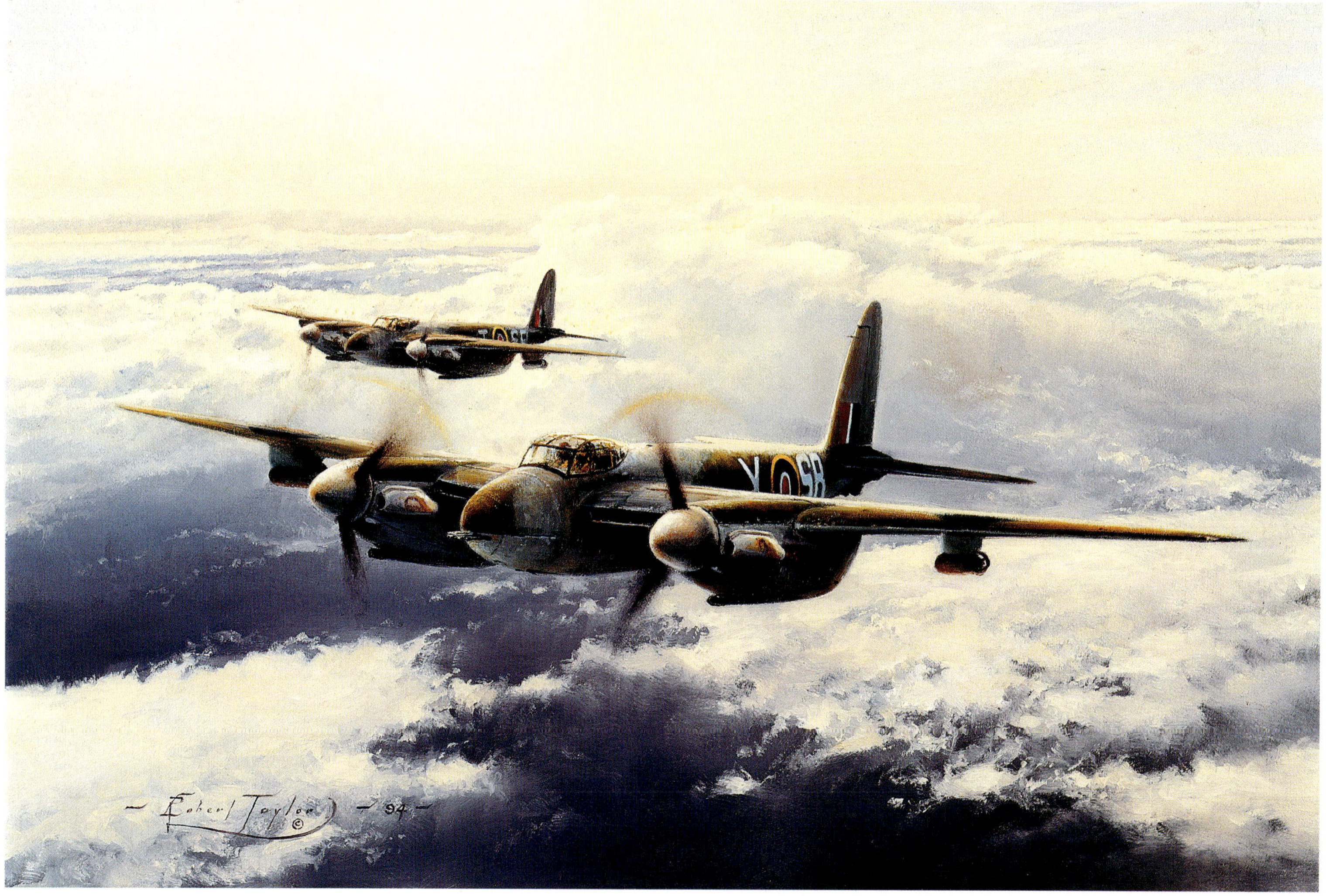

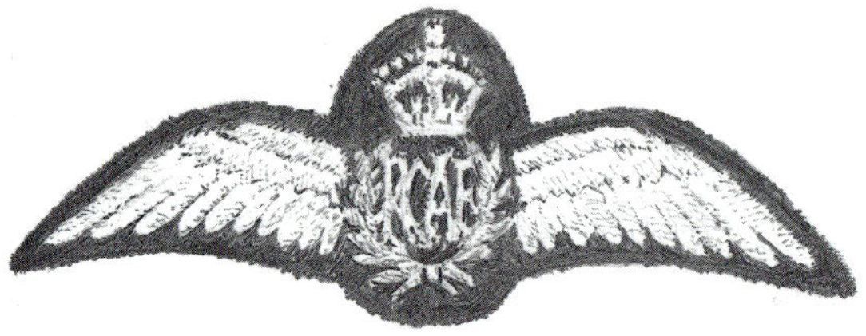

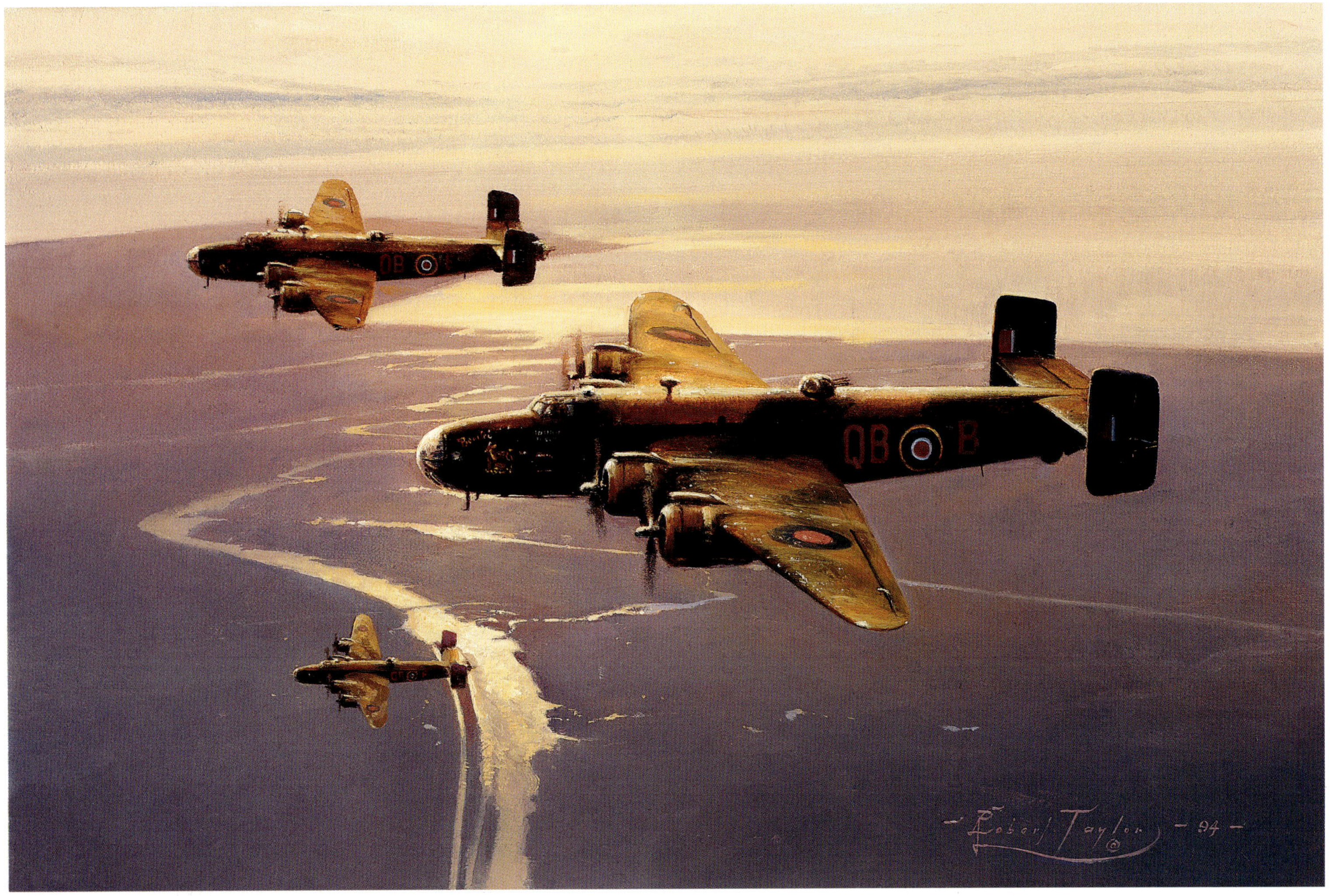

MAPLE LEAF HALIFAXES

The Canadian Bomber Group was unique in the annals of RAF Bomber Command in that it was made up entirely of Canadians. No 6 Group, Royal Canadian Air Force grew from humble beginnings to comprise no fewer than fourteen heavy bomber squadrons at its peak. The highly respected Canadian aircrews built a reputation of fearless determination and an astonishing record of success.

Formed in Yorkshire in 1942, they flew operationally until the end of the war, completing no fewer than 40,800 missions. In a single month during the period following D-Day the group's Halifax and Lancaster crews completed 3,740 operational sorties, dropping a greater weight of bombs than the Luftwaffe delivered on London throughout the entire war.

Headquarters for the group was situated at the huge Victorian castle at Allerton Park, and shortly following formation on the night of 3 January 1943, twin-engined Wellington bombers of 427 Squadron chalked up the new group's first operational mission, laying mines off the Frisian Isles. As the new, four-engined 'heavies' came into service, No 6 Group began equipping with Lancasters and Halifaxes, the Halifax bomber ultimately becoming synonymous with the Canadians.

The second companion painting completed for the *Escort* suite, entitled *Maple Leaf Halifaxes*, is illustrated on this page. These are Halifax BIIIs pictured returning over East Anglia as dawn breaks, following a raid over Germany during the summer of 1944.

I received a flattering letter from Canada soon after these prints were published. It is reproduced here, not to impress, but for the revealing remarks it contained appertaining to the thoughts and fears of aircrew as they flew into battle:

"Words can never express or describe my emotions upon seeing your painting Maple Leaf Halifaxes. *QB-B was my aircraft, and believe it or not, having checked my log book, I also flew QB-P and QB-E, the other two Halifaxes in your painting ... You have captured the true atmosphere to an uncanny degree. I keep gazing at the painting and can almost feel the crews' thoughts as we crossed the enemy coast: quiet excitement, fear, the tenseness of self-preservation and the desire to do a good job ... the whole gamut."*

Jack Dundas DFC, of 424 (Tiger) Squadron, the man who flew the three aircraft I had depicted, happily for me, acquired the painting. To know that my efforts with the brush can bring back such emotions is a humbling feeling.

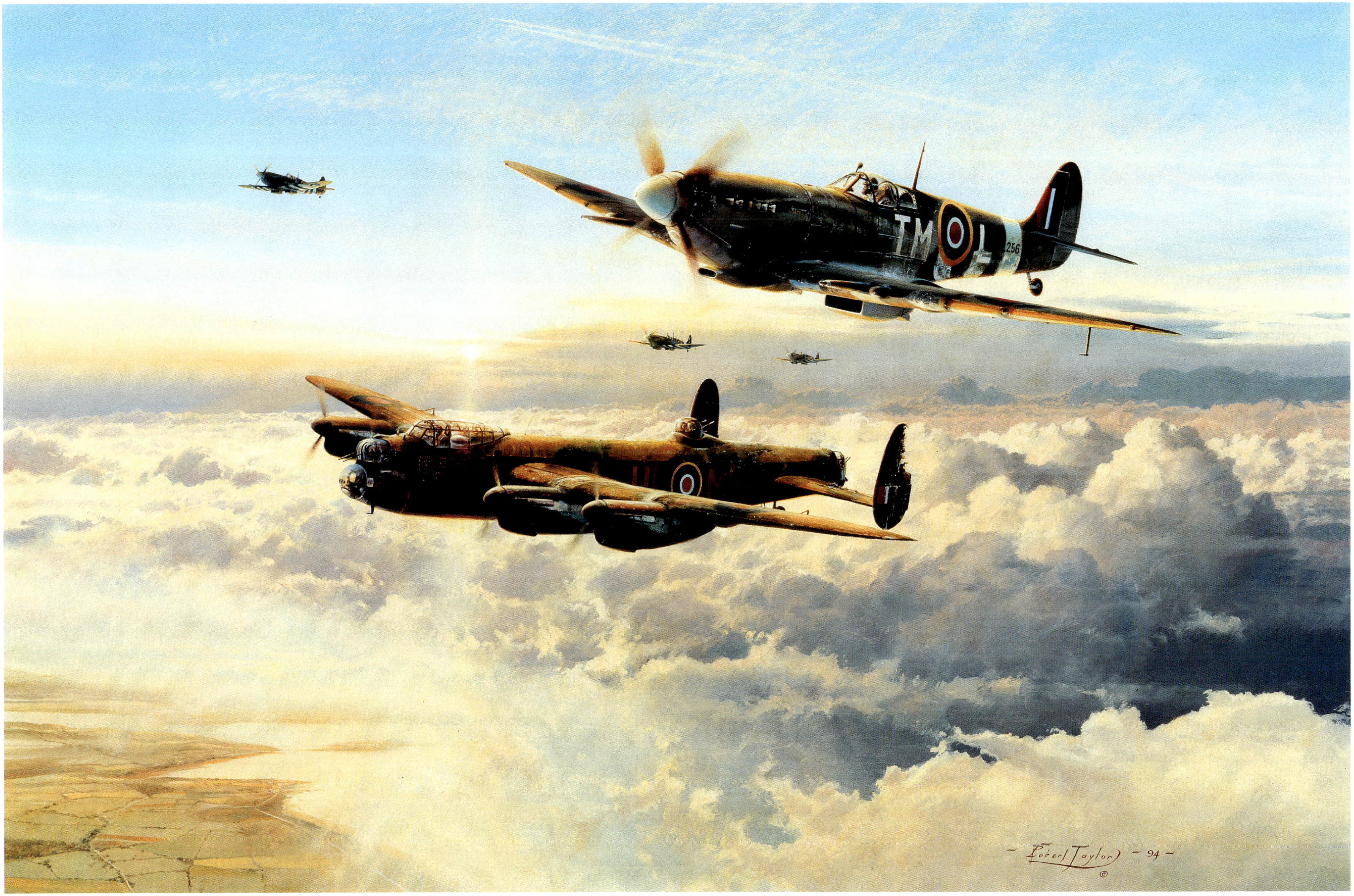

ESCORT FOR THE STRAGGLER

Private collection

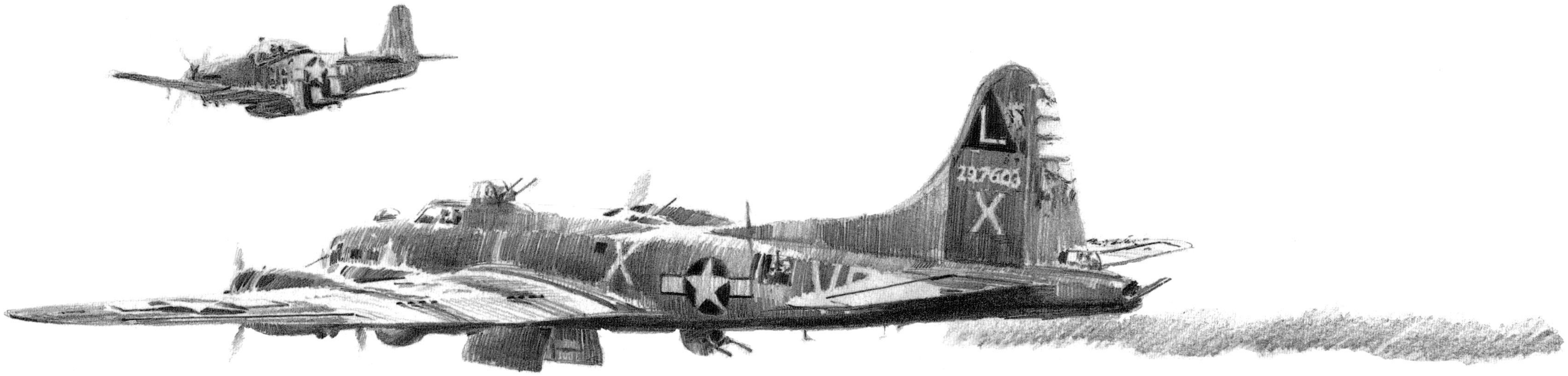

COMING HOME

The USAAF arrived in England with their brand-new B-17 bombers in 1942, and announced their intention of flying unescorted missions into occupied Europe in broad daylight. Flying their innovative Flying Fortress bombers, armed to the teeth like no other bomber had been before: that is how the B-17 was designed to be flown to war, and by heck, that is how were going to take them to war ...

The idea of sending large formations to bomb German installations in broad daylight, without fighter escort, sounded suicidal to the crews of RAF Bomber Command. They had tried daylight bombing during the early part of the war and had incurred devastating losses. Even when fighter escort could be spared, the well equipped fighters of the Luftwaffe had picked off the relatively slow machines like cherries off a tree. As a result the RAF had switched to night bombing, using the cover of darkness to afford at least some protection for their crews. As far as RAF crews were concerned, daylight bombing without fighter escort was not something to be attempted lightly.

The theory behind the B-17 concept was that bombers would fly in carefully designed 'box' formations, and that their fearsome firepower – machine guns were mounted from one end of the aircraft to the other – would enable them to repel any fighter attack the Luftwaffe could mount: the gunners would put up such a wall of flying lead that nothing would be able to penetrate their protective screen. It was a plausible idea. As with so many well laid plans, many unanticipated things arise between the drawing board and reality, and so it was with the saga of the B-17. When the aircraft first went into battle – or to put it more precisely, were first attacked by enemy fighters – the bomber crews found that great as their firepower was, it was no match for the agile German fighters, many flown by battle-hardened pilots with a couple of years' air combat experience under their belts. Like the RAF, they were quickly forced to change their thinking, and to their credit they did. It was not long before fighter escort was the order of the day.

In spite of its shaky start (and there is no denying the courage of those early B-17 crews), the B-17 Flying Fortress became America's most successful four-engined bomber, and today has become the symbol of the legendary USAAF bomber crews of World War II.

The B-17 was a truly beautiful airplane. Its streamlined fuselage gave it a graceful appearance almost too aesthetically pleasing for it to be sent into war. Yet it was the aircraft's 'accoutrements of war' that provided its special character. Bristling with guns it was an awesome sight, and slow and lumbering as it may have seemed to the pilot of an attacking Me109 or Fw190, it must have taken some courage to fly into the hail of bullets its gunners let loose when attacked.

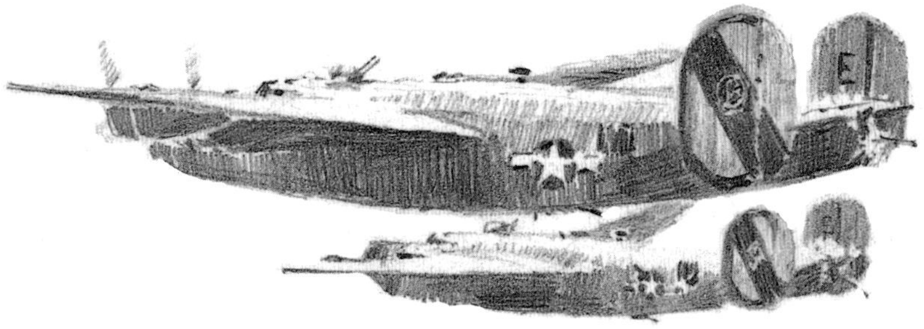

In 1992 more than 20,000 American Air Force veterans returned to England to celebrate the 50th anniversary of their arrival in Britain with the USAAF in 1942. I was commissioned to paint two pictures to commemorate that important anniversary, and it seemed natural that one painting should feature fighters and the other bombers. To me, the B-17 was clearly the aircraft to choose to represent the bombers – but such arbitrary decisions can lead an artist into very hot water.

'What about the B-24 Liberator?' I am asked; and, 'How come you artists always paint the four-engined planes? What about the B-26 Marauder? That aircraft had a better strike record than any other bomber in the US Air Force in World War II.' There are always good reasons for proposing different planes to represent the Air Force, but whatever those arguments, the fact is that as the Lancaster came to symbolise RAF Bomber Command, the B-17 Fortress became the symbol of the USAAF Bomber Groups that took part in World War II in Europe.

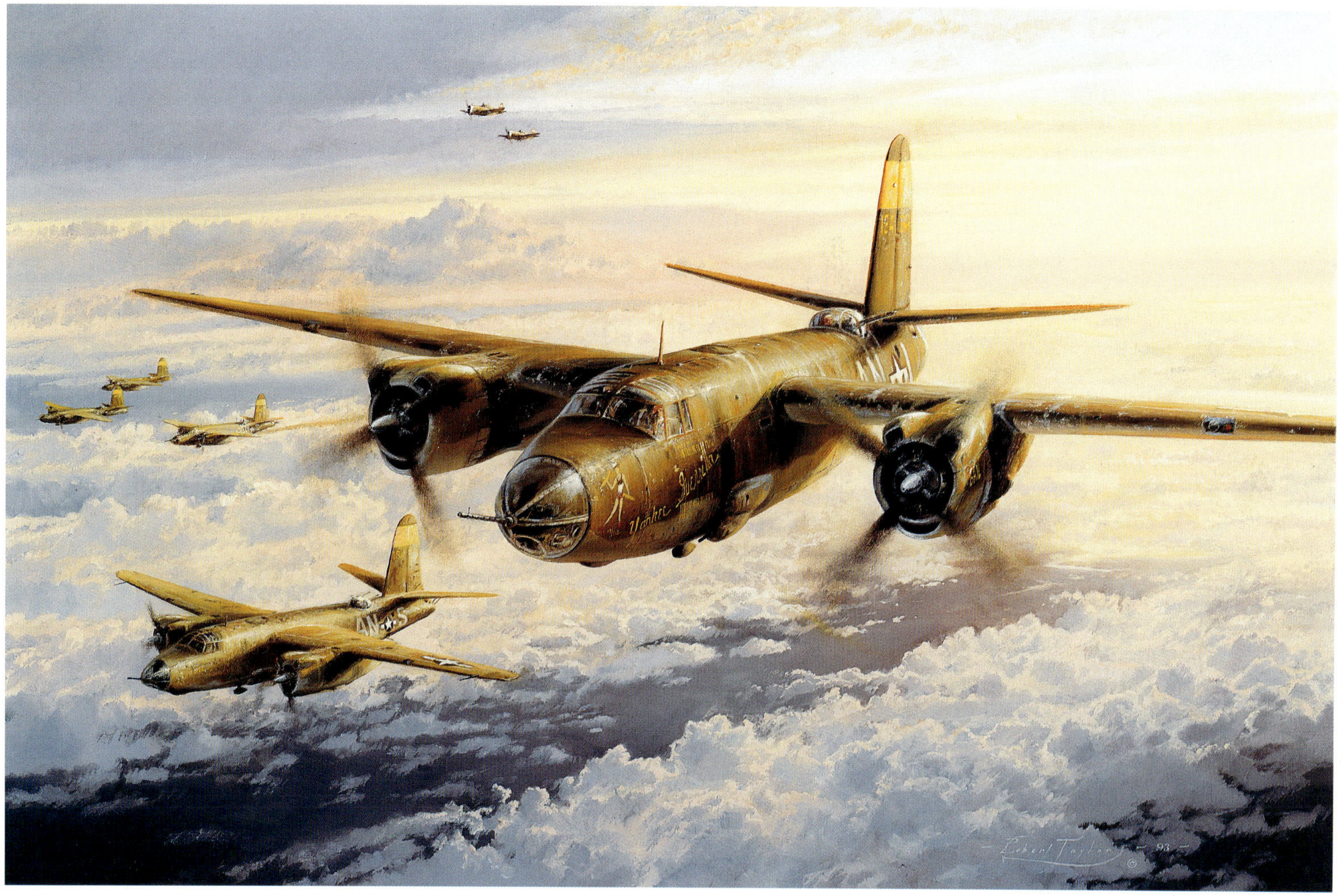

MARAUDER MISSION

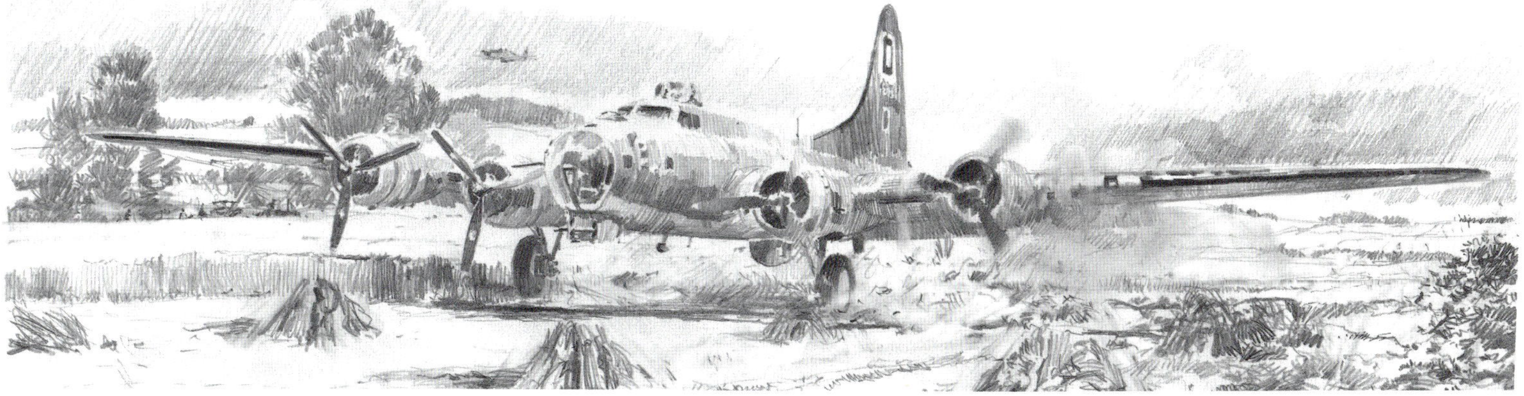

For this particular painting, as I saw it, the choice had long since been made for me by others: it would be a B-17.

Taking heed of all the foregoing comments, I decided to try to incorporate the B-24 Liberator into the painting; but before I did so, I needed to make sure that the two types *would* have returned from a mission together. A short telephone call to the Eighth Air Force guru Roger Freeman cleared away any doubts I may have had on this score.

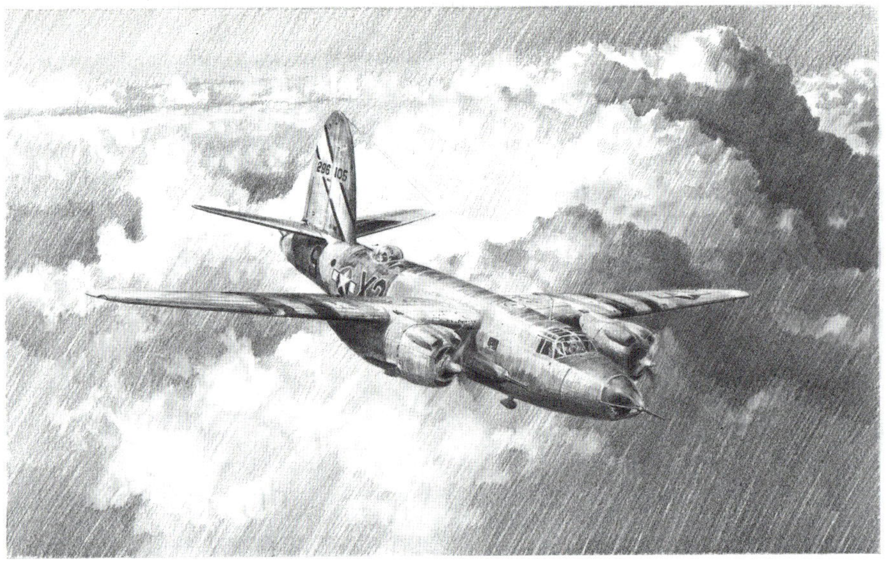

A B-26 Marauder of the 397th Bomb Group encounters heavy weather returning from an attack on the German V-1 rocket sites in the Pas de Calais.

The painting I finally conceived to commemorate the American Air Force's arrival in Europe in 1942 was *Coming Home*. In this painting I tried to evoke something of the awesome reality of the bomber mission by leaving a number of questions concerning the main aircraft in the picture unanswered. She is clearly damaged, but how badly? There is obvious damage to the tail section, but there are signs of more serious trouble. Though well into her journey home, the B-17's bomb doors still hang open, indicating that the tail isn't the only part of the plane to have taken hits. Are bombs still hanging in their racks which can't be released, and if so, what is likely to happen when the plane lands – if they are lucky enough to make it all the way back to base? Is that faint oil streak trailing behind the aircraft hydraulic fluid, and is it becoming increasingly difficult to handle? Is that inner port engine overheating, might the pilot have to feather the prop, lose power and drop out of the relative security of the formation? Are there injured aboard?

These were not the occasional traumas of war: these were life and death scenes enacted mission after mission by the bomber crews every day they went to war.

While endeavouring to capture something of this atmosphere, I also wanted to inject a good feeling into the painting – to try to get everyone rooting for that B-17 crew, and to indicate in some way that they would make it. In my effort to achieve this I painted a big, warm evening sky – a friendly sky, and I stationed a P-51 Mustang in close attendance just in case there were any of those nasty Fw190s still lurking about.

The painting to the left, *Out of Fuel and Safely Home*, shows another hazard crews sometimes faced at the end of a long, weary mission: the crash landing. Pilots were then glad enough to put down on the first piece of friendly soil, their tattered aircraft unable to go another mile.

OUT OF FUEL AND SAFELY HOME

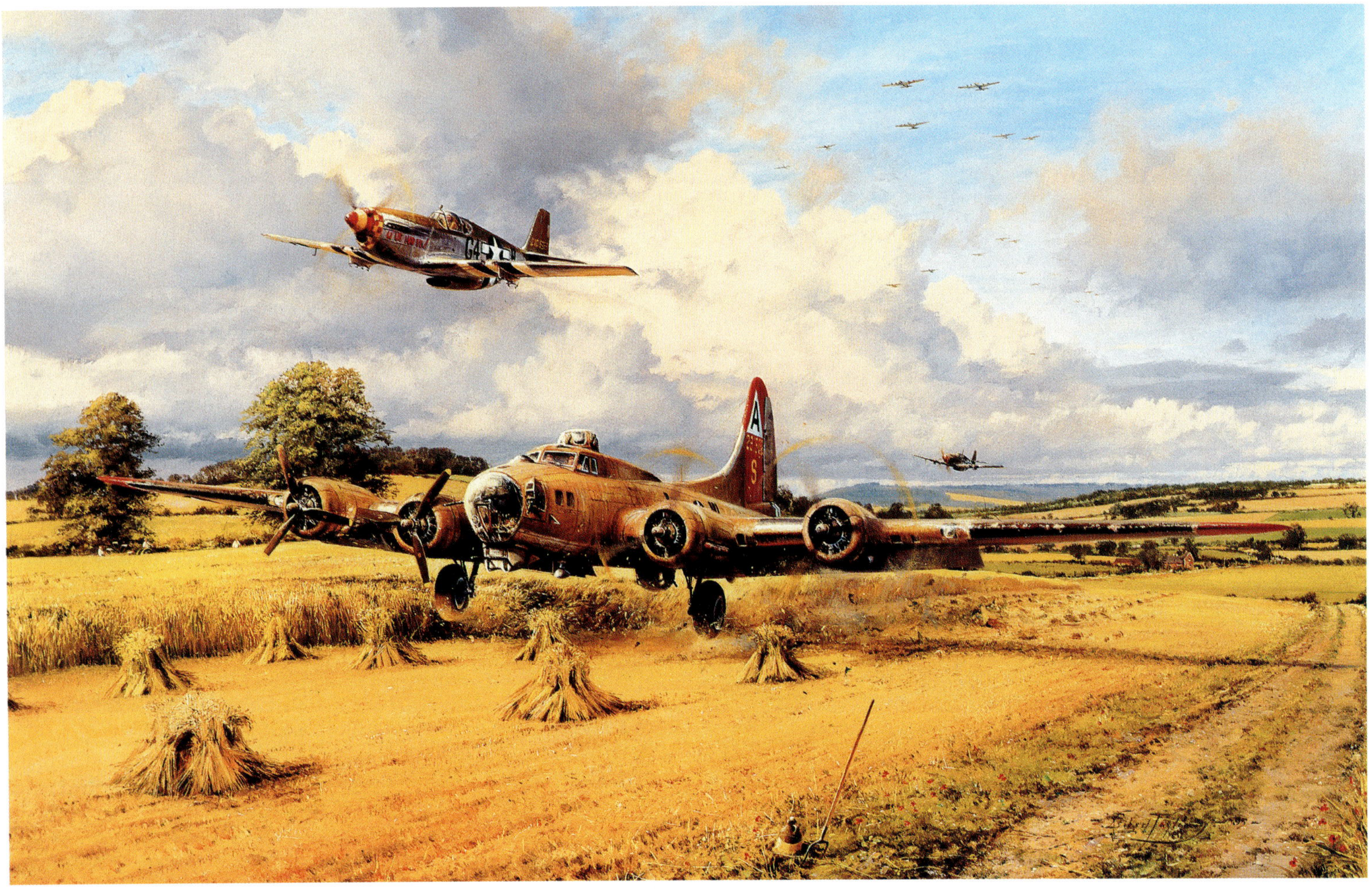

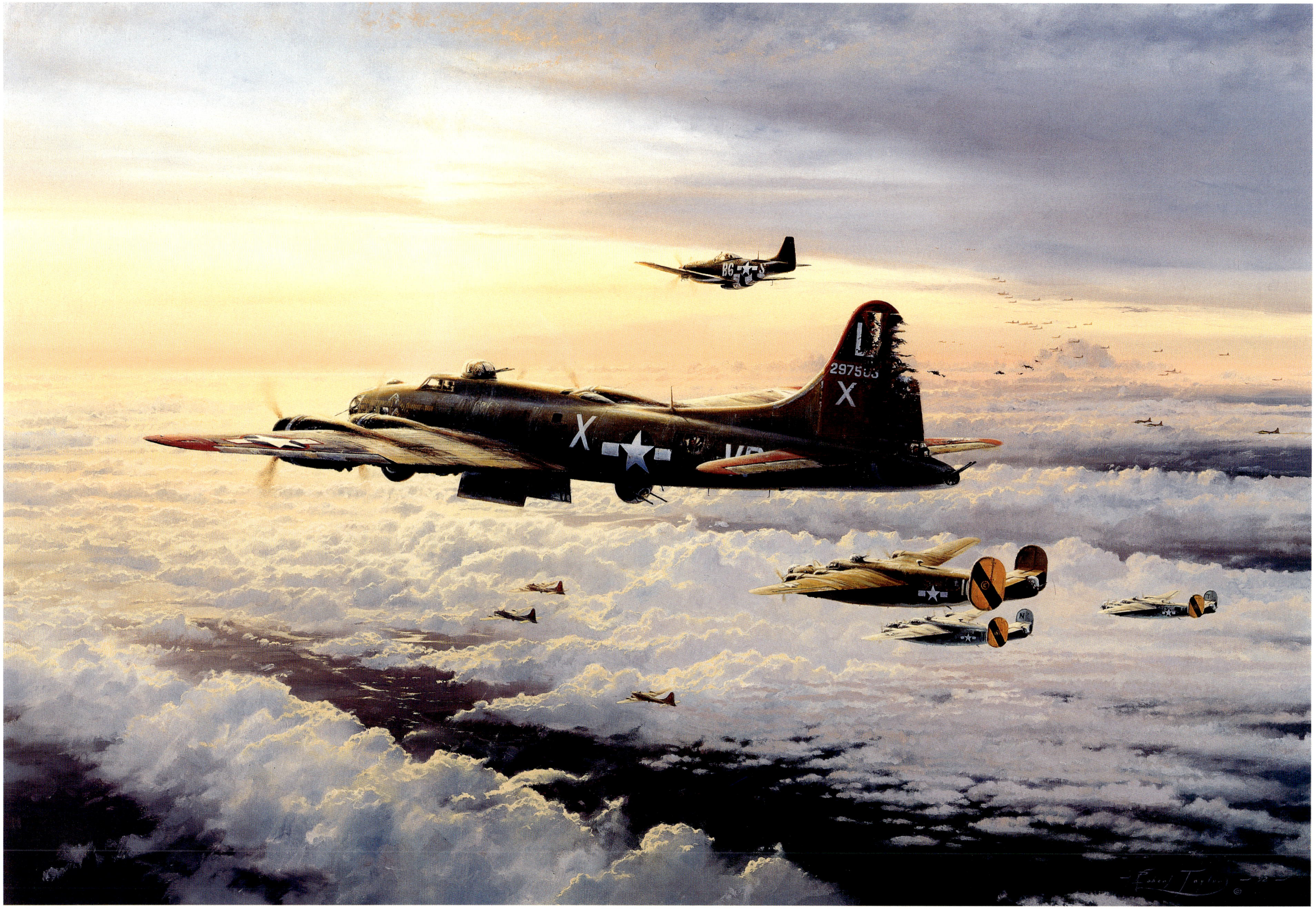

COMING HOME

In the collection of Mr Edgar Leicher

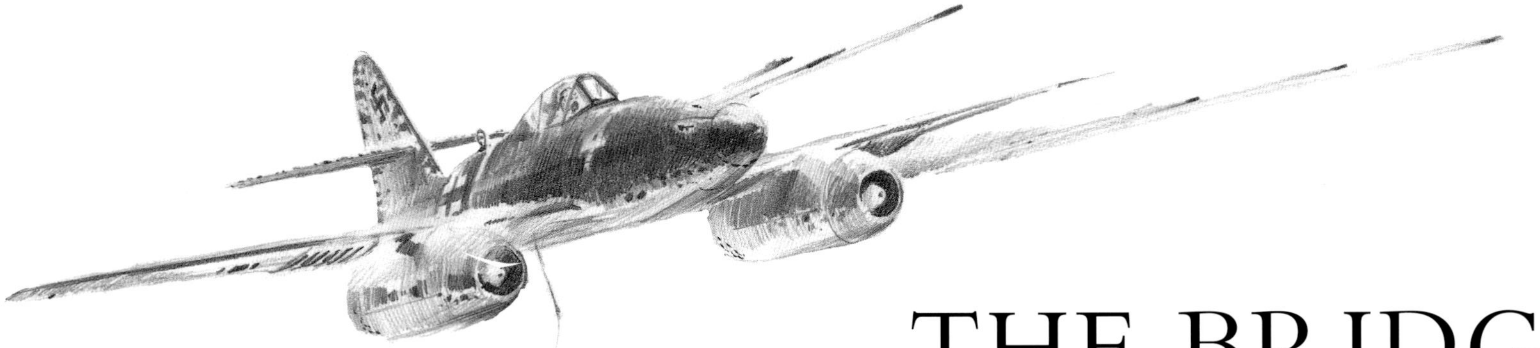

THE BRIDGE AT REMAGEN

The eighteenth-century royal portrait painter and first president of London's Royal Academy, Sir Joshua Reynolds, advocated that the artist must sometimes deviate from the strict historical truth in pursuing the grandeur of his design. He made the point that this is not falsifying the facts, rather a taking of poetic licence in order to strike at the imagination of the viewer. When attempting any painting it is our audience's imagination that we, as artists, are trying to stimulate, and unless we succeed in this we fail in our quest to entertain. Part of the entertainment for the viewer should come from his or her search for explanation, and from the resulting interpretation of the image before them. If an artist can provide the raw material for that exercise he will have accomplished something worthwhile.

In trying to recreate on canvas an event such as the attack on the bridge at Remagen, a present-day aviation artist has no option but to use liberal helpings of poetic licence in order to strike at the viewer's imagination. In fact he must employ every ounce of his own imagination in the first place, for the facts, the detailed visual facts (save perhaps a handful of hurriedly snapped photographs made at the time) are already lost in the mists of time.

To conceive any artistic concept which aims to evoke something of the atmosphere of those heroic long-ago days, and to do so in such a way that people might get some feeling of being there, is a challenge so daunting that if contemplated for too long, it might prevent most of us ever making that first mark on the canvas. The artist has but one chance to make his visual statement – he is allowed no accompanying words of explanation, no footnotes – it must all be said in one single visual image. It works, or it doesn't, and we stand or fall by the way we are able to translate what we see in our minds into something that touches the imagination of our audience. It is with such thoughts that one sits down to ponder how best an event such as the attack on the bridge at Remagen could be brought to the canvas.

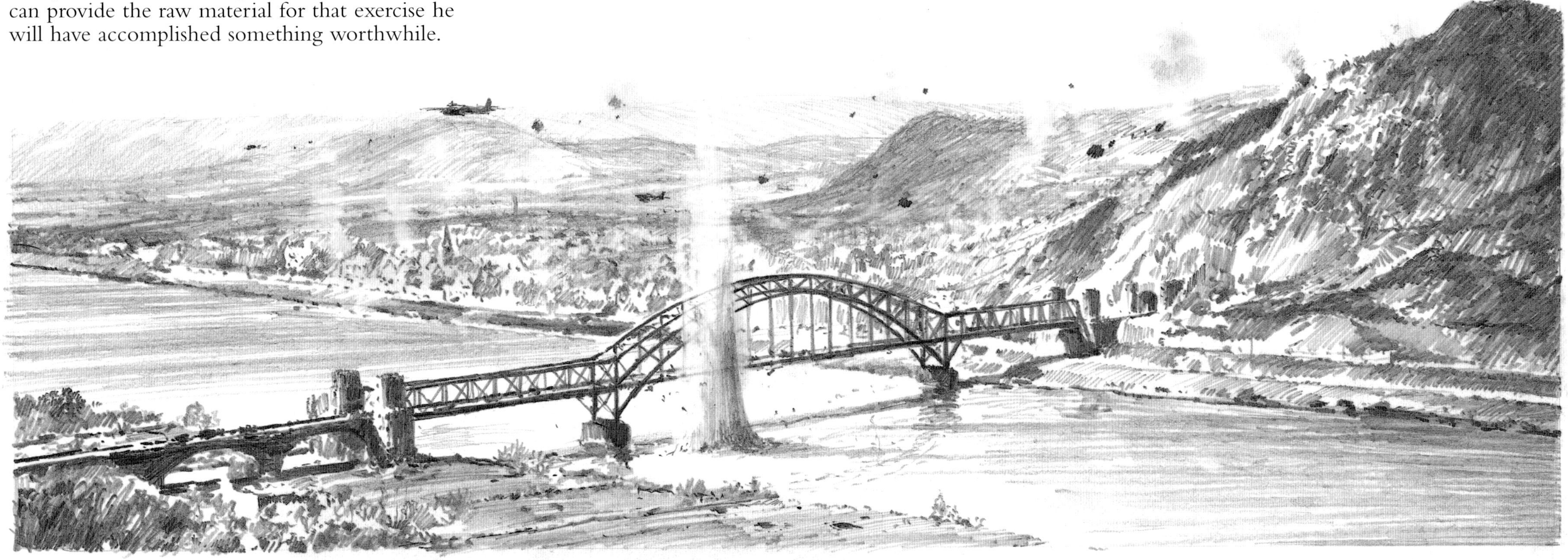

For my part I aim to immerse myself in the folklore, the legend of the event, in every way possible. This I do by reading everything that I can lay my hands on, sifting through what sparse contemporary photographs are available, talking to those who were there – although often their memories have faded with the passing of time – and above all, by letting my imagination run with all the material I have gathered. When pictures start to form in my mind I start to draw, small sketches at first, often on scraps of paper, backs of envelopes, until gradually the picture begins to take form. Once the overall concept has become clear the ideas start to come more quickly, and the project gathers momentum. But in the case of the Remagen painting, I had one problem which took me some time to resolve.

I had studied a number of photographs of the Rhine and the landscape around Remagen, taken at about the time of the famous battle for the bridge. I also obtained some good contemporary reference showing the contours of the surrounding hills and the shape of the river – some things don't change. What I was unable to find was enough good reference of the buildings, and since these were to feature fairly prominently in the painting, I had to set about solving this difficulty.

I had already decided the angle from which to view the attack on the bridge, and I didn't want to change this just because the reference material didn't seem to be available. The task I set myself wasn't an easy one: I obtained the earliest photograph I could find taken after the war, carefully eliminated all buildings which by their architecture had obviously been built after the war, and completely constructed via a large pencil drawing, a view of Remagen as it must have been back in 1945. This kind of exercise requires considerable detective work, is time-consuming, and requires a fair amount of imagination, but it is very satisfying.

The Me262 was a beautiful aeroplane, having an airframe configuration seemingly way ahead of its time. I am reminded of this repeatedly: my home is right under the flightpath on the approach to Bristol international airport, though fortunately about 15 miles distant so noise is not a bother. Watching aircraft pass overhead I frequently notice the shape similarity of some of the smaller jetliners with that of the Me262, designed half a century earlier.

STORMBIRDS OVER THE REICH

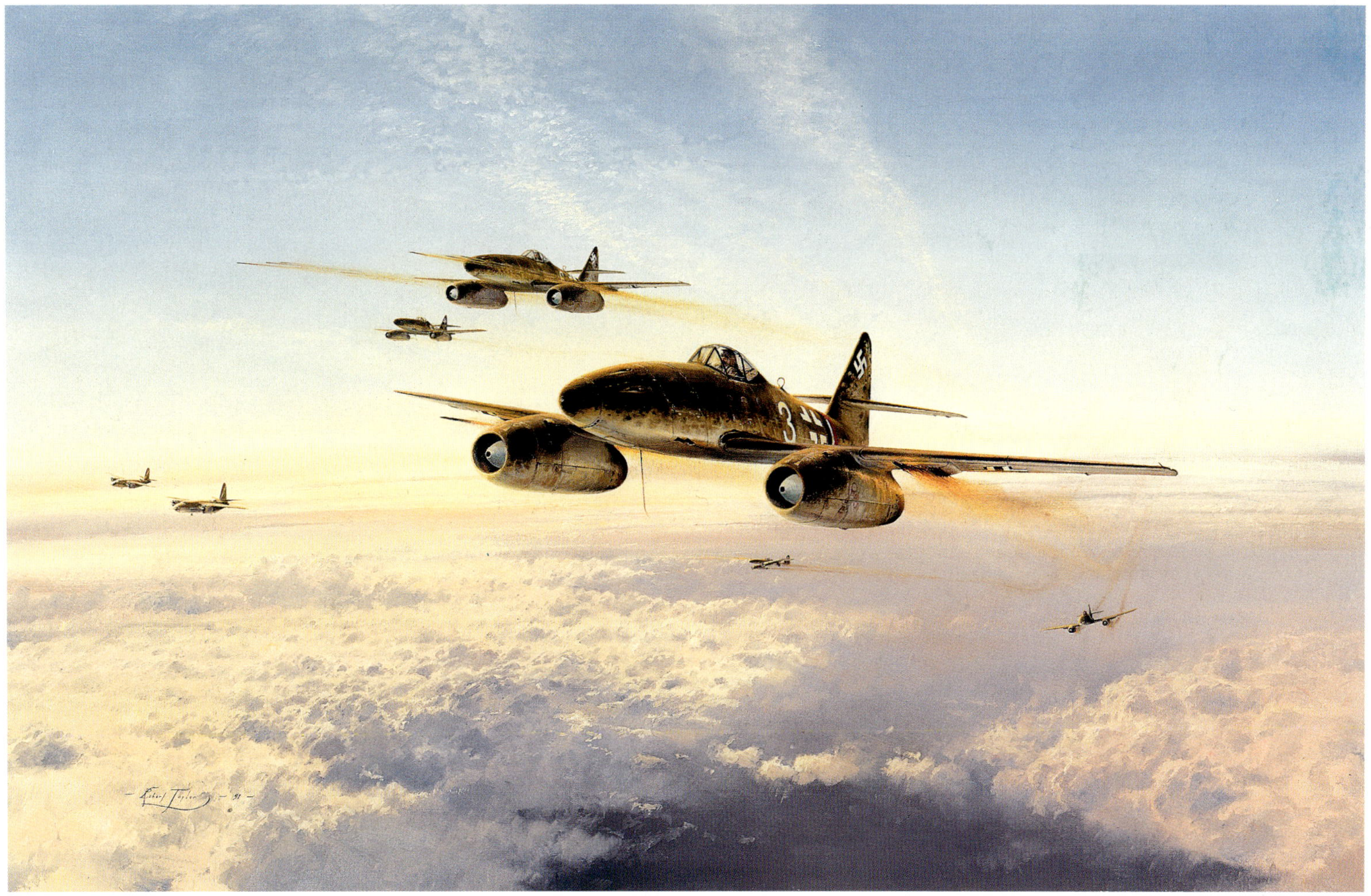

After my publisher released prints from the painting they received a letter from an American infantryman who took part in the battle for the bridge at Remagen. Tom Yochim wrote:

My rifle company crossed the Ludendorff Bridge at Remagen at dawn on 8 March 1945. I witnessed at first hand the German jet planes strafing the bridge, the anti-aircraft batteries shelling us from the hill above Erpel, the mines that were floating down the river and other frightening hazards ... Mr Taylor's painting does a remarkable job of portraying both aspects of the overall scene on the day of the crossing.

It is very gratifying to know that all the effort put into the research and preparation of a painting has paid off, and also to have it confirmed with some authority that my imagination did not get too carried away.

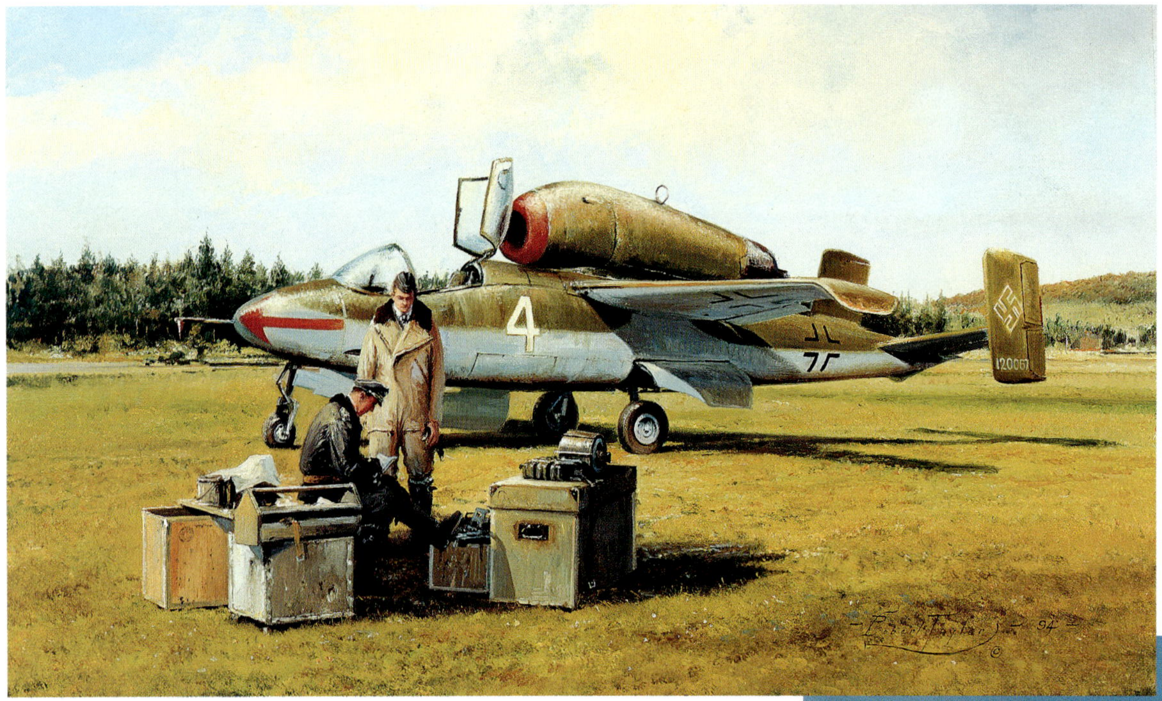

PRE-FLIGHT BRIEF

NIGHT INTERCEPTORS

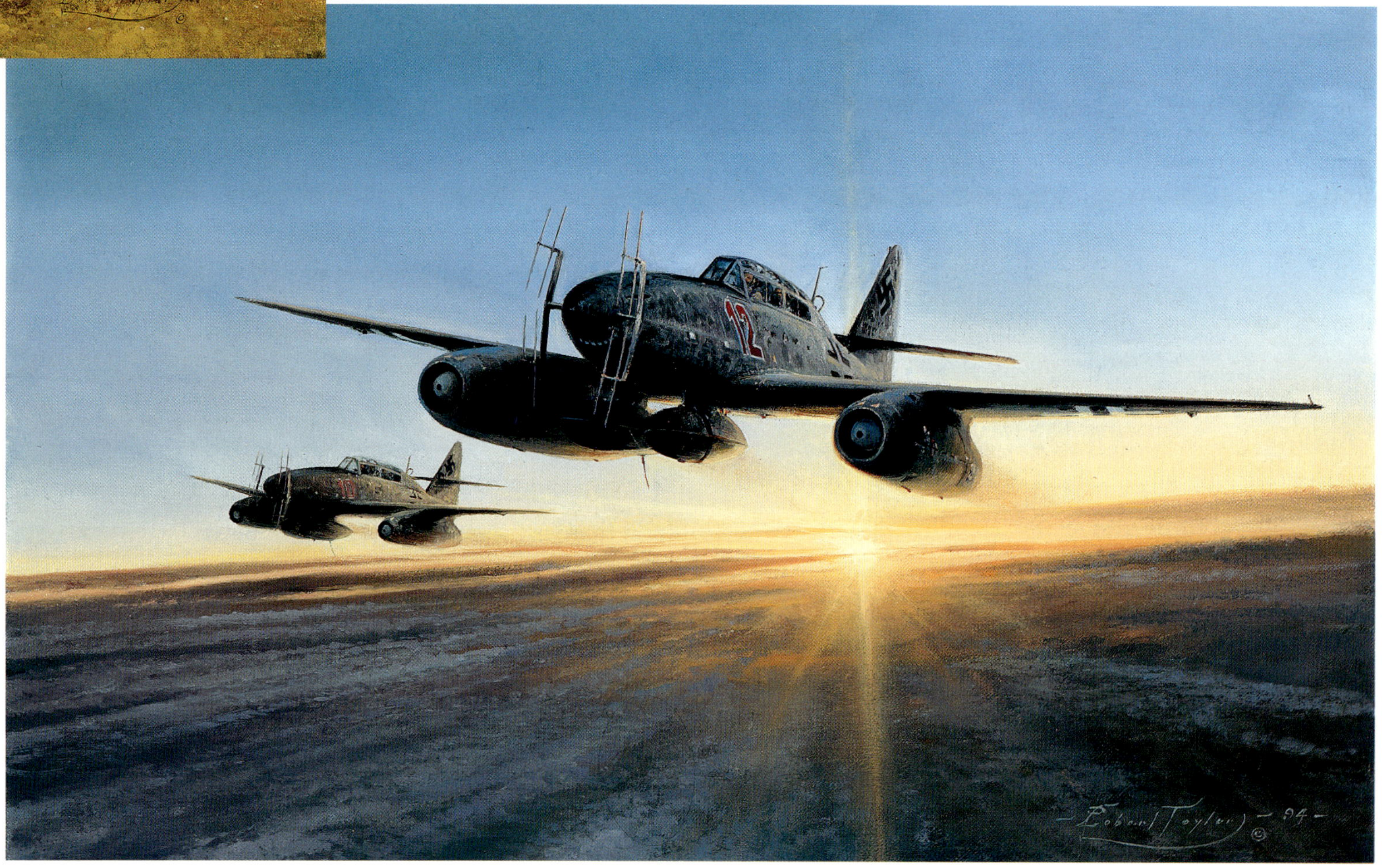

One of the unique things about the Luftwaffe's attack on the bridge at Remagen was the use of both of its new jet attack aircraft: the Me262 and the Arado. Although the attack was not successful in knocking out the bridge, it was nevertheless a unique event in aviation history, not to mention the considerable courage it took on the part of the participating Luftwaffe pilots.

I painted two other smaller pictures as companions to *The Bridge at Remagen*, as it seemed like a good opportunity to record all three of the Luftwaffe's World War II combat jets, and the roles they flew in. The first (shown on the right) depicts the Me262 in its nightfighter role, this being apparent by the conglomeration of radar antennae protruding from the nose of the aircraft. The second shows the distinctive Heinkel 163. This diminutive little jet was made almost entirely of wood, the jet engine unceremoniously mounted, seemingly as an afterthought, on top of the airframe. In this picture the pilot is preparing to make a test flight, and is having a last-minute discussion with ground staff.

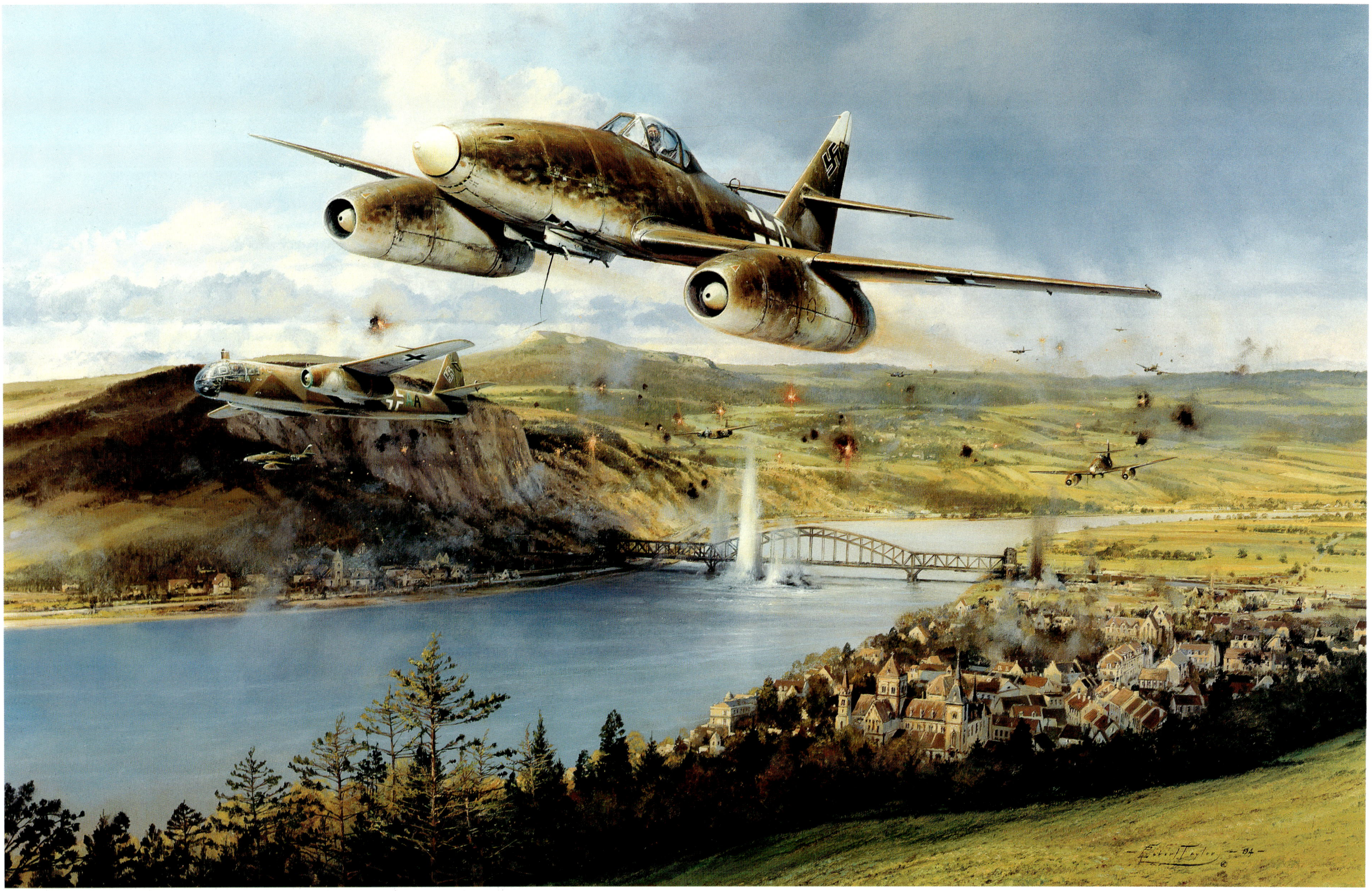

THE BRIDGE AT REMAGEN

In the collection of Mr Edgar Leicher

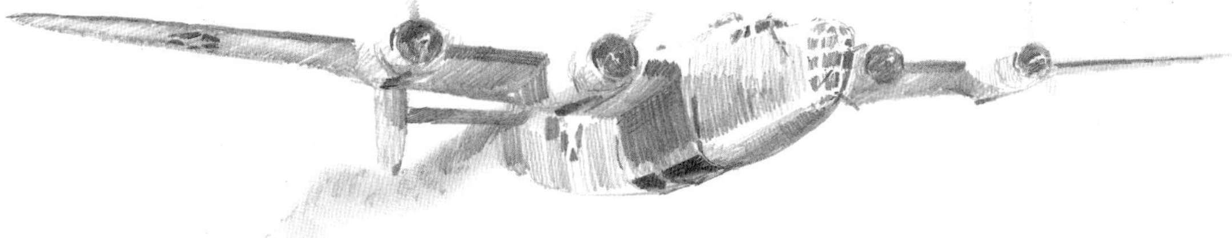

PLOESTI – THE VITAL MISSION

Clipping the wings off an aircraft in flight can – and usually does – have a disastrous effect! I know because I have tried it many times, sometimes in desperation when trying to get an aircraft to fit into a normal-shaped picture; on most occasions my efforts get no further than the drawing board and end up in the wastepaper bin. Most World War II four-engined heavy bombers, including the B-24 Liberators which flew to Ploesti, had a large wingspan, and in contrast to today's big swept-wing aircraft when viewed from the front, the old heavies look to be all wing. With some, and in particular the Liberator, the enormity of the wing width seems to be exaggerated by the narrowness of the fuselage. The outcome of this, from the artist's point of view, is that by the time the entire aircraft is squeezed wing-tip to wing-tip into the canvas, you can't see much of the fuselage, and the cockpit area almost vanishes.

To bring the aircraft nearer and get a good close-up look at the plane, especially the cockpit area and even the pilots' faces, the artist has no option but to slice off some wing. It is something none of us likes doing, however. Normally no airplane looks complete with bits of its wings missing, and in any case it is difficult to maintain the balance of a painting with parts of a plane chopped off; so finding a way of drawing attention away from the surgery is always a knotty problem to solve.

There were a number of things I wanted to do

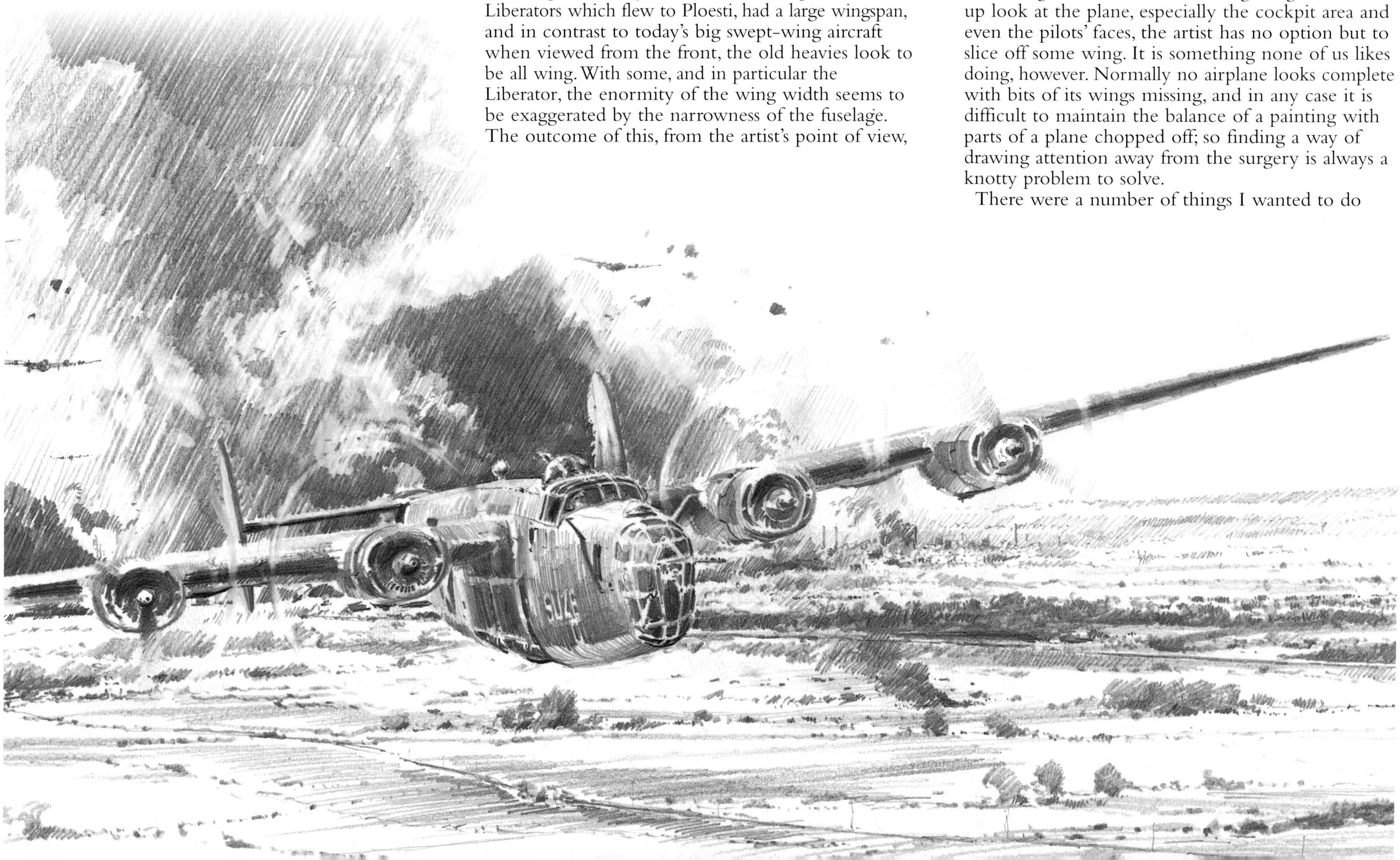

when I set about painting *Ploesti*. First, it was a low-level raid so the B-24s needed to be shown close to the ground. Next, it was important to show the burning oil installations, and the intense barrage of flak the crews had to fly through. Third, I wanted the main aircraft to be close enough to see the pilots' faces. Lastly, and perhaps this was most important of all, I needed to achieve all these aims within an image that would instantly tell people that this was Ploesti, without them having to read the title of the painting.

I used up the best part of a drawing pad working out the composition, deciding amongst other things exactly where the B-24's wing would be severed; the sketch opposite shows my final drawing. When happy with this I set about correcting the balance of the picture. This was achieved by careful positioning of the B-24 at the top of the picture. This secondary aircraft needed to be very eye-catching to give the composition the required equilibrium, and I carefully dropped its port wing slightly to compensate for the opposite tilt of the lead aircraft. My point concerning balance can be demonstrated easily by turning to the colour plate on the next page and, by using the hand or a piece of paper, obscuring for a moment the top aircraft. Without that smoking B-24 the painting looks heavily loaded to the left, and the lead airplane seems to be sliding gently out of the bottom left-hand corner of the painting.

Because I wanted the lead aircraft slightly above the horizon, the burning oil refinery is viewed just below Suzy Q, helping the effect of the low altitude of the attack. The bright sunlight on the fuselage glinting against the great palls of dark smoke provides a dramatic backdrop for the lead B-24. The composition allowed me to paint the faces of the pilot and the 44 Bomb Group commander, Leon Johnson, who led the raid from the right-hand seat of Suzy Q.

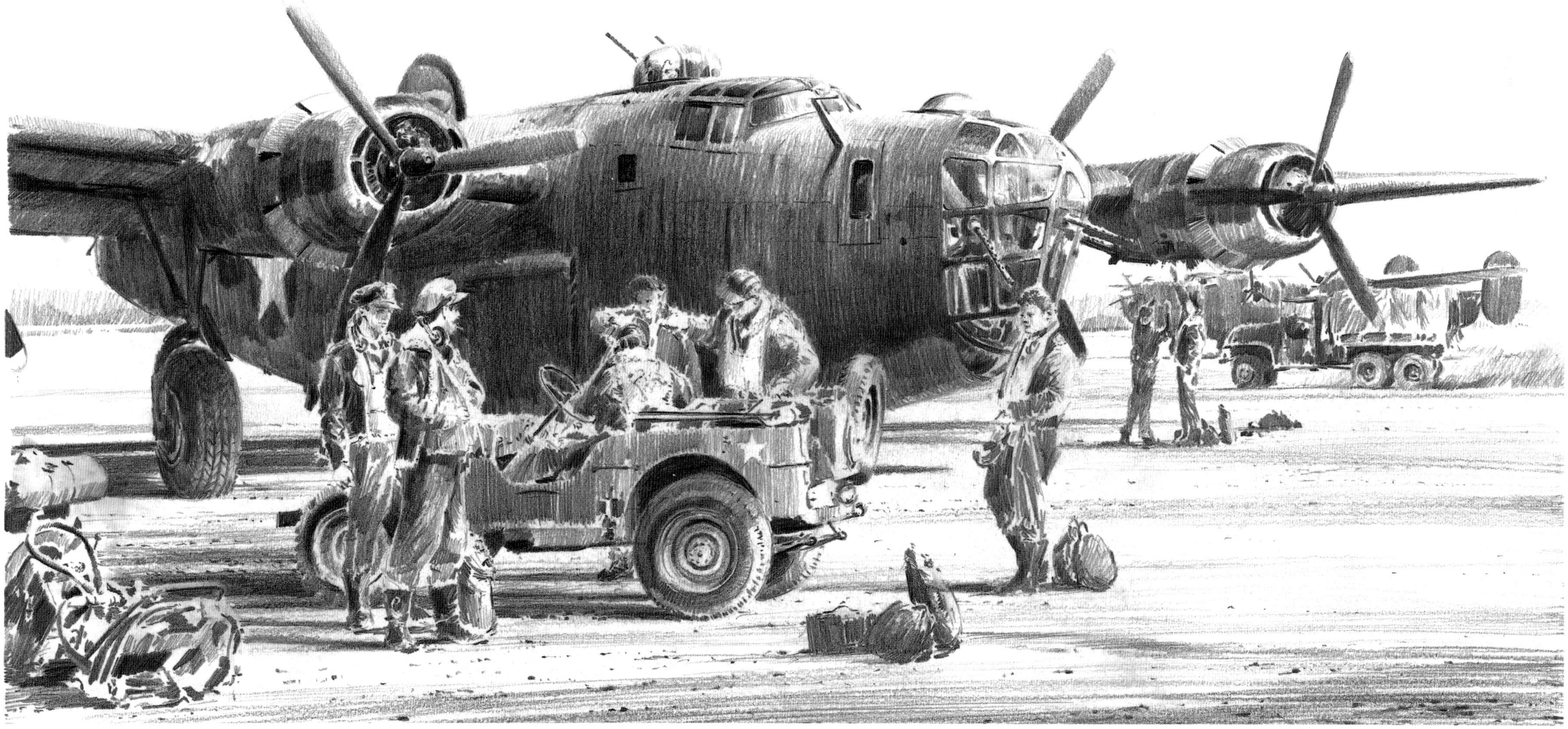

'One of the Lucky ones' - A B-24 Liberator crew first back from the epic raid on the Ploesti oil refinery. August 1943.

I am frequently asked how long it takes me to complete an oil painting, in what order I do things, and how I get started. I have explained elsewhere in this volume the process of research, how I arrive at a plan via the preparation of conceptual drawings, and how long all this can take. But the question here I believe concerns this: faced with a large expanse of clean white canvas, how do I set about making those first tentative brushstrokes, and how long does it take me to finish a painting?

Usually I am able to start a new painting with ease and confidence, because by the time I approach the new canvas I have already planned everything in considerable detail. I know that many artists simply start painting with only a vague idea or plan, and see where the act of painting takes them. This may work for them, but not for me. By the time I actually start putting paint on to canvas I have quite a good idea as to where everything is going, and even have the colour scheme mapped out in my mind.

The first task is to cover the canvas completely in paint, and in so doing, to position all the main components of the painting: artists usually refer to this process as 'blocking-in'. In the illustration on this page, the painting is completely blocked in, and although no detail has yet been painted, it can be seen that the picture has already taken on its basic form, and that the overall colour scheme is apparent. This part of the painting process is completed fairly quickly; the stage shown here, for example, took only two days.

The blocked-in canvas provides a solid base of ground colour upon which to work. I leave the freshly painted canvas for a few days, allowing the paint to become reasonably dry; this allows me to work over it with fresh colours without them mixing with the ground colour, thus keeping the new paint clean and bright. I find it important to paint the ground colours fairly accurately while blocking in, because the next stage of painting requires much detailed work and this necessitates the use of thinner paint; so drastic changes of colour at this stage are a nuisance. The remaining work to bring the painting to completion can take anywhere between two and four weeks of concentrated effort, depending upon the amount of detail in it.

A careful comparison of the blocked-in canvas on this page with the finished painting shown to the right, will reveal some subtle changes which became necessary as the detailed work on the painting developed. Some of the changes are more obvious than others, and it may be more interesting to let you discover these for yourself.

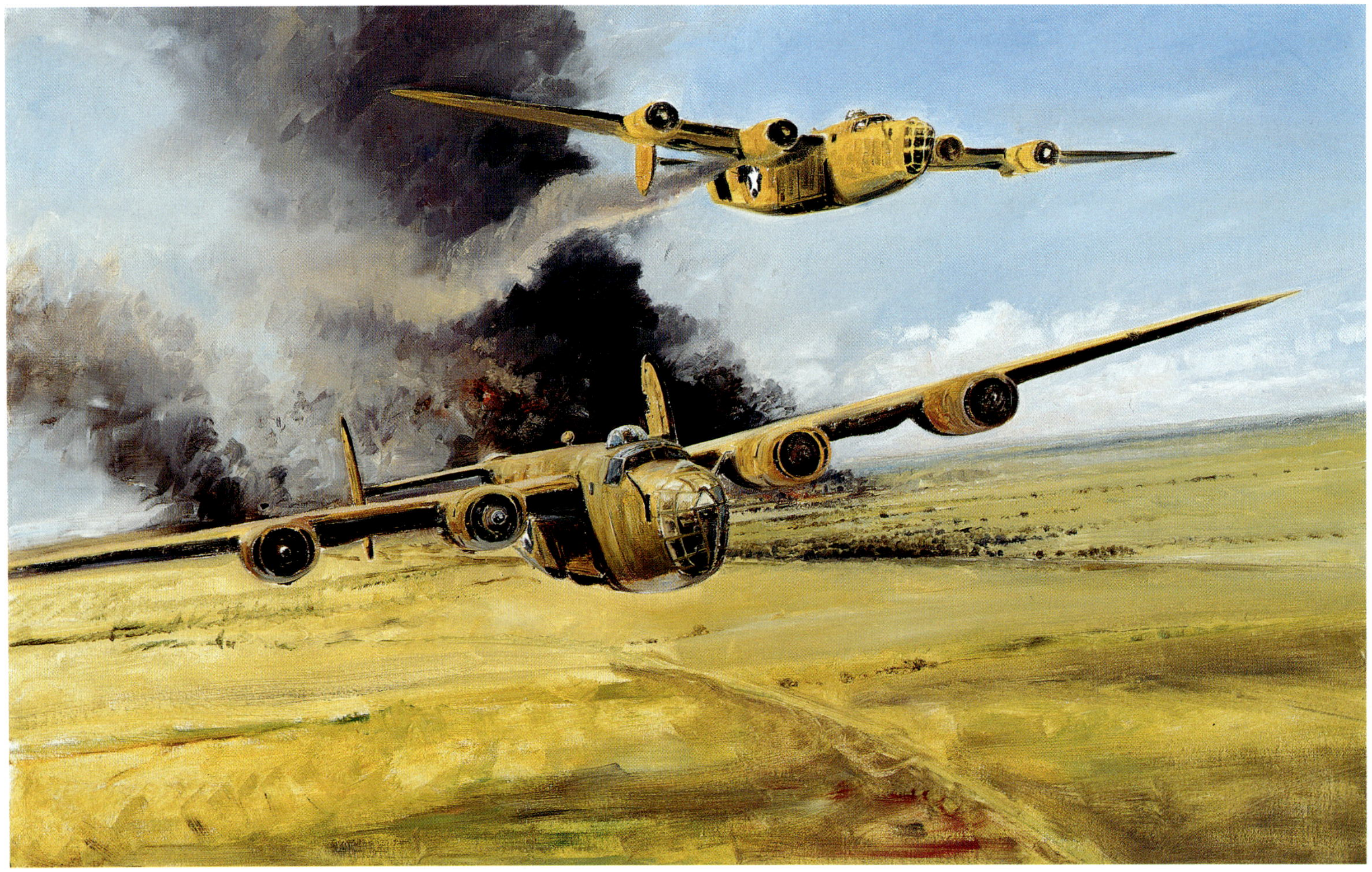

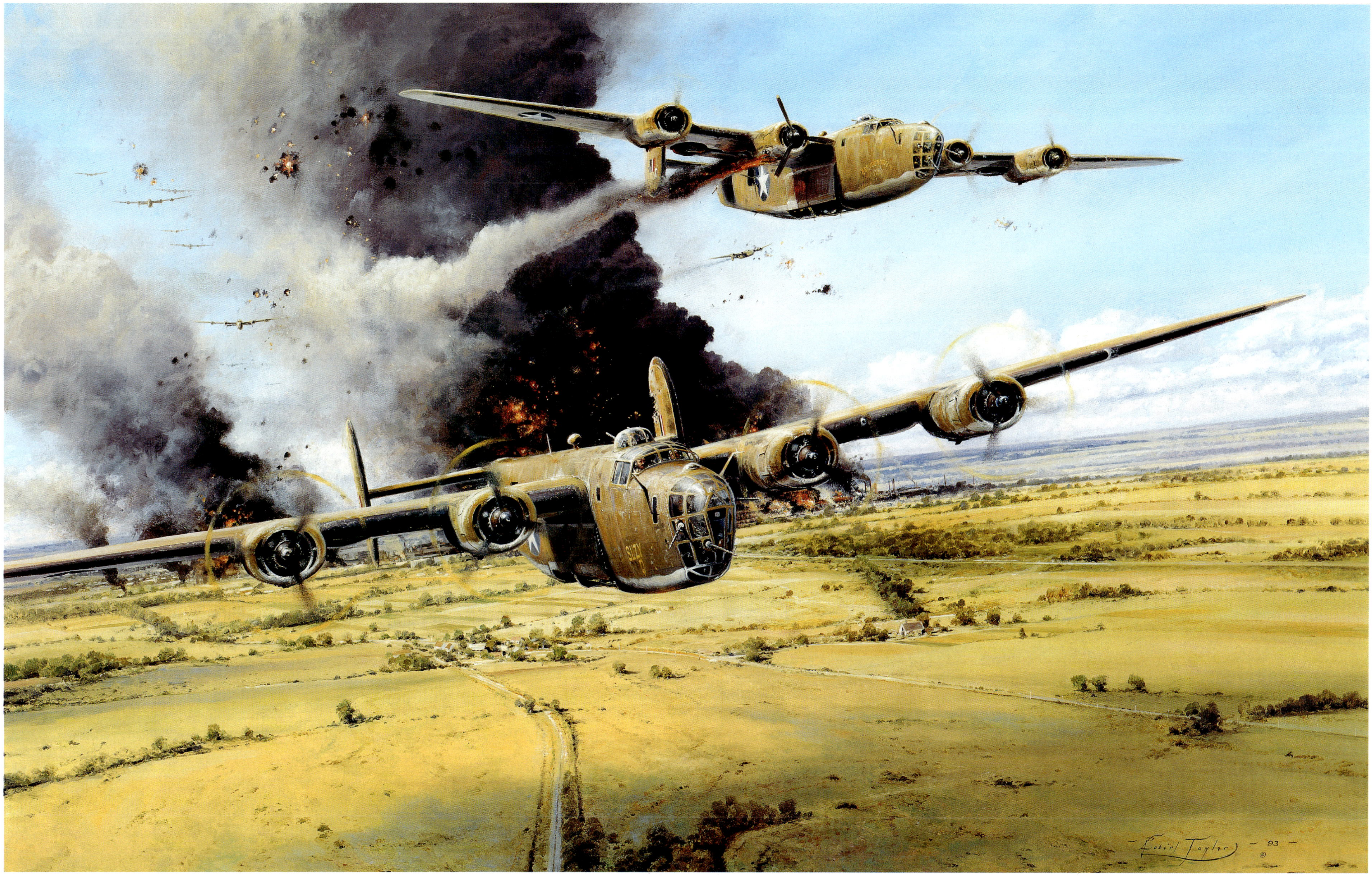

PLOESTI – THE VITAL MISSION

In the collection of Mr Bill Ward, Fine Art Services

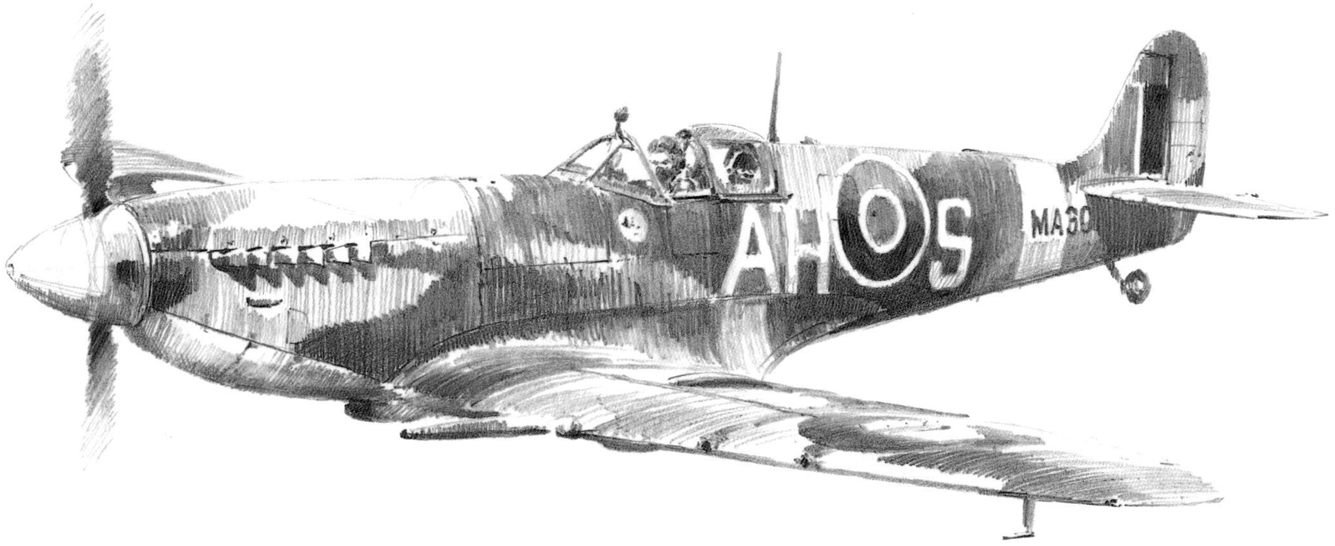

AFTER THE BATTLE

A light wind blew in from the English Channel on the morning of 6 March 1936. The weather wasn't perfect for flying but the unbroken cloud layer was high, and Vickers Supermarine's chief test pilot was keen to get going. Wedging his considerable frame into the narrow cockpit of a sleek pale blue prototype, 'Mutt' Summers fired up its Merlin engine and taxied out across the grass field. Moments later he lifted gracefully into the air for the first time in what was arguably to become the greatest single-seat interceptor fighter of all time. Within a decade this classic little fighting machine, and the pilots who flew it, were to become legend.

The Spitfire was, and to many still is, the most beautiful aircraft ever built. Mention the word 'Spitfire' to a man who flew one and watch the expression of pure nostalgia wash over his face. This remarkable little fighter left a deep and lasting impression upon every pilot who flew it, and when talking about Spitfires to men who flew them in combat it is not difficult to become caught up in their powerful emotions for the aircraft. Its perfectly proportioned design is art in its purest form. It is always a thrill to watch and listen to a Spitfire in flight and I doubt I shall ever feel any differently about Mitchell's graceful, elegant little fighter.

One airshow I always try to attend each year is the Flying Legends display at Duxford, a 1930's airfield set in the heart of the rolling Cambridgeshire countryside. A Royal Air Force Battle of Britain base back in 1940, much of Duxford is still as it was in the war years, and today it is home to one of the world's most fascinating air museums. Operated by the Imperial War Museum, it hosts several flying displays during the summer months, the Flying Legends event being for me a highlight of the year. Almost all the legendary warbirds of the 1939–45 air war that are still flying are demonstrated by today's pilots with the same verve with which their predecessors took them into battle half a century ago.

Attending last summer's show, I was busy signing copies of my previous books at a large exhibition of my work presented at Duxford by Vector Fine Arts. Outside the marquee the airshow was in full swing, with the exciting noise of piston-engined aircraft performing before the assembled crowds. Sitting next to me was the well known WWII Spitfire Wing Leader, Air Vice Marshal H.A.C. Bird-Wilson, known affectionately to everyone as 'Birdy'. We were surrounded by a horde of aviation enthusiasts – most of whom, I should add, were hanging on every one of Birdy's words – when quite suddenly the place emptied.

The distinctive sound of a Merlin engine in full song told me the reason instantly. A Spitfire had taken centre stage and was thrilling the huge crowd. I hurried to join Birdy who was already watching, transfixed and spellbound, as the little thoroughbred wheeled and turned in the summer sky. When the aerial ballet came to an end Birdy gave the pilot an approving salute and turned to me and said, 'Now that's *real* flying.' I was sure I detected the trace of a tear in his eye.

The pilots who flew most of the twenty-four variants of this legendary fighter usually agree that the Mark IX was the finest of all, and it is this particular type which I chose for my painting *After the Battle*. When the Mark IX came into service it gave the Spitfire pilots that vital edge over the Me109s and Fw190s of the Luftwaffe, a superiority the Spitfire continued then to hold for the rest of the war.

After playing around with a number of different concepts, I decided to show the Mk IX Spitfires in classic pose, set in a panoramic scene above the distinctive English landscape, patchworked as it was back in the 1940s with small multi-coloured meadows and wandering hedgerows. These Mark IXs belong to 611 Squadron, among the first to be equipped with the new Mark, and based at Kenley in the summer of 1942. The Spitfires are seen returning from a combat mission in which they have tangled with the Luftwaffe over northern France. To emphasise the recent action I have shown superficial damage to the rudder of the lead aircraft and streaks of burnt cordite trailing back from the machine-gun ports.

The drawing below is one of a number of concept sketches I made in preparation for this painting. This one shows Spitfires in combat with Me109s over the Needles – the western tip of the Isle of Wight, off the south coast of England. Following completion of my eventual final design, I painted two smaller pictures of Spitfires as part of this particular project, one of which is shown on the page overleaf. This depicts Mark I Spitfires of 610 Squadron lifting off a typical grass airfield in southern England during the course of the Battle of Britain.

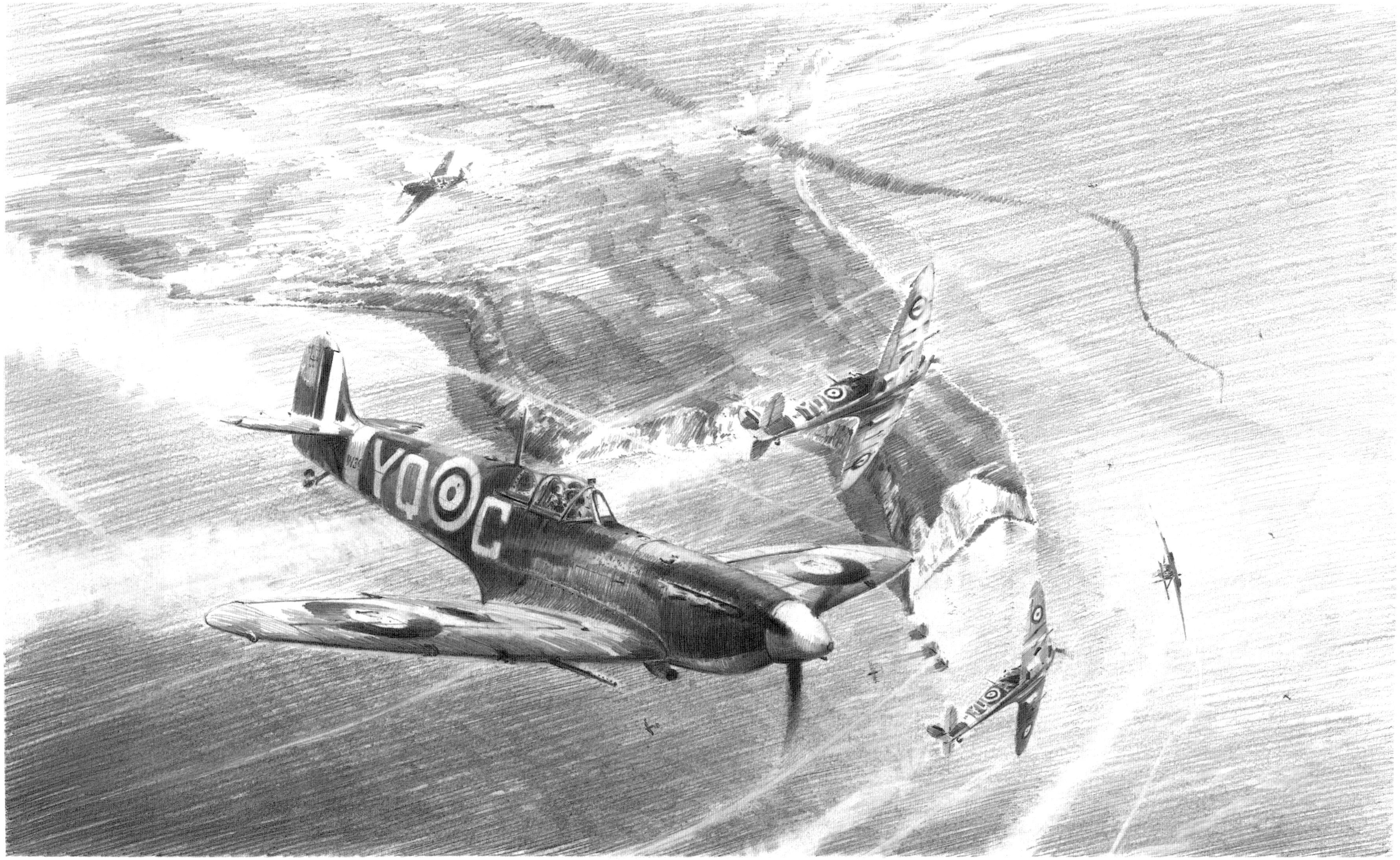

'Spitfires over the Needles' – Spitfires from the Tangmere Wing engage with Me109s over the Isle of Wight.

A close-up view of a painting of an aircraft such as this draws attention to, and places emphasis upon the artist's use of light and shade. Planning the lighting for a painting should come as second nature to an artist; it is of critical importance if a painting is to be effective. Always conscious of this I spend hours working out the areas of light and shadow before I start work on the canvas.

Because of the complexity of shapes that make up an aircraft the artist is unable to make guesses with light and shadow, and my technique to avoid making any basic mistakes is quite simple: I make a large scale-model of every aircraft I paint, and place this on a rotatable spindle on a plinth, which I set up outdoors on a bright sunny day. I fiddle about until I find the precise angle of lighting I am looking for, then shoot a few photographs to capture the light just as I want it before the sun moves on. I then prepare a rough drawing in soft-lead pencil showing the sharply contrasting areas of light and shadow and I keep this before me throughout the painting of the picture. To emphasise the point it is interesting to note where the sunlight and shadow fall on the lower wing of the Spitfire in this painting.

By way of example, in this painting I purposely placed a strong accent on the cannons, the idea being to take advantage of the strong directional flow they seem to give to the aircraft – pointing the way, so to speak, and helping to give the illusion of movement. In order to do this the sun is positioned high above and to the right of the Spitfire so that the left-hand cannon, as it is viewed, falls in bright sunlight, contrasting sharply with an area of shadow on the wing. The right-hand cannon, also in sunlight, is painted using dark shadow underneath to give the cannon a clear line against the lighter colours in that area of the painting.

Still on the subject of lighting, I have used a powerful thundercloud as a backdrop to the painting, this one carefully constructed to give a dark area immediately behind the brightly lit top edge of the fuselage and the glinting cockpit. This helps to give the aircraft a three-dimensional effect, but also adds both interest and drama to the picture. I always use authentic cloud formations as the basis for painting them; I believe that to try to invent clouds by painting them from memory is a sure way to come up with a painting that doesn't look realistic.

SPITFIRE SCRAMBLE

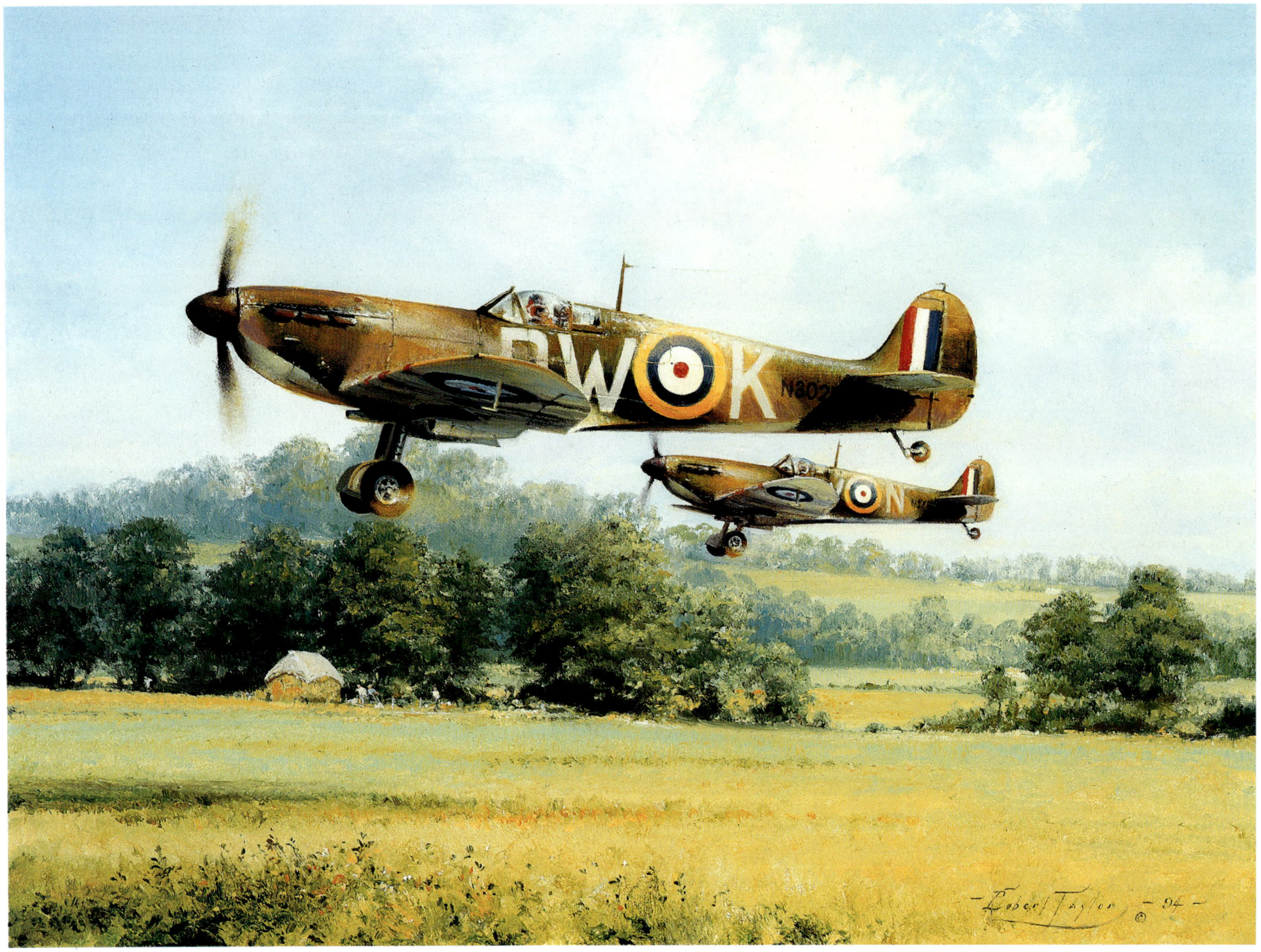

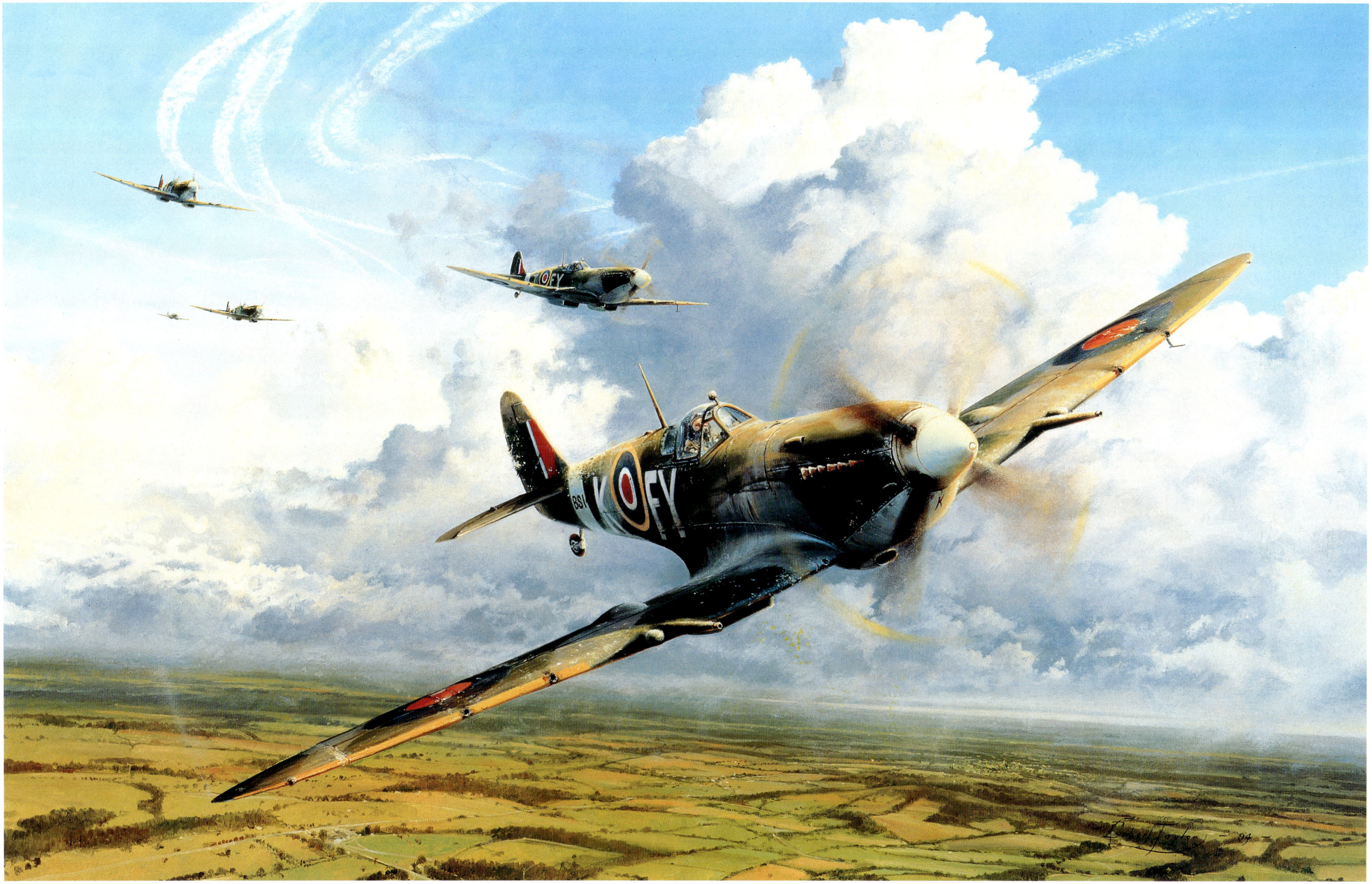

AFTER THE BATTLE

In the collection of Mr Eugene Eisenberg

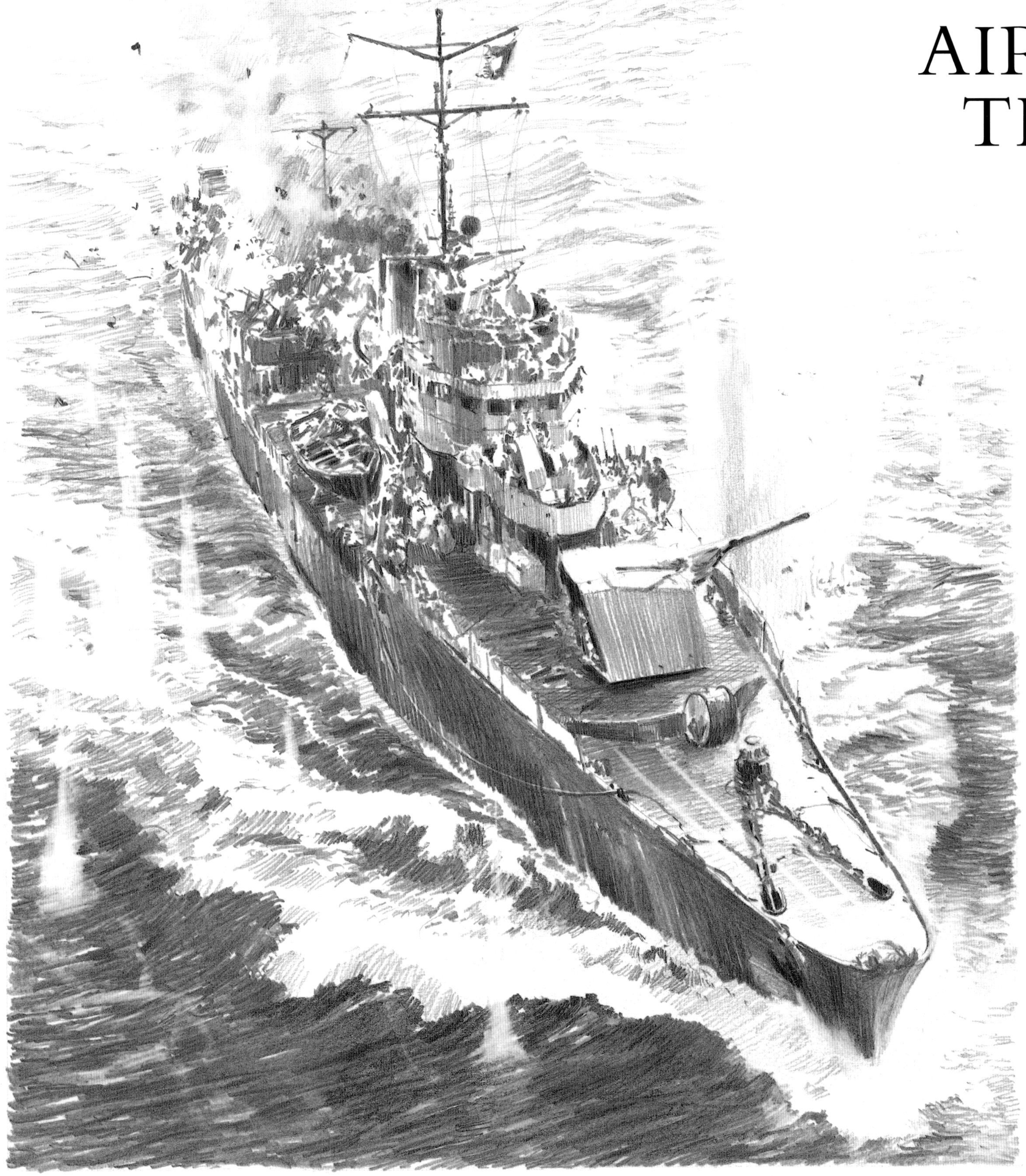

AIR APACHES ON THE WARPATH

I have to admit that very few photographs have ever given me much inspiration for paintings; more often my enthusiasm is aroused during discussion with pilots, aircrews, groundcrews, eyewitnesses of events or people who were otherwise involved in the scenes I portray. With *Air Apaches on the Warpath*, however, it was different.

Hoping it might spark an idea for a painting, my good friend Dwight Van Horn gave me a copy of a book chronicling the fortunes of the 345th Bomb Group's B-25 Mitchells in the Pacific – a scenario Dwight had been cajoling me to paint for a long time. I was truly astonished by the quantity and originality of the high quality photographs the book contained, and became fascinated by the story of the 345th. The result was my painting, *Air Apaches*.

Photographs are invaluable as a means of reference for an artist, but not in the way most people think. There are many thousands of wartime aviation photos available but, perhaps surprisingly, unless they contain good background material, I find most are useful only for the information they provide about aircraft markings. Certainly it is unacceptable for an artist to copy directly from a photo as a means of painting a picture, because of the distortion created by the camera lens. Often it is difficult to know if the photo has been taken close up with a regular lens, or from a distance using a telephoto lens. Even where the angle of the two photographs is identical, the two different lenses will produce two quite different images of the same aircraft.

What was so inspiring about the book I received from Dwight Van Horn was that it contained such a variety of excellent quality action images, showing with great clarity a huge number of different locations in the Pacific where the war was fought. He didn't have to persuade me any further that I should paint a Pacific scene featuring the 345th B-25s in action. The drawing on this page is of a Japanese destroyer under attack from B-25s.

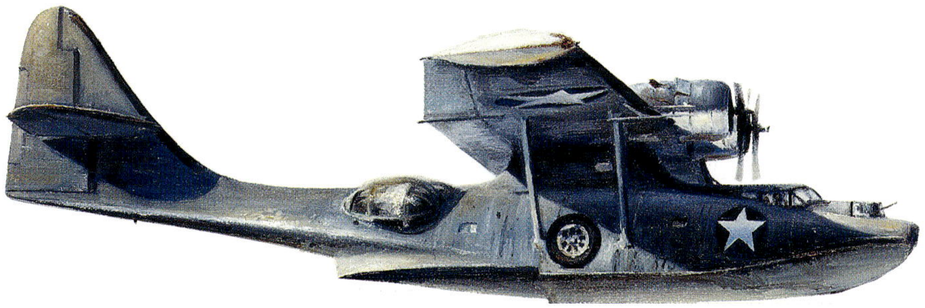

Pilots who flew in the Pacific have often remarked to me that their worst fears were not combat with the enemy, but the possibility of having to bale out or ditch somewhere in the ocean; the chances of being found and picked up were remote in the vast expanse of the Pacific. When researching *Air Apaches* I came across a remarkable rescue story involving a Catalina pilot and the crews of three B-25 aircraft which had been brought down in the ocean.

In February 1944 it had been decided to neutralise the important Japanese supply and staging base at Kavieng, situated on the western tip of the island of New Ireland; this was to be achieved by strike from the air rather than by invasion. As it happens, among the many aircraft which took part was 'Rita's Wagon', the B-25 featured in *Air Apaches on the Warpath* – but that's another story.

While aircraft continued to pound the heavily defended Kavieng, several others were circling downed comrades in the water off the peninsula. In an effort to save them, two B-25 crews flew off in search of a Navy Patrol Squadron PBY Catalina which couldn't be raised on the radio.

Having found the rescue aircraft but still unable to communicate by radio, they had to direct the 28-year-old Navy pilot, Lt Nathan Gordon, with hand signals. The PBY arrived over the downed crew of 'Gremlin's Holiday' to find them being shelled from the shore. Despite this, Gordon put his Catalina down in the eight-foot swell, and cut the engines while his crew hauled all six airmen aboard. Nathan fired up the engines again and took off.

No sooner were they airborne than the radio reported another crew in the water. Gordon again set his PBY down in the swell, this time picking up three further B-25 crewmen. With nine men rescued from certain capture and probable death, Gordon headed his laden craft for home. Ten miles into the journey an urgent call told him that a third B-25 crew was wallowing in the water just 600 yards offshore.

With nineteen aboard, Gordon hauled the Catalina round and again put the amphibian down in the water, cutting the engines as he did so. Amidst a barrage of bullets and shells from the Japanese shore batteries, another six B-25 crewmen were hauled aboard. Nathan was now faced with having to lift his heavily overloaded PBY out of the difficult swell while under constant fire. Somehow he managed it, and fifteen grateful B-25 crewmen lived to tell the extraordinary tale. Nathan Gordon was justifiably awarded the Congressional Medal of Honor, America's highest award for bravery.

The drawing on this page shows the PBY Catalina flying boat, a gorgeous, characterful aircraft of which happily a number still survive in flying condition to this day.

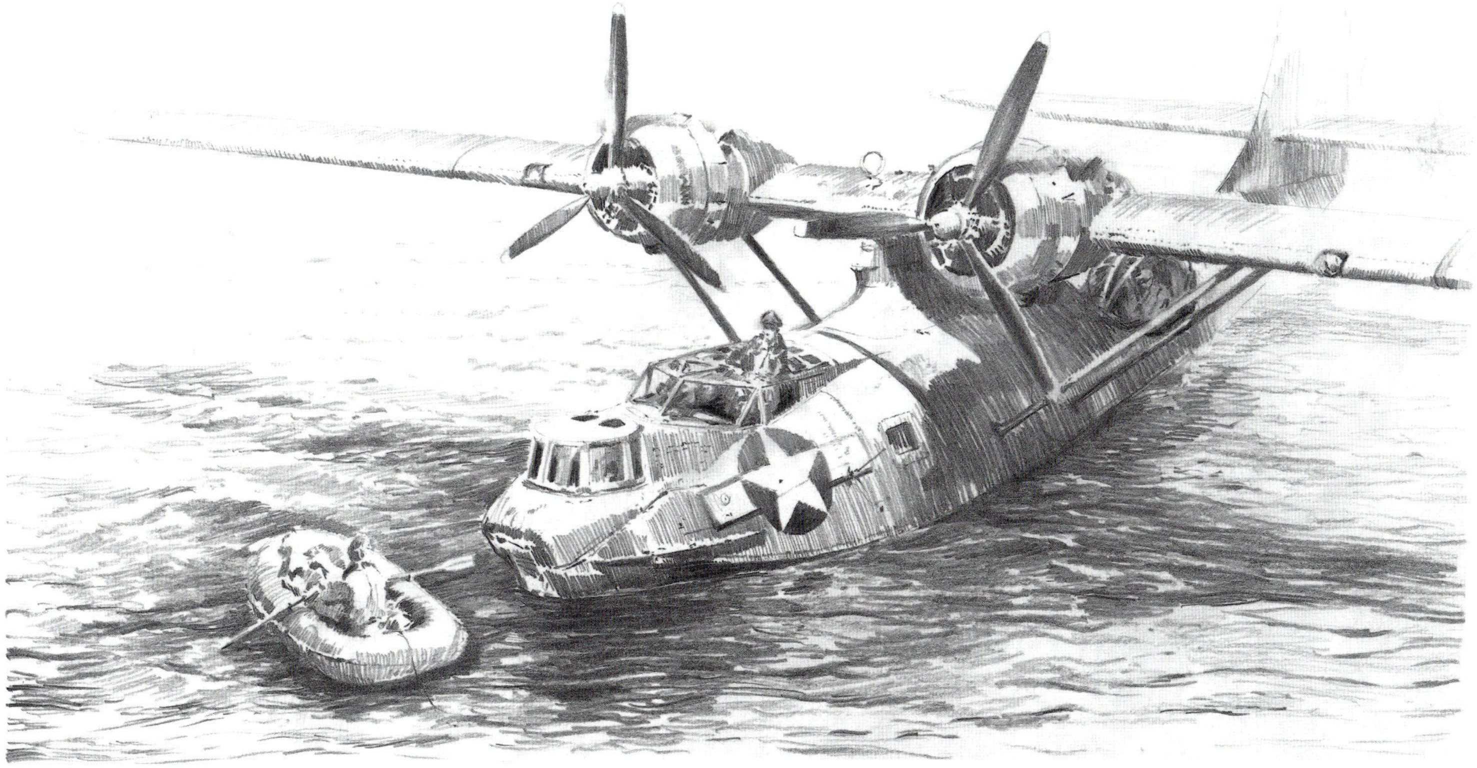

A downed fighter pilot is picked up by a PBY Catalina

Intelligence had reported enemy shipping in the region of New Hanover on 16 February 1944, and the 345th despatched forty-one of their B-25 strafers to hunt down and attack the enemy force. The 345th's Mitchells were ideal for the task. Each had been ingeniously fitted with eight forward-firing .50-calibre machine-guns, converting their medium bombers into devastating low-level attack aircraft. Thus equipped, their crews had built a formidable reputation, neutralising Japanese airpower on the ground and devastating their vital shipping supply lines.

The painting shows the 345th's Mitchells as they make their attack, the 420-ton Japanese Subchaser No 39 being the focus of their attentions. In the foreground a B-25 from the 500th squadron, 'Rita's Wagon', completes her run over the target. Having raked the ship with machine-gun fire, her bomb explodes near the stern, damaging the steering gear. Following closely behind, the next assault is about to start as 'Brother Rat' begins her diving attack.

The Japanese crew is defiantly fighting back, a bursting shell from one of the ship's guns rocking the B-25 as it skims the masthead. The air would have been full of tracer and flying shrapnel and I have included plenty of evidence of this in the painting. The close-up of 'Rita's Wagon' shown below provides a good view of the B-25's forward-firing machine-guns.

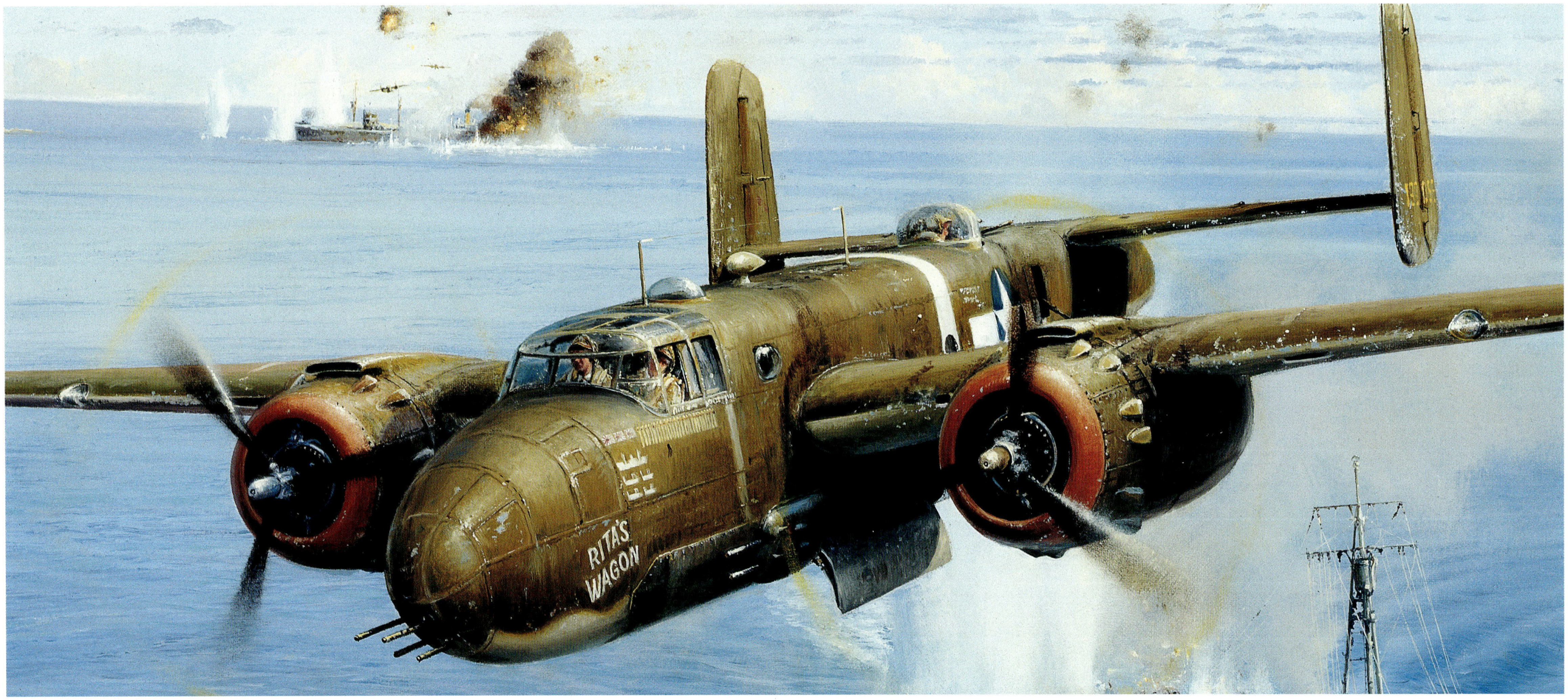

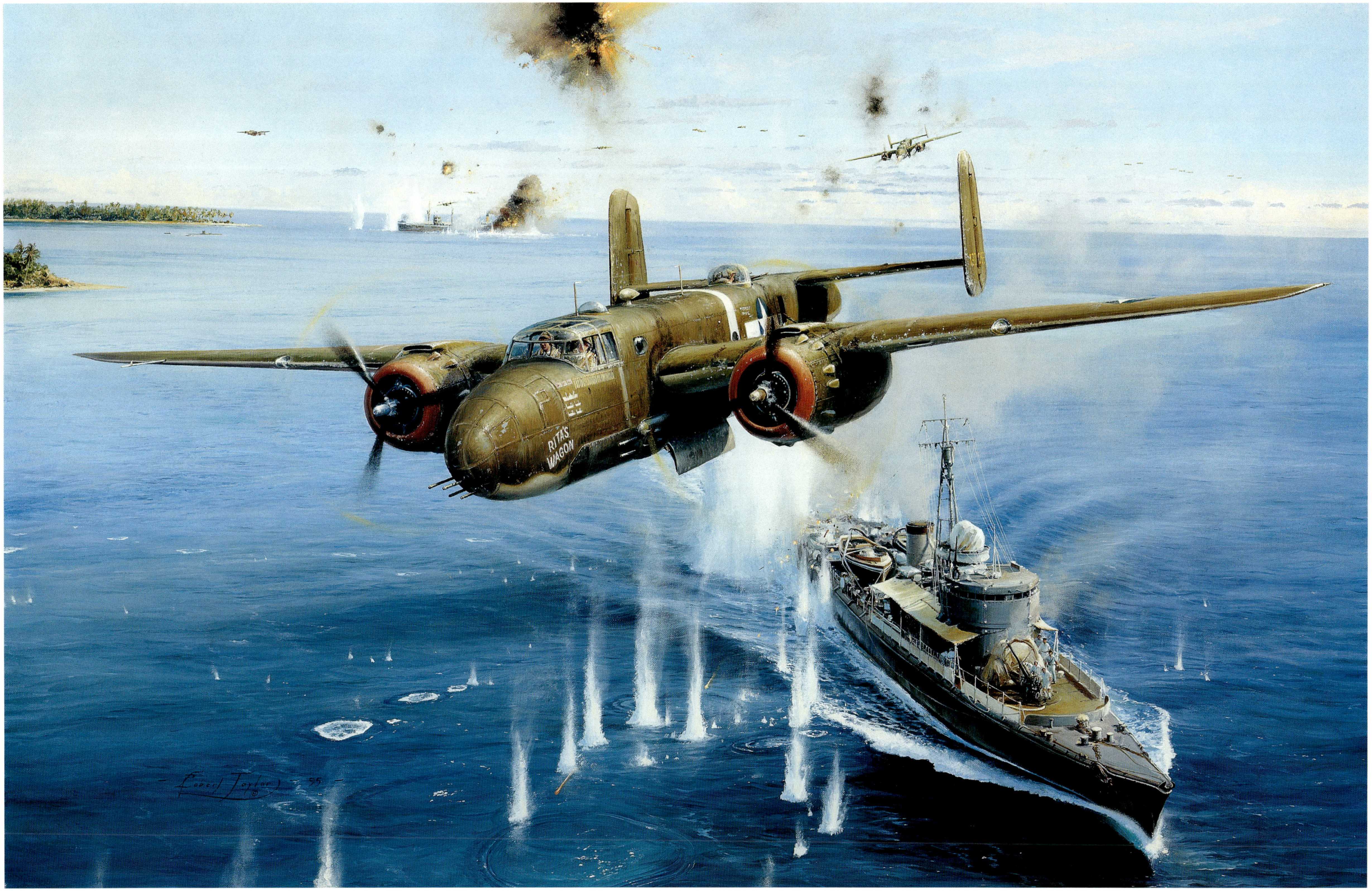

AIR APACHES ON THE WARPATH

In the collection of Mr Eugene Eisenberg

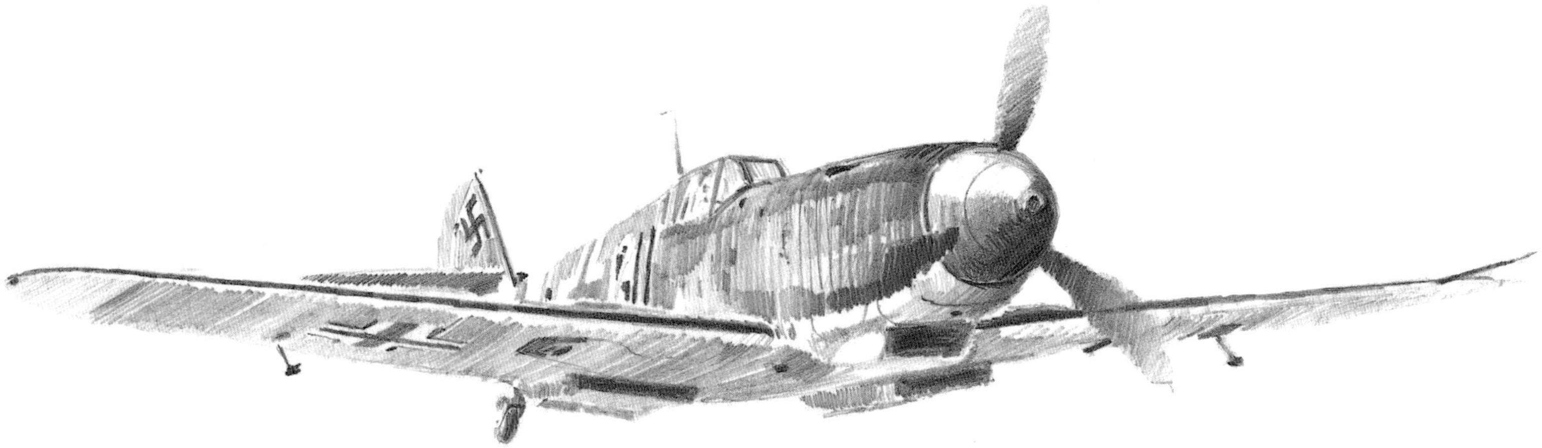

HARTMANN TRIBUTE

Colonel Erich Hartmann became a legend in his lifetime. As a novice fighter pilot he was posted to JG-52, the Luftwaffe's crack fighter wing on the Russian Front. He was lucky to survive his first combat – in fact he crash-landed, ignominiously walking back to base. He continued this inauspicious start to his combat career with a number of mishaps, showing no early signs of the skills required of a fighter ace. What was apparent to the more experienced JG-52 pilots was that the newcomer had an abundance of courage and determination, two attributes that a budding fighter pilot cannot be taught.

Among the first to notice these qualities in the frail-looking new pilot was Walter Krupinski, a jovial carefree character known throughout the Russian Front as The Count. Already an experienced ace, Walter took the youngster under his wing – literally, too, because he appointed Hartmann to fly as his wingman. It was while flying with the intrepid Walter that Erich Hartmann scored his first victory, and the rest is history: by the time the war was over, the blond-haired pilot with the boyish features had become the most feared pilot on the Eastern Front, and the top-scoring ace in history.

I had previously painted two pictures showing the great ace in action, both in air-to-air scenes, so I was looking for a new angle when considering how I would paint *Hartmann Tribute*. I decided to view his aircraft from the ground, the sketch below being one of my working drawings.

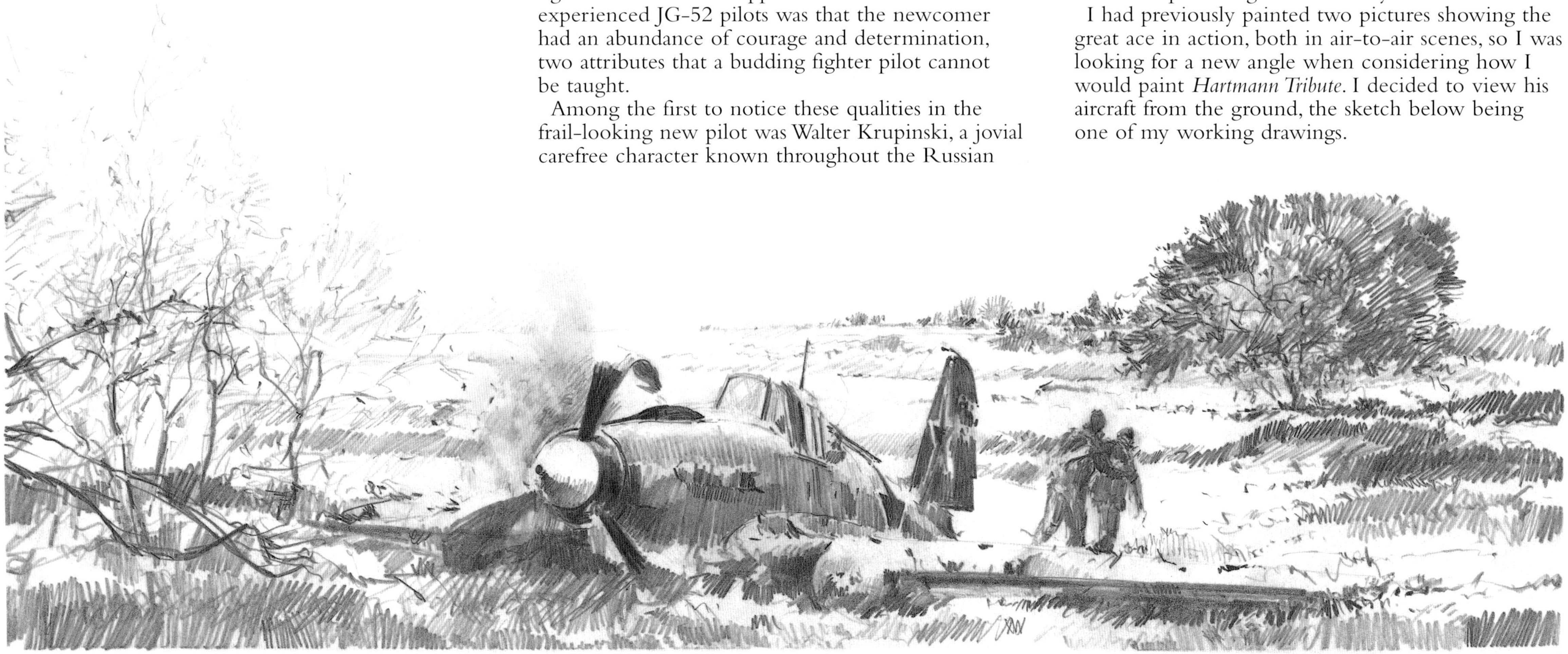

Some of the most heroic air-combat fighting on the Russian Front involved the Free French Squadrons. Formed in 1942 from part of the 3rd Free French Fighter Group, 'Normandie', the first squadron of fourteen Yak-3 pilots reached Russia, first seeing action in March 1943. Fighting right across East Prussia up until the capitulation of Germany, the ninety-six pilots of the Normandie-Niémen flew 5,240 missions and scored 273 confirmed victories. However, forty-six of them never returned from this hellish battlefront.

In 1944 the squadrons won the citation 'Niémen' from the Russians, for their courage during the battle to cross the river Niémen into East Prussia – a citation of honour which remains with the squadron today.

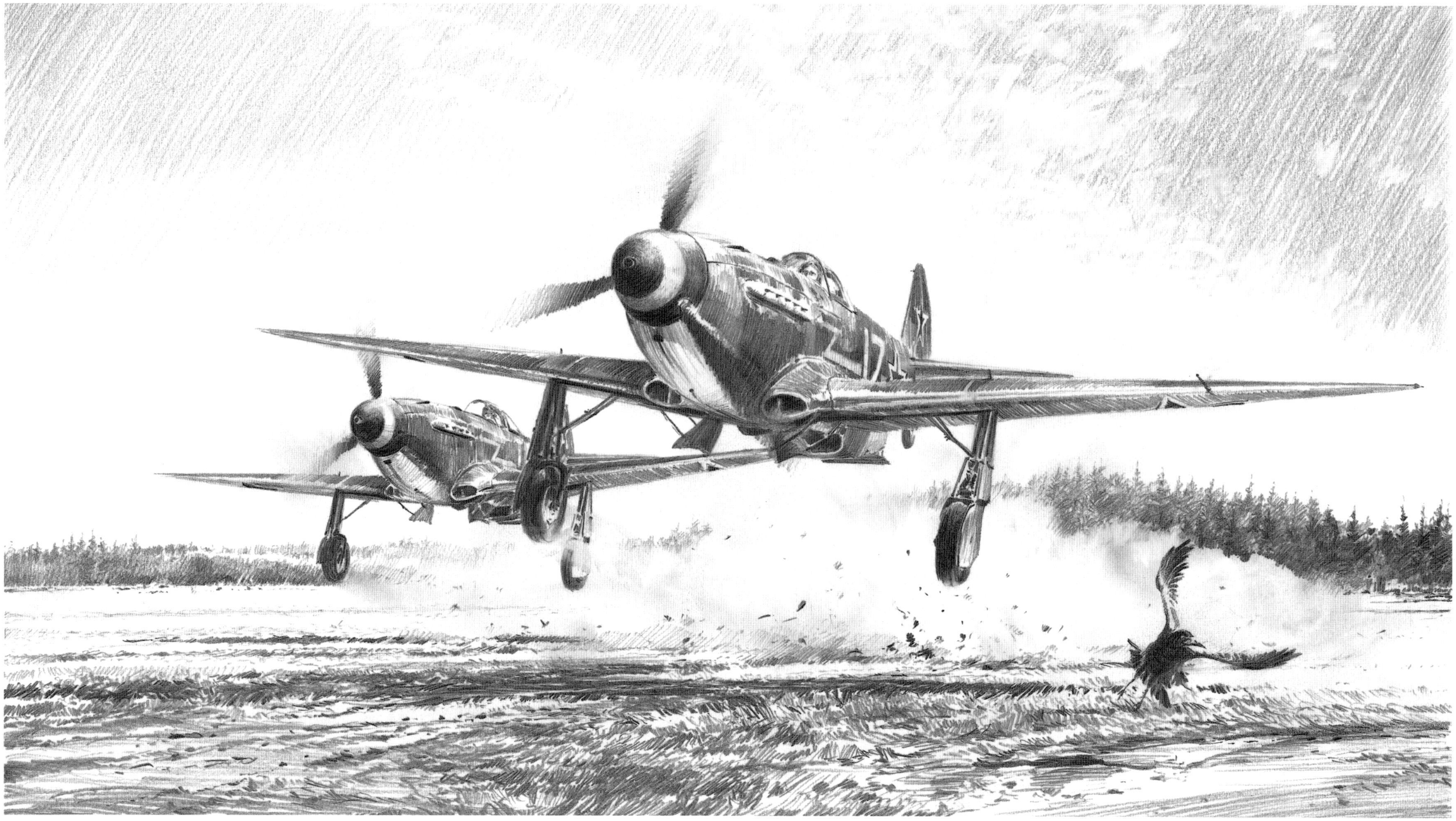

Yak 3 fighters of the Normandie-Nieman Squadron scramble from a rough airstrip on the Russian Front in 1944.

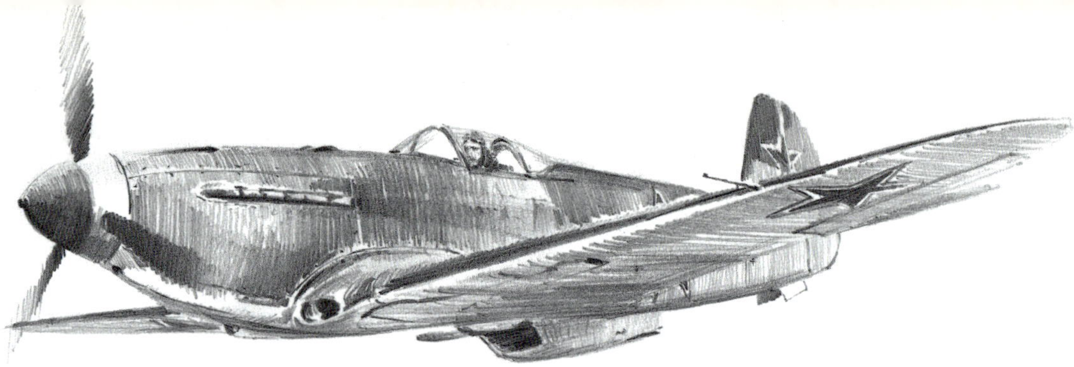

The Normandie - Nieman Squadron's trusty Yak 3 – a fighter with classic lines of the era.

One of the most popular fighters with the Russian pilots was the Yak 3, and certainly it was one of the best looking. As regards performance, however, the Yak 3 was not in the same league as the Me109, and because of the vast experience of their opponents the Russians paid dearly in the air fighting against the German pilots.

Happily quite a number survived the war, and in 1992 two of their leading aces did me the honour of signing a complete edition of prints from one of my paintings, *Russian Roulette*, shown below.

One of the problems which an aviation artist constantly faces when composing air combat paintings is the distance between opposing airplanes. Erich Hartmann was one of the most obliging fighter pilots in this respect in that he 'waited until the enemy filled the gunsight' before firing; however, it was more usual for aircraft to be several hundred yards apart when the shooting took place. This precludes the artist from showing any side views of the action, unless of course an unacceptably wide canvas is used.

One way around the problem is to show the head-on attack. This was a tactic favoured by the bravest and most determined of fighter pilots, the manoeuvre usually ending in a battle of wills. Collisions were not infrequent, and it is said that more head-on attacks were decided that way than with bullets.

The advantage to the artist of this hair-raising form of aerial combat is that by showing the aircraft almost at the point of the pass, he can legitimately paint both opposing fighters nice and large on the canvas. I chose this scenario for *Russian Roulette* and the title chose itself.

Having determined the approximate position of the aircraft, the next decision is which airplane will be viewed from the front and which from the rear, the answer often depending upon the shapes of the two contenders. Usually I will make a drawing of the encounter, observing it both ways to see which works best. In this particular incident, however, I had the luxury of finding that both aircraft looked really quite good viewed from the front or the rear, and since I had not painted the Yak before, I decided to show this one from the front.

Painting an aircraft for the first time is, I imagine, rather as flying a new aircraft type must be to an experienced pilot: it holds no fears, but takes a little getting used to. I followed my usual procedure of making a scale model, and spent some time studying all the angles. I had already taken a close look at a Yak 3 at the Museum of Flying on a visit to Santa Monica, California, so by the time I came to work out the composition for the painting I had a good feel for the Russian fighter.

RUSSIAN ROULETTE

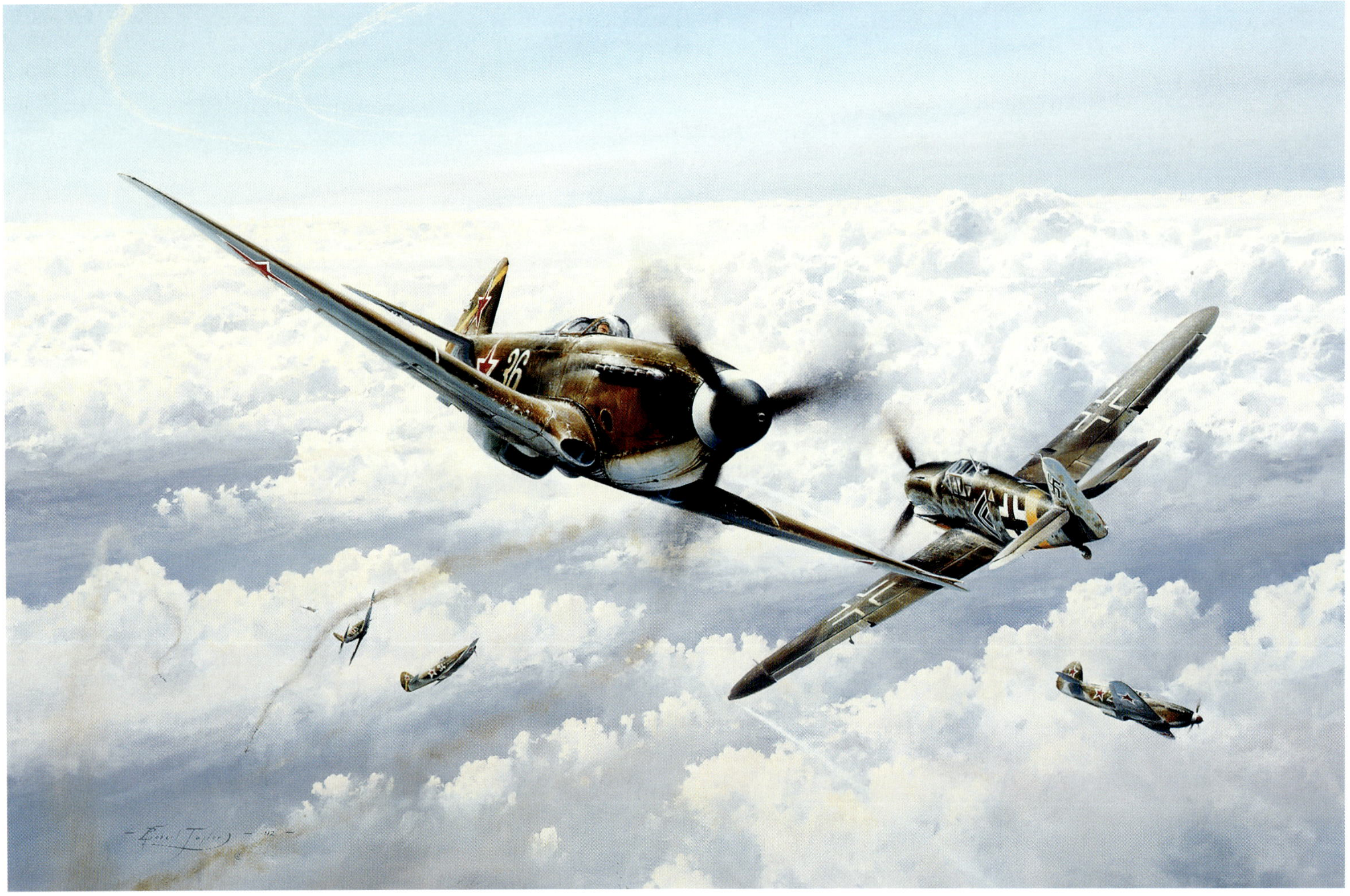

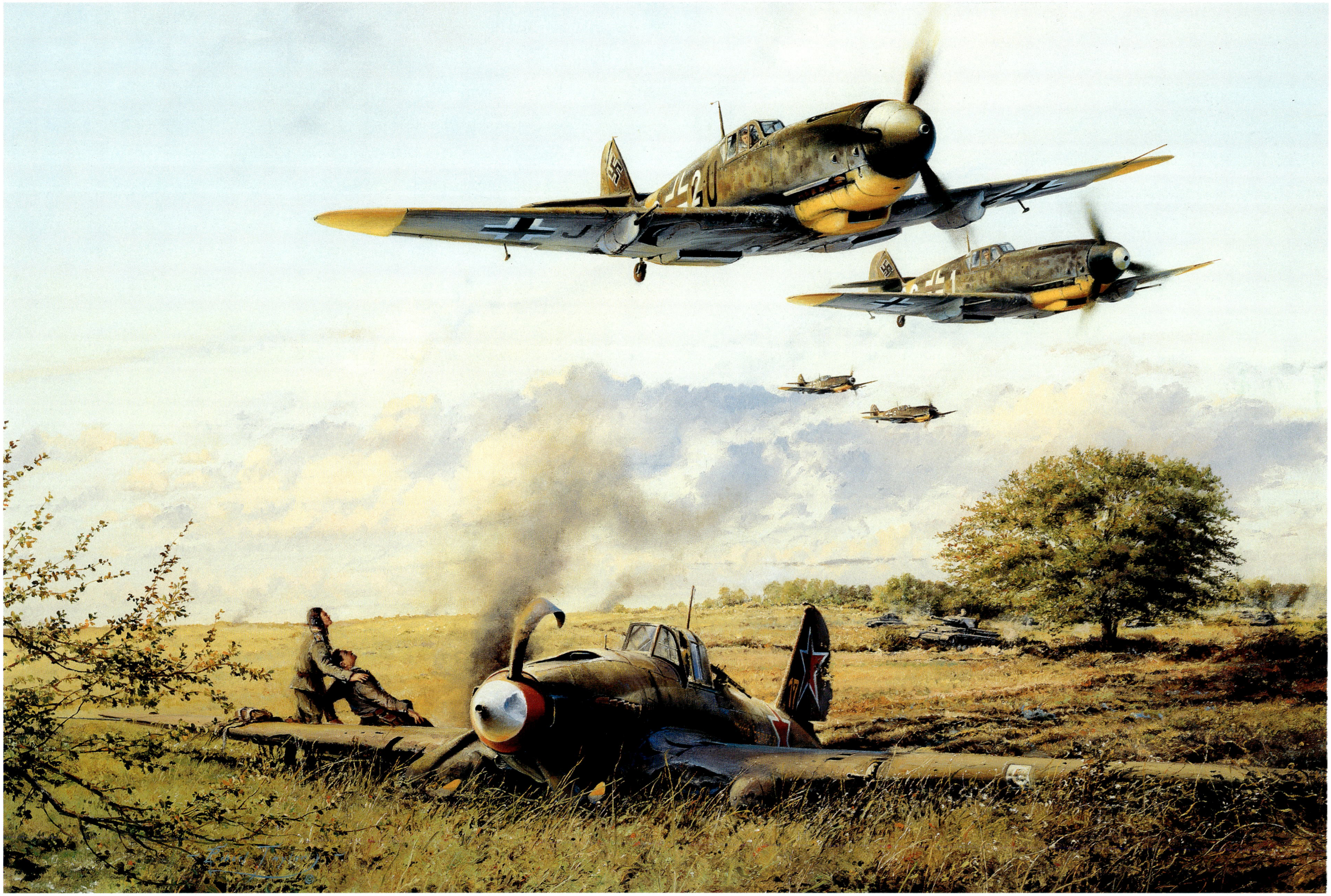

HARTMANN TRIBUTE

In the collection of Mr Edgar Leicher

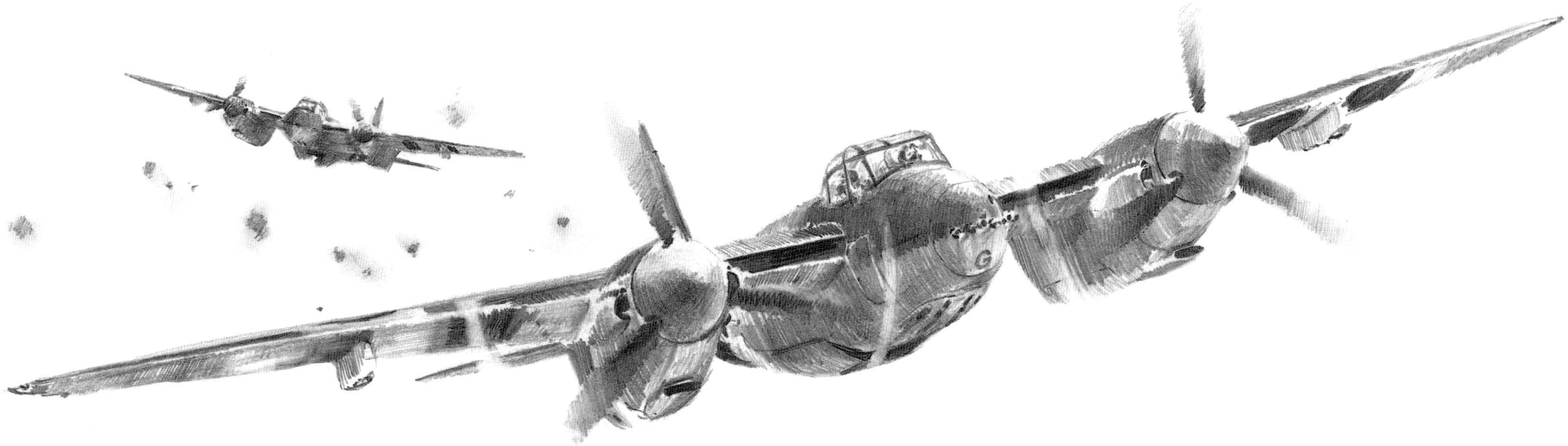

RANGERS ON THE RAMPAGE

Although I have painted pictures covering most eras of aviation, for a number of years I have specialised in the period covering World War II. During this time I have accumulated many friends who help me on a regular basis with research, such a vital part of painting pictures featuring scenes from the past. This group of knowledgeable enthusiasts each has his or her own area of special interest, and it continually astounds me how much they know about their subjects. An example of the value of accurate reference material to an artist painting retrospectively, as I do, was the information I needed for *Rangers on the Rampage.*

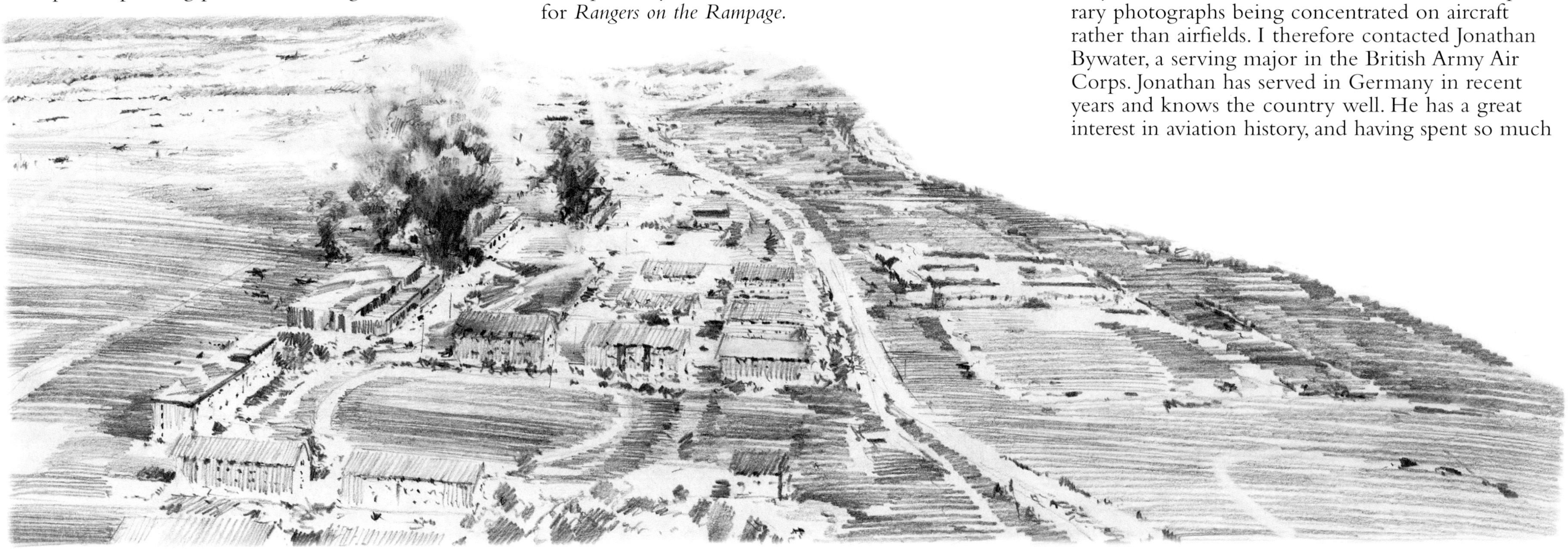

This painting was to feature the Mosquito in its role as a low-level attack aircraft, and I needed visual reference of German airfields upon which I could base the one in the picture. I was having difficulty finding anything other than photographs showing only small areas of airfields, most of the contemporary photographs being concentrated on aircraft rather than airfields. I therefore contacted Jonathan Bywater, a serving major in the British Army Air Corps. Jonathan has served in Germany in recent years and knows the country well. He has a great interest in aviation history, and having spent so much

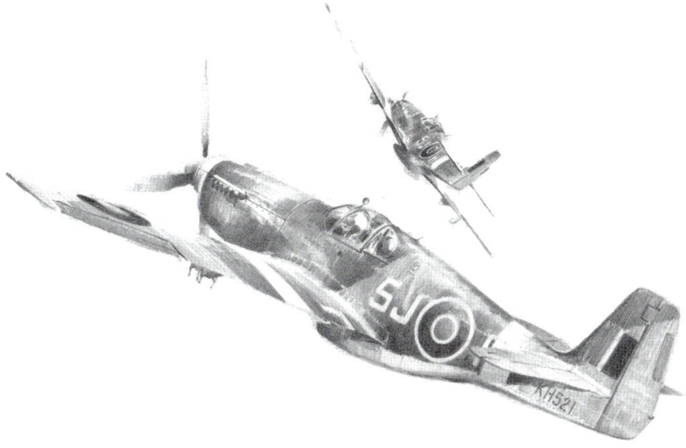

Mustangs of 126 Squadron

time in Germany, has developed a special interest and knowledge concerning the Luftwaffe during World War II. I discussed my needs with him and within a couple of days received all the reference material I needed. Without this kind of help I would spend more time researching than painting.

The airfield depicted is based on Hildesheim, situated about twenty miles south of Hanover, and the reference material available to me was a mixture of contemporary and modern photographs. The airfield was used by the British army until quite recently, the hangar clearly visible in the picture having stored their Chieftain tanks; the hangar obscured by smoke housed the Army Air Corps Lynx and Gazelle helicopters. The airfield and buildings survived the war reasonably intact in spite of the attack witnessed here, but the town of Hildesheim was heavily damaged during the final phases of the war.

Using the collection of photographs available, I made some sketches of the airfield in order to determine the overall composition, and to decide where I would position the Mosquitos. I selected an angle which gave me a series of features in the overall landscape which had converging 'lines' in order to take the eye into the middle distance, the various roads and the river all contributed nicely. The strange-looking patterns on the grass airfield were put there so as to appear from the air like ditches, in an effort to disguise the airfield from visiting Allied bombers. They were rather a nuisance to paint, interfering somewhat with the perspective in that area of the painting, but I had to include them in the interests of accuracy.

The De Havilland Mosquito was one of the best aircraft of the period. Made almost entirely of wood and powered by two powerful Merlin engines, it was faster than any other piston-engined aircraft that flew during the war. Because of its great power and manoeuvrability it was used in almost every role enacted by the RAF, one of the most exhilarating of all being the low-level 'Day Ranger' missions. Given a free hand at squadron level to select targets of opportunity deep inside enemy-held territory, the Ranger Mosquito crews wreaked havoc in the air and on the ground all over occupied Europe.

Rangers on the Rampage aims to give some impression of these exciting yet dangerous sorties.

Typical of the Day Ranger squadrons was No 418 (City of Edmonton) Squadron, Royal Canadian Air Force. Flying the Mosquito Fighter-Bomber MkVI, they completed over 3,000 effective missions, destroyed 172 enemy aircraft (73 on the ground), damaged a further 103, and in addition brought down 83 buzz-bombs. The painting below, *Mosquito Sting*, shows Mosquitos of 418 squadron RCAF making a low-level attack on the airfield at Vaerlose, Denmark, in 1944.

MOSQUITO STING

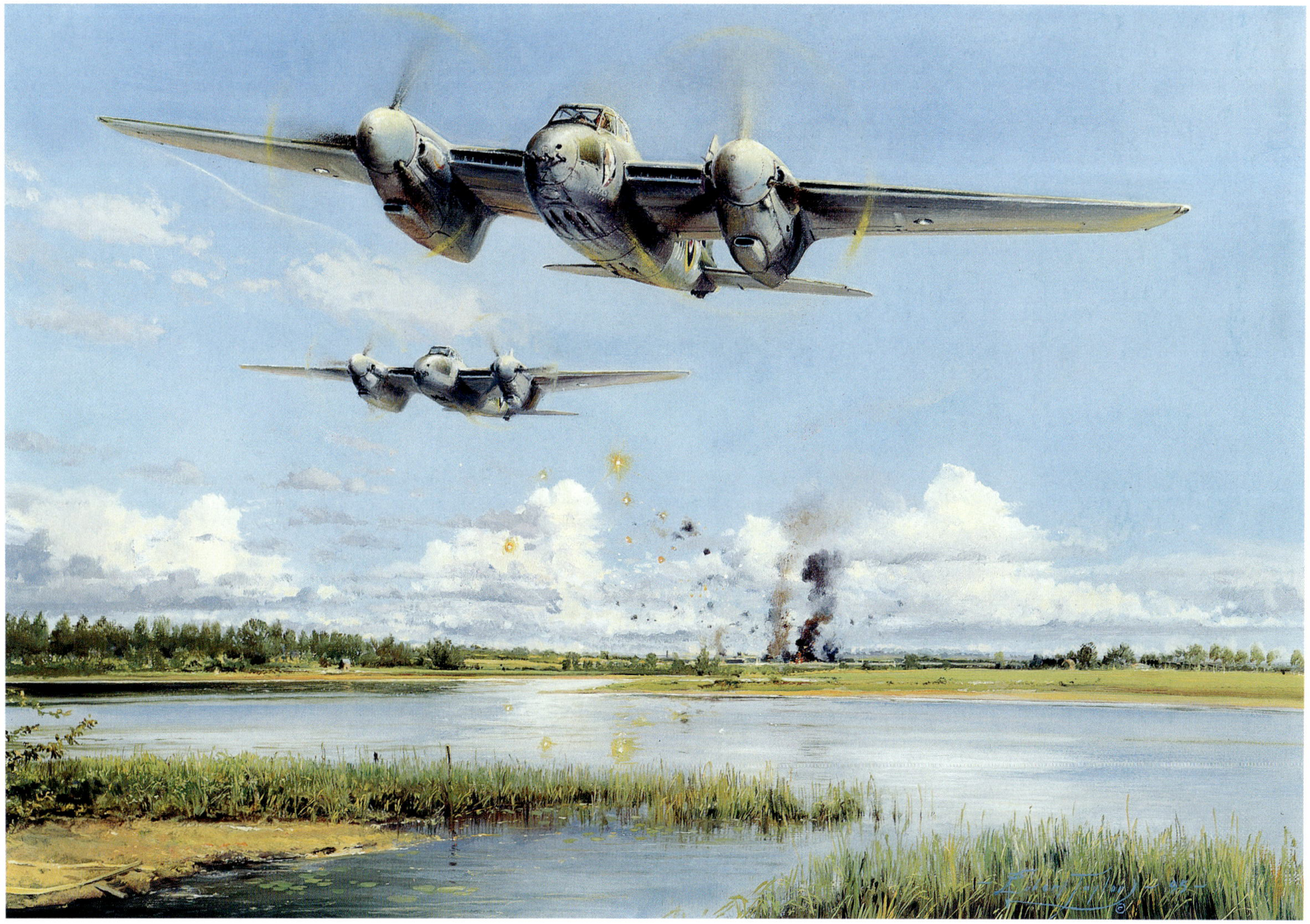

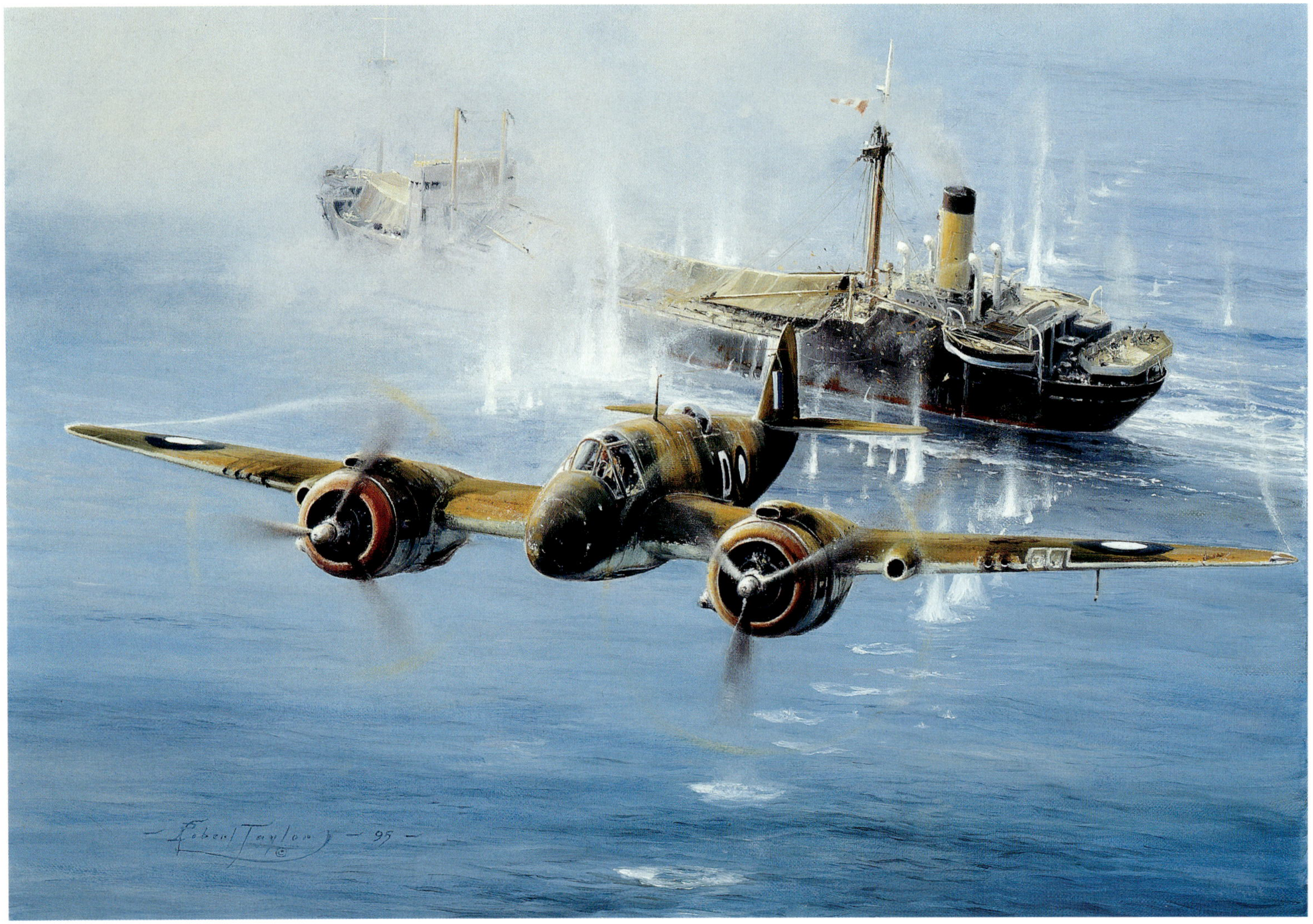

SHIPPING STRIKE

The free-ranging Mosquitos almost always hunted in pairs. I would have liked to have included a few more of them in the painting, but to have used this kind of artistic licence would have compromised the authenticity of these missions. For this reason I painted the main aircraft fairly large in the picture, and relied upon flak and exploding bombs to introduce plenty of action to the scene. The close-up view clearly shows the forward-firing machine-guns in the nose, and close scrutiny will reveal the bomb doors almost, but not quite closed following the attack. Both Mosquitos still carry their invasion stripes, these being clearly visible on the underside of their wings.

The buildings in the foreground were, as one would expect of a military base, very regimented in their layout, and I had some difficulty with them throughout the painting. They were always going to be prominent, but it was important that they didn't dominate the foreground. To this end I painted the horizon on a slight angle, which means that the buildings appear off the perpendicular and so don't catch the eye quite so readily. The main façade of each building has three storeys, each having twenty-seven windows, nine of which are dormers in the roof. Painting the barracks took forever!

Another British aircraft which built a reputation as an excellent low-level attacker was the Bristol Beaufighter. Though lacking the Mosquito's supreme performance, it was a tough and manoeuvrable plane, well suited to the number of roles in which it served during World War II. The painting on this page, *Shipping Strike*, shows a Beaufighter of No 30 Squadron Royal Australian Air Force – the first Australian squadron to be equipped with the Beaufighter – making a typical low-level attack on enemy shipping off the coast of New Guinea in 1943. Under the command of Brian 'Black Jack' Walker, No 30 Squadron's exploits in the Far East became legendary. The aircraft seen in the picture is flown by the squadron commander.

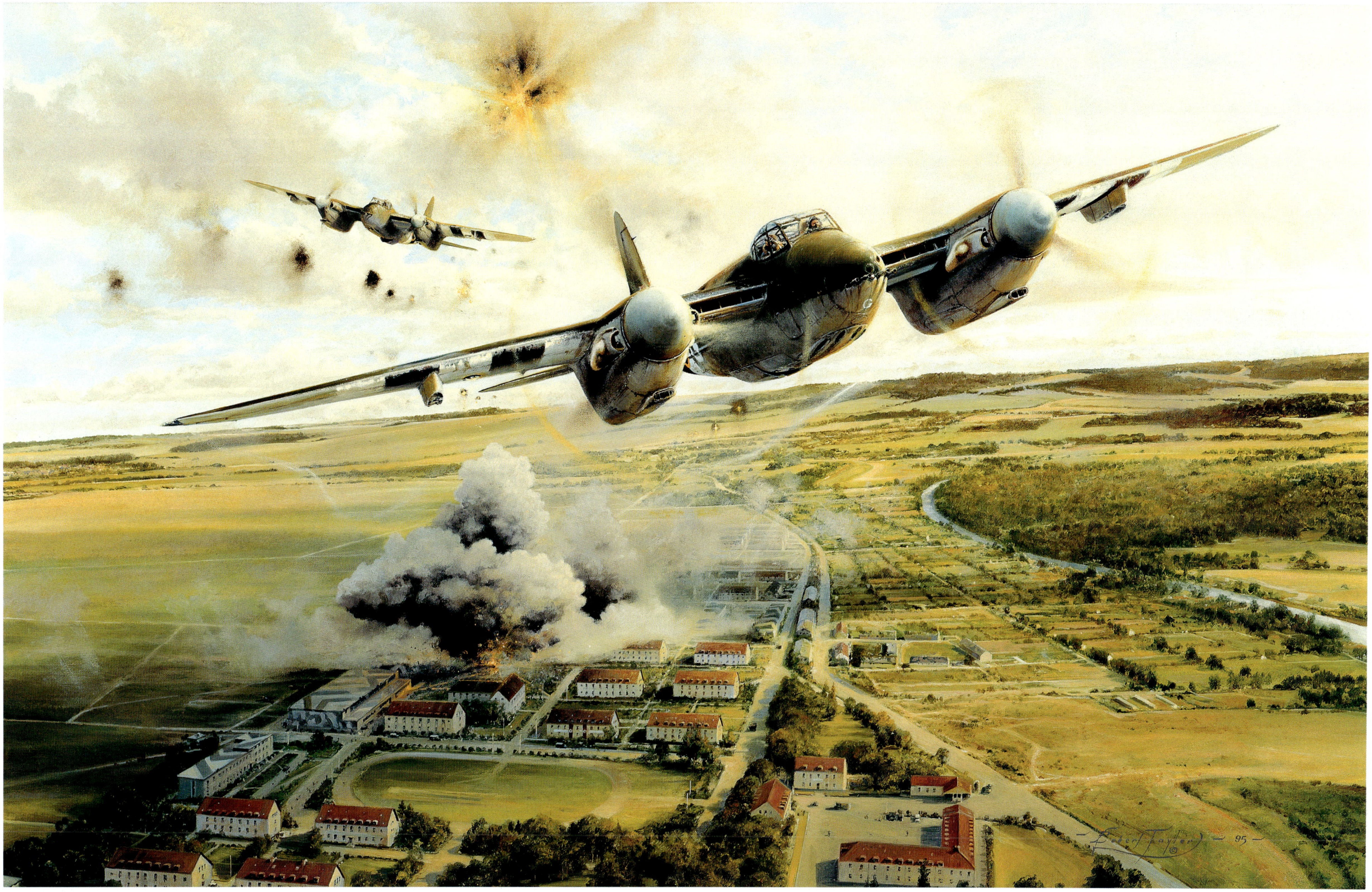

RANGERS ON THE RAMPAGE

Private collection

CHENNAULT'S FLYING TIGERS

Thirty days overdue from the United States, a Norwegian freighter slipped quietly into Rangoon harbour. Believing that there were Japanese-equipped German raiders operating in the western Pacific, she had navigated a circuitous route for she carried a precious cargo of one hundred Curtiss P-40C fighters.

A month later, on 11 July 1941, a Dutch liner set sail in great secrecy, headed for the same destination. Aboard was a rag-tag bunch of flyers seeking adventure: disguised as missionaries, doctors, businessmen, students and tourists, these were Navy and Air Force pilots, and a few commercial and test pilots. This mixed bag of adventurers was to become General Claire Chennault's American Volunteer Group, known as The Flying Tigers, and within the following year this outwardly casual gathering of young men would become legend.

To the north of the vital port of Rangoon lay the long, winding Burma Road, China's only remaining link with the outside world since the expanding Japanese forces had placed a stranglehold on its seaports. That particular war was already three years old. Aware of the strategic importance of the roughly hewn and tortuous thoroughfare, the Japanese Air Force gave the road a continual pounding. As the cargo from the two ships came ashore at Rangoon, resistance to the air attacks had all but evaporated, and the Chinese army was in danger of having its vital supply line permanently severed.

But within six months of their arrival in Burma, the pilots of the AVG, assisted by some two hundred ground personnel, had become a cohesive, highly effective fighting force. With little support from home and almost without replacement aircraft or spares, the P-40 pilots of the AVG became the scourge of the Imperial Japanese Air Force, and heroes to the Chinese people. In a six-month period of combat, with no more than fifty or sixty serviceable aircraft at any one time, and often outnumbered five or six to one, they destroyed some three hundred Japanese planes while probably damaging another three hundred, and caused incalculable damage to Japanese ground resources. Practically single-handed they succeeded in keeping the Japanese out of India.

Their brief but illustrious existence came to an end when the AVG was absorbed into the US Army Air Corps on 4 July 1942; thus Chennault's Flying Tigers passed gloriously into history.

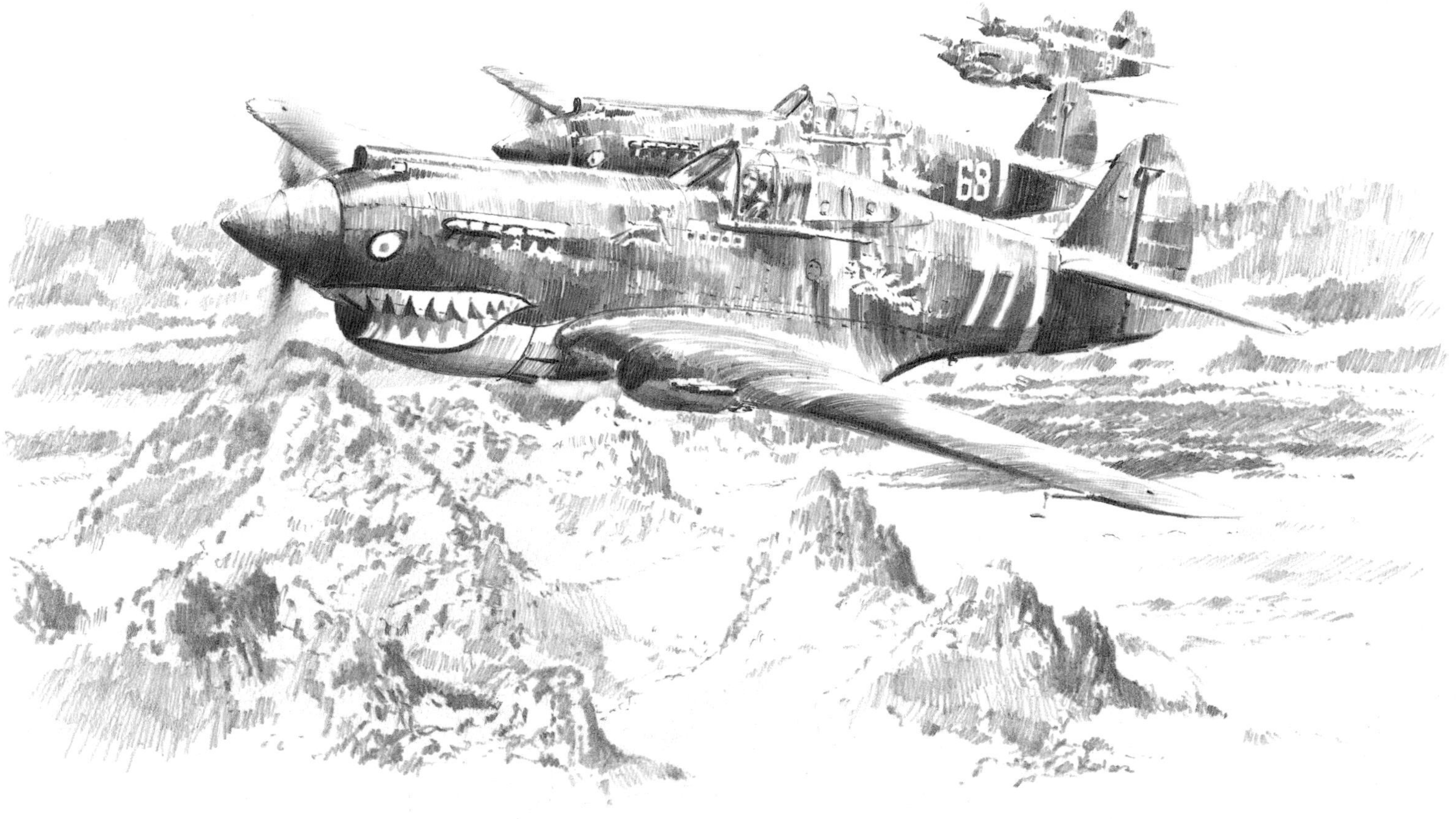

Shark mouthed P40c of the 3rd Pursuit Squadron (Hells Angels) fly in tight company.
Over a period of nine months the AVG amassed 286 confirmed kills against only four combat losses.

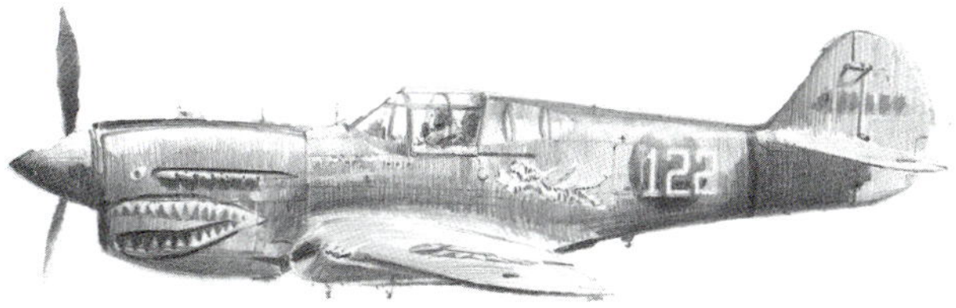

Novelists could not have scripted a more exciting or unlikely scenario, and it is not surprising that films have been made about the Flying Tigers, books written, and paintings painted. When researching for this picture I learned that, contrary to popular conception, the famous shark's teeth insignia painted on the engine cowl was *not* copied from the British squadrons operating in the North African desert: as far as the AVG was concerned, its origins lay with Chinese folklore.

Erik Shilling, one of the AVG pilots, had learned from a local missionary that the Japanese had an obsessive phobia about sharks. Being an island nation of fishermen, and since the shark is the scourge of all fishermen, it seemed the perfect insignia for the job in hand and Shilling arranged for the shark's mouth, complete with vicious-looking teeth, to be painted on one of the aircraft. Chennault was so taken with the idea that he ordered the aggressive design to be painted on all the AVG's P-40s. The sharply coned spinner and the large air intake just below it were of the ideal shape, and when the eye of the shark was added, the design gave the P-40s a fearsome appearance. The design was continued after the Flying Tigers were absorbed into the US Army Air Corps, being proudly displayed by the P-40 pilots who followed the illustrious AVG into battle. The tradition of the Flying Tigers is permanently honoured, and there has been a US Air Force squadron proudly wearing the famous shark's mouth insignia ever since.

I also learned the origins of the 'Flying Tigers' title. One of the AVG pilots, A.B. Christman, had been an artist with Walt Disney, and a colleague at the studios in California had created an emblem consisting of a winged Bengal tiger set against the Chinese Star. This also appealed to Chennault, and when the design was painted on all AVG aircraft, the group became known as the Flying Tigers.

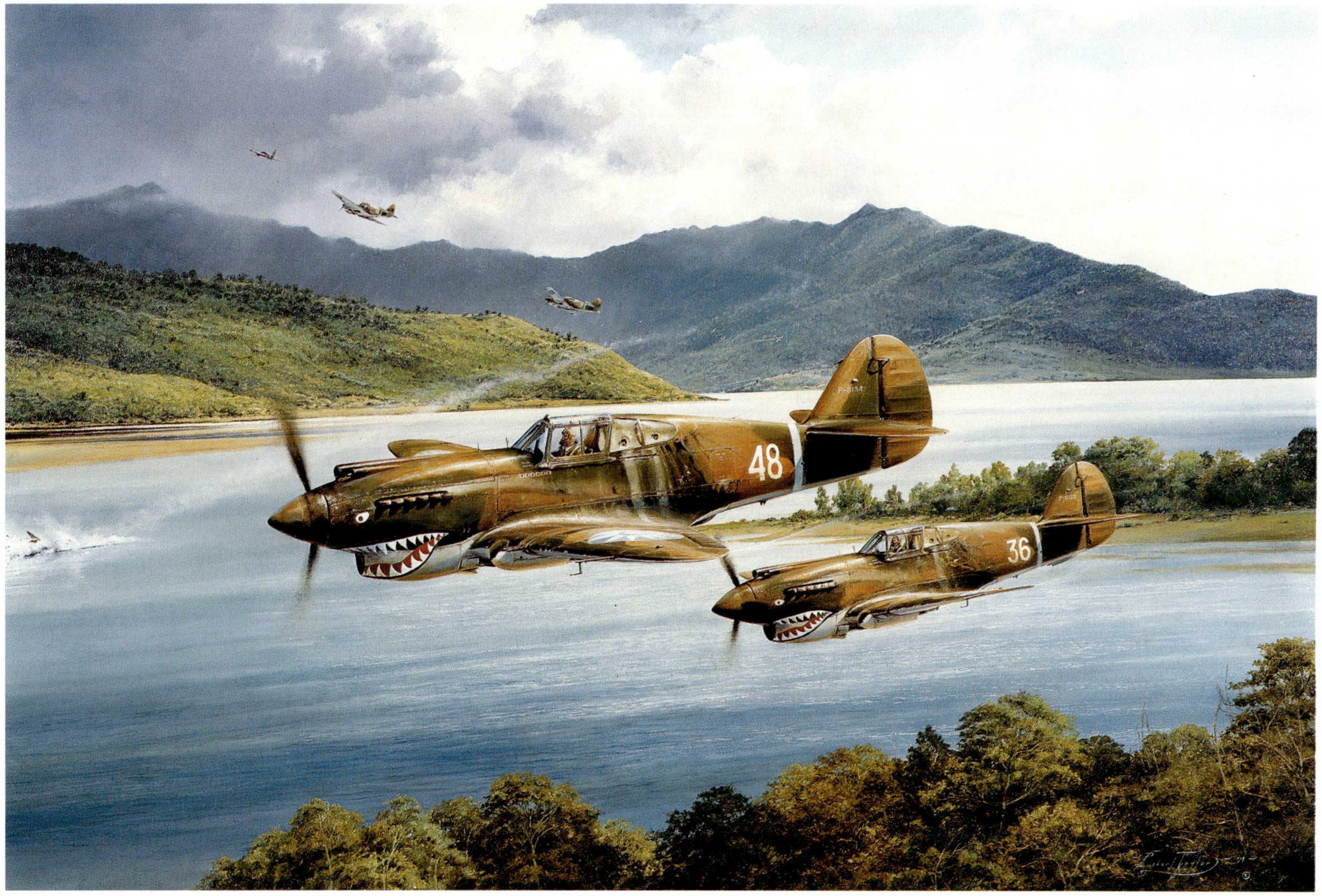

CHENNAULT'S FLYING TIGERS

In the collection of Mr Eugene Eisenberg

Brightly coloured insignia, ornate squadron markings and even art became the hallmark of the USAAF, most aircraft being adorned with some unique form of graphic design. Paintings on the noses of aircraft reached almost high-art proportions, by far the most popular being lavishly portrayed ladies accompanied by an appropriate name or description. This colourful approach to the serious business of war added a much needed lighter touch, and was indicative of the flamboyant nature of the young Americans who flew in World War II.

The painting above, *Chennault's Flying Tigers*, depicts a typical AVG action. In the foreground, two P-40s of the 2nd Pursuit Squadron, the 'Panda Bears', pull out of their diving attack just above the tree-tops of the Burmese jungle; their victim, a Japanese bomber, hits the water to starboard. Two more P-40s bear down on a second Nakajima, while in the background the air is busy with low-level combat.

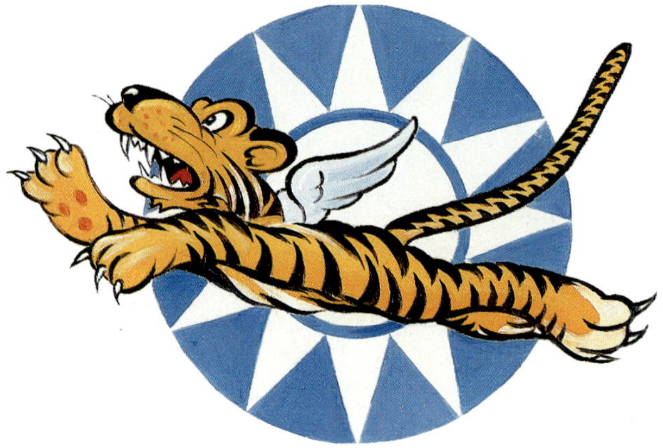

I have discussed elsewhere in this volume the close-up study of paintings, and the insight this provides for those interested in an individual artist's particular technique and painting style. The detail shown on this two-page spread shows the main P-40 in the painting *Chennault's Flying Tigers* at almost the exact size it was painted on the original canvas. The complete painting is shown on the previous page.

In all my paintings I endeavour to achieve realism in my work, and with this one it was no different. The Flying Tigers were plagued with a lack of spares, and it is testimony to the ingenuity and dogged persistence of the small band of ground crews that the AVG's P-40s were kept flying, let alone in fighting shape. Mechanical maintenance was of prime importance, so engines had top priority along with control surfaces, and appearance came at the bottom of the list. Aircraft were patched up as best as was possible; there was little paint available and not much time to apply it anyway, so the aircraft of the Flying Tigers were not exactly in showroom condition. I knew this and painted them accordingly.

I therefore carefully chipped paint off the leading edges of the wings and from the engine cowl behind the spinners; the panels around the engine were given that slight unevenness that comes with continual removal and refitting; and more paint was removed from the panel fixing points and along the rivet lines, denoting the constant activity of ground crews. Streaking from the fuel filler caps is a film of dust and grime attracted by wet gasoline, a feature noticeable on all P-40s. This grimy area of the fuselage unfortunately coincided with the spot chosen to paint the squadron emblem, presenting the difficult task of first painting the emblem, then half obliterating the handiwork with a layer of 'dirt'!

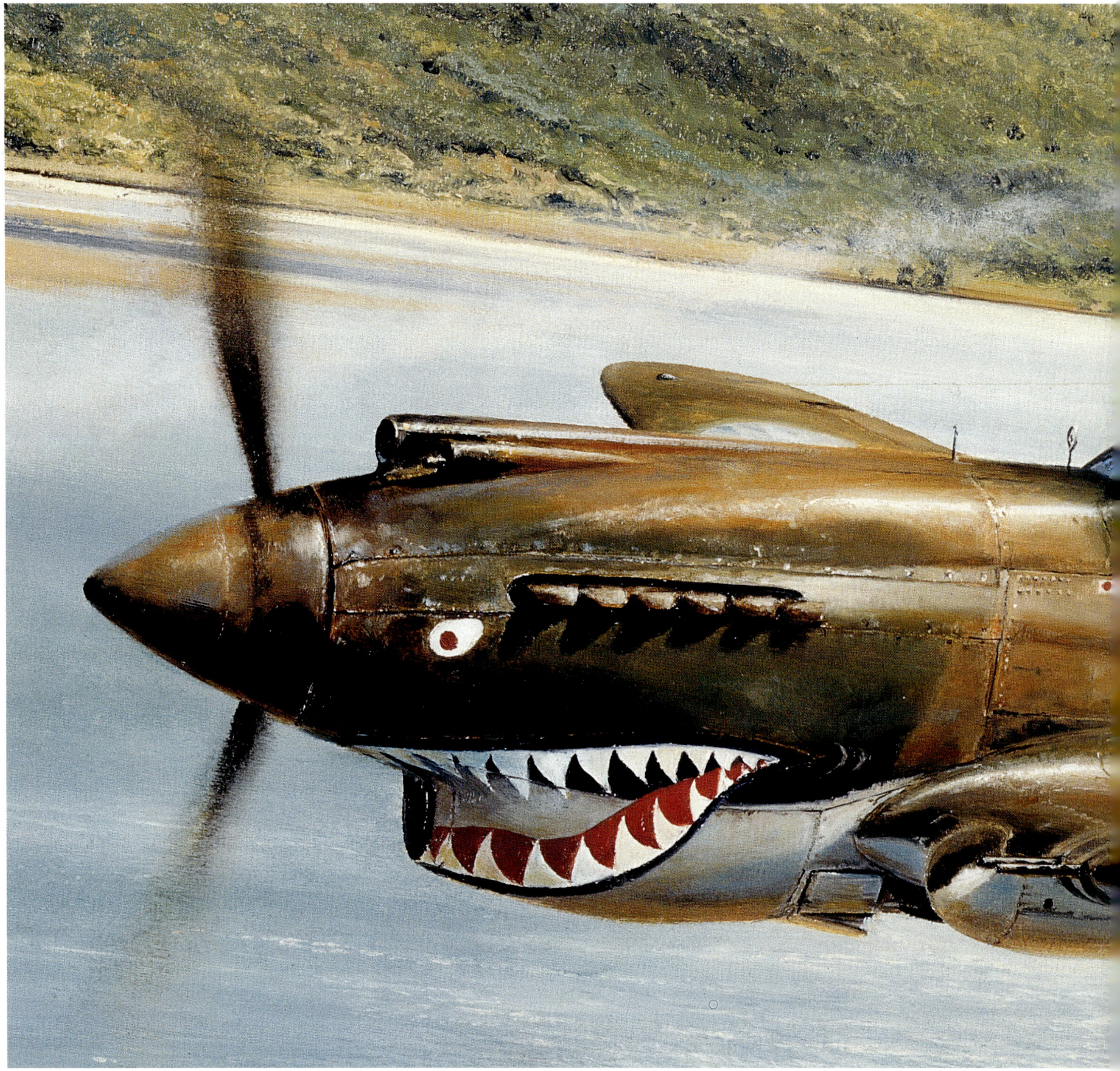

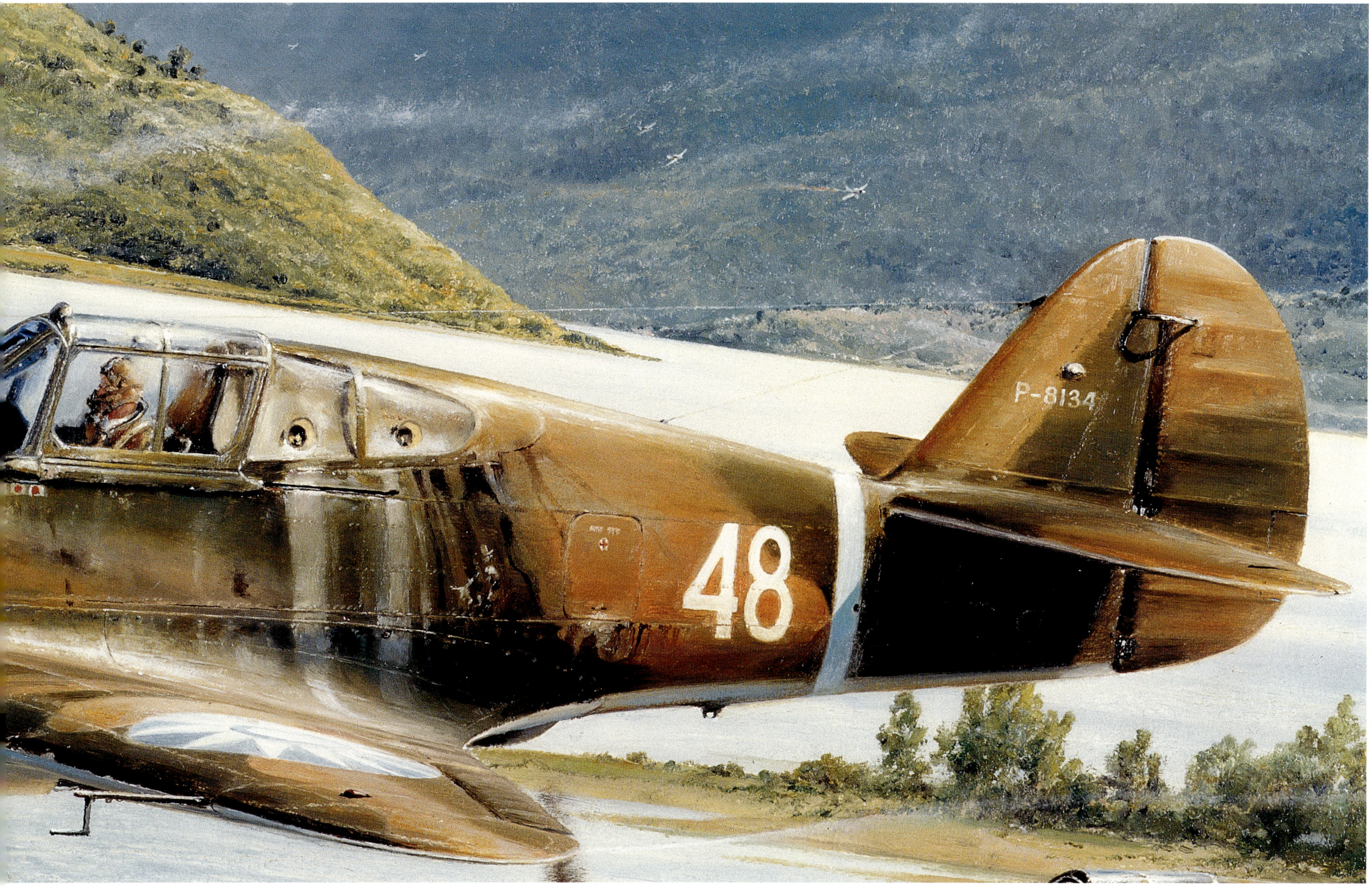

CHENNAULT'S FLYING TIGERS

(detail)

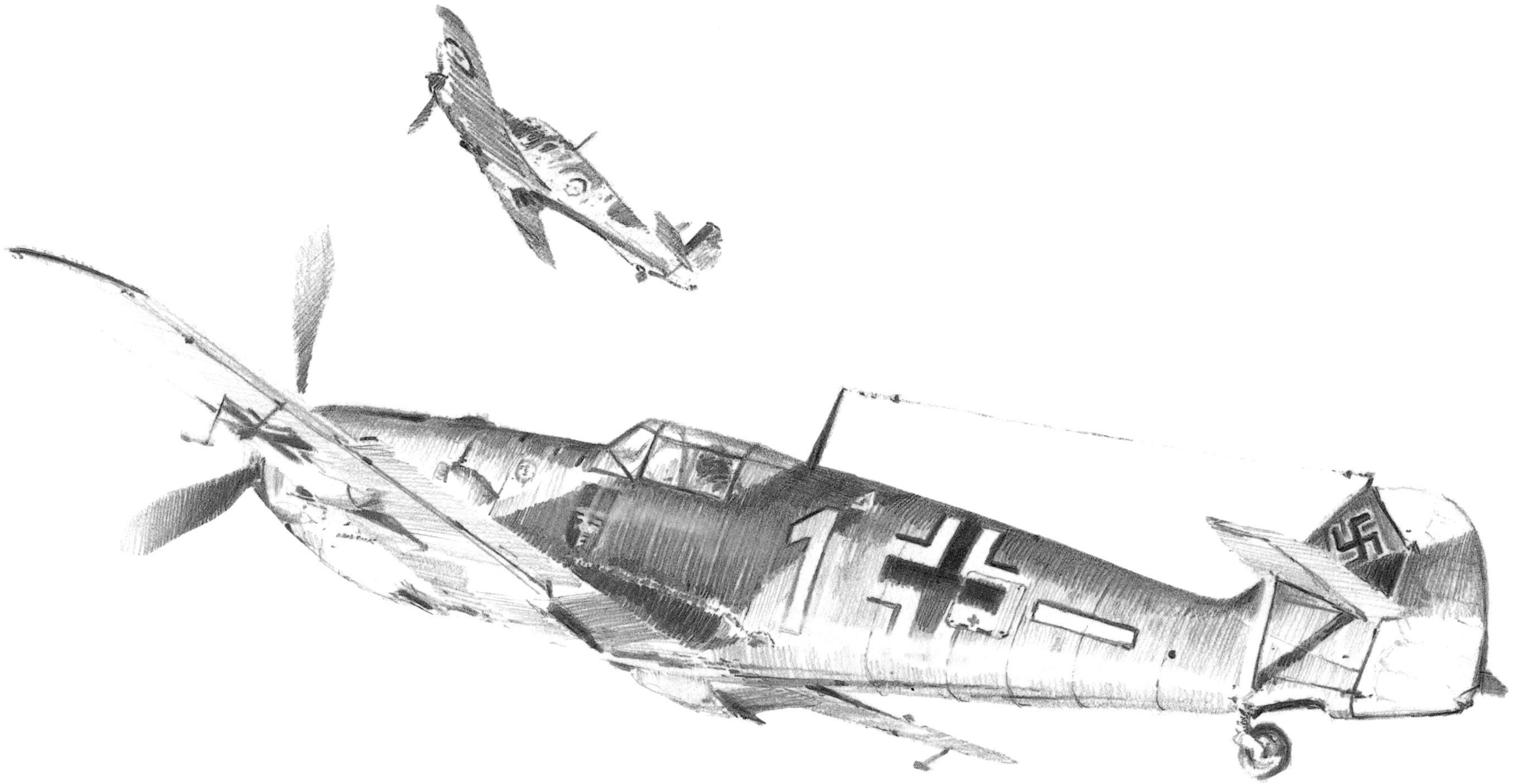

STEINHOFF TRIBUTE

The tremendous air battles between the Luftwaffe and the Royal Air Force, fought high over London and south-east England in the summer of 1940, were the most decisive of the war. Both sides in the desperate contest knew that the outcome would determine the course of the war. Had the Luftwaffe not been repelled during those summer months Hitler's planned invasion of Britain would have followed quickly, and the war might have been lost. Every day throughout the long, hot summer the RAF's pilots climbed their Spitfires and Hurricanes to meet the incoming armadas of German planes, and in the ensuing months history witnessed the most sustained period of air fighting in the annals of aviation. This great aerial contest, which became known as the Battle of Britain, produced many of the famous air aces of the war. Johannes Steinhoff, 'Macky' to his friends and comrades, was one of the greatest.

As a young man Macky Steinhoff yearned to fly, commencing his training in 1935. Like all young flyers of the day, he knew nothing and cared even less of the politics and motives behind the fast emerging Luftwaffe, and when he was given the task of forming the first night-fighting squadron in 1939 with gleaming new Messerschmitt Me109s, it was a dream come true. Moreover if his country was to go to war, as a professional military man he would play his part with dignity and honour; and with those sentiments he led 10 (night-fighter)/JG26 to war.

I met Macky Steinhoff many times. He was a man of great dignity, personality and courage, and a man of many talents. He was badly scarred on his face and hands, the consequence of a terrible crash while taking off an Me262 towards the end of the war; yet it was indicative of his strong character that you never seemed to notice this disfigurement while in his company. That he became Chief of Staff in the new German Air Force, and ultimately chairman of the NATO military committee with the rank of general, is testimony to his fortitude and determination.

Throughout his life Macky was a great horseman, and during his latter years his fine white Lippizaner stallion was his pride and joy. He travelled a great deal, and loved visiting his family in Colorado, and in spite of his busy schedule somehow managed to find the time to write several books. He was also an accomplished painter in watercolours, and would question me in great detail on painting techniques whenever we met. When he died I lost a greatly respected friend: I clearly remembered his words regarding the Battle of Britain – *'Looking back, I felt that the early part of the war, particularly the Battle of Britain, had been a gentleman's conflict'* – and these served as inspiration for the picture I painted in tribute to this legendary Luftwaffe fighter leader.

Throughout the Battle of Britain the opposing fighter pilots fought each other with tremendous determination. At the time, although there was considerable respect for each other, there was no love lost between them and, like the duels of the knights of old, their aerial dogfights were fought with gallantry but to the bitter end. There was chivalry on both sides, and this was apparent whenever a pilot was captured, it being customary in those early years for the victor to visit the vanquished whenever possible – always provided the latter had lived to tell the tale!

When the Battle of Britain was over there was a brief respite, for the RAF pilots which allowed many who had fought continually throughout to take a short rest from operational flying. The system of resting pilots between tours was a luxury not afforded to the Luftwaffe pilots. Many such as Macky Steinhoff continued to fly front-line combat missions virtually without a break throughout the duration of the war, a number of the great Luftwaffe aces completing over a thousand missions.

After the war, many of those pilots who had fought on opposite sides met to discuss their experiences, and some became lifelong friends, that unique camaraderie which exists between fighter pilots sealing their friendship. On the frequent occasions that I met Luftwaffe pilots it was in the jovial, friendly company of the RAF pilots they had once fought. Seeing them laughing and joking together, to this day I find it difficult to imagine how this happy band of warriors could have fought each other, and their lasting friendships emphasise only too vividly the futility of war.

The painting below depicts the Mk Va Spitfire of one of the RAF's most famous Battle of Britain pilots, Douglas Bader. After commanding No 242 Hurricane Squadron during the battle, Bader then went on to lead the famous Tangmere Wing Spitfires, until he was brought down over northern France and taken prisoner in 1941. Using the Wing Commander's privilege, Douglas Bader's Spitfire carried his initials, which in turn led to his famous call sign 'Dogsbody'.

BADER LEGEND

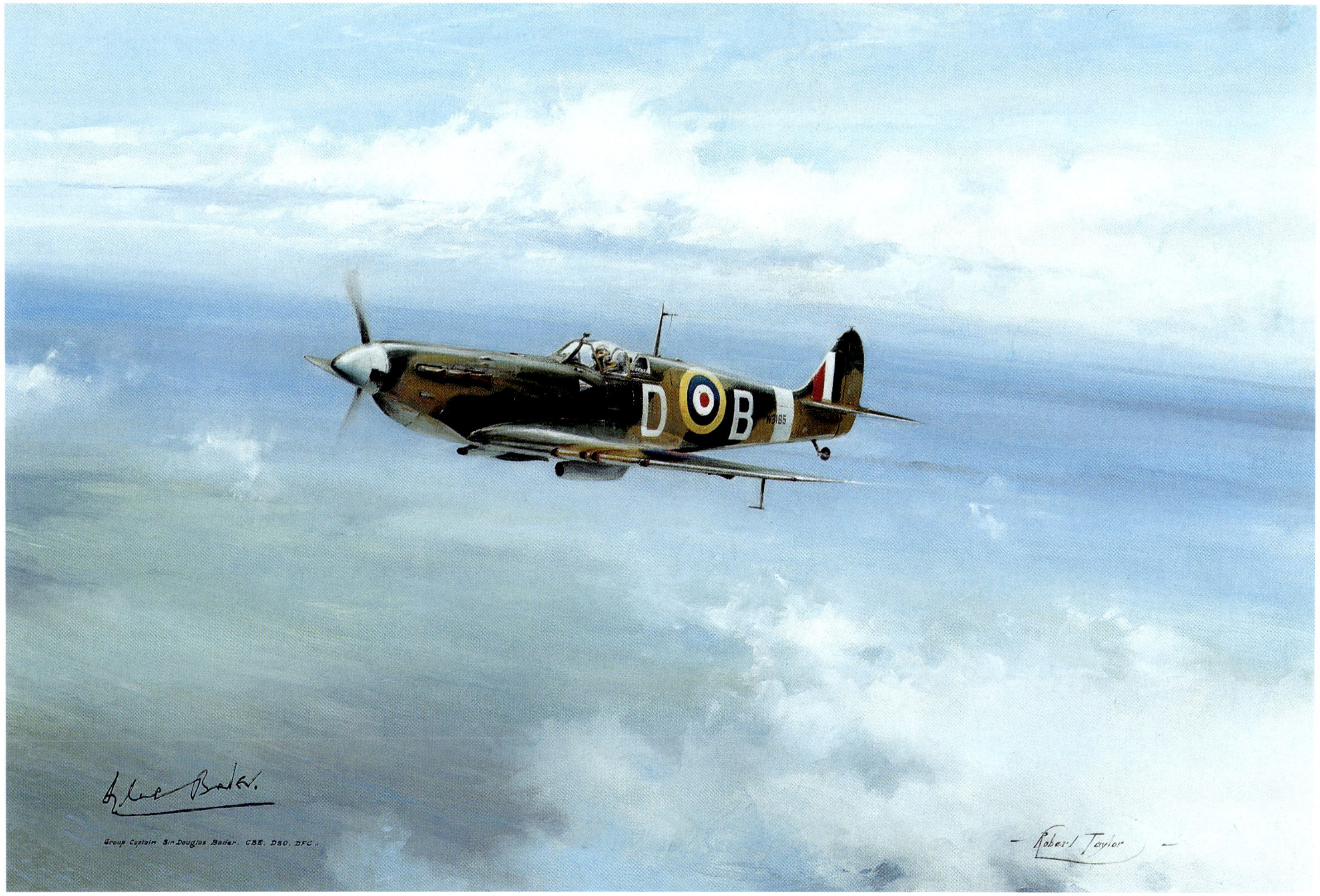

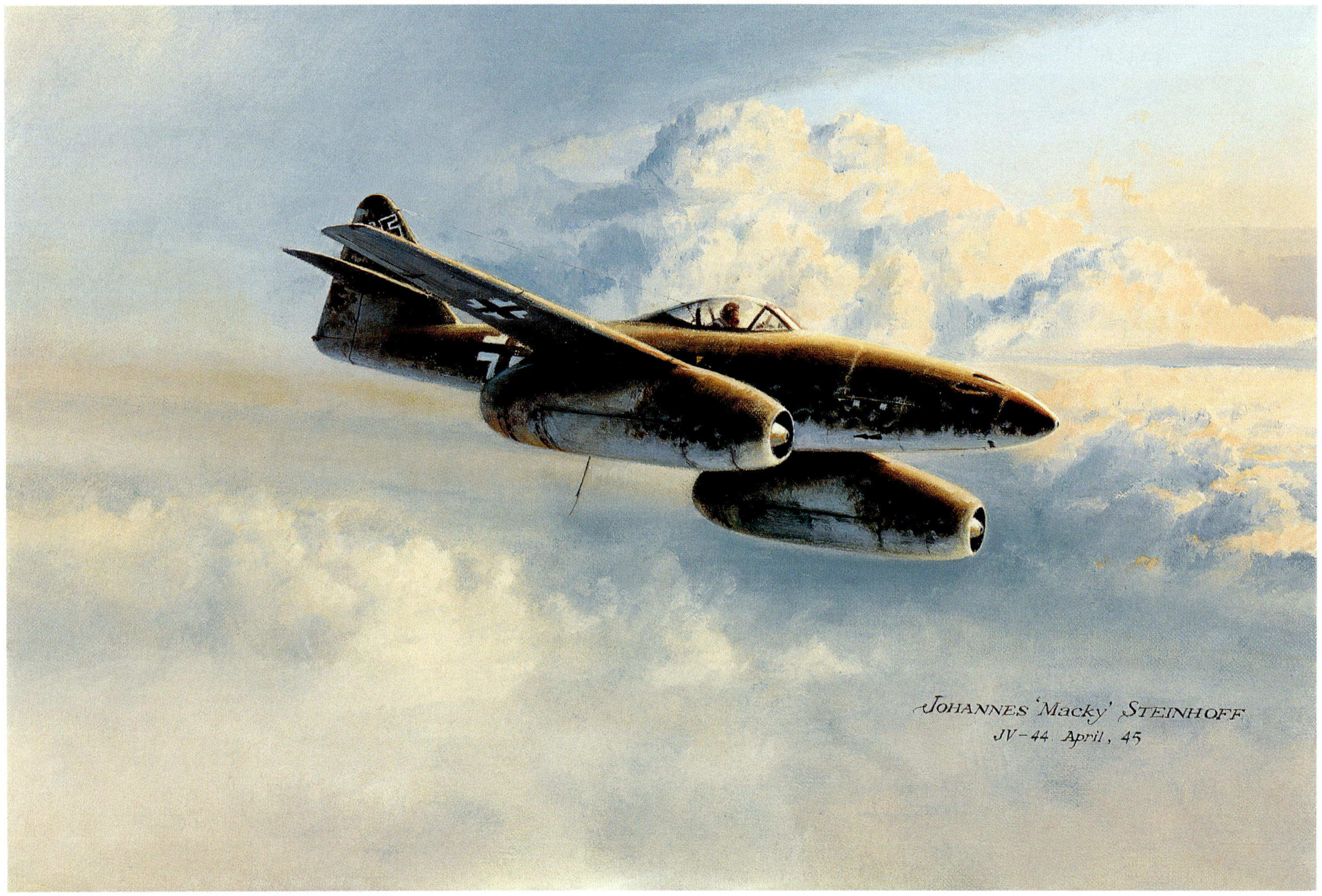

MACKY STEINHOFF'S Me262

After five years of almost continual combat flying in Me109s on both Western and Eastern Fronts, in late 1944 Macky Steinhoff took command of JG-7, the Luftwaffe's first jet unit. He later joined Adolf Galland's JV-44, and it was while flying with Galland's 'Squadron of Experts' that he survived the horrendous crash: taking off his Me262 from Munich-Riem, it hit a shell crater, overturned and burst into flames. Miraculously Macky survived, but his burns were so serious that he lived with the legacy of that incident for the rest of his life.

Macky was in every sense a gentleman. Knowing how he had always reflected upon the 'gentlemanly way' in which the Battle of Britain had been fought, when commissioned to paint a tribute to him I felt it appropriate to paint him in action in a typical Battle of Britain scene. It is August 1940: Heinkel 111 bombers have attacked airfields and radar stations along the south coast, and a frantic dogfight has developed above the white cliffs of Dover as the bombers head for home. Flying with JG-52, Macky's Me109s have clashed with Hurricanes of the RAF's No 32 Squadron, and Macky is desperately defending one of the He111s which has suffered at the hands of the Hurricane pilots. Directly behind his Me109 is the port of Dover from which so many small ships had set out during the evacuation of Dunkirk a few months earlier.

The small oil sketch on this page shows Macky Steinhoff's Messerschmitt Me262 jet fighter. Steinhoff flew with many other leading Luftwaffe aces in Adolf Galland's JV-44, a remarkable group of top-scoring, highly decorated fighter aces brought together by Galland towards the end of the war. But as Luftwaffe supremo Hermann Goering continued to demonstrate total incompetence, and knowing that the war was lost, Galland, Steinhoff and company came together in a last ditch effort to defend their homeland against the Allies' final assault. Though they all knew it was a hopeless task, being professional fighter pilots to the core, they would fight to the bitter end. And they did.

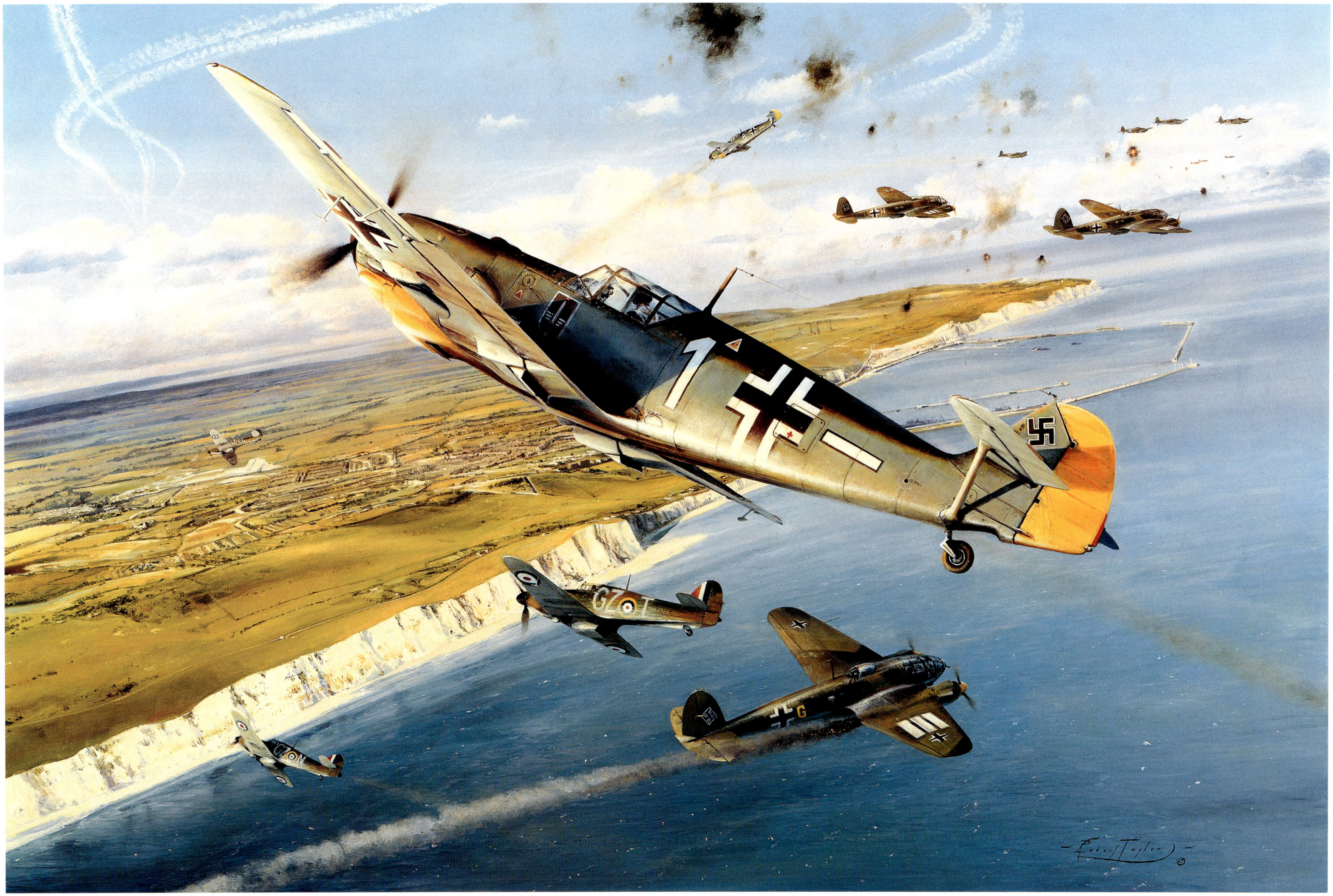

STEINHOFF TRIBUTE

In the collection of Mr Edgar Leicher

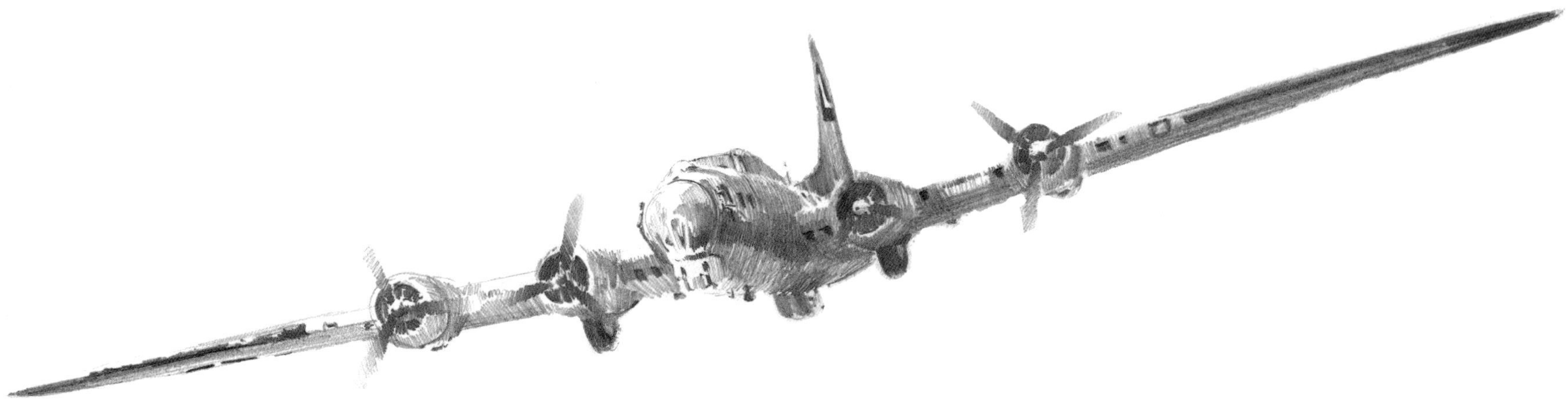

WINTER'S WELCOME

The unique beauty of the English countryside has appealed to artists for centuries. As a teenage apprentice picture-framer I used to marvel at the works of the great English landscape artists – their paintings portrayed such natural unspoiled beauty and tranquillity of lifestyle, conveying a special kind of nostalgia that I always found spellbinding, and their magnificent masterpieces constantly drew me back to their great canvases. The patchwork fields with their random hedgerows, the ancient woodlands, the characterful village cottages dotting the landscape and the ever-changing seasons, always gave me a feeling of excitement and an overpowering urge to paint.

One might think that landscape painting is not, perhaps, something an aviation artist needs to bother himself with; but, like many things in life, when one looks a little more closely into a subject, there are many things to be seen which at first glance are not obvious.

In some ways aircraft are inextricably linked to the landscape, and certainly that was the case back in the 1940s. Most airfields were set in the heart of rolling countryside, often with quite breathtaking views surrounding them in all directions.

I have always felt that an aviation painting should comprise more than a simple study of an airplane, and since my early days of painting professionally, I have constantly looked for ways to add dimension and secondary interest to my work. I go even further, believing that any good aviation work should be able to stand on its own as a finished painting, without relying upon the aircraft that appear in them.

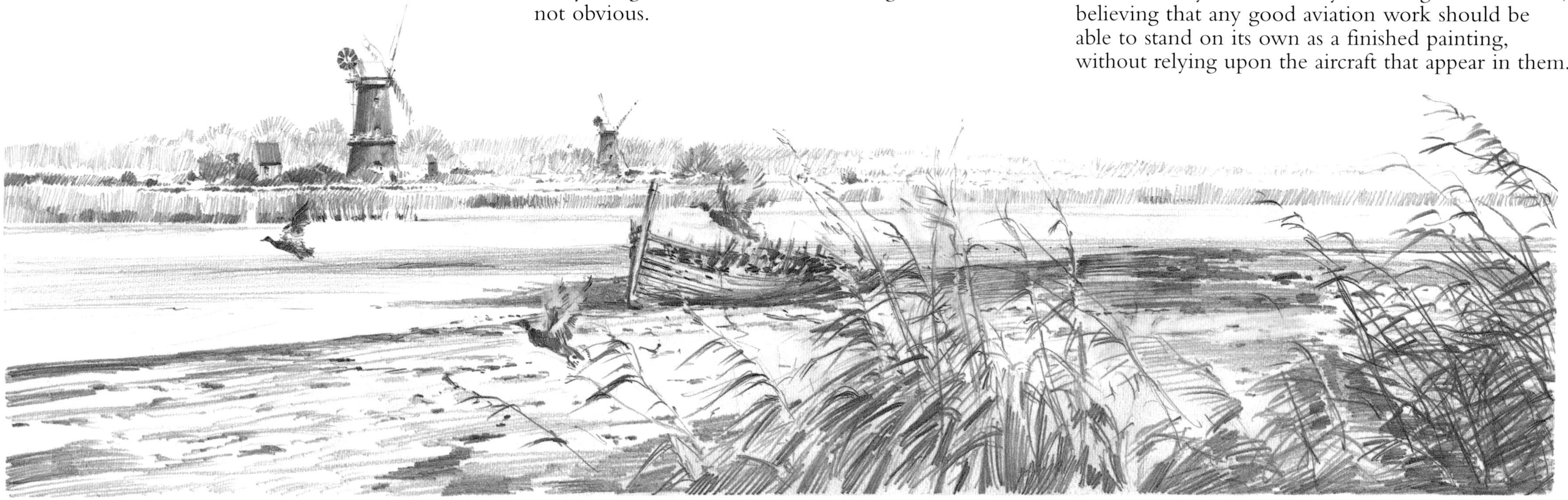

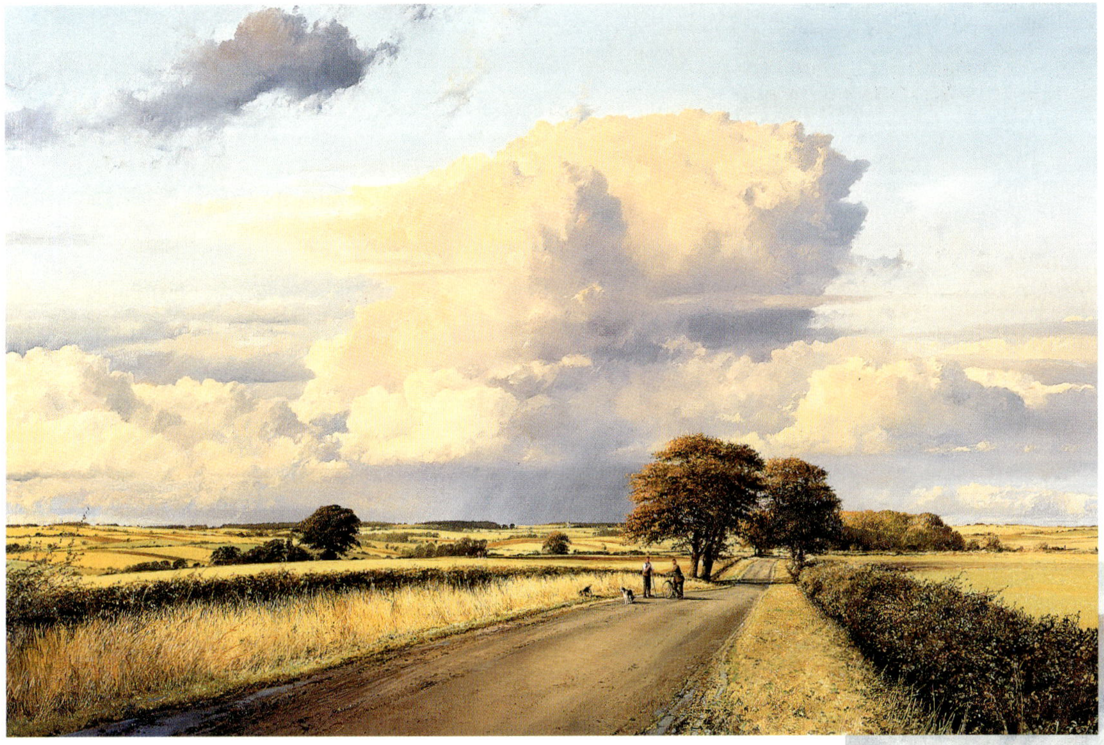

The two illustrations on this page show a painting I completed in 1991 entitled *Return of the Belle*. In the first, shown on the left, the landscape is almost finished and although my preparatory drawings will have told me exactly where the aircraft will be painted, at this point I have yet to position them on the canvas. The illustration below shows the completed painting with the B-17s inserted. My wife Mary said she preferred the picture as it was before I added the airplanes!

RETURN OF THE BELLE

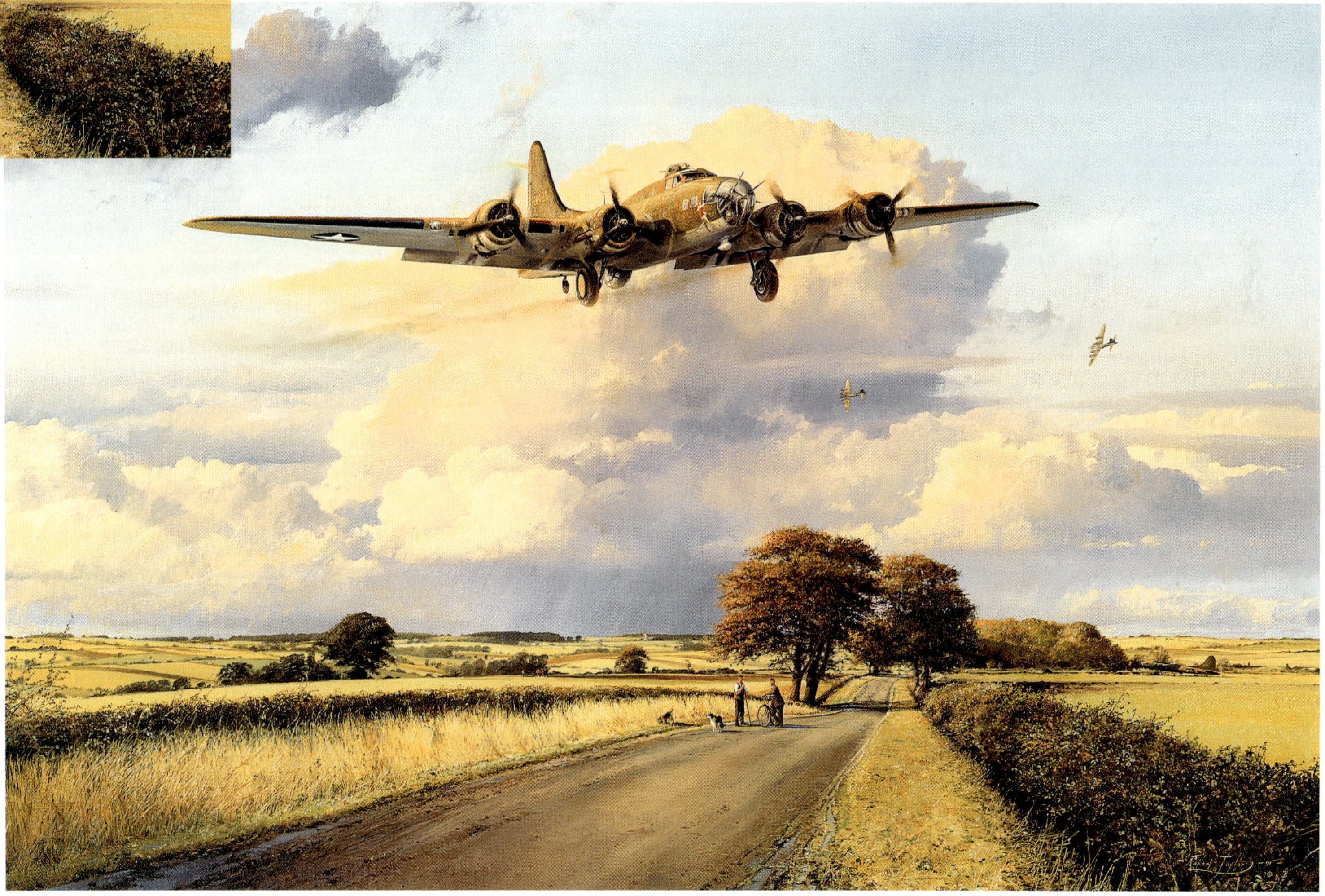

Obviously if all the aircraft are removed from a painting the composition will in most cases look somewhat empty. However, the point I am making is that if the artist takes the trouble to compose a painting so that all the background components are carefully constructed, and in sympathy with the principal subject, the painting will have interest beyond the purely technical, and in so doing will come to life.

As I have mentioned in the chapter discussing the Ploesti painting, I usually block in all the main components of a painting at a very early stage, including the positioning of the aircraft. On occasions, however, particularly where a landscape forms the basis of the painting, I paint the entire landscape first, just for variety. Two examples of this routine are shown in this chapter.

The use of landscape in a painting where aircraft are depicted returning from a mission provides not just a pretty backdrop, but reflects an interesting situation where the machines of war have been forced upon the solitude of rural life.

This fascinating juxtaposition gives a reminder of the dual lives led by aircrews during war, one hour in the hostile environs of battle, the next in the safety of the countryside hundreds of miles away from the battlefront.

Another work where I completed the landscape before painting the aircraft is *Winter's Welcome*. In this painting I have been careful to ensure that nothing of secondary interest competes with the main subject of the painting – the B-17 Fortress coming in to land. This is achieved by allowing the B-17 to occupy almost the full width of the canvas, and at the same time not allowing any of the items in the landscape to attract too much attention. On this subject, it is easy to get carried away with all the other details that catch the eye, but the temptation must be resisted if the painting is to retain credibility and balance.

The tractor is a pre-war Fordson. As war broke out the early tractors had started to push the old waggons and horses off the farms. The war delayed their advance for a short time, many tractors being commandeered for use on RAF bases, but once the war was over the march of progress put paid to the trusty horse, and the slow peaceful way of life down on the farm was gone for ever.

In the foreground, a horse-drawn hayrake lies idle awaiting the spring. Two milk churns sit by the gate ready for collection. To the right a pair of cock pheasants take to the air, startled by the noise and sight of the fast approaching bomber.

Looking across the fields to the small village in the middle distance, there is the traditional small church, farmhouse and group of farm cottages found in all small English villages. The keen eye will spot the red telephone booth.

A comparison of the unfinished picture with the completed painting will show some minor changes I found necessary after inserting the aircraft. Also I have added a few new items of interest. The main area of change was to the large cumulus cloud in order to give the main B-17 some added dimension. It may be of greater interest if I leave readers to discover for themselves where the other changes were made.

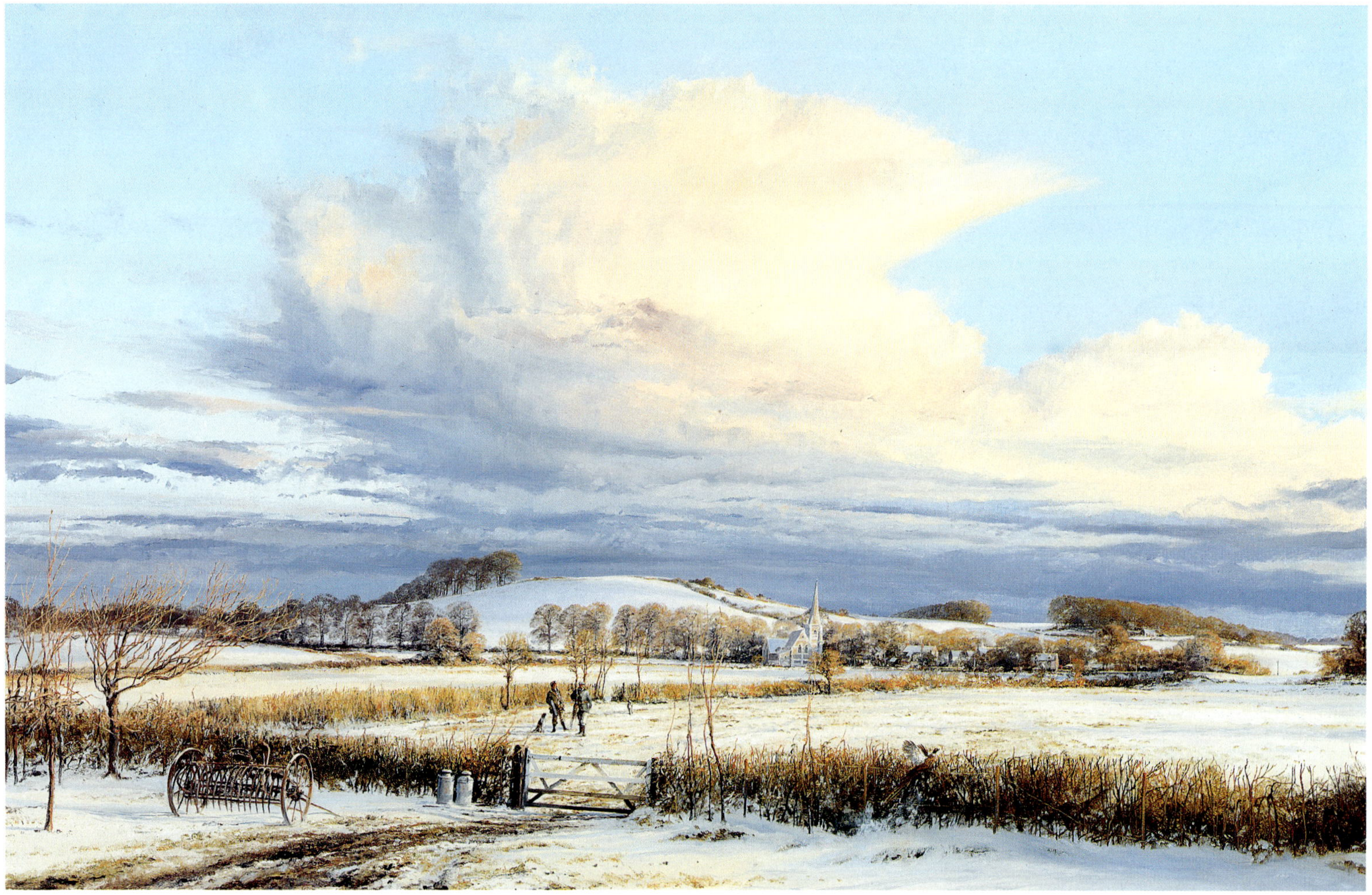

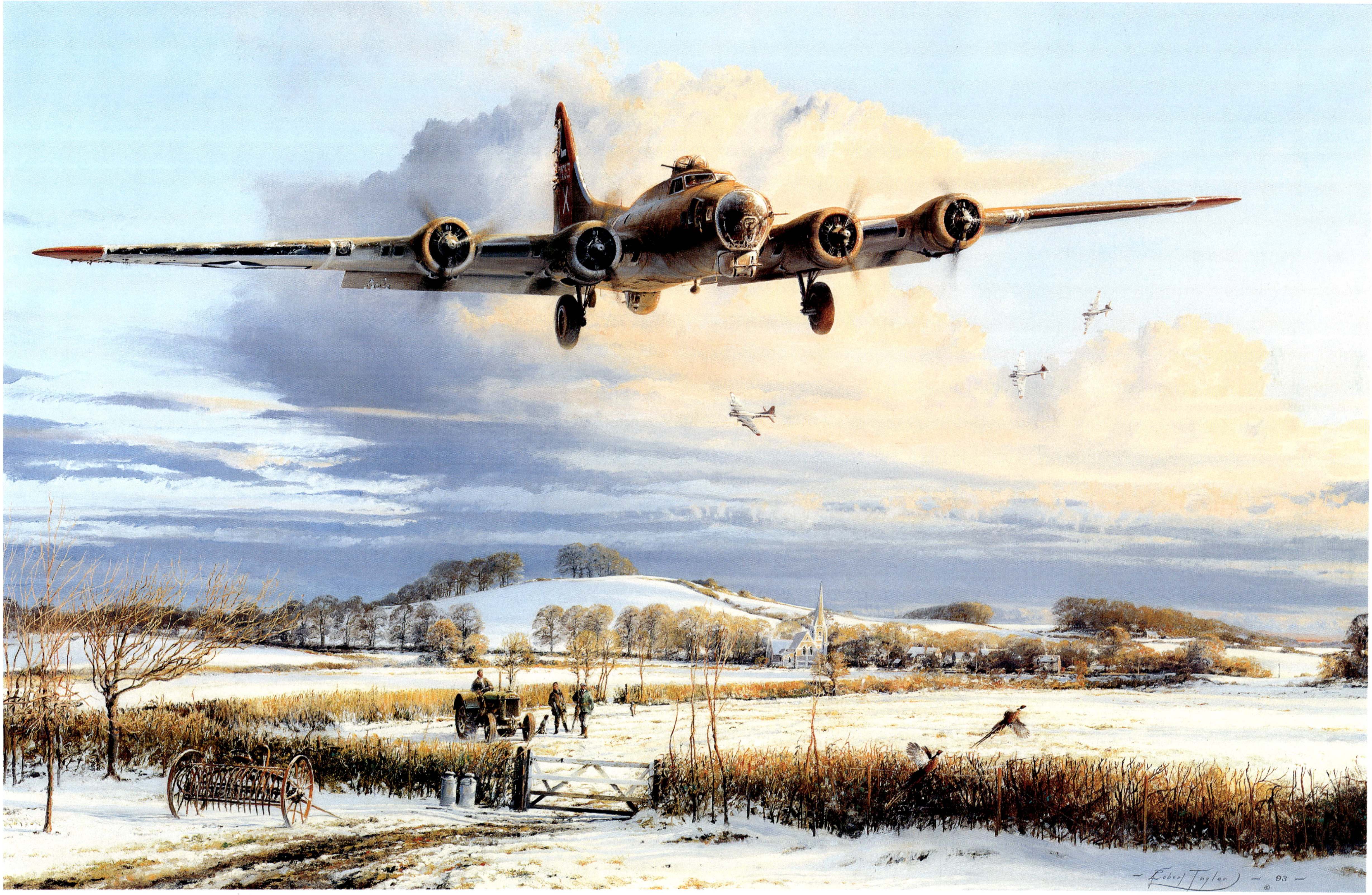

WINTER'S WELCOME

In the collection of Mr Eugene Eisenberg

THE DOOLITTLE TOKYO RAIDERS

Painting well known historical events with an element of originality becomes increasingly difficult as time goes by. The more famous the event, the more times it is likely to have been painted by other artists, and thus the fewer the options regarding a new and original slant. Nevertheless it is always a challenge to come up with a picture which goes beyond the obvious, and if this is possible without detracting from the historical accuracy of the event, then that is what I will usually try for.

When I set out to paint *The Doolittle Tokyo Raiders* in 1991, I was aware of several other artists' renditions, and naturally it was my aim to come up with a scenario that was somewhat different. I had noticed that most other works concentrated on the moment of Doolittle's actual take-off from the deck of the aircraft carrier *Hornet,* and so that was immediately discounted from my list of possibilities.

Although the take-off sequence had been ruled out, I felt nevertheless that it was important to include the *Hornet* in the painting. It was the first time a group of bomber aircraft had been flown off the deck of a carrier, and there was much speculation as to whether the feat could be accomplished. The tension aboard ship would have been electric as Jimmy Doolittle launched his B-25 off the heaving deck. The entire raid depended upon a successful launch, and if Doolittle failed to get airborne the raid was to be cancelled. Those few minutes surrounding the launch, and the moments immediately following when it became clear that a full-scale launch of the entire battle group would go ahead, were therefore the most crucial of the mission, and somewhere in there I looked for an aspect that hadn't been portrayed before.

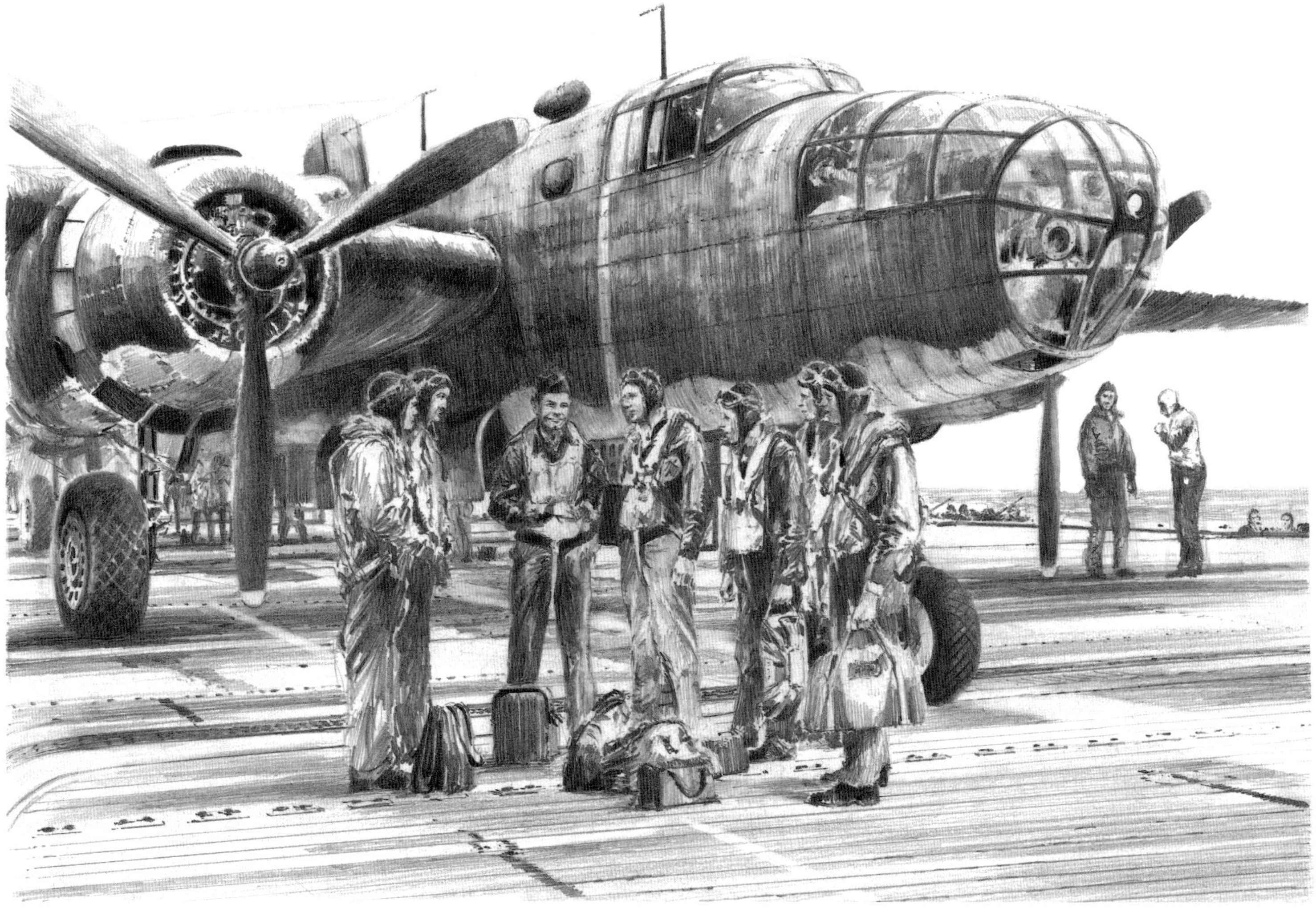

Early morning aboard the Hornet April 18th, 1942.

Remember what I told you - the Emperor's palace was strictly off limits"!

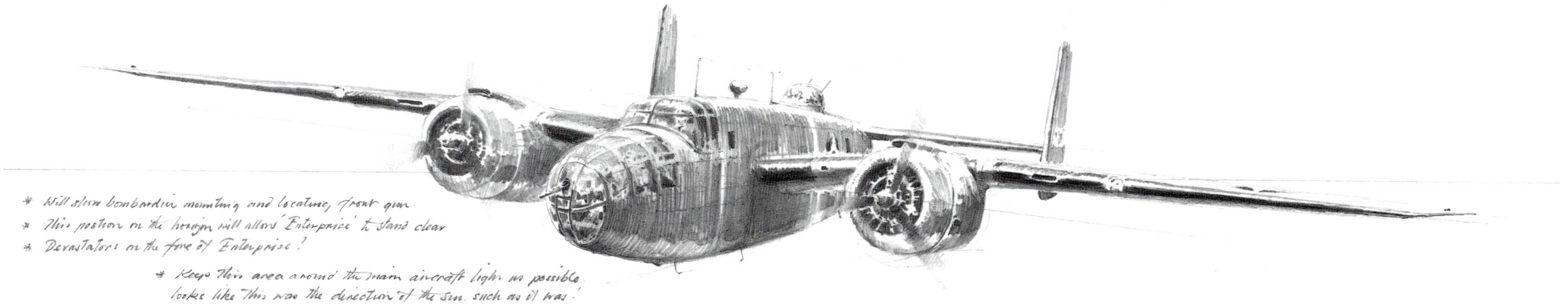

Studying all the detail available concerning those few minutes, I discovered that Doolittle had made a climbing turn after take-off, coming around to fly directly overhead the *Hornet* to check his compass with that aboard ship. Bearing in mind the importance of navigation on an 800-mile over-water mission, I felt that this was significant enough to warrant painting. Furthermore, by selecting this particular moment I was able to portray Doolittle's aircraft large on the canvas, and also paint a good view of the *Hornet* without the two competing with each other. And by viewing the scene from a little higher up than a take-off would have permitted, I was able to broaden the vista to include other ships of Halsey's Enterprise Task Force, thus conveying something of the overall atmosphere of the moment.

There was a fair sea running on that April day in 1942, but this in fact aided the pilots in their difficult and highly dangerous launch from the heaving deck: each pilot timed the short run across the deck to coincide with the swell, reaching take-off point as the bow rose to its full height above the waves. In the detail from the painting below, the second B-25 has just launched, with the *Hornet*'s bow towering at its peak above the turbulent swell.

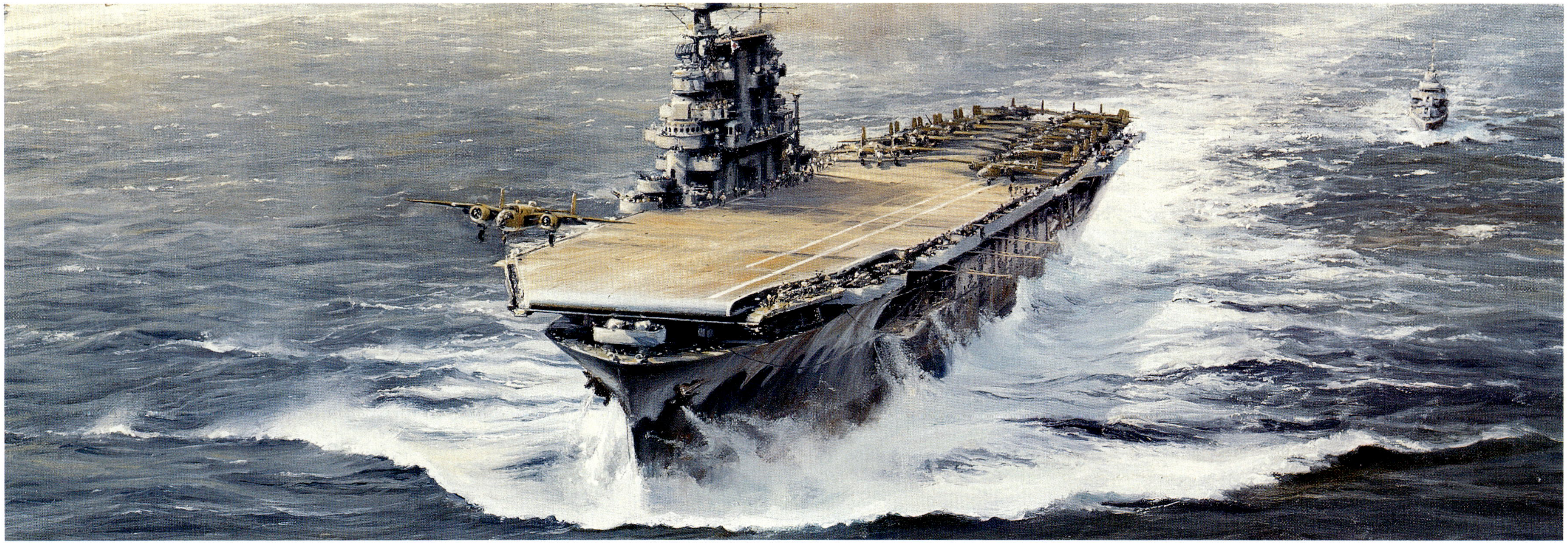

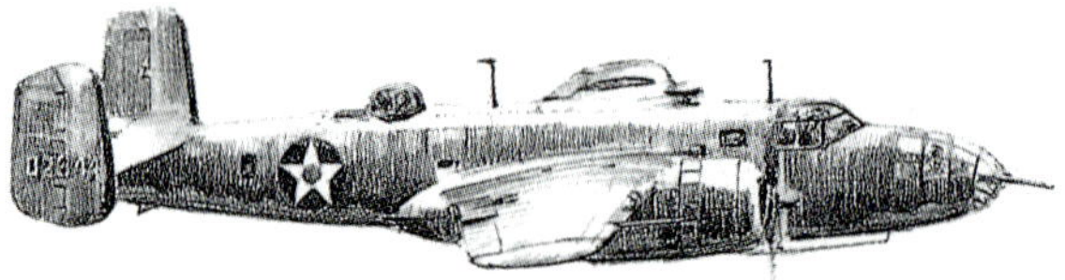

The courageous Doolittle raid on Tokyo was one of the most written and talked about missions of the war. Almost everyone interested in the era knows its every detail and all about the remarkable man who led it and so I knew that whatever scene I painted would come under the close scrutiny of a host of 'experts'.

It was 18 April 1942, just four months after the Japanese attack on Pearl Harbor, and it had been decided that a strike at the heart of Imperial Japan would greatly alarm the enemy who had thought their homeland safe from attack. Furthermore such a raid would be morale-boosting for the American forces, who up to that time had spent much of the time on the receiving end. Under the mercurial leadership of Lieutenant-Colonel James H. Doolittle, it was planned that sixteen Army Air Force B-25 Mitchell medium bombers would make a daring attack on the Japanese capital and other industrial centres. The huge distance determined that any such raid would have to be launched from a carrier, and even then there would be insufficient fuel for any return trip; the crews would have to fly on to China and fend for themselves as best they could. Volunteers were called for.

On the morning of 18 April the *Hornet* found herself in rough seas under squally skies, but Doolittle and his crews were all ready to go and were not going to let the marginal weather conditions stop them. With Doolittle taking the lead, sixteen aircraft got airborne without mishap, and headed for Tokyo.

All sixteen reached their targets. However, nine were attacked by fighters and all the aircraft were lost – but miraculously most of the crews survived to fly and fight again later in the war. The attack came as a complete surprise, and influenced the Japanese High Command into attempting to extend its perimeter in the central and southern Pacific regions – with disastrous results. Colonel Jimmy Doolittle was awarded the Congressional Medal of Honor for his part in this raid, one of the most audacious of World War II.

The painting below is another study of the B-25 bomber General Jimmy Doolittle flew off the *Hornet* to lead the raid on Tokyo in April 1942. The original painting measures only 18 x 12 inches. Usually when artists paint small oil sketches these are done quickly, often with quite large brushes and without any attempt at detail, the main purpose being as a preliminary study for a full-size painting. I tend not to work in this way, however, preferring to use pencil sketches in the preparation of a painting. Somehow I seem to be able to determine all the basic colours I will use in the final painting as I work with the pencil. When I paint small canvases such as that below, I tend to complete them with almost the same degree of detail as my larger works. Although these are sometimes described as oil sketches, in my case in reality they are small paintings.

DOOLITTLE'S B-25

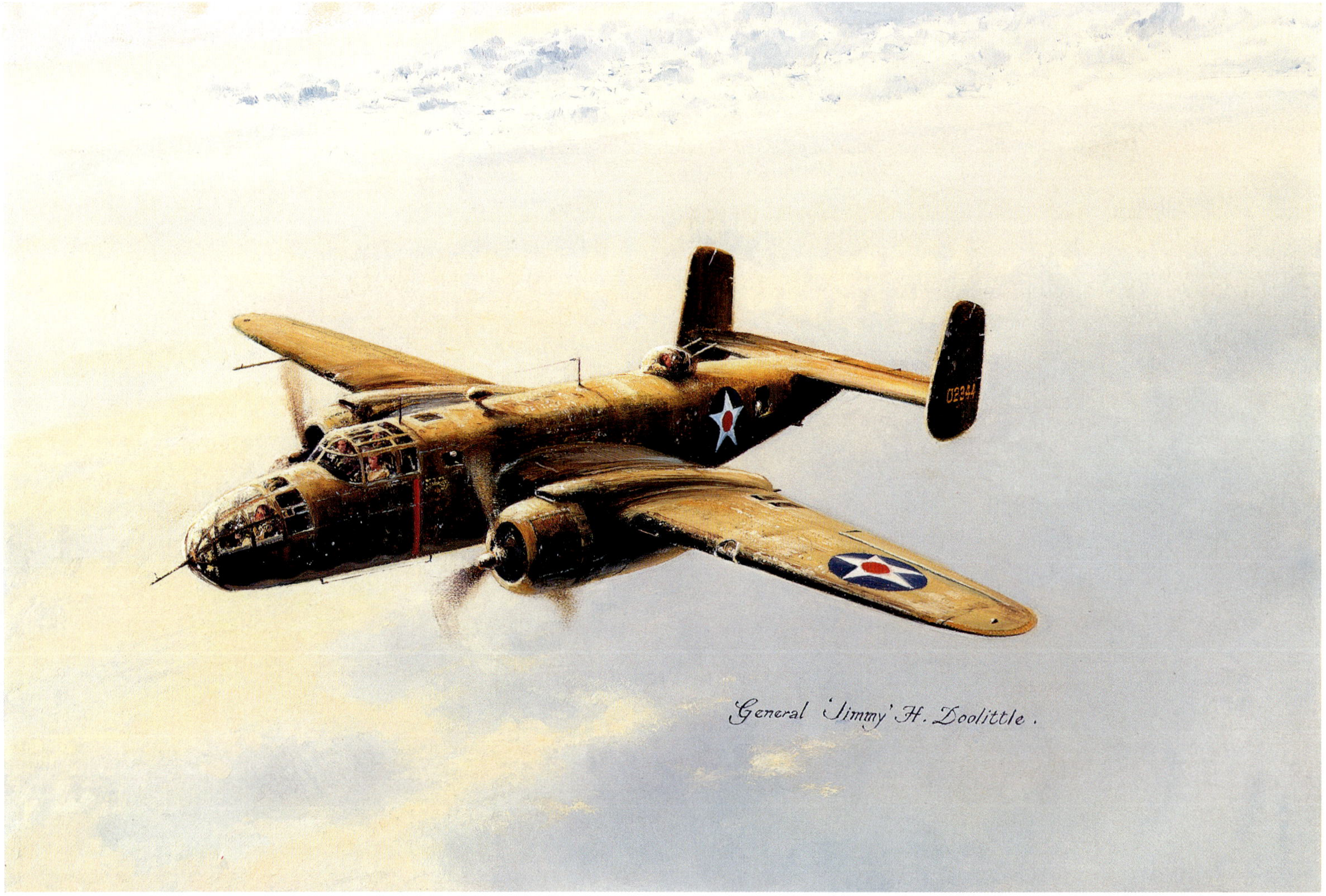

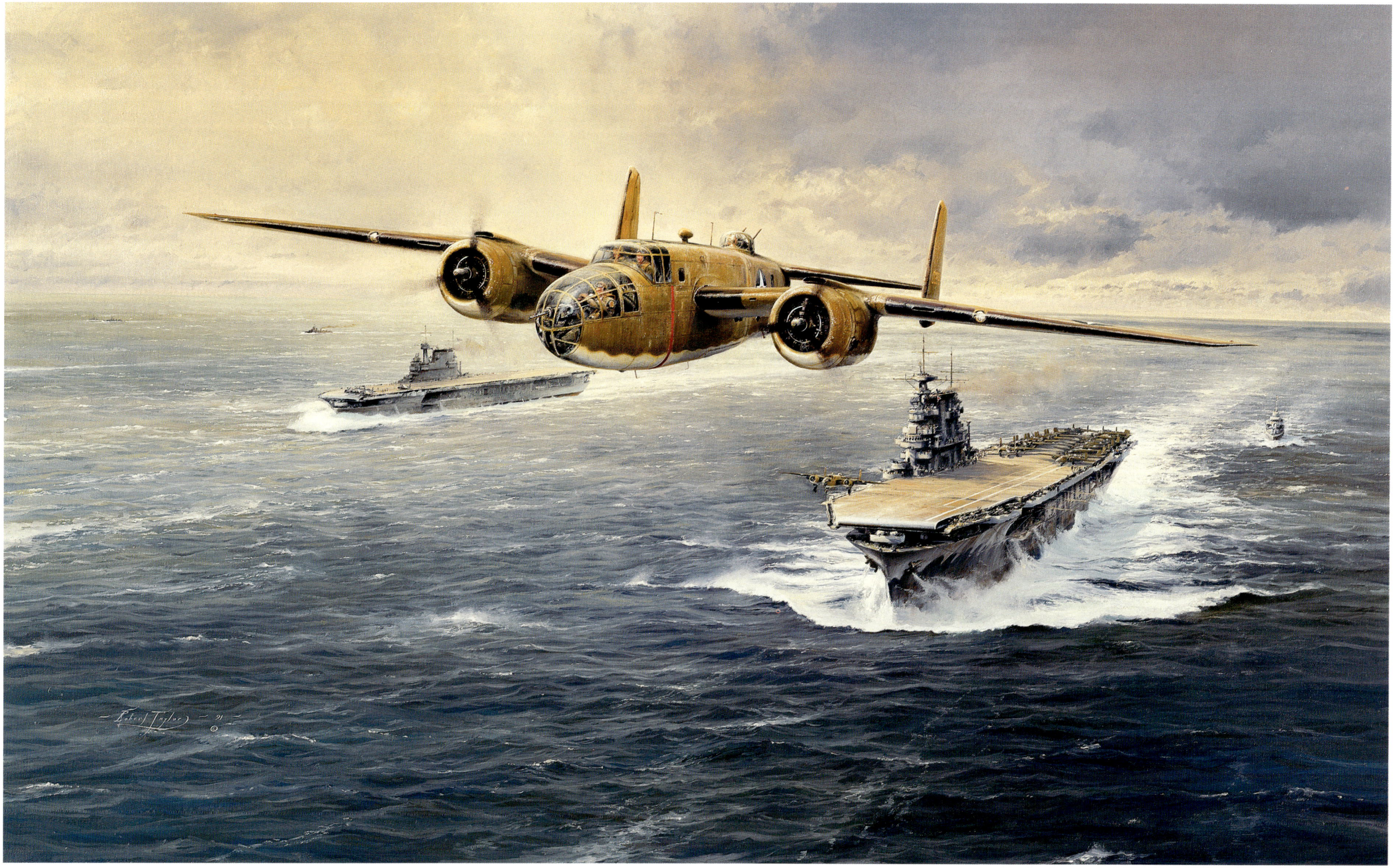

THE DOOLITTLE TOKYO RAIDERS

In the collection of Mr Eugene Eisenberg

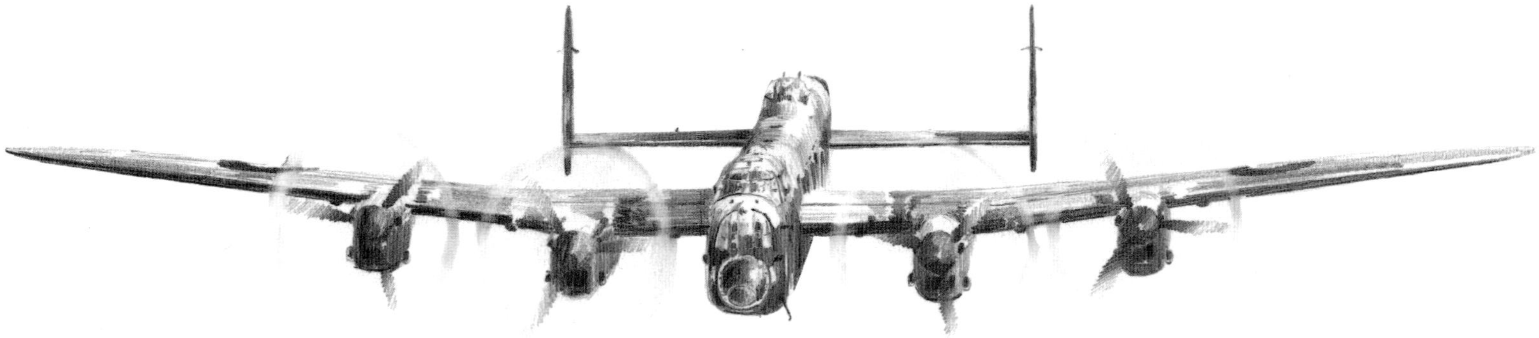

TARGET PEENEMUNDE

Early on in the war, the RAF had discovered to their cost the perils of flying daylight bombing raids, and had quickly determined that the bulk of their efforts would in future be concentrated on night-time missions. Throughout the war they flew tens of thousands of them. Because the summer nights of northern Europe are so short, the bomber forces would begin to form up as dusk fell; they would then fly their mission, and often not return until dawn was breaking.

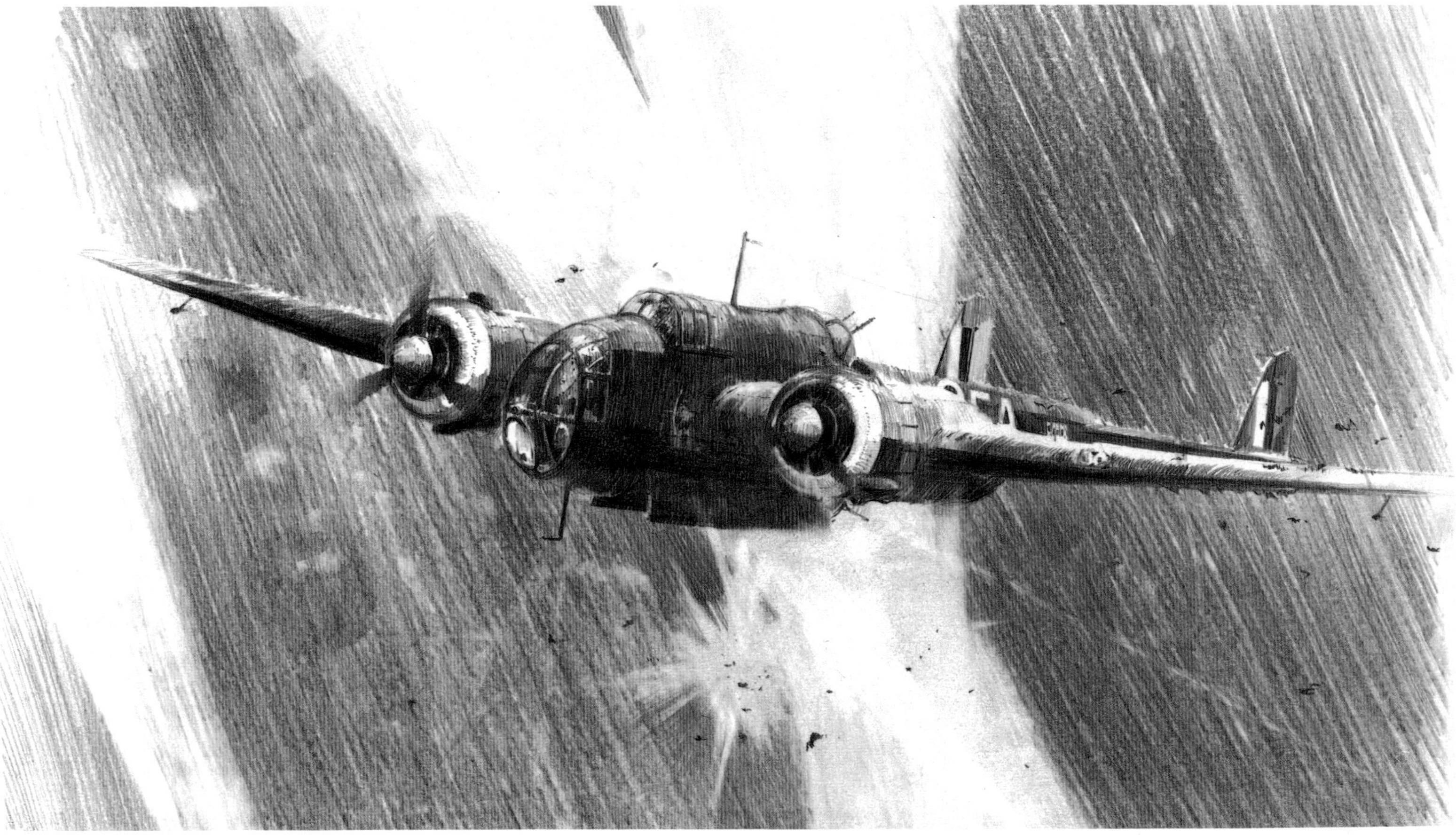

FL R.A.B. Learoyd piloting a Hampden bomber attacks and destroys the viaduct on the Dortmund Ems canal on the 12th Aug. 40.
For his gallantry under intense anti aircraft he was awarded the Victoria Cross.

One such mission trip took place on the night of 17 August 1943, when a total of 596 aircraft of RAF Bomber Command climbed out over the east coast of England and headed into the darkening sky. Spearheaded by the Pathfinder Force, they set out on what called for, and what became, one of the most precise bombing raids of the war.

Their target was some 600 miles distant, a secluded research establishment near the remote Baltic town of Peenemunde. There, a group of Germany's top scientists were developing Hitler's secret weapon, the V-2 rocket projectile. With this fearsome flying bomb he planned to devastate London and other major cities in England, and terrorise the British people into submission. When Allied intelligence discovered the plan, the RAF was given the task of destroying the installation at Peenemunde, whatever the cost.

As the night offensive against Germany progressed it had become obvious to its commander, Arthur Harris, that a system of clearly identifying and marking targets in the darkness was essential in order to maximise the effectiveness of the raids. This led to the formation of the Pathfinder Force: comprised of Bomber Command's most experienced crews, the Pathfinders led the raids, navigating the large bomber formations overhead the targets, marking them in the darkness by dropping flares.

At Peenemunde, the masterbomber's aircraft was navigated into position right over the target at 12,000 feet by Norman Scrivener, dropping its flares at precisely 12.10am. 'Scrive's' Lancaster made nine dangerous passes over the target, directing operations while the main bomber force pounded the rocket installations. During the fifty-five minutes duration of the raid, Hitler's secret weapon establishment was almost totally destroyed.

I toyed with the idea of painting the actual raid in a night-time scene, but because this particular work was to be reproduced as a limited print edition, I decided that the limitations of depicting aircraft in the dark were too great. I therefore chose the moment the masterbomber's aircraft departed from the English coast, giving a clear view of the No 83 Squadron Pathfinder Force Lancasters as they set out on their dangerous but highly successful mission.

Although night raids afforded crews the protection of darkness, they were by no means immune to attack from enemy aircraft. As the war rumbled on, the Luftwaffe became adept at using radar to locate and intercept the RAF planes. The drawing below shows Victoria Cross recipient Bill Reid. Attacked twice whilst piloting a Lancaster on the night of 3 November 1943, Bill was badly wounded in the head, shoulders and hands; with a shattered wind-screen the cold was intense, and his aircraft was crippled and defenceless. However, he refused to be turned from his objective and after releasing his bombs over the target, he set course for home steering by the stars alone. Weak, exhausted, and without oxygen, it was his tenacity and bravery which brought his surviving crew safely home.

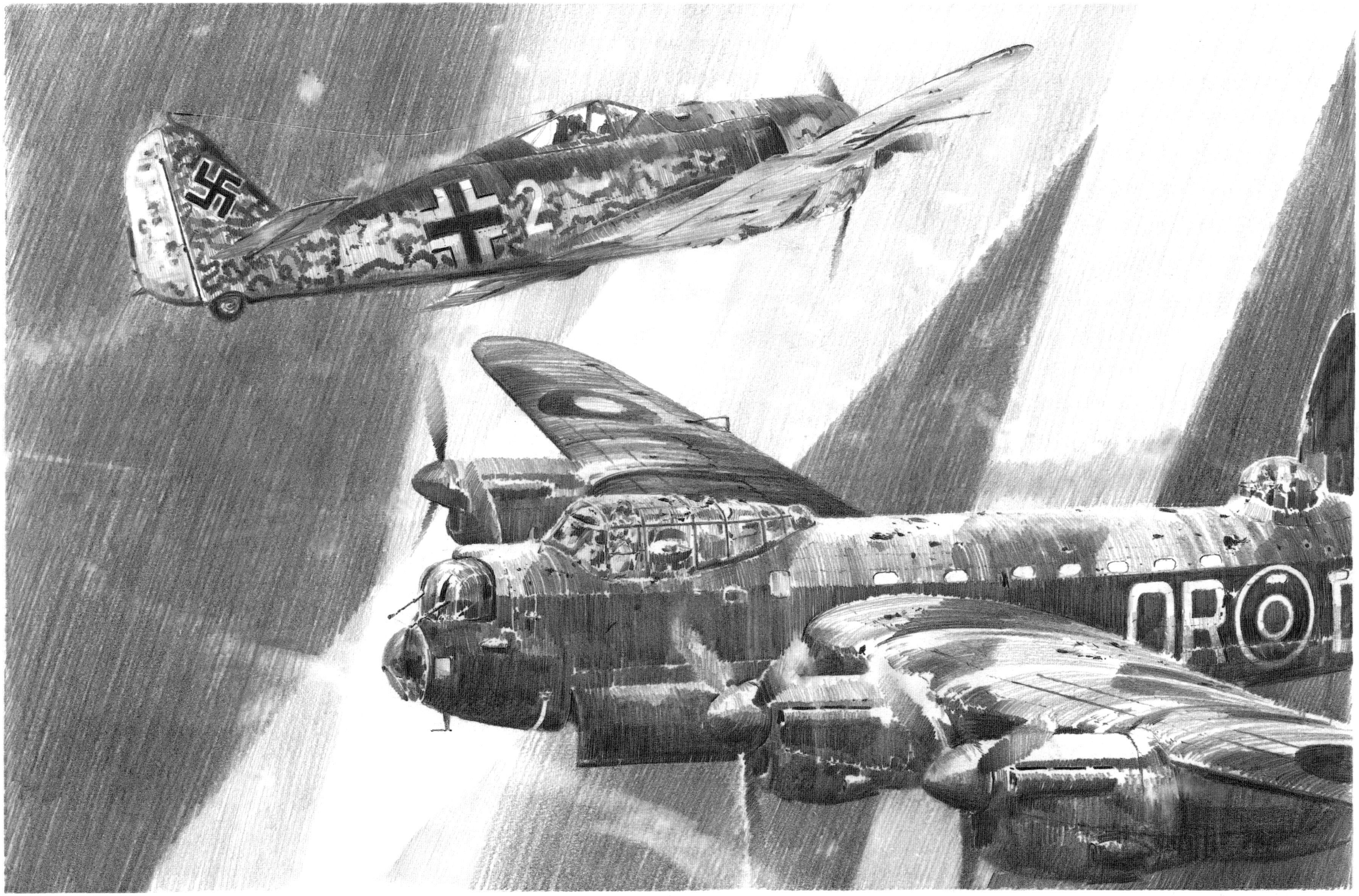

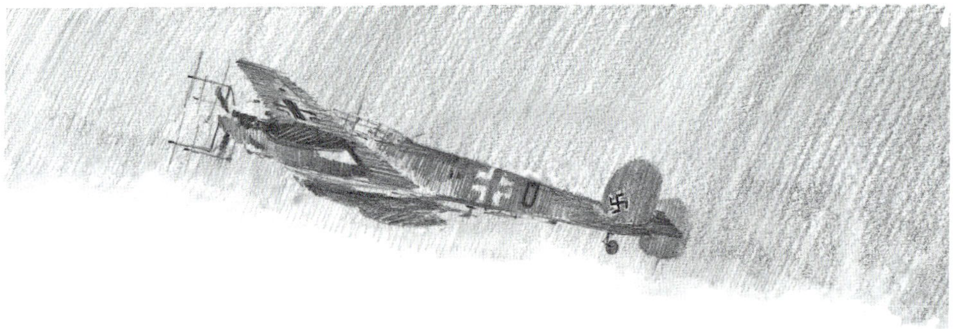

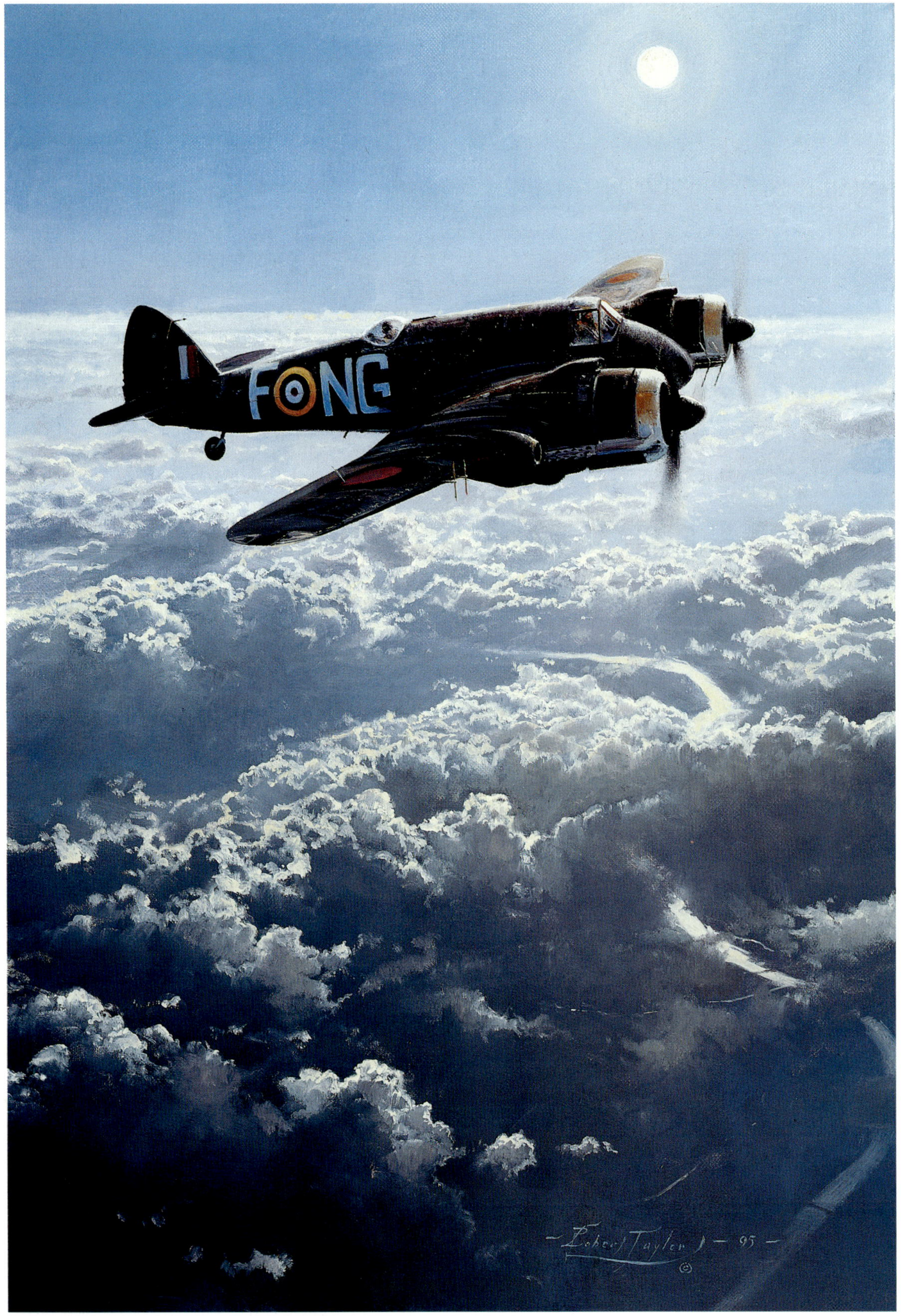

MOONLIGHTING

Air combat at night is an artist's nightmare. Painting is all about light and shade and colour, and after dark there isn't much of this to work with; in fact, to make any night-time painting effective, considerable licence must be taken, otherwise there is little for the viewer to see. A Navy pilot once suggested to me that a night landing on a carrier on a dark night would be an easy subject to depict, requiring only a tube of black paint. Looking at some paintings in museums of modern art these days I often think I might be able to get away with it!

The movie-makers have overcome the lack of light quite simply for night-time scenes: they film in broad daylight using a dark blue filter. This form of licence is both practical and effective, and it is this kind of ingenuity which an artist painting a night scene must employ.

When painting aircraft at night there is no opportunity to make use of light shining from windows, open doors, street lights and the like; the moon being our most commonly used ally.

The painting featured on this page, *Moonlighting*, makes use of the light of the moon to show what would be the otherwise indistinguishable Beaufighter of John Cunningham. Known as 'Cat's Eyes Cunningham' for his extraordinary vision in the dark, Cunningham's aircraft is seen here on a typical night mission. Hunting alone with his navigator, the night interceptor pilot would roam the sky lurking in wait for incoming raiders. As soon as the enemy was located he would begin to stalk his quarry, steadily closing to very short range before making his attack. Usually his opponent was unaware of his presence until the bullets started to fly.

To the Luftwaffe the Beaufighter was a feared opponent: for the artist portraying it some fifty years on, the aircraft is a joy to paint. Referred to by the German pilots as the Snub-nose Battleship – the Japanese called it the Whispering Death due to the quietness of its sleeve-valve engines – its distinctive, somewhat bulbous conformation provides some lovely shapes to work with.

I have nothing against the sleek, ultra-aerodynamic shapes of modern jets, many of which are quite beautiful. However, I must admit to finding the huge variety of distinctive designs and characterful shapes of the aircraft prior to the jet age a little more interesting and challenging to paint.

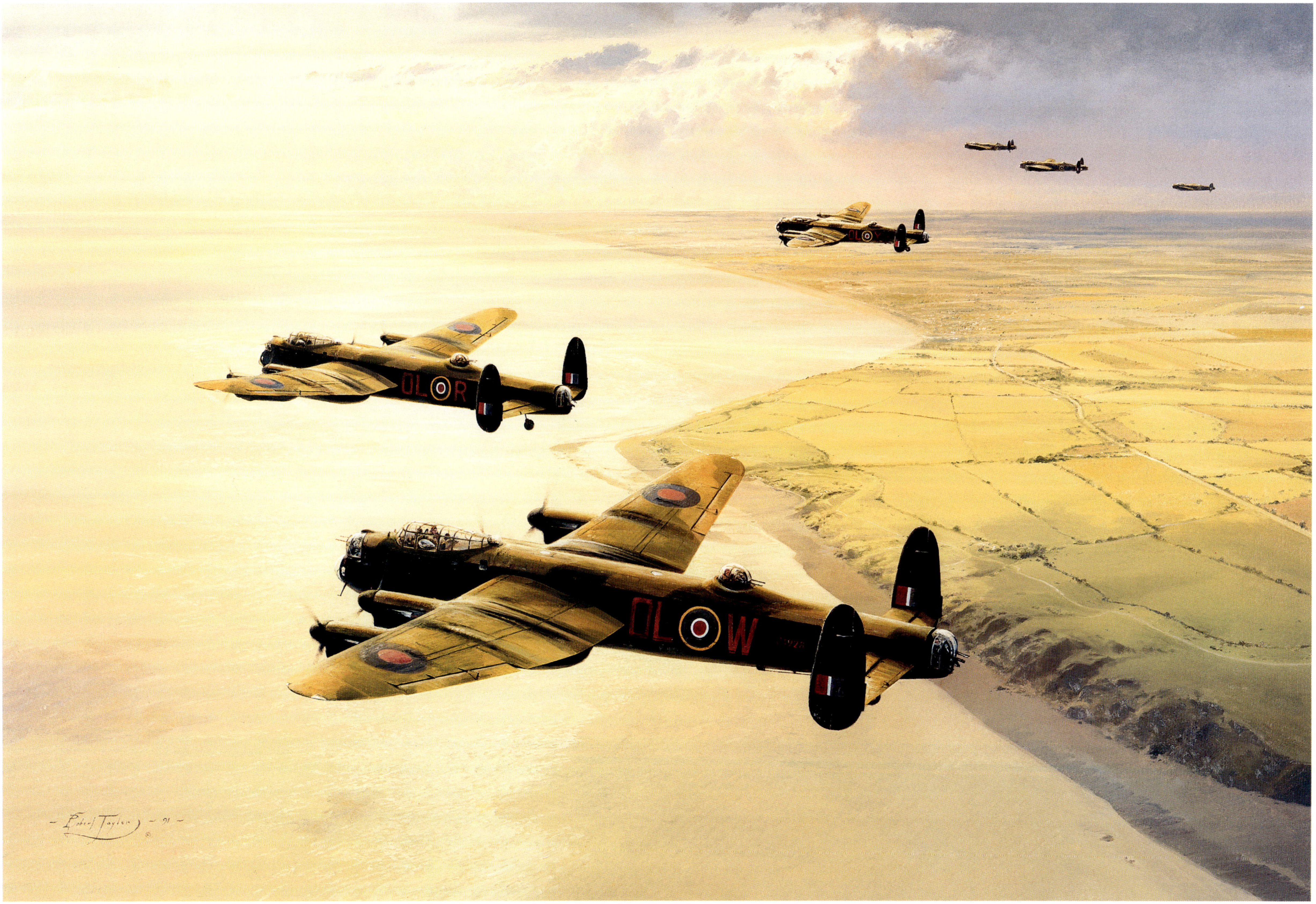

TARGET PEENEMUNDE

In the collection of Mr Eugene Eisenberg

D-DAY – THE AIRBORNE ASSAULT

Sid Harwell piloted the No 2 aircraft in the lead formation of the D-Day invasion, dropping elements of the 101st Airborne Division at St Mère-Eglise before dawn on the morning of 6 June 1944. After flying his C-47 Dakota back to England, he collected a CG-4 Waco glider laden with troops, and again headed for the Normandy beach-heads. Turning his C-47 for home after releasing his glider he was astonished at the sight before him: 'The sky was jam-packed full of aircraft of every description, stretching all the way back to the English coast. The airspace was literally full. I didn't know we had that many aircraft!' Sid's description stuck in my mind as I deliberated how to paint a picture depicting the D-Day airborne assault on 6 June 1944.

After completing a few rough sketches I realised that although these told me how I would get Sid Harwell's feeling of the crowded sky, none of them seemed to engender the atmosphere of D-Day. The furious activity on the beaches is the first image that comes into most people's minds at the mention of D-Day, and it wasn't until I included a view of the beaches below the aircraft that the picture began to work in the way I wanted it to.

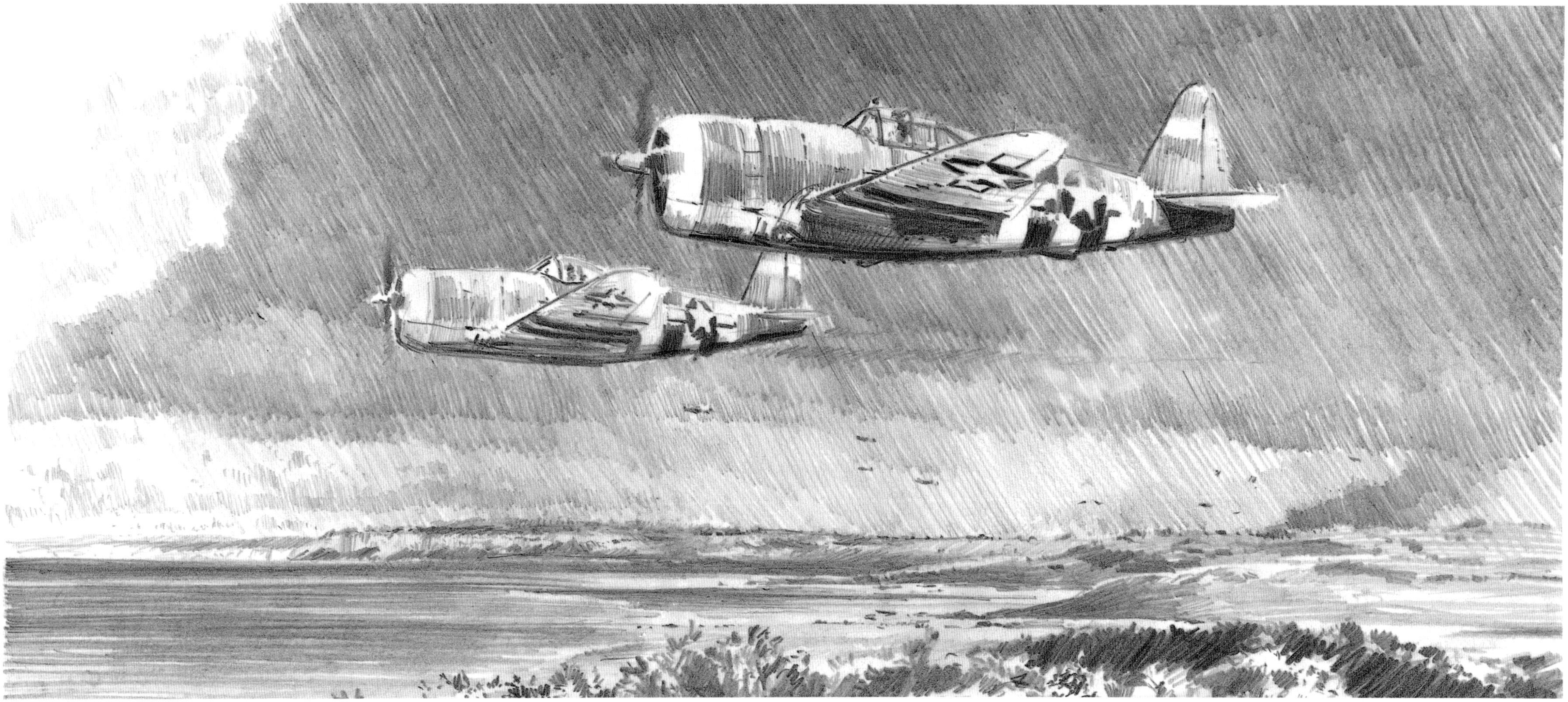

The morning of 6 June had dawned dull and grey with the cloudbase at just a few thousand feet, and to have portrayed the early stages of the invasion would have meant a cold and somewhat sombre painting. I like my paintings to have a certain warmth, and so I chose to depict a scene in the late afternoon; by this time on D-Day the sun had appeared between broken cloud, thus enabling me to paint a brighter picture while sacrificing none of the authenticity.

The C-47 Dakota was the automatic choice of aircraft for the D-Day painting; it was the backbone troopcarrier of the war and played a key role in every important invasion in World War II. Although the Waco glider was not necessarily the best of the towed aircraft to take part, I like the look of it and decided to use it in favour of the more cumbersome-looking Horsa glider. The choice of P-51 Mustangs as the escort planes – in fact any number of types could have been featured – was based on the shape of this sleek fighter. I wanted the escort formation to be positioned above the C-47s, and other contenders such as the P-47 Thunderbolt or the P-38 Lightning were a little too bulky, especially when viewed from slightly underneath.

Painting a lot of airplanes into a picture while at the same time maintaining a realistic image, is fairly challenging. I fiddled about with the positioning of the main aircraft in the composition for some time until I got the right shape to the formation. I was trying to create the appearance of a spearhead to the arrangement, so that visually the airplanes seemed to be moving from right to left, but so their positions didn't look too contrived. By superimposing two of the P-51s over those to their right I felt I achieved this, although picking the exact spot on the canvas for each one took quite some time to get right.

I moved the lead Dakota as far to the left as I dared, partly to give me enough room to show the Waco glider it is towing, but also to give it the lead, as it were, in the painting. The second C-47 is carefully placed so the tow cable from the lead aircraft runs right across the fuselage, thus drawing attention to this unique feature; at the same time it conveniently takes the eye back to the main glider in the painting.

All the aircraft are from the American Ninth Air Force. The C-47 Dakotas are from the 438th Troop Carrier Group, towing CG-4 Waco gliders. The P-51 Mustangs are the earlier B models flying with the 354th Fighter Group. The distinctive black-and-white invasion stripes were painted around the wings and fuselages of all Allied aircraft as a means of easy identification.

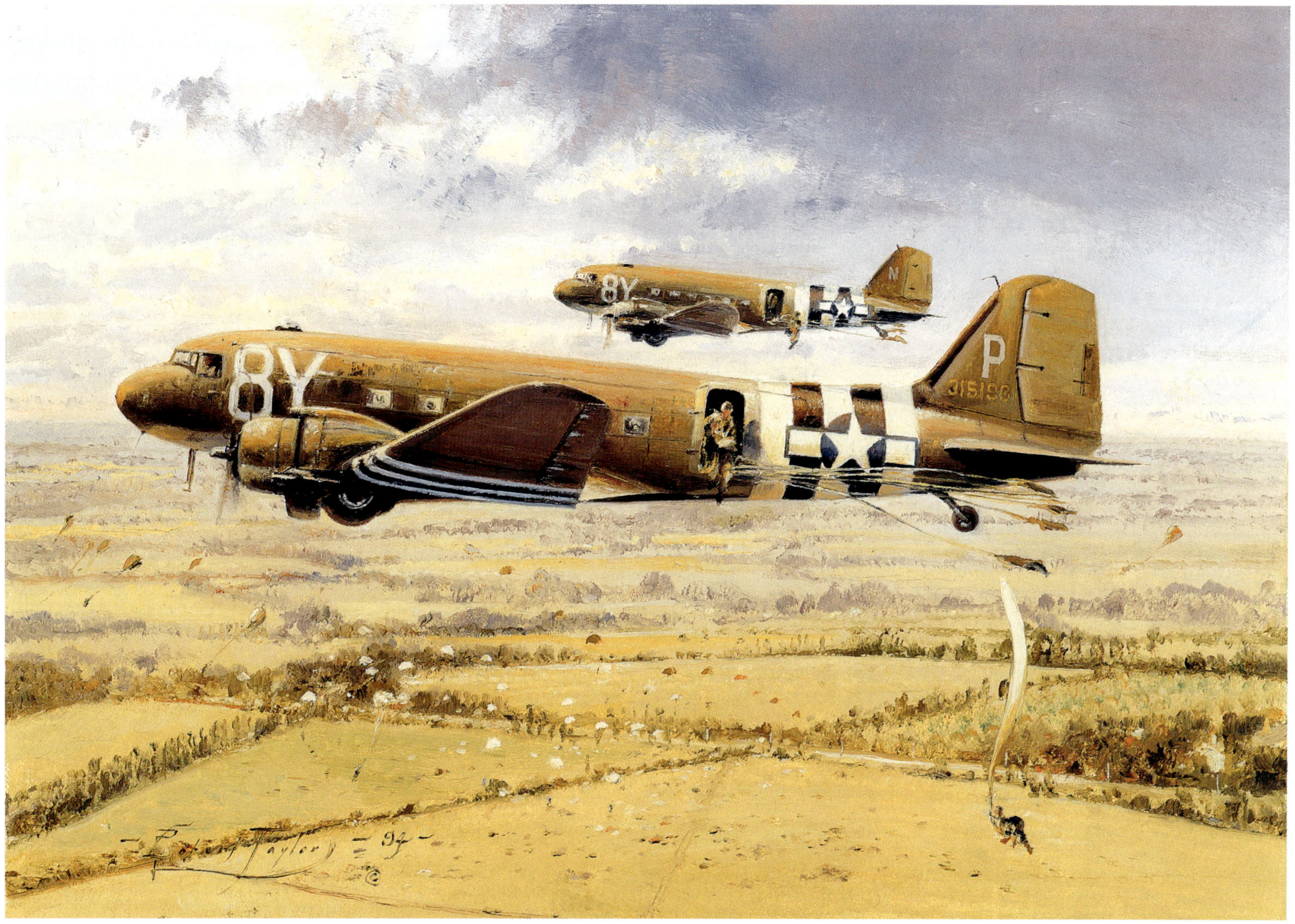

INTO BATTLE

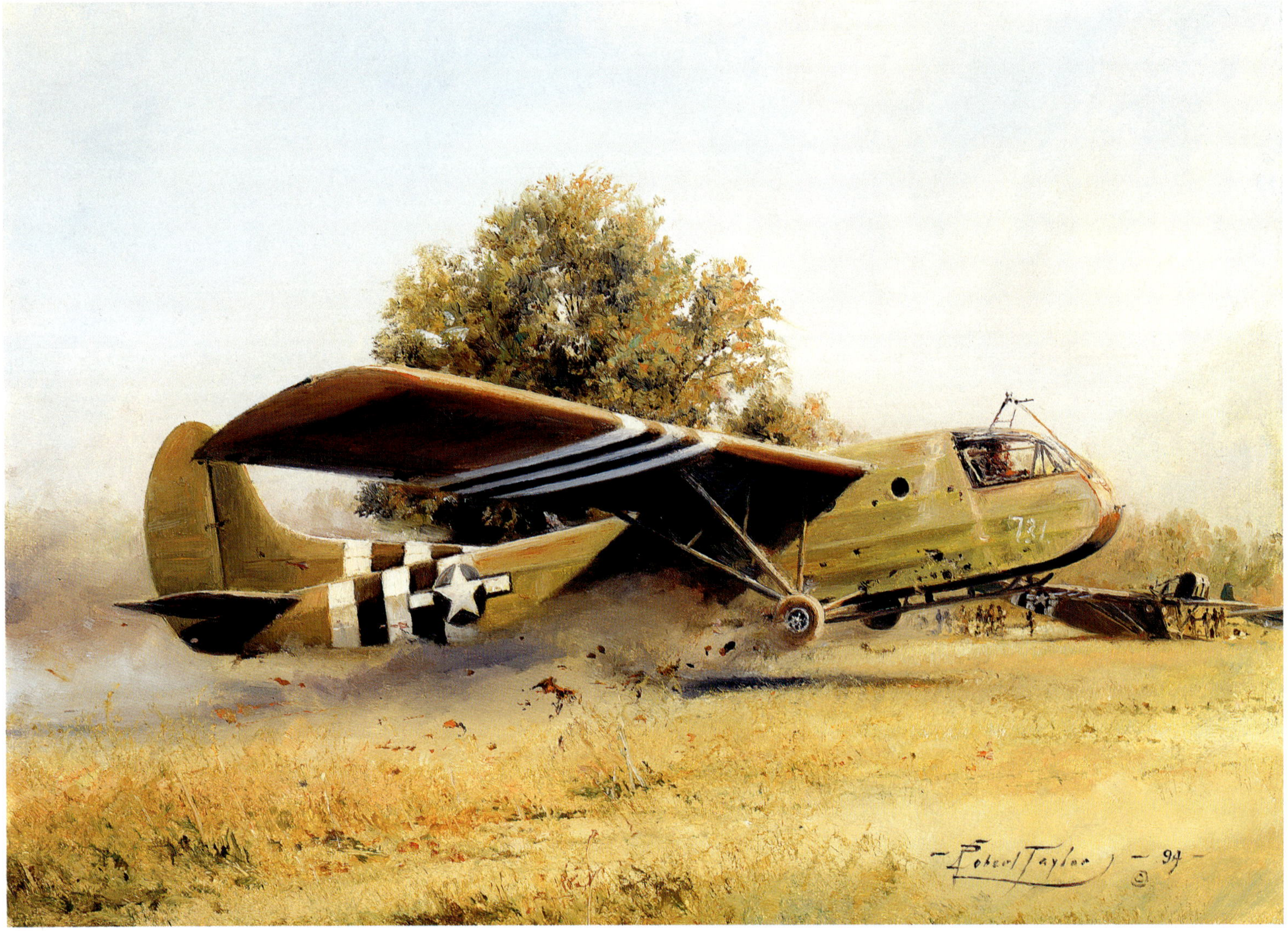

CRASH LANDING

I painted two 'companion pieces' to the D-Day painting, the idea being to highlight the part played by the airborne forces: the first (shown on the previous page) is a study of the C-47 Dakota in the role for which it is best remembered – dropping troops into battle. A paratrooper in full battle kit is just leaving the aircraft door, while the man ahead of him tumbles away, his parachute just starting to open. Static lines flow back from the despatch door indicating that four other paratroopers are already on their way down.

The air below the C-47 is scattered with billowing parachutes floating to earth from other troopcarriers which have already passed over the dropping zone.

As I painted this scene I reflected upon the courage it must have taken to plunge headlong into the fray on the end of a parachute, the troops often being fired upon while dangling helplessly on their way to earth. There can't be many worse ways to go into battle than this.

The second painting, shown on this page, depicts a CG-4 Waco glider during its perilous last moments of flight as the pilot brings his frail, powerless, fully laden aircraft bouncing into a crowded Normandy battlefield. Having only one opportunity to judge his approach into an unprepared field, the glider pilot's chances of making a smooth arrival were almost nil and the best he and his human cargo could hope for was a piece of clear space and a decent crash-landing. Many were not that lucky, striking other gliders, trees or other obstacles as they landed, sometimes breaking up before they came to rest. I have given this glider pilot and his valuable cargo a break – a clear piece of reasonably flat ground – as I reckon they need all the good fortune they can get.

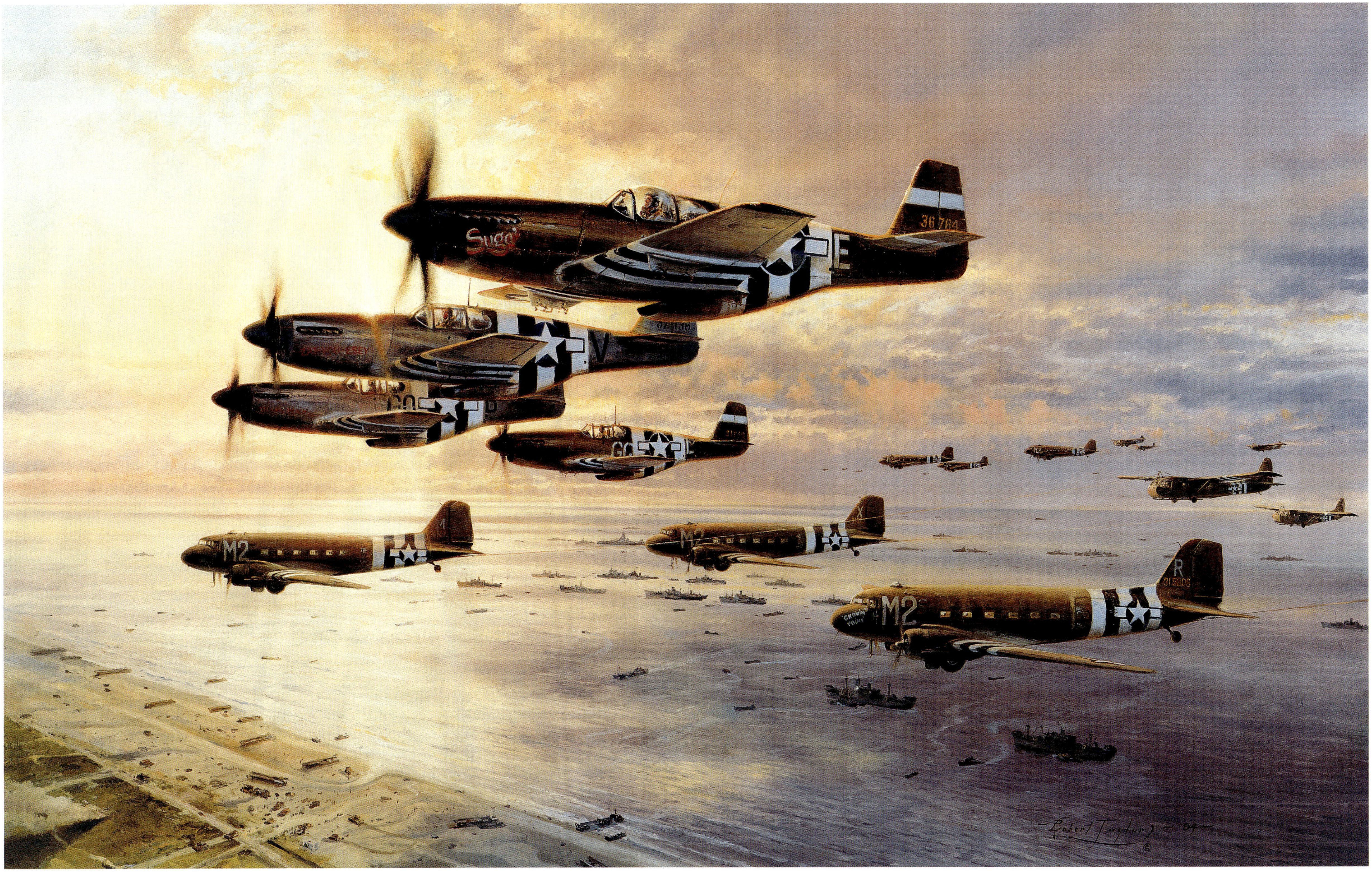

D-DAY – THE AIRBORNE ASSAULT

In the collection of Mr Eugene Eisenberg

THE BATTLE OF THE CORAL SEA

When attempting a painting featuring an historic battle, particularly one which may have lasted many days or even weeks, or in the case of the Battle of the Atlantic several years, the artist is faced with hundreds of different choices. As time goes by, old battles become remembered increasingly for fewer and fewer incidents, memories becoming focused on the most dramatic events, and it is usually these which are chosen by artists to portray. The fundamental choices to be made for a painting such as *The Battle of the Coral Sea* concern what particular incident to depict, whether this has already been painted by others, and if so, what the possibilities are for recreating a new aspect of that incident.

No matter how much I think I know about a particular battle, I always refresh my memory before I start work on ideas for a painting. This I do by re-reading the subject, talking to people who were there, questioning historians, obtaining new information from museums, and so on. This helps me at the same time to become immersed in the subject, which is the way I like to approach every painting I do. This renewed research is always fascinating, absorbing, and invariably turns up something I hadn't discovered before; and it is during this very early stage of preparation that I get most ideas for the painting itself.

The Battle of the Coral Sea was the first naval engagement fought without visual contact between the opposing forces, and with it opened a new chapter in naval warfare. Carrier went against carrier, and for the first time the greatest threat to the fleet came not from the mighty guns of battleships, but from the air. History was made in the Coral Sea as flyers from the decks of aircraft carriers commanded the arena. Naval aviation had come of age, and the events of that decisive engagement in May of 1942 were a portent of what was to come.

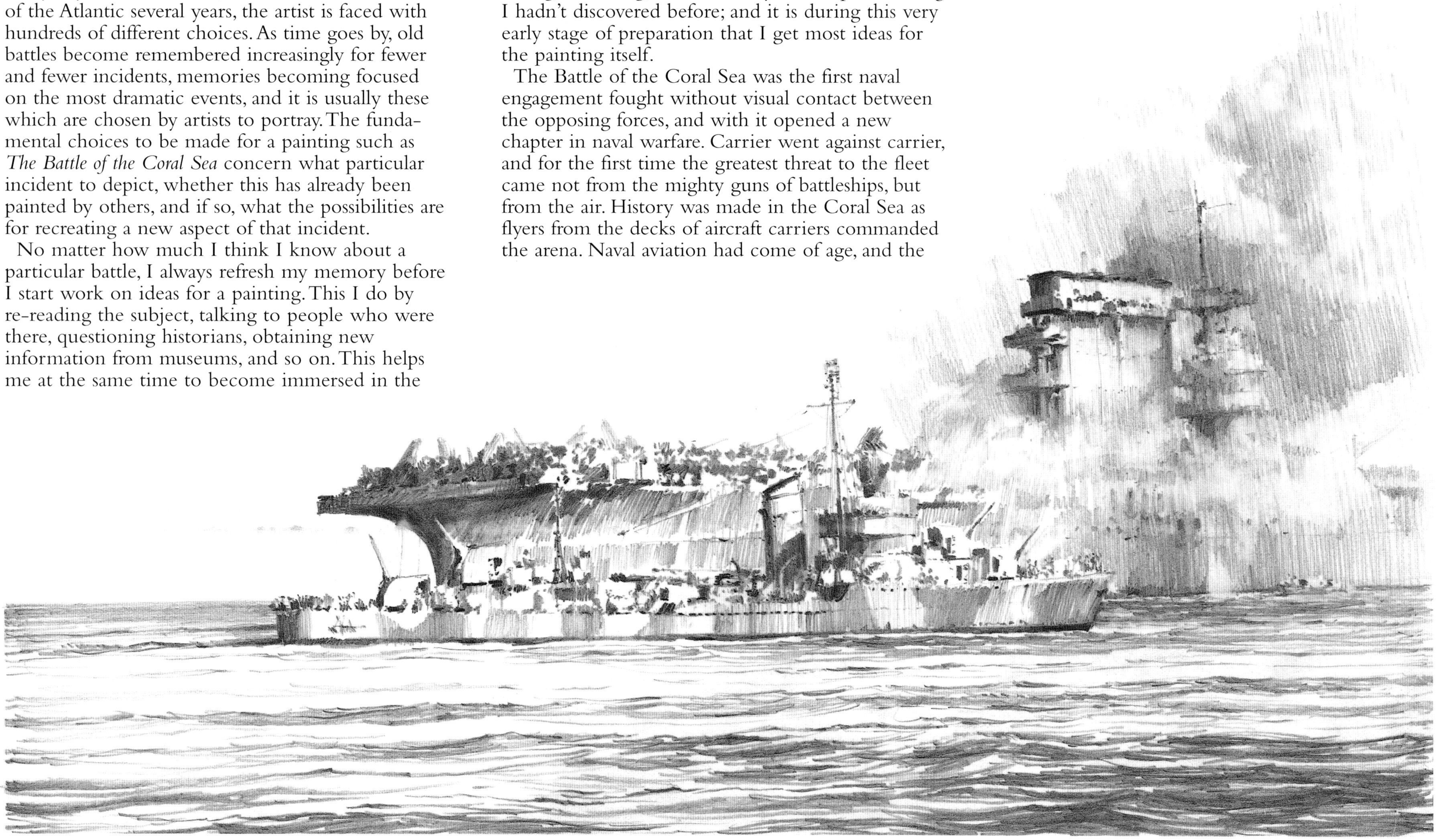

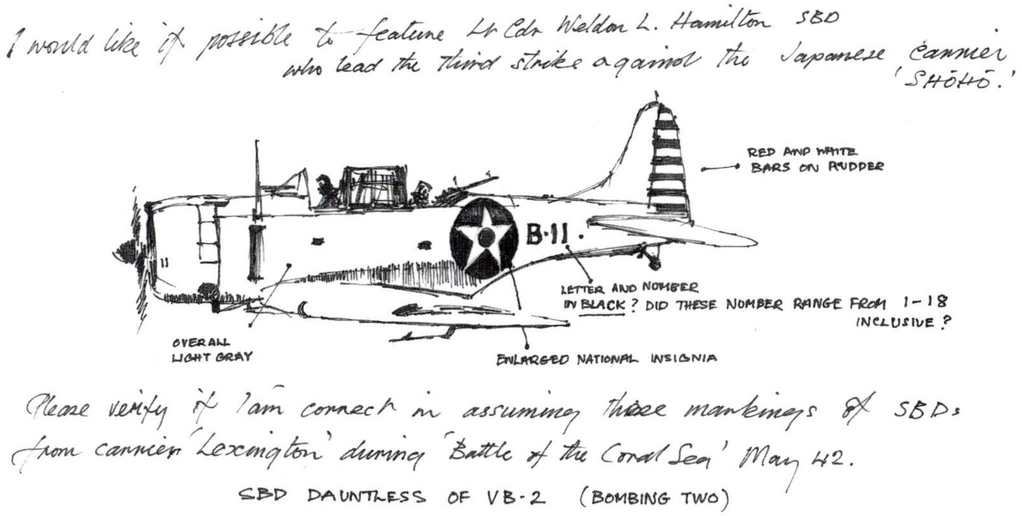

Like most things which are created, more time goes into the thought, research, design and experimentation than into its actual making. I certainly find this seems to be so when painting reconstructions of historic events. There is always an endless amount of information required, much of it needed before any sort of image can be formed in the mind. In my case, because I prefer to have everything about a picture decided before I start painting, I probably spend more time in research mode than most artists; although I suspect I catch up during the painting stage. Once I have started painting I like to avoid too much chopping and changing, and rarely make any fundamental alterations to the composition or content of a piece.

I had previously painted two different scenes from the Battle of Midway, and a number of other works featuring events from the war in the Pacific, but this was to be the first painting depicting a Pacific battle as early as the Coral Sea. During my research one of the first things that caught my attention was the brightly coloured markings of the naval aircraft in service at that early stage of the conflict. Shortly after Coral Sea the Navy decided to make their aircraft slightly less conspicuous, and did away with almost every shade of paint except blue. As a result the war at sea in the Pacific was essentially a 'blue' war: the sea, the sky and the aircraft all having the same basic colours; all very practical I am sure, but having no consideration for artists of a later generation! So when painting the Dauntless aircraft that flew at the Battle of the Coral Sea, it was good to find that I could legitimately introduce a nice splash of red into the planes in this picture.

Having chosen the exact aircraft to be featured, I made a quick sketch (shown above) of the SBD Dauntless and sent this to my ever-helpful friends at the Admiral Nimitz Museum in Texas, asking for confirmation of the size and colour of insignia, and the positioning of letters and numbers of the *Lexington*'s SBDs involved at Coral Sea. As usual, they obliged with the alacrity and efficiency the legendary admiral would have approved of and expected. Meanwhile I busied myself with making sketches and drawings until I was satisfied with the composition.

In all, the research for *The Battle of the Coral Sea* was spread over several months and, as with the majority of my paintings, involved the assistance of many kind people. The original canvas measures 40 x 24in, and from the commencement of painting took me about five weeks to complete.

The sketch below shows a Douglas Devastator carrier-borne torpedo bomber of the type involved in the attack on the *Shóhó*. The 'gun-barrel' object mounted on the fuselage just in front of the pilot is his site used for the release of the torpedo, the angle of which was crucial to the success of the weapon. The smaller aircraft is an F4F Wildcat.

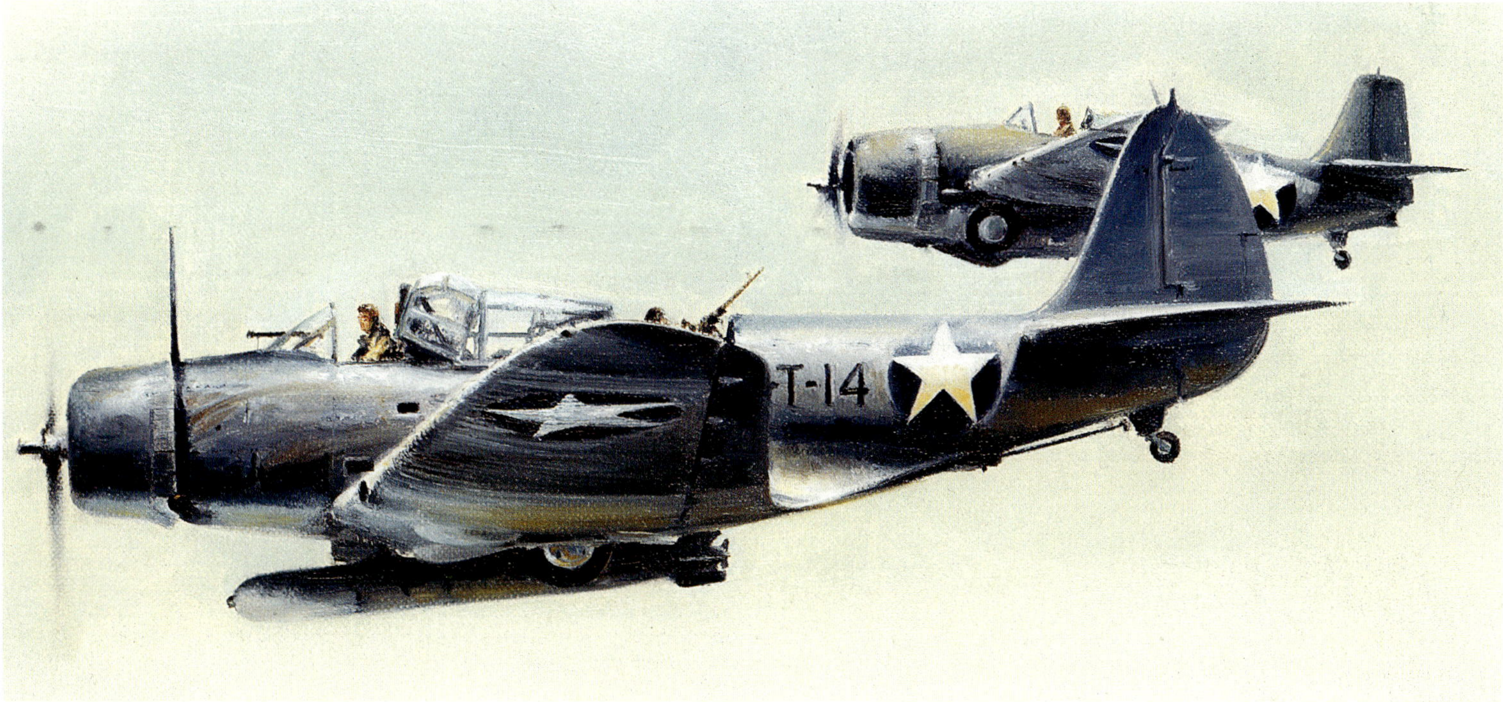

Unlike the beautifully painted and polished vintage aircraft we see at airshows and in museums today, the paintwork of those that fought the great aerial battles of yesteryear were far from pristine. Although airframes and engines were carefully, even lovingly maintained by groundcrews, there was neither the time nor the materials available to keep their charges looking like the day they left the factory. No *concours d'élégance* on the front line: it was how they flew that mattered.

I enjoy painting the old warplanes looking as they did, with little crinkles and undulations in the fuselage, rivet heads polished with wear, and exhaust stains spoiling the paintwork. I enjoy also having the opportunity to paint the faces of the crews as they fly their planes in combat, emphasising the vital human element of war in the air. No aircraft provides this better than the SBD Dauntless. The detail below serves to highlight these comments.

The SBDs in the painting have completed their mission and are affording themselves the luxury of a last look at their handiwork as they form up for the return to the carrier; they are from VB-2, Bomber Two, based on the USS *Lexington*. Below, other Dauntless dive-bombers and Devastators finish the task. The *Shóhó*'s days in the Pacific are almost over.

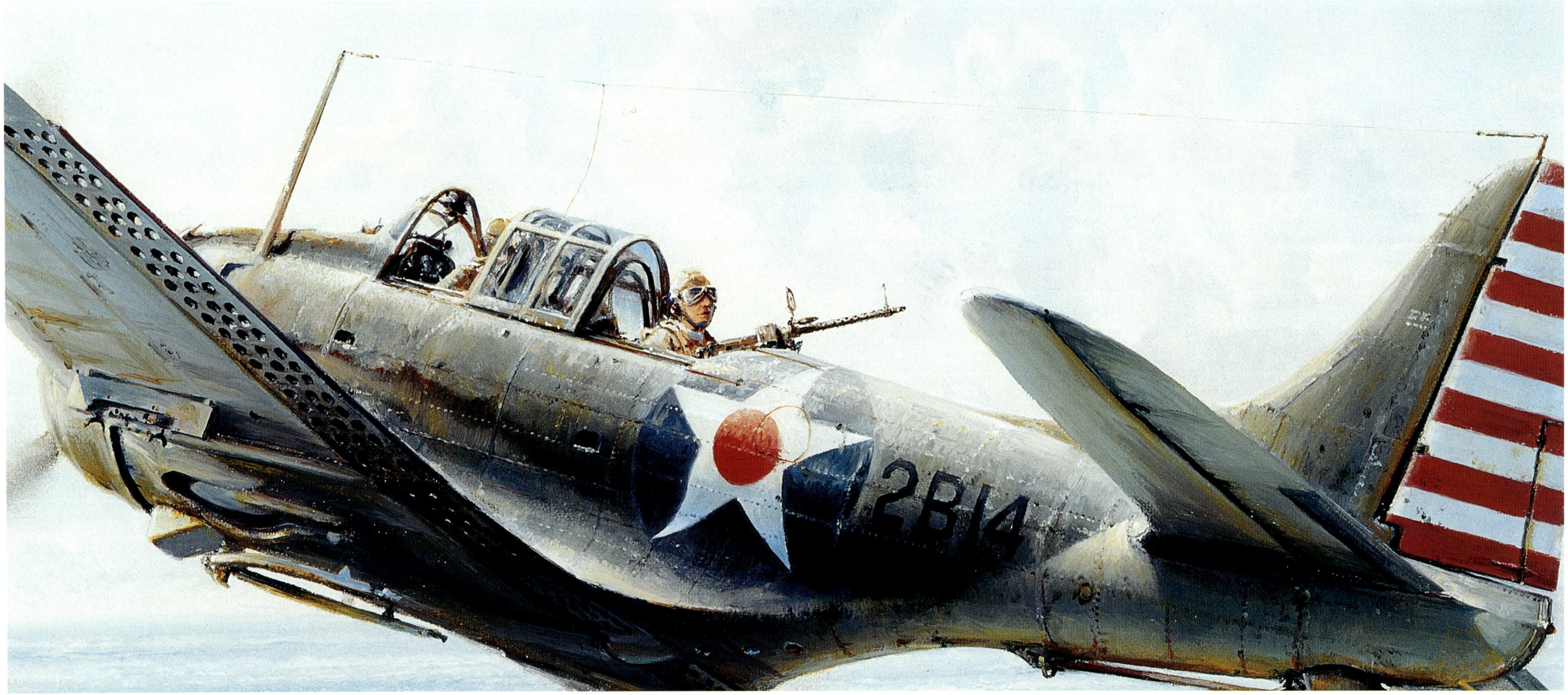

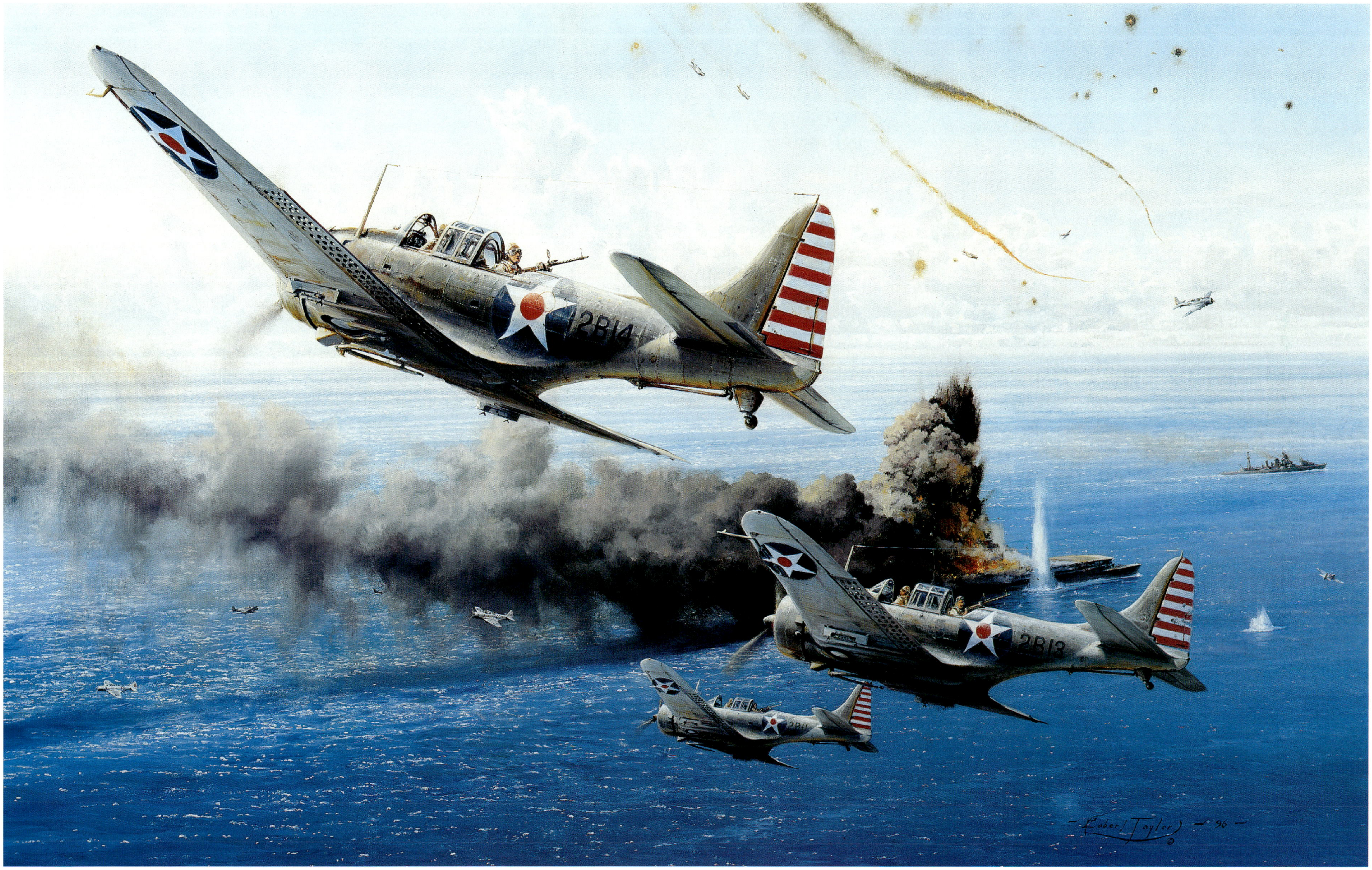

THE BATTLE OF THE CORAL SEA

In the collection of Mr Eugene Eisenberg

OUTWARD BOUND

Whenever I paint an airfield scene I receive a pile of correspondence from the ground-crew fraternity asking why I don't do it more often. The fact is I enjoy painting the old wartime airfields enormously. They provide such variety and scope, and *Outward Bound* is a good example of what I mean. It is one of my favourite paintings.

The air bases during World War II were always a hive of noise and activity, with people and vehicles scurrying about all over the place, twenty-four hours of the day. Everywhere planes were being refuelled, re-armed, taxiing, taking off, landing, having engines run up for checks, and guns tested and sighted in the butts; and if they were not, they were in maintenance, with cheerfully noisy mechanics swarming all over them. Nobody had much time for rest, and during periods of high activity it was not unusual for the crew chiefs to catch what sleep they could in the hangar. In a painting such as *Outward Bound* the aim is to catch some of this urgent activity and atmosphere.

The scene depicted is based on the well known fighter station that was RAF Duxford during the first part of World War II. A Battle of Britain airfield in 1940, it became home to the 78th Fighter Group in 1943 with the arrival of their P-47 Thunderbolt escort fighters. Here, P-47 Razorbacks from the 78th FG, complete with long-range drop-tanks, taxi from their dispersal positions in readiness for take-off, their mission being to escort heavy bombers – already formed up and on their way to Germany. The invasion stripes date the scene as being in the late summer of 1944.

Because the painting was commissioned to commemorate the 50th anniversary of the USAAF fighters in Europe, I included a few P-51 Mustangs already airborne from a neighbouring base, and parked a P-38 Lightning by the Nissen hut, thereby including all three escort fighter types that flew with the Eighth Air Force during their campaign in Europe.

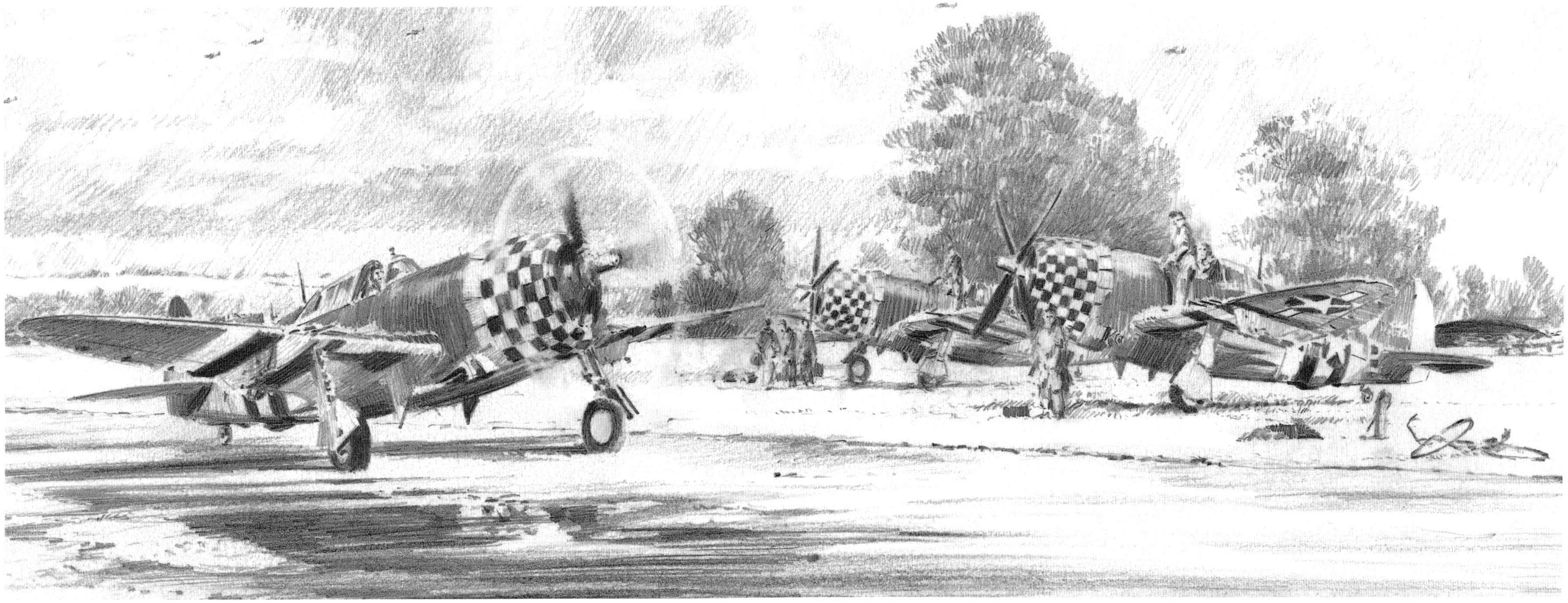

The P-47 Thunderbolt was not the prettiest of the World War II fighters, and I have always found it difficult to paint effectively in flight, its somewhat bulbous shape always seeming to slow it down! On the ground, however, where there is no need to create an illusion of speed, it is quite a different proposition. The enormous fuselage, gigantic cowl and air-intake, substantial undercarriage with all its accoutrements, and its massive propeller, all serve to give this huge fighter a thoroughly businesslike appearance, and it seems to take on a different character.

The P-47s in *Coming Home* are the earlier B models. I have always preferred the appearance of the 'Razorback' B to the later D model which was fitted with a bubble canopy and a slimmed down fuselage. Pilots who flew both types will not agree with my sentiments, I am sure, the bubble canopy giving far better all-round visibility in the air; but the glass-panelled cockpit with the high tapering fuselage behind it seemed to provide a far greater aesthetic balance for the massive engine in the front. On the ground, the tall undercarriage ensured that forward visibility was just about zero, and when taxiing, pilots had to use their brakes to weave the aircraft from side to side to avoid accidental collision.

All three P-47s in the painting were earlier models and would therefore have seen plenty of service by late 1944, and so I have painted them with this fact in mind. The big radial engines always shed a little oil, which would escape onto the fuselage just behind the ventilation flaps, seen here in the open position for taxiing; inevitably the oil attracted dust and grime, and this always formed a distinctive sweeping pattern along the side of the fuselage, these stains showing clearly on the P-47 in the foreground.

The checkerboard squadron markings on the cowl, the invasion stripes under the wings and around the fuselages, the stars and bars and the drop-tanks all help to make these P-47 Thunderbolts wonderfully interesting to paint. Adding to the interest, the pilots would always taxi with the canopy slid open, which conveniently gives the artist the opportunity to do a little portrait painting; and of course an airfield scene would not be complete without including some of the ground crews who kept the fighters in the air.

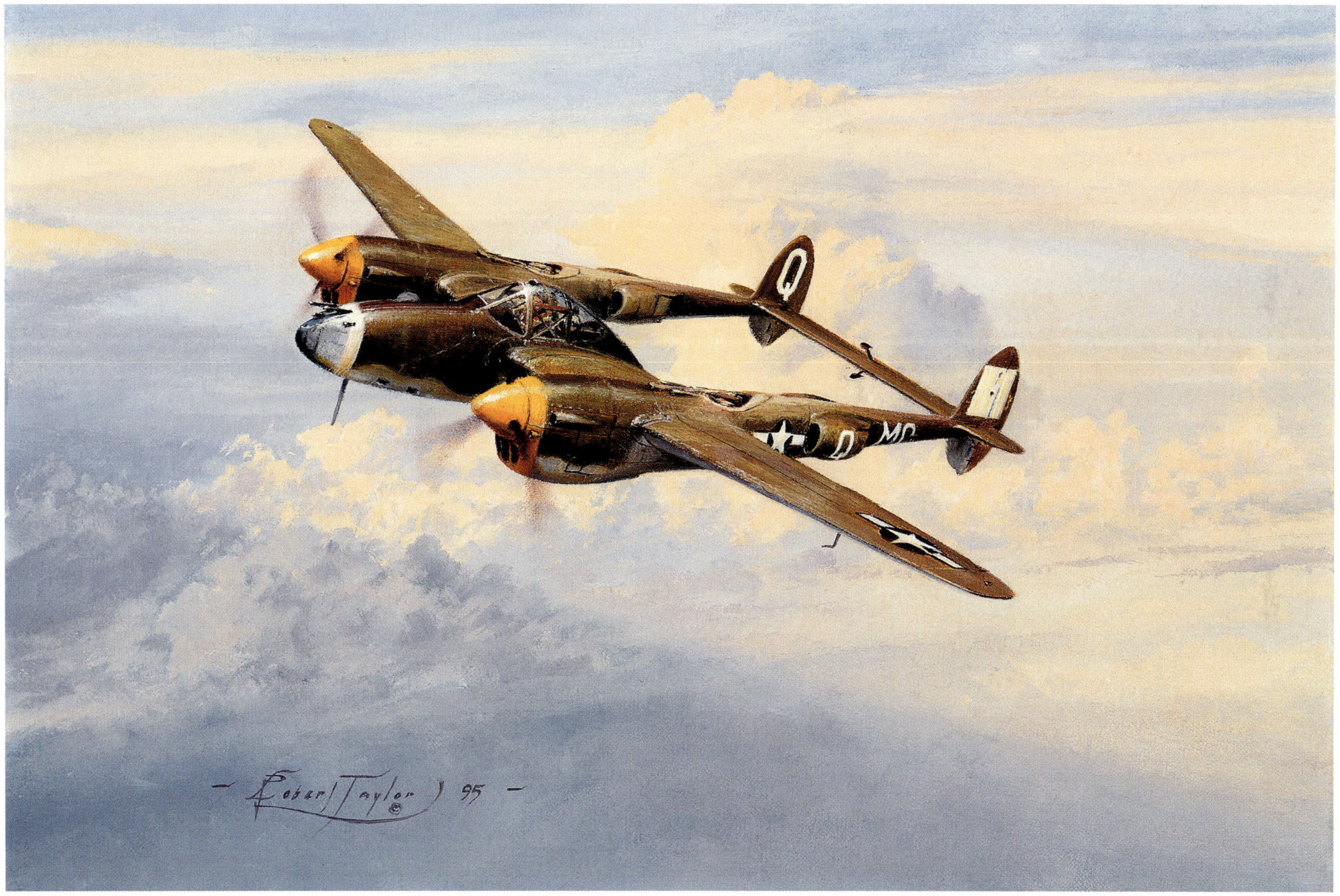

WIDE HORIZONS

The painting above is a small oil study of a P-38 Lightning in flight. Though seen here without its long-range drop-tanks, the P-38 came into its own as a long-range escort fighter, this particular aircraft having flown with the 20th Fighter Group in Europe.

When completing any kind of aviation picture I feel it important to take great pains with the composition and the painting of the sky. After all, the sky is the exclusive domain of the airplane, and I believe it deserves every bit of attention and skill an artist is able to muster; personally I make no exceptions to this rule, even for small paintings such as this – hence its title, *Wide Horizons*.

The painting below is another featuring P-47 Razor-backs, these Thunderbolts flying with the US Ninth Air Force. The Ninth became the largest air force ever assembled under one command, and it provided the bulk of the air armada for the Normandy invasion in June 1944. This huge tactical air force comprised no fewer than 3,500 airplanes equipping fighter, bomber, troop carrier, reconnais-sance and liaison squadrons, and in the lead-up to D-Day was despatching up to 1,000 aircraft each day against targets in Normandy and the Pas de Calais.

In *Thunderbolt Strike,* P-47s of the 404th Fighter Group are spread out across the landscape as they cross the French coast following an attack upon an airfield behind the port of Le Havre. Tracer shells wind up towards them from the ground defences as their pilots make a hurried exit from enemy territory. The nearest aircraft has taken some hits, causing superficial damage to the tail section – but not enough to stop this rough, tough Thunderbolt from returning to its base across the Channel. The third aircraft is trailing something nasty and a P-47 in the distance is smoking badly, but with only one hundred miles of water to cross, both will probably make it home. Fires are burning around and behind the port of Le Havre, just visible through a summer rain shower; a pair of gulls, frightened by the sudden whirlwind of noise, take hurriedly to the air.

To obtain the illusion of speed – difficult at the best of times, and doubly so with the P-47 – I have painted the Thunderbolts as nearly in profile as I felt comfortable with. I don't generally paint aircraft in profile if I can avoid it, because the wings virtually disappear, but in the case of the cumbersome-looking P-47 it is the angle that best gives the impression of speed!

The carefully shaped, dark summer storm-clouds were painted to add drama to the picture and to provide a sharp contrast for the aircraft. The arrow-shaped formation of the nearest four aircraft is deliberate, giving the group a strong directional pattern against the sky, and also helping to add a feeling of motion. I chose this particular piece of coastline for the same reason, its overall shape contributing nicely to the general flow of the composition.

In reality the dear old P-47 Thunderbolt was as quick as almost anything around at the time, and frighteningly so in a dive – a point I feel I should make lest any of my P-47 pilot friends think I am maligning their beloved steed!

THUNDERBOLT STRIKE

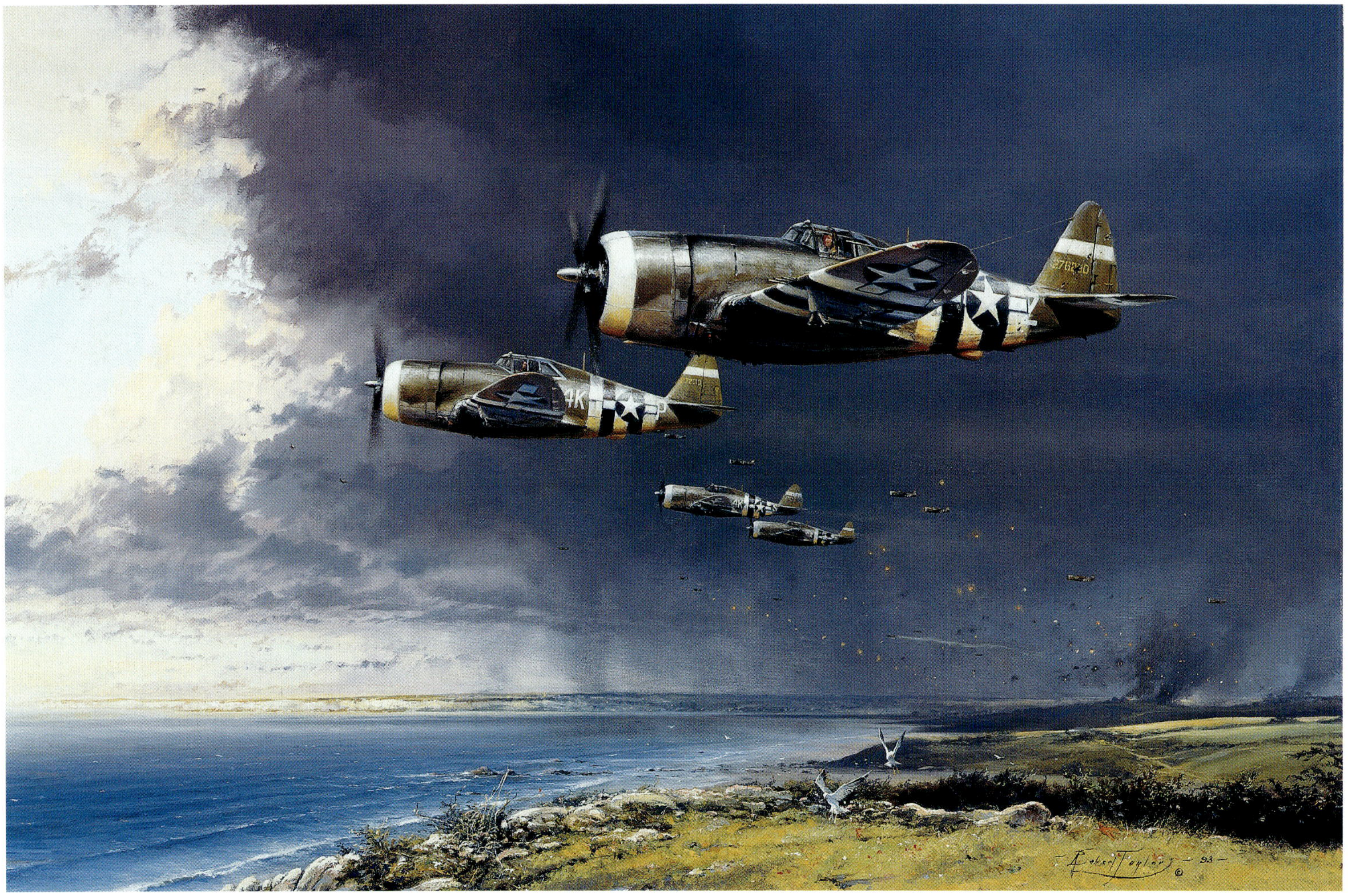

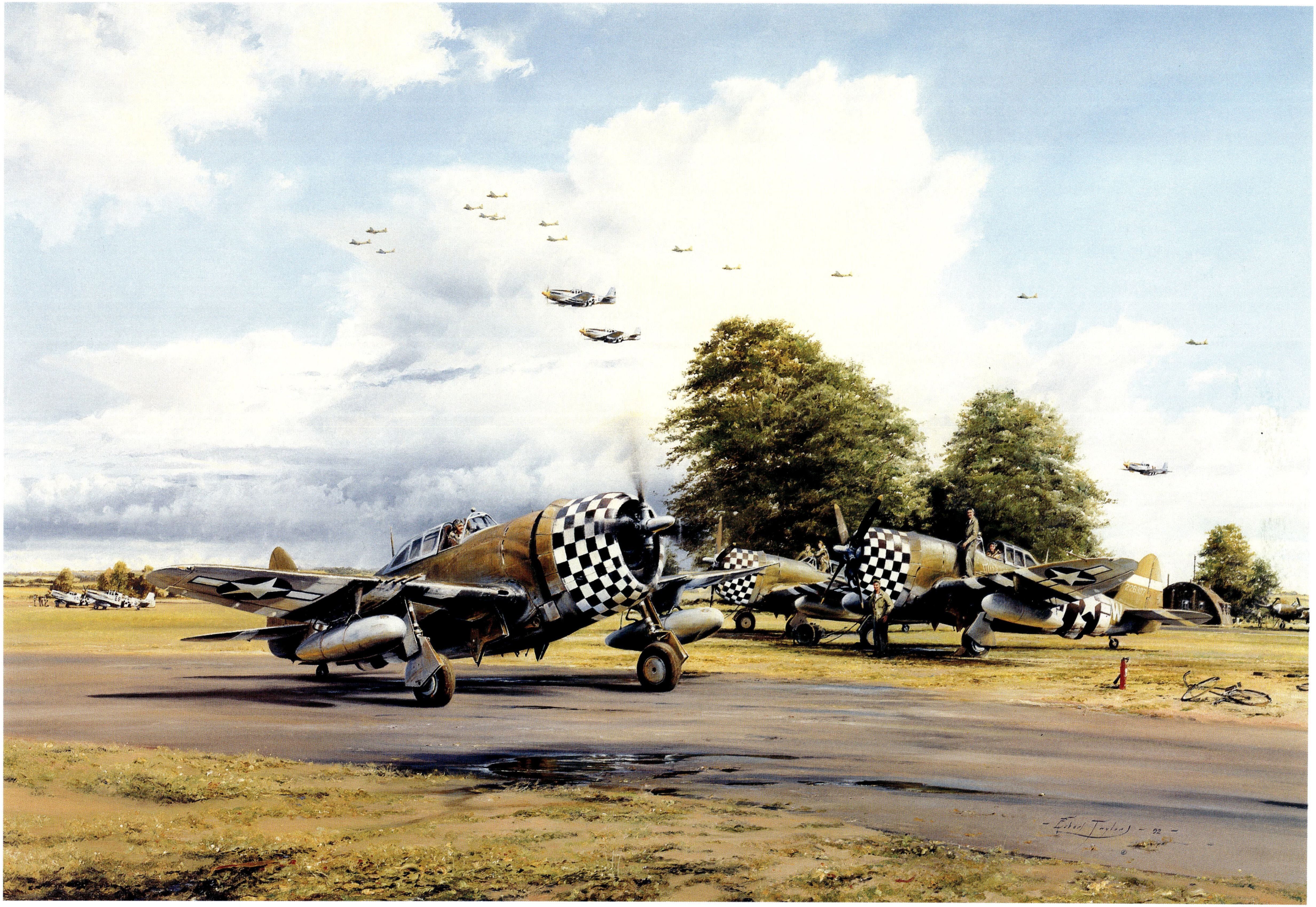

OUTWARD BOUND

In the collection of Mr Eugene Eisenberg

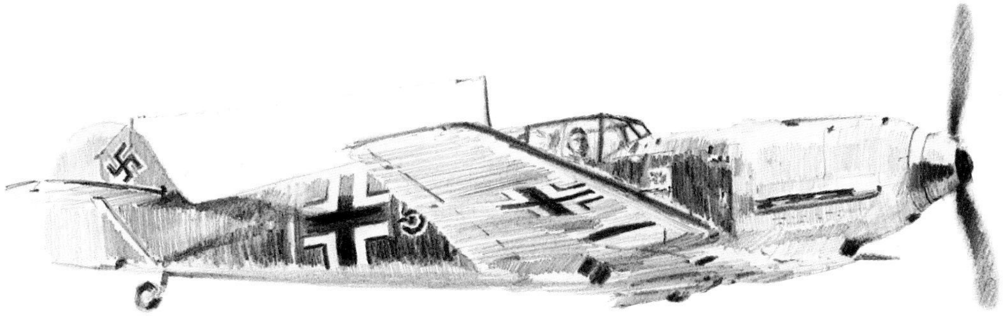

ACES ON THE WESTERN FRONT

Hermann Goering fell decidedly out of Hitler's favour after the RAF pilots had held his beloved Luftwaffe at bay during the Battle of Britain. Their failure to destroy the RAF and thus bring England to its knees caused the cancellation of Hitler's planned invasion, and was an acute embarrassment for Goering. Anxious to make amends, he promised his Führer a new aerial offensive against Britain.

The Luftwaffe's early fighter group commanders were experienced pilots such as Adolf Galland, Werner Molders and Hannes Trautloft, and they had questioned and complained about their leader's strategy and tactics throughout the recent air fighting over south-east Britain; but they were ignored. The abuse they took from Goering – who called his pilots cowards when the battle was lost – did nothing to restore the waning faith these professional airmen had in their narcissistic leader.

By 1941 France had capitulated and was occupied by German forces, and Goering deployed his air force all along the north coast of France in preparation for his promised offensive. What his new Western Front air offensive master-plan was, none of his pilots knew, for other than promising it would come, no details were ever divulged. Meanwhile Luftwaffe bombers blitzed English cities by night, while the fighters continued their duel with the RAF fighter pilots, who were now venturing across the Channel on to the attack.

While aerial battles raged above, the French people were having to come to terms with the awful reality of Nazi occupation, their lives interrupted day and night by the constant activity of aircraft and the comings and goings of troops in their towns and villages; nevertheless they continued as best they could. My painting *Aces on the Western Front* aims to show something of this situation, and I painted the beach scene in front of one of the most historic landmarks on the French coast, Mont St Michel, to place emphasis on this wartime phenomenon.

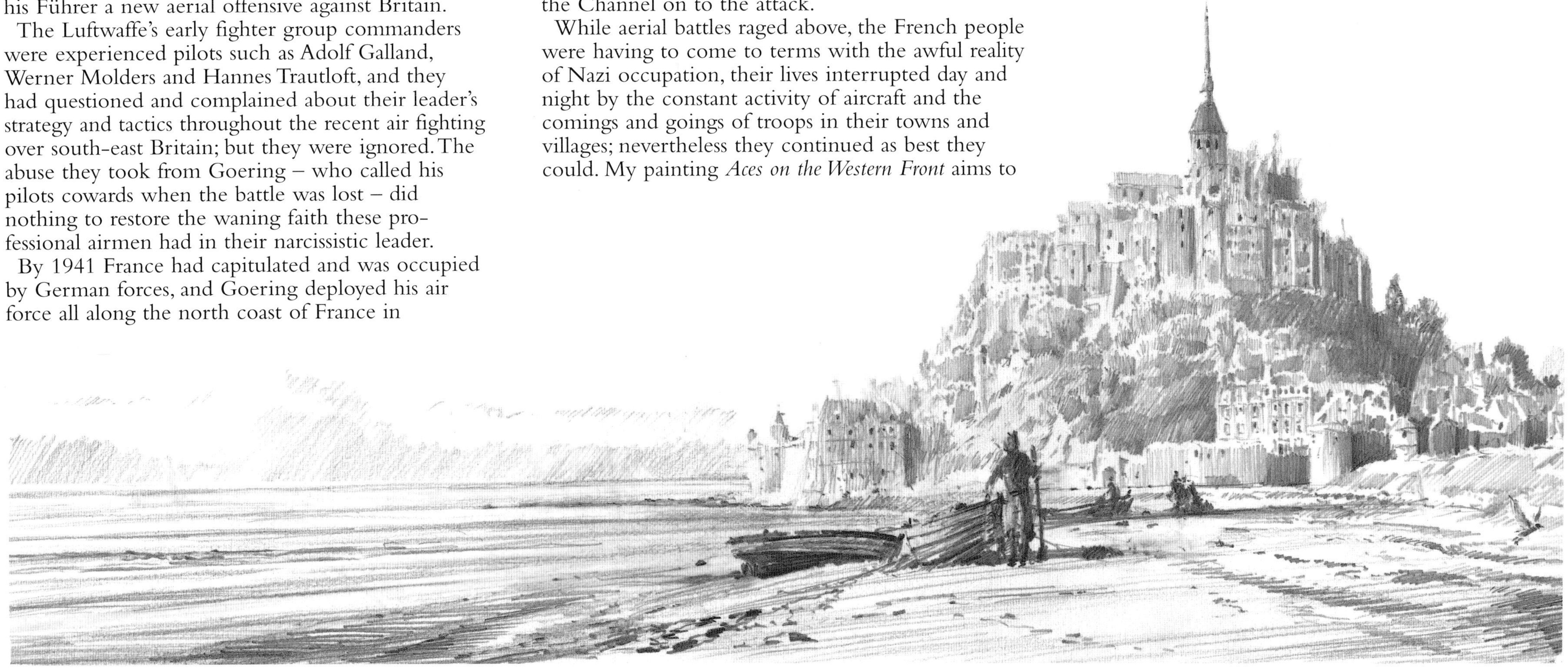

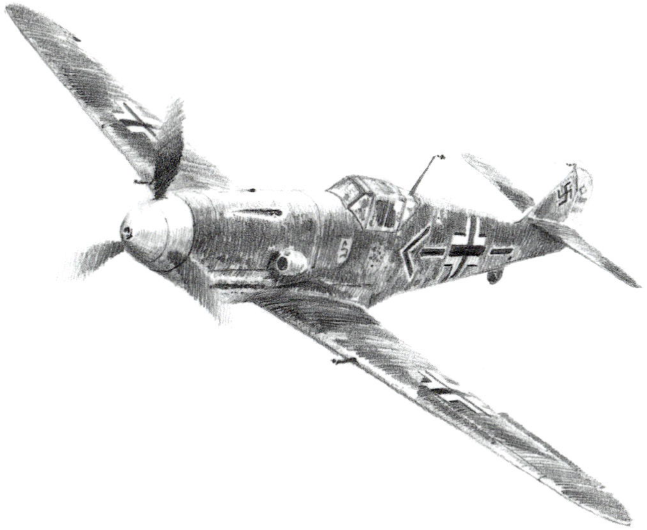

Mont St Michel was built by the Normans between the eleventh and sixteenth centuries. Constructed on a solid granite rock rising 250ft out of the sea, this ancient monastery has witnessed conflict over almost a thousand years. I felt it would make a poignant backdrop for a scene depicting what was the very latest in fighting technology back in 1941.

In spite of the obvious difficulties, the local populace still had to set about their daily routines in order to keep the wolf from the door; and with hundreds of thousands of invading troops ready to plunder the best of what food was available, feeding the family was a constant challenge.

Fishing was always a traditional source of food but had become a hazardous affair, and where possible was limited to in-shore waters. Venturing out by day, even with the authority of the local German commander, was to run the risk of being shot at by marauding, trigger-happy RAF pilots; and at night there was the danger of being mistaken for a clandestine Allied operation and arrested by the Gestapo. Nevertheless some in-shore fishing did take place, the local fishing folk preferring to keep their boats painted in the traditional peacetime colour schemes so as not to be confused with military craft; in this picture fishermen are seen doing what men of the sea are for ever doing: maintaining their boats. With repairs completed and the remnants of their endeavours tidily burning on a small fire high on the beach, the painting of the hull of the nearest boat is halfway through. It can be seen from the original sketch, shown on the opposite page, that I changed the position of the activity in the foreground to give this more prominence.

My youngest son Richard modelled for the boy in the painting, and the two men were real fishermen from the Cornish fishing port of Looe which my family and I visit regularly. In the detail from the painting shown on this page, all three are looking up at the Me109s as they roar overhead. The young French boy is no doubt excited by the sight of low-flying aircraft, too young to appreciate their significance. The thoughts running through the minds of the two fishermen can be guessed with accuracy!

The Me109's seen returning from a mission across the Channel are from JG-54, led at the time by Dieter Hrabak.

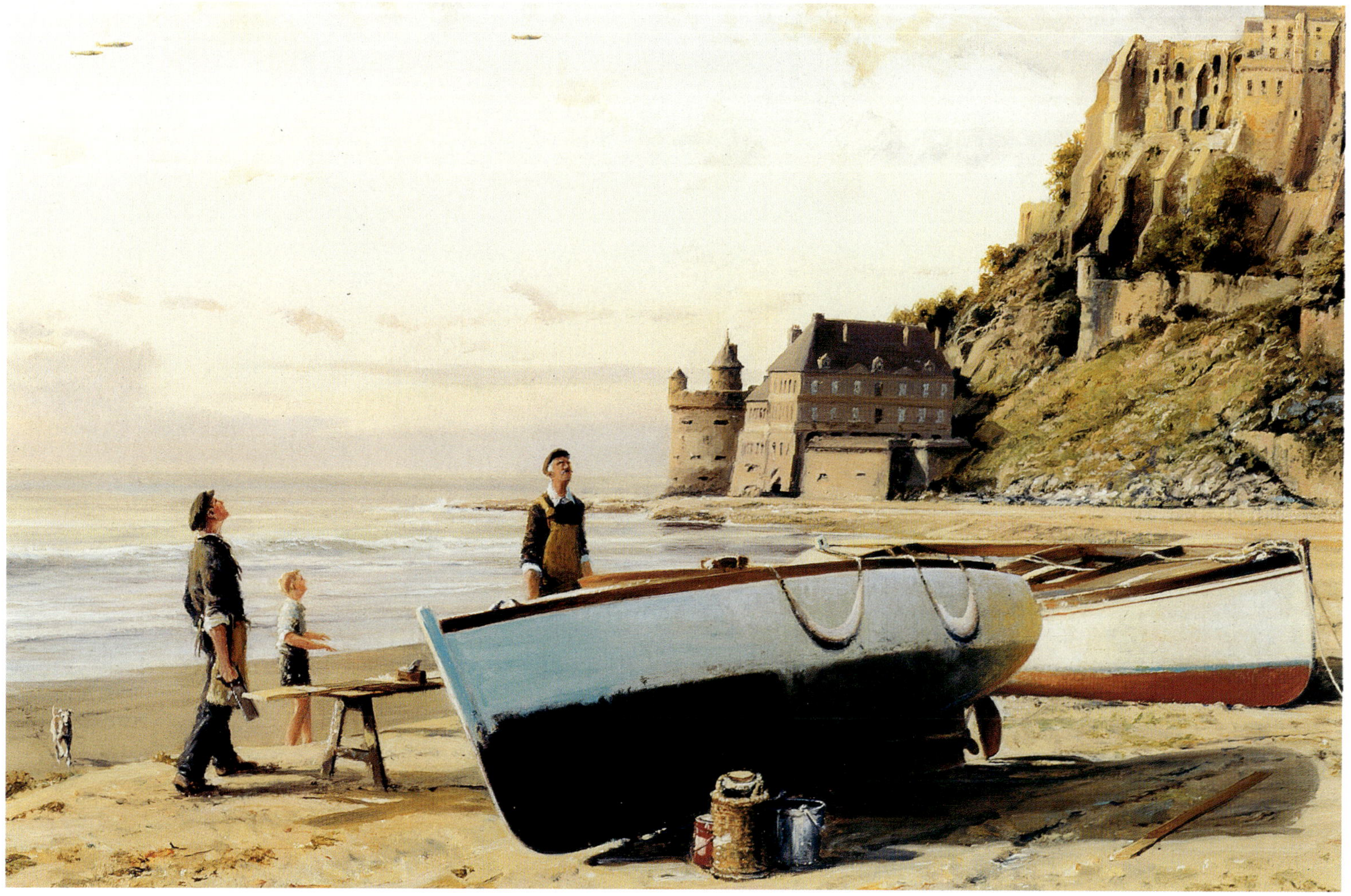

After the mauling received from the RAF during the Battle of Britain, a number of Luftwaffe fighter wings on the Western Front were depleted of pilots and were withdrawn from the front line to rebuild. With the opening of the Eastern Front, many of the Luftwaffe's top aces who had survived the campaign in the West – such as Dieter Hrabak, Gunther Rall, Walter Krupinski, Johannes Steinhoff and Herbert Ihlefeld – were selected to lead the revitalised squadrons and wings assigned to the Eastern Front. Among these was JG-52.

Initially based in Germany, JG-52 had fought the aerial battles of France and Britain; however, having lost many pilots it was posted to Rumania to regroup. Soon back in action, the wing flew in defence of the Rumanian oilfields, in the Battle of Crete, and then assumed the first fighter role in Russia. It was on the Russian Front that JG-52 pilots notched up their remarkable scores, the wing becoming the most successful of the war.

The detailed section shown below is from a picture featuring Me109G's from JG-52 in action against Russian Yak 9s. This typical head-on attack was a tactic favoured by many of the experienced Luftwaffe aces, and one not shied away from by the Russian pilots. Like the Spitfire, the Me109 was continually developed throughout the war.

KNIGHTS OF THE EASTERN FRONT

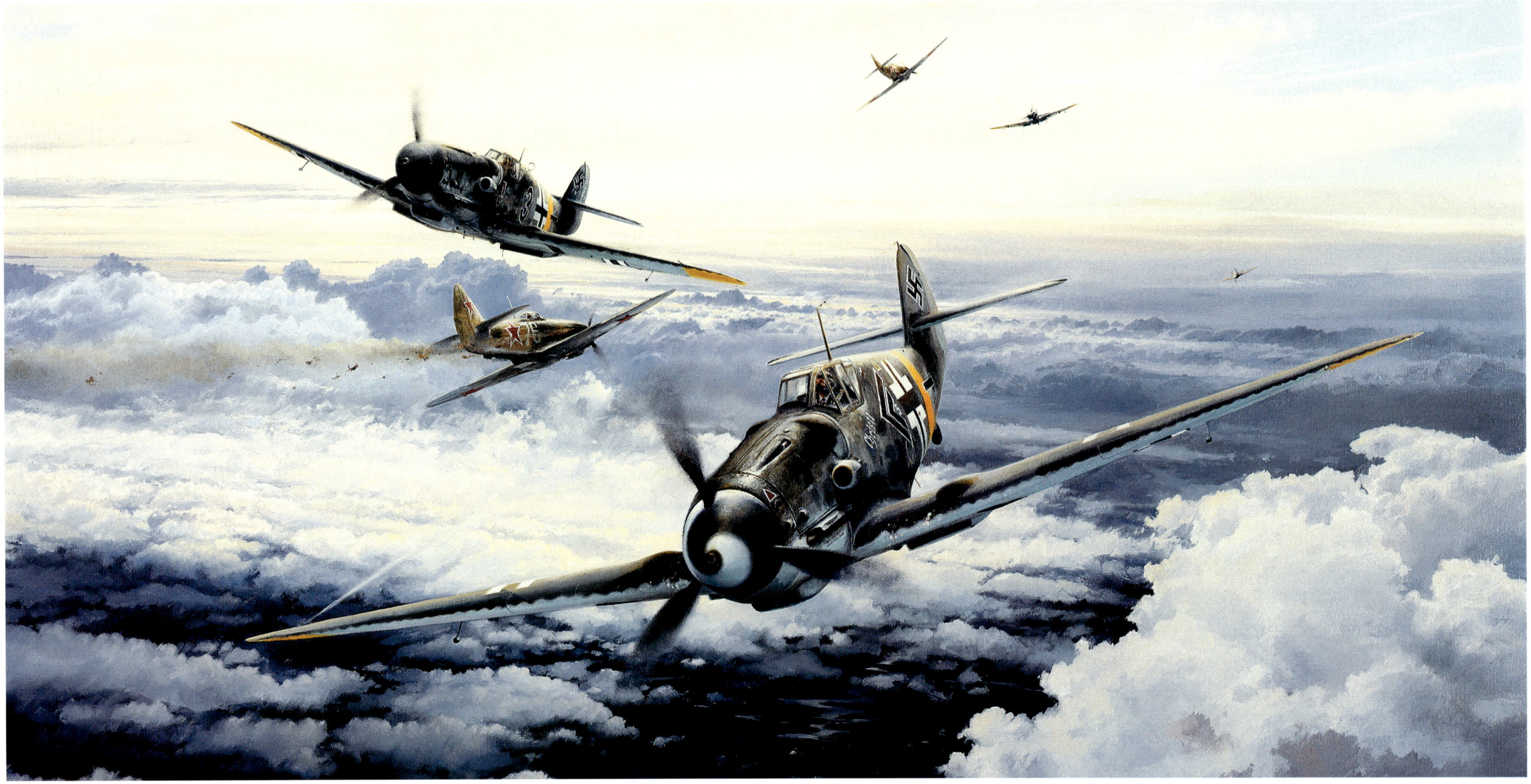

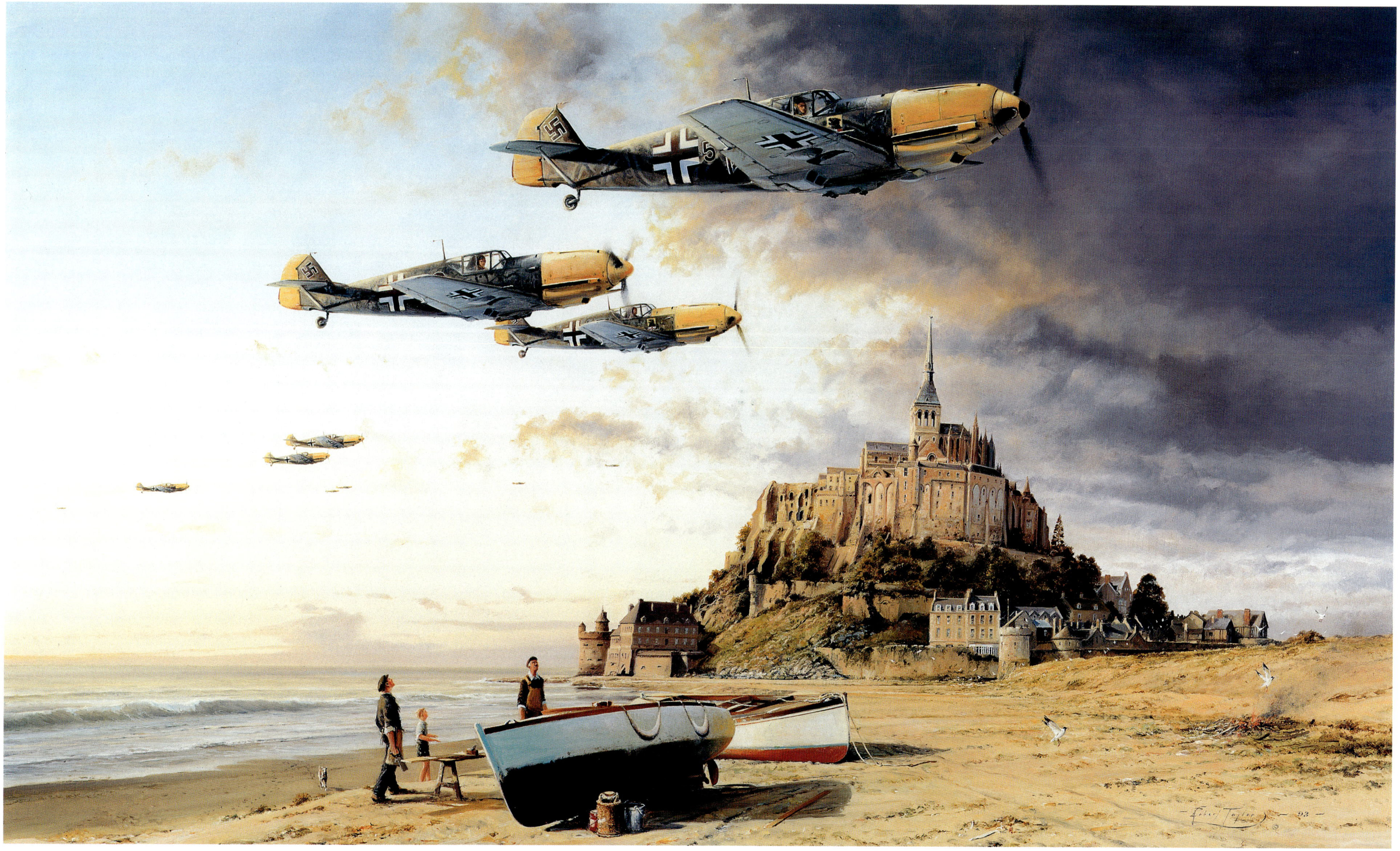

ACES ON THE WESTERN FRONT

In the collection of Mr Edgar Leicher

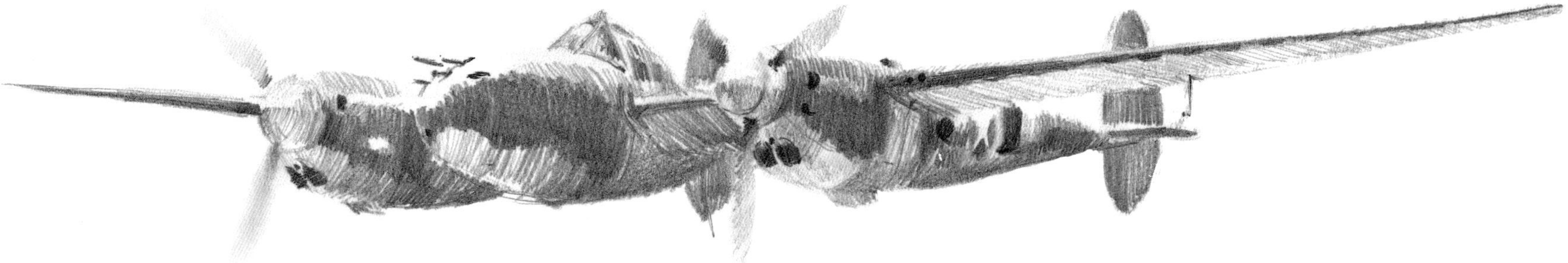

COMING IN OVER THE ESTUARY

Bosham is a small coastal village on the south coast of England. Although the quaint cottages, the old boat houses and the church are in better repair than they were fifty years ago, the view from across the estuary shows few signs of the late twentieth century and it seems to me that little must have changed during the past fifty years.

I was touring along the south coast, sketching and making notes for future paintings. There is a wealth of material for the landscape artist all around the coasts of Britain, but the small towns and villages along the south coast are those I know best. It was over and above this stretch of coast that much of the Battle of Britain was fought, and later, when the RAF were first able to go on the offensive, the fighters and bombers set course for northern occupied France.

As I sat in peaceful solitude on the edge of the estuary making a sketch of Bosham, I tried to visualise the scene as it might have been fifty years earlier. Barely a day went by during that six-year period when the air was not filled with the constant drone of aircraft coming and going about the business of war. With only the sound of the incoming tide lapping at my feet it was difficult to look back that half century and imagine that same scene with England in the grip of conflict.

When making sketches of Bosham I wasn't sure what type of aircraft would go into the ultimate painting, and the drawings were duly filed away on the return to my studio. It was a while later, when I was commissioned to paint a picture featuring the P-38 Lightnings of the American 364th Fighter Group, that I dug out the sketches of Bosham (I knew when I made them they would come in handy!).

The 364th were involved, among other activities, in low-level strafing in the build-up to, and the period following the Normandy invasion in the summer of 1944. Setting out from their base in England they would often cross the coast at a mere 100 feet, make the Channel crossing at wave-top height, and hedge-hop into the target to hit the enemy without warning. The village of Bosham would have seen many aircraft setting out and returning from such missions, and I retrieved my sketches to contemplate a composition containing P-38 Lightnings. *Coming in over the Estuary* was the result.

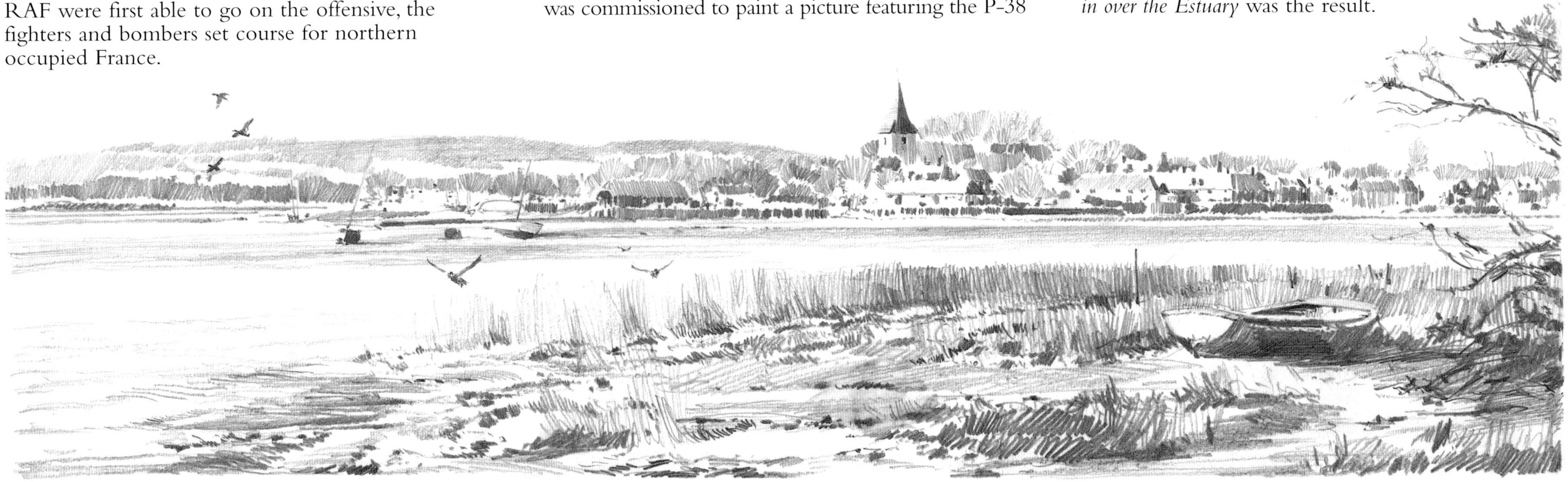

Before deciding exactly how I would paint this P-38 picture I made a number of sketches of the Lightning. I particularly like constructing aviation pictures around landscapes, viewing the scene, as most of us do, from ground level; however, this does mean that the aircraft has to be viewed from beneath, and not all airplanes look their best when studied from below. At one point I considered discarding the Bosham scene to avoid looking up underneath the P-38s, and the drawing of the Lightning below was made while I was considering an alternative aspect. But I changed my mind in favour of Bosham, and put the drawing, which at this stage comprised only the P-38, to one side. I resurrected the sketch some time later, completing it by drawing in the clouds.

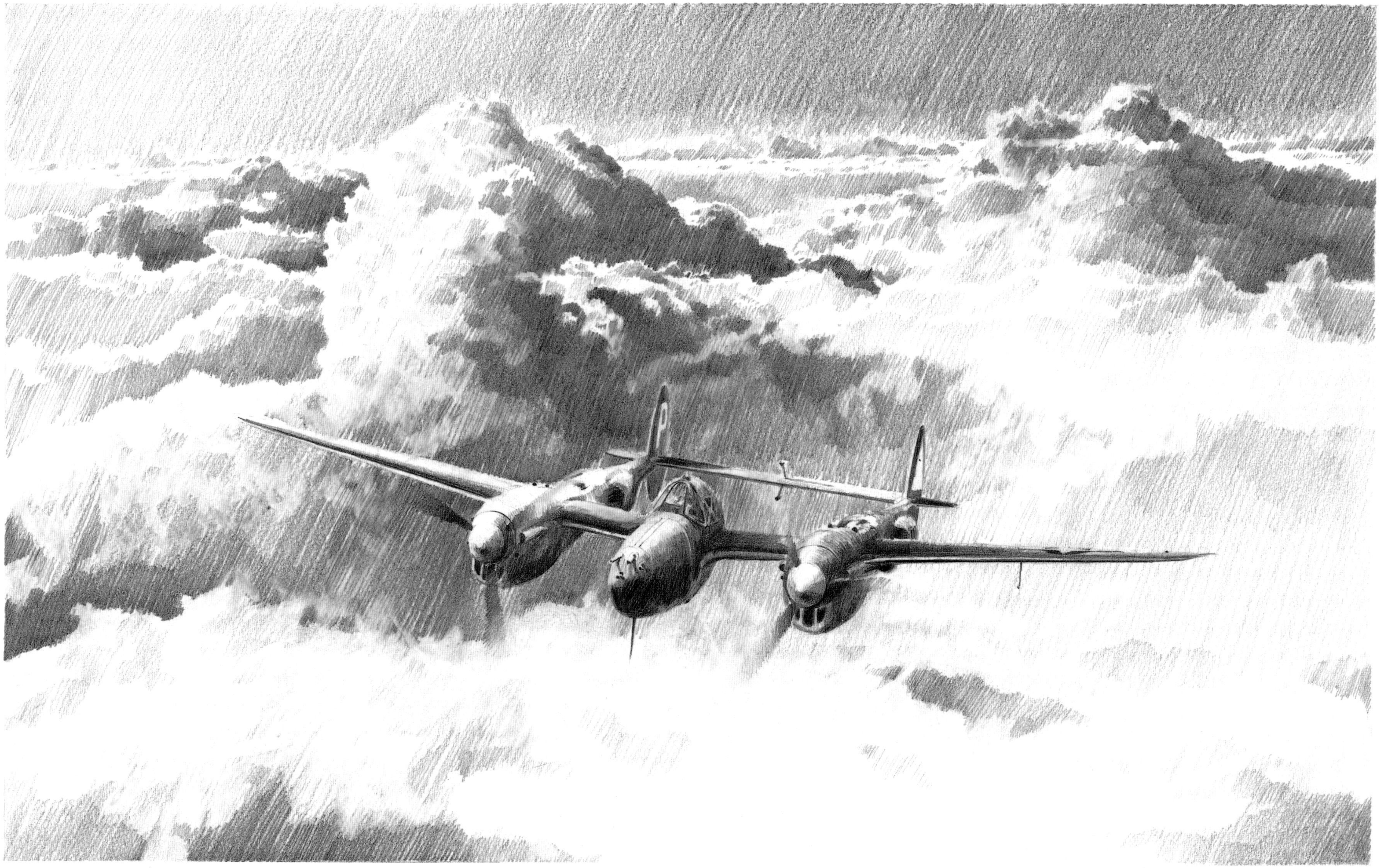

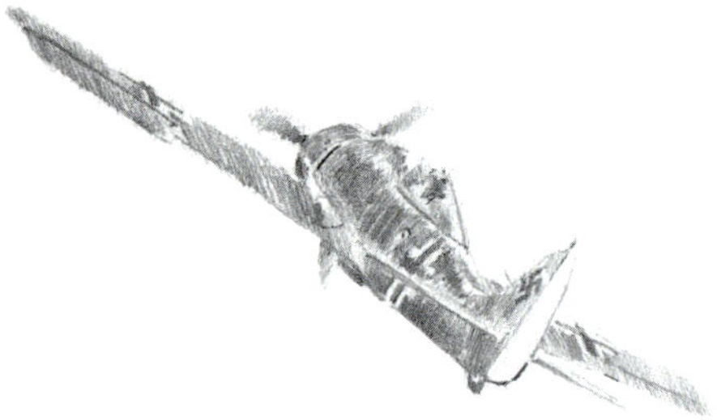

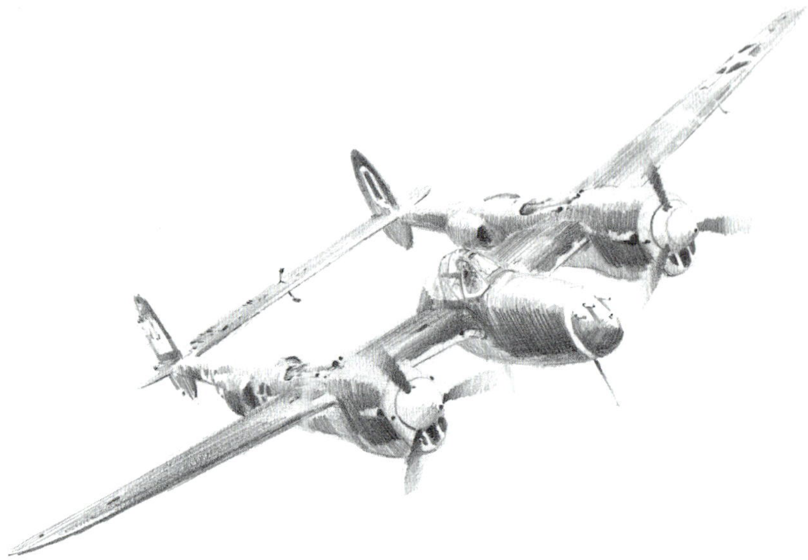

Most American bomber crews have a special affection for the P-38 Lightning because it was the first fighter capable of escorting them all the way to targets deep inside Germany, and all the way home again. When the first Lightnings arrived in England in 1943, the bombers of the 8th Air Force were taking a hammering from the German fighters. The endurance of the P-47 Thunderbolts was such that they could escort the bombers only as far as the German border; after that they were on their own, and the Luftwaffe knew it: the German fighter pilots waited for the P-47s to turn back to refuel, and then pounced. Bomber losses were high.

Though no match for the nimble Me109s and Fw190s in a dogfight, the American P-38 pilots bravely took on the enemy whenever they approached the bomber formations. By getting the best out of their machines and displaying dogged determination and courage, the Lightning pilots more than held their own and bomber losses were dramatically reduced.

Gunther Rall, the great Luftwaffe ace, flew against the Americans in the final defence of Germany. He told me that although the Luftwaffe fighter pilots knew their aircraft held the advantage over the P-38, they respected the American pilots greatly, and the presence of a Lightning escort always made the task of attacking bombers both difficult and dangerous.

HOSTILE SKY

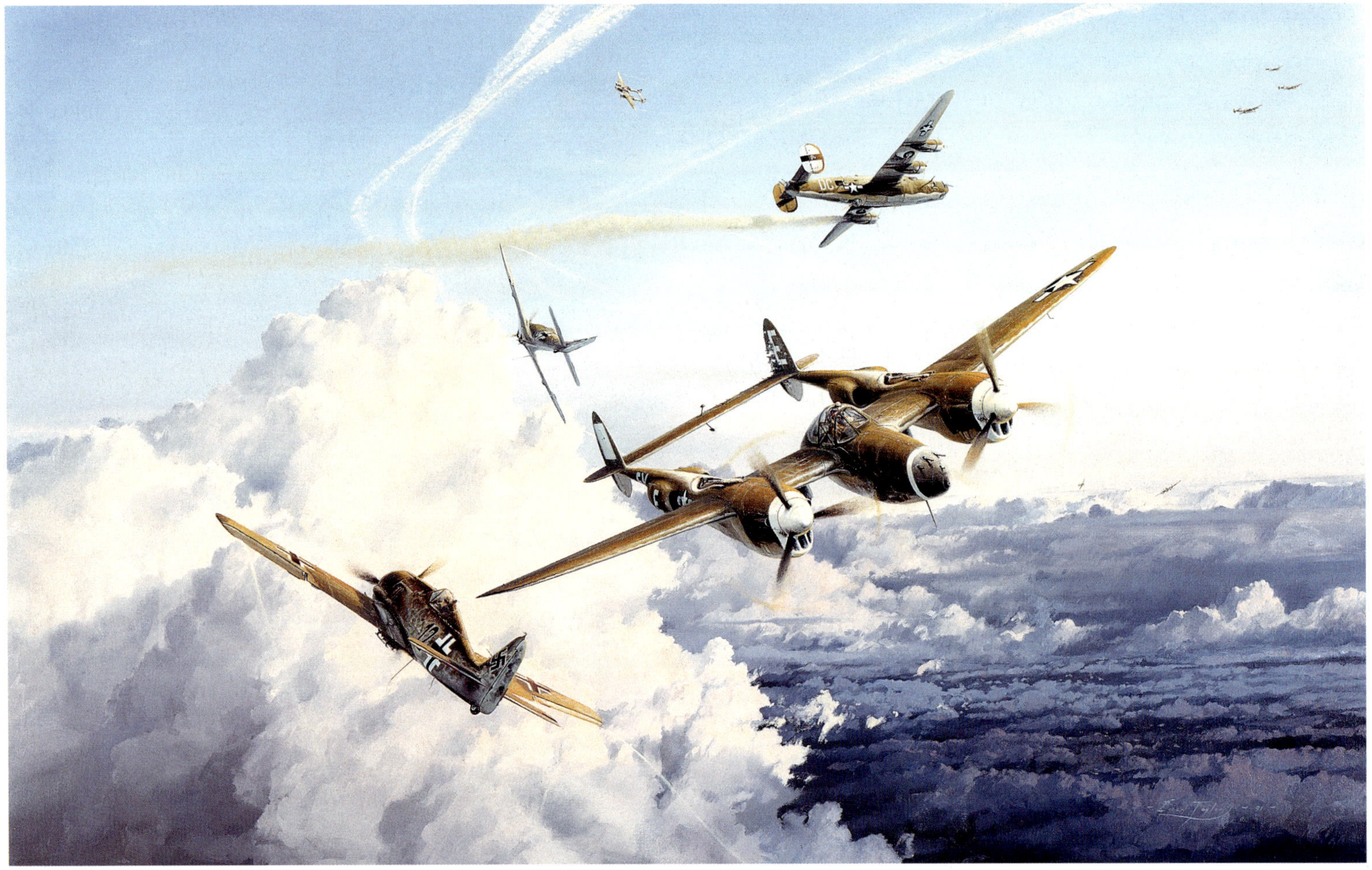

From the artist's point of view, the P-38 Lightning presents an interesting shape to work with. Furthermore, the highly distinctive P-38 is a good example of one of the many innovative designs that came out of that particular period in aviation history. War always brings about an acceleration in design ideas, and this, combined with the fact that in the late 1930s and early 1940s aviation was still in relative infancy, brought about a huge surge of design ideas.

Over forty different fighter types were flown by Allied pilots during World War II. These came from twenty-eight different aircraft manufacturers with, in most cases, a different design team working on each project. It is no wonder that so many different shapes and sizes evolved, and this must surely be one reason why the aircraft of that particular era are so fascinating.

The painting on this page, *Hostile Sky*, shows P-38 Lightnings in the fighter escort role. A B-24 Liberator has been hit and is losing touch with the formation, and the Luftwaffe pilots are concentrating their attentions on the unfortunate aircraft – but help is at hand. Two Fw190s, having made a diving pass through the formation, are zooming back up for an attack on the damaged bomber: but seeing the desperate situation, a P-38 escort pilot has made a daring head-on attack, splitting the determined Fw190s and thwarting their attempt to finish off the B-24. Another P-38, also aware of the situation, is turning into the path of the German aircraft, and at this point the outcome of the contest could go either way.

In painting this scenario it was my intention to create doubts in the minds of viewers and leave the question of the outcome unanswered.

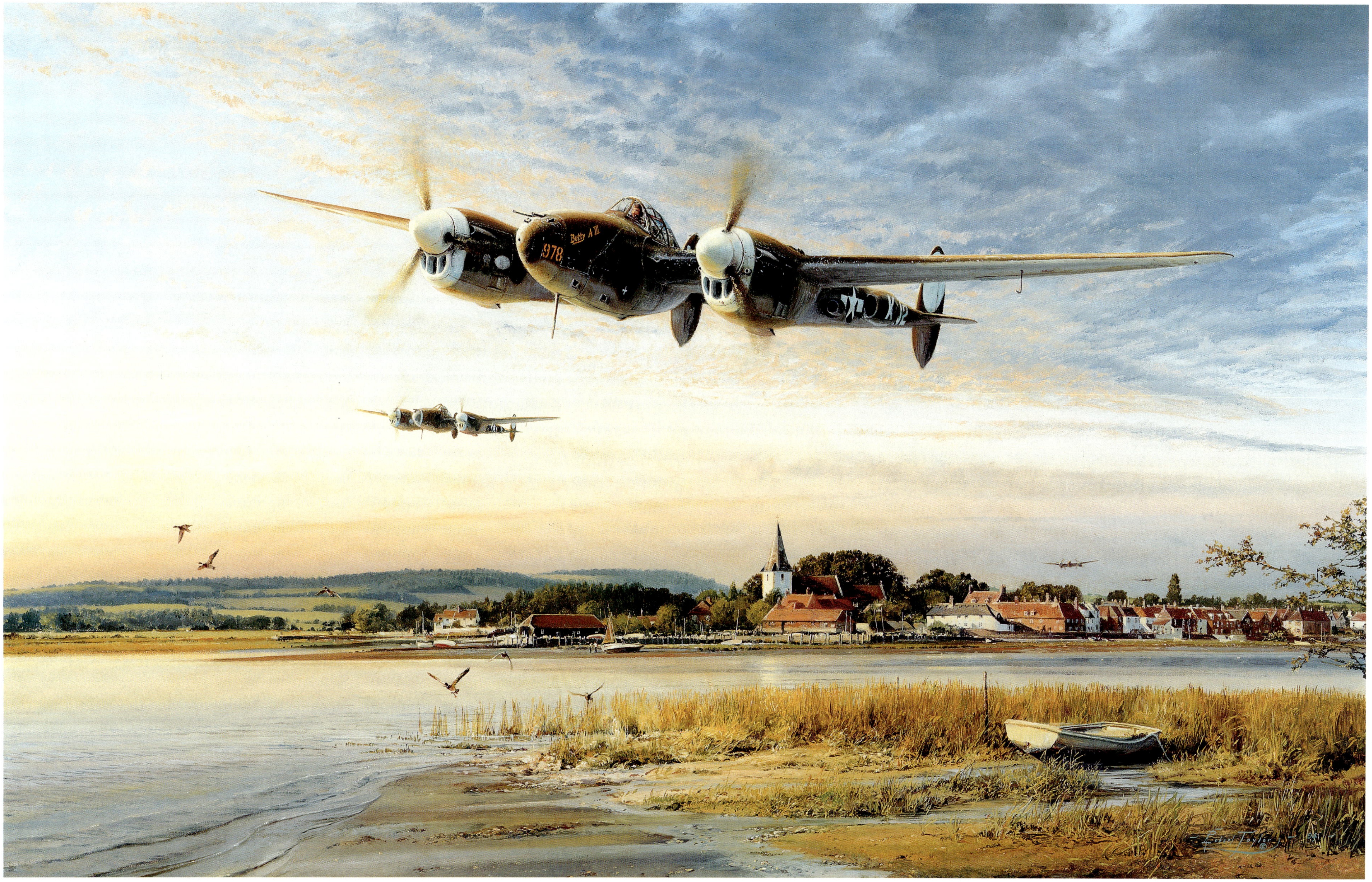

COMING IN OVER THE ESTUARY

In the collection of Mr Bill Ward Fine Art Services

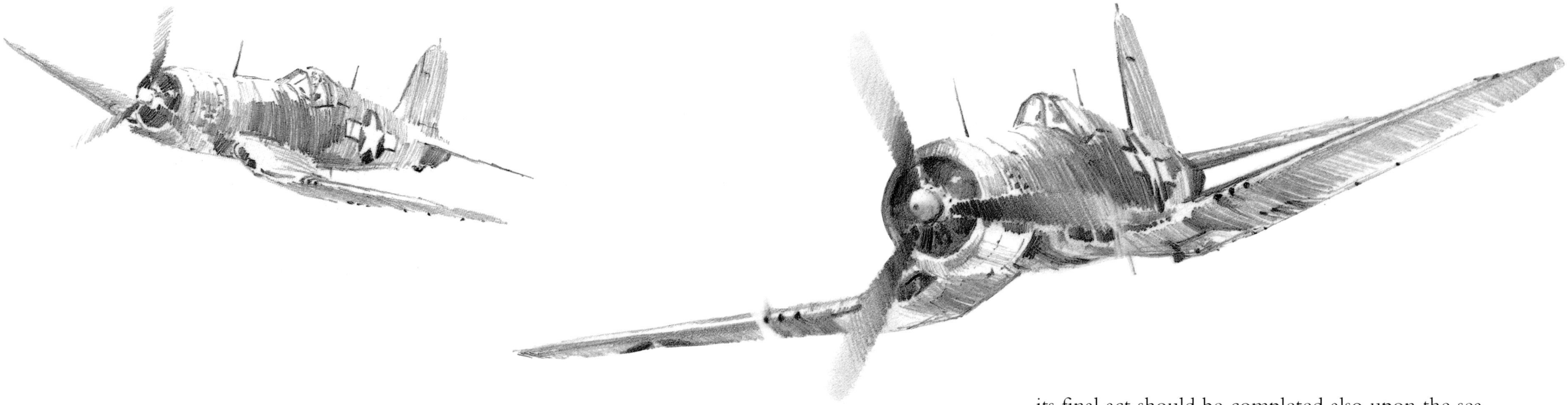

VICTORY FLYOVER

The signing of the surrender document that ended World War II was carried out aboard the USS *Missouri* in Tokyo Bay at 9.25am on 2 September 1945. It was one of those events that almost everyone knows about, and certainly one of the most documented events of the twentieth century.

I read an eyewitness account of the scene in a book published not long after the war ended. The writer poetically described the atmosphere of the occasion '... as if it had been staged by a Hollywood director: shafts of radiant sunlight broke through the morning mist, flooding the historic scene with brilliant colour, as a mighty rumble began to fill the air. Then, right on cue, a great armada of American airplanes swept across Tokyo Bay: Corsairs, Hellcats, Avengers, Helldivers, Mustangs, Thunderbolts, Fortresses and Superfortresses, as if heralding the peace ...'

When I read those words a vivid impression of the scene jumped into my mind with an intensity much greater than any contemporary photograph could have inspired. I find that words often have a unique power to stimulate the imagination; they can surpass even the most striking picture.

My main concern here was whether the resplendent scene I had in my mind would be sufficiently accurate to use for the basis of a painting. After an amount of careful research and a little reconstruction here and there, fortunately I was able to satisfy myself that it was, and the final image is almost exactly what came to me in that instant.

That the surrender ceremony should be consummated aboard a mighty battleship was truly a master stroke of stage management. It had been a war fought across the awesome expanses of the Pacific Ocean; a war started from the sea, and fought largely on and over the sea, and it could not, to my way of thinking, have been more appropriate that its final act should be completed also upon the sea.

Somebody asked me why I chose the F4U Corsair to feature as the main aircraft in my painting. I was surprised by the question and not truly sure of the answer. Any one of those airplanes that took part in the great flyover on 2 September, plus a few that didn't, could have qualified for the title role in the painting, and there was no great message intended in the selection of the Corsair.

I could have said that I chose the F4U because it was generally considered to have been the best carrier-borne fighter of the war, or pointed out that many of the great aces flew the aircraft in the latter stages of the war, or said simply that it is a great aircraft to paint; but the way I saw it, it didn't really matter. What did matter was that I should somehow try to recreate the electric atmosphere of that historic occasion with accuracy, at the same time placing my own interpretation upon that poetic description written by someone who had actually witnessed the scene and been so impressed by it. The moment captured is that just following the signing ceremony, which had ended so poignantly with MacArthur's words 'These proceedings are closed'. The first day of peace has dawned full of excitement, and now the celebratory flyover is in full swing, heralding a new era of hope and expectation for the nations of the world. The painting is crammed with the machines of war, but their guns are now at last silent. No longer will the drone of approaching aircraft set alarm sirens wailing and propel all hands to action stations: today they will stand and cheer.

It seems amazing to think that the USS *Missouri* was still a sufficiently modern fighting force to take part in the recent Gulf War, almost half a century after that historic occasion in Tokyo Bay. Now there's testimony to that old adage 'they don't build 'em like they used to'. This magnificent Iowa class battleship, the likes of which will never be built again, now enjoys a quiet retirement lying in Puget Sound, Washington, awaiting her fate. Will she be allowed to live on gracefully as a museum ship, a tribute to the men who fought that long and arduous war in the Pacific, or will she again be dragged out of retirement to fight a new battle in some far-flung corner of the world? Or will she be unceremoniously converted into razor blades? Whatever her ultimate fate, she and her sister ships of the Pacific Fleet will long be remembered for the vital role they played in twentieth-century maritime history.

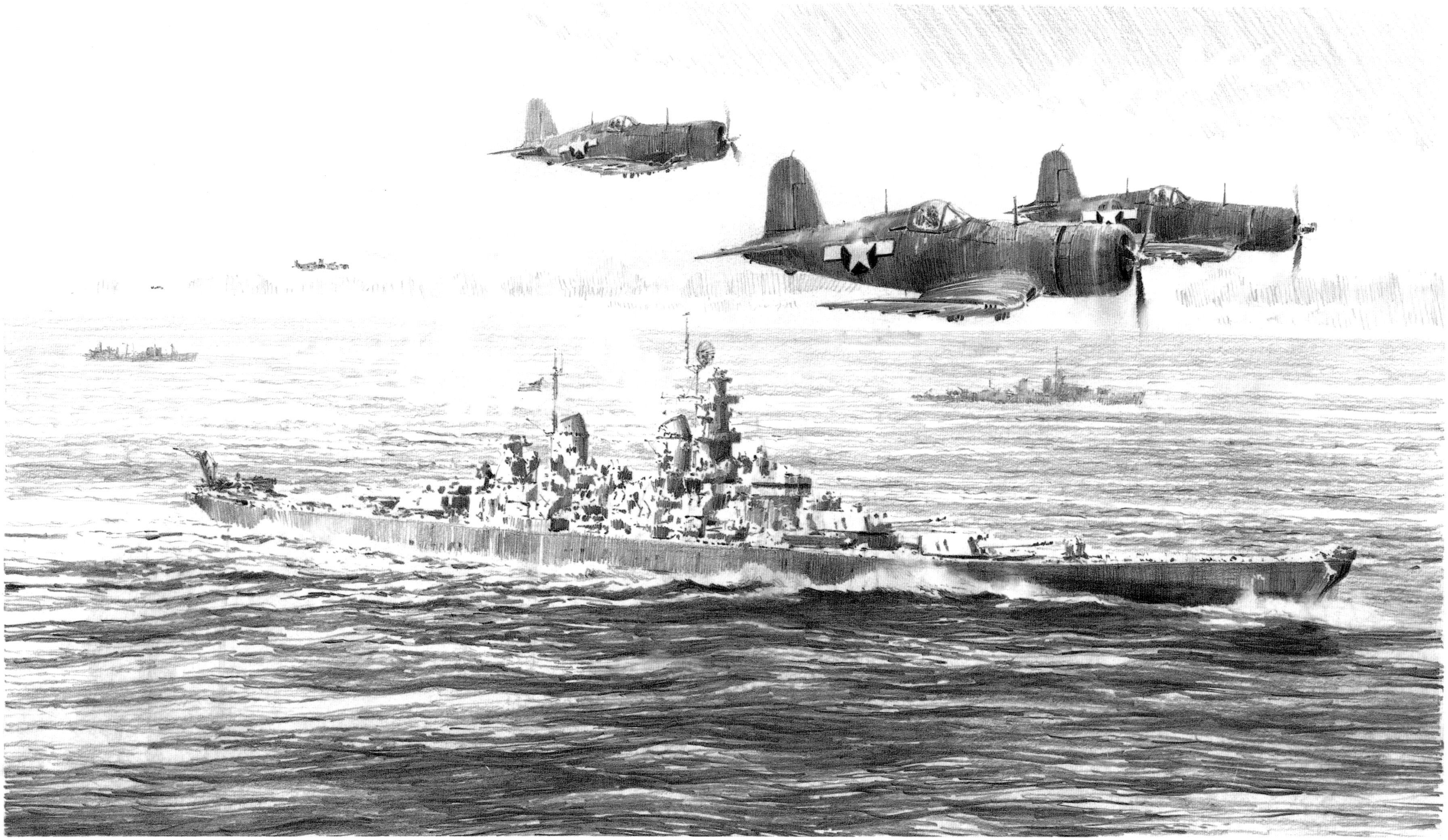

'Bound for Tokyo' – The USS Missouri, escorted by F4U Corsairs, heads for Tokyo Bay, September 1945.

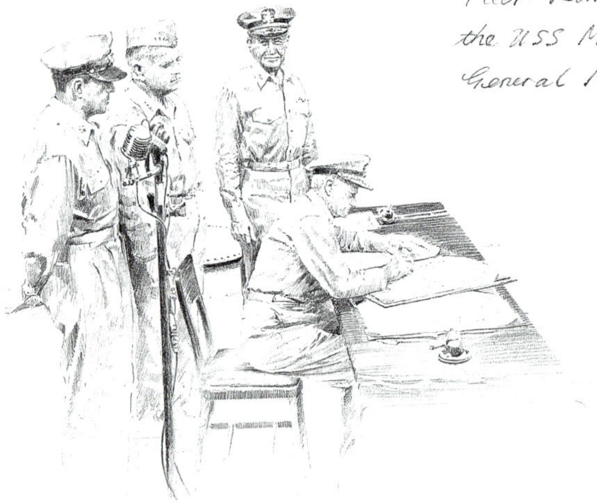

Fleet Admiral Chester Nimitz signs the surrender document aboard the USS Missouri, Toko Bay, 2nd September, 1945. Also present are General MacArthur, and Admirals Halsey and Sherman.

General Douglas MacArthur, Fleet Admiral Chester Nimitz, and Admirals Halsey and Sherman presided, with representatives from all the Allied nations in attendance, while Emperor Hirohito's Foreign Minister, Mamoru Shigemitsu, and General Yoshijiro Umezu of the Japanese Imperial Headquarters, officially brought the cataclysmic war in the Pacific to an end. I made a small pencil drawing of Admiral Nimitz signing the instrument of surrender, which was reproduced as a printed remarque on each of the prints published from the painting. The drawing is shown above. I carefully painted the Corsairs in the foreground to ensure that they looked as if they had just finished fighting a war, chipping paint off everywhere, working in oil streaks along and down the sides of the fuselages, and generally giving them a very 'war-torn' appearance. There are some twenty marine craft in the painting and over a hundred and fifty airplanes.

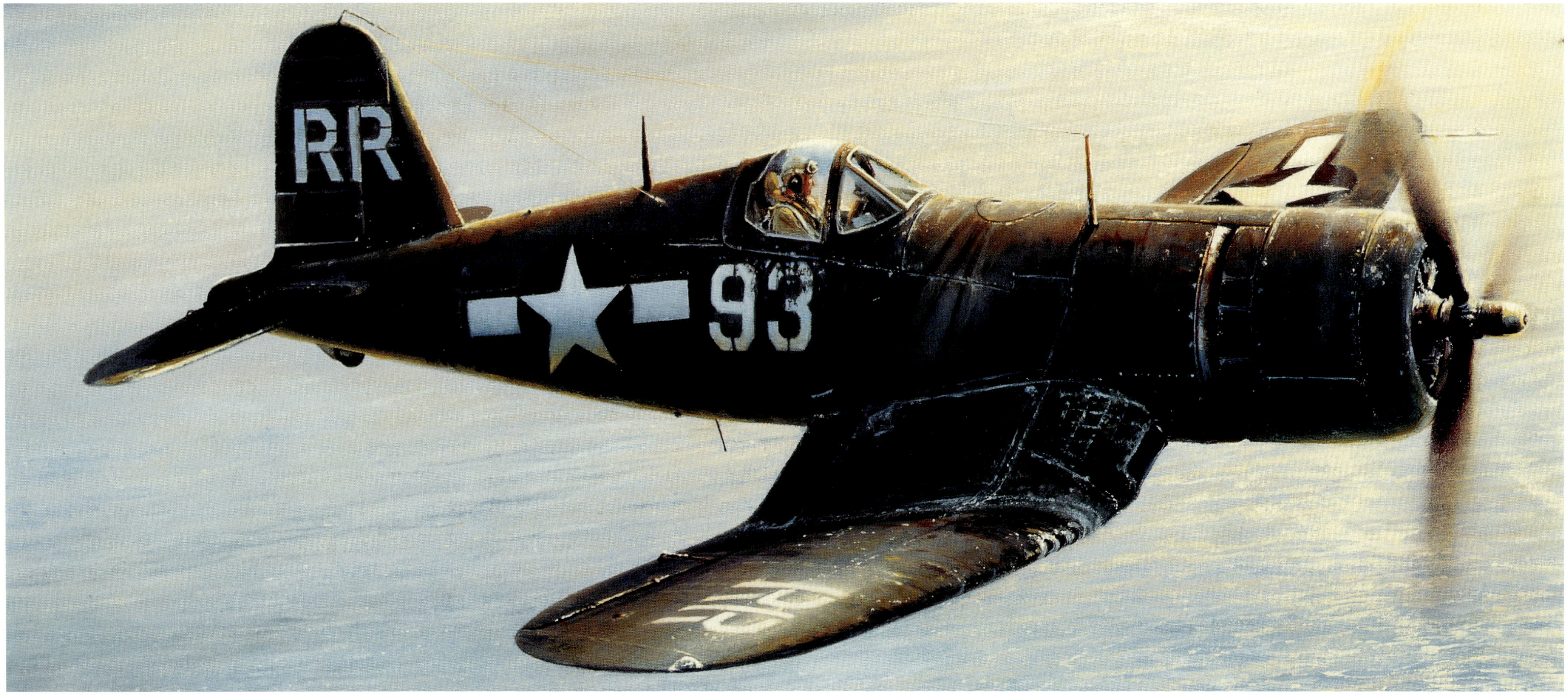

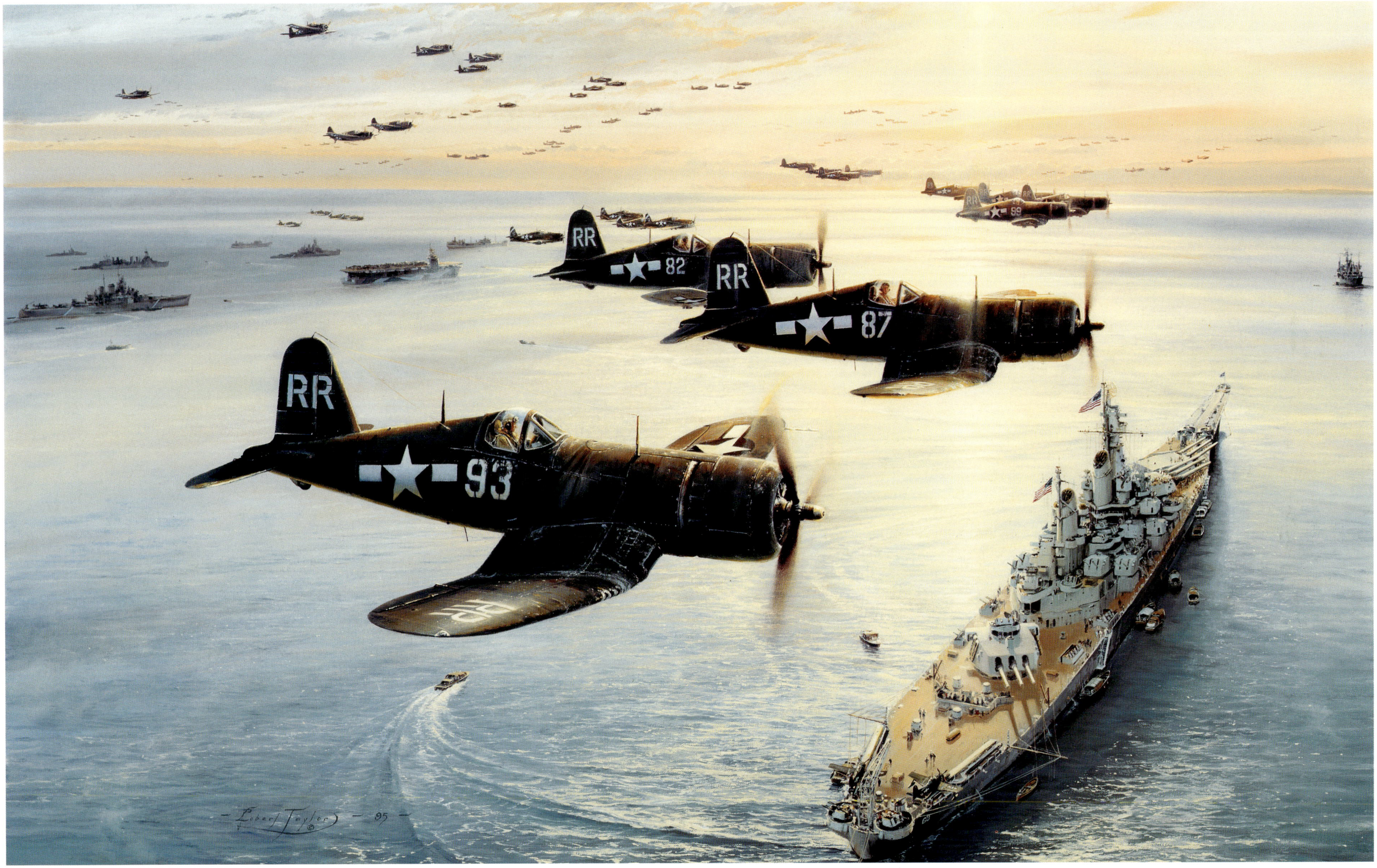

VICTORY FLYOVER

In the collection of Mr Eugene Eisenberg

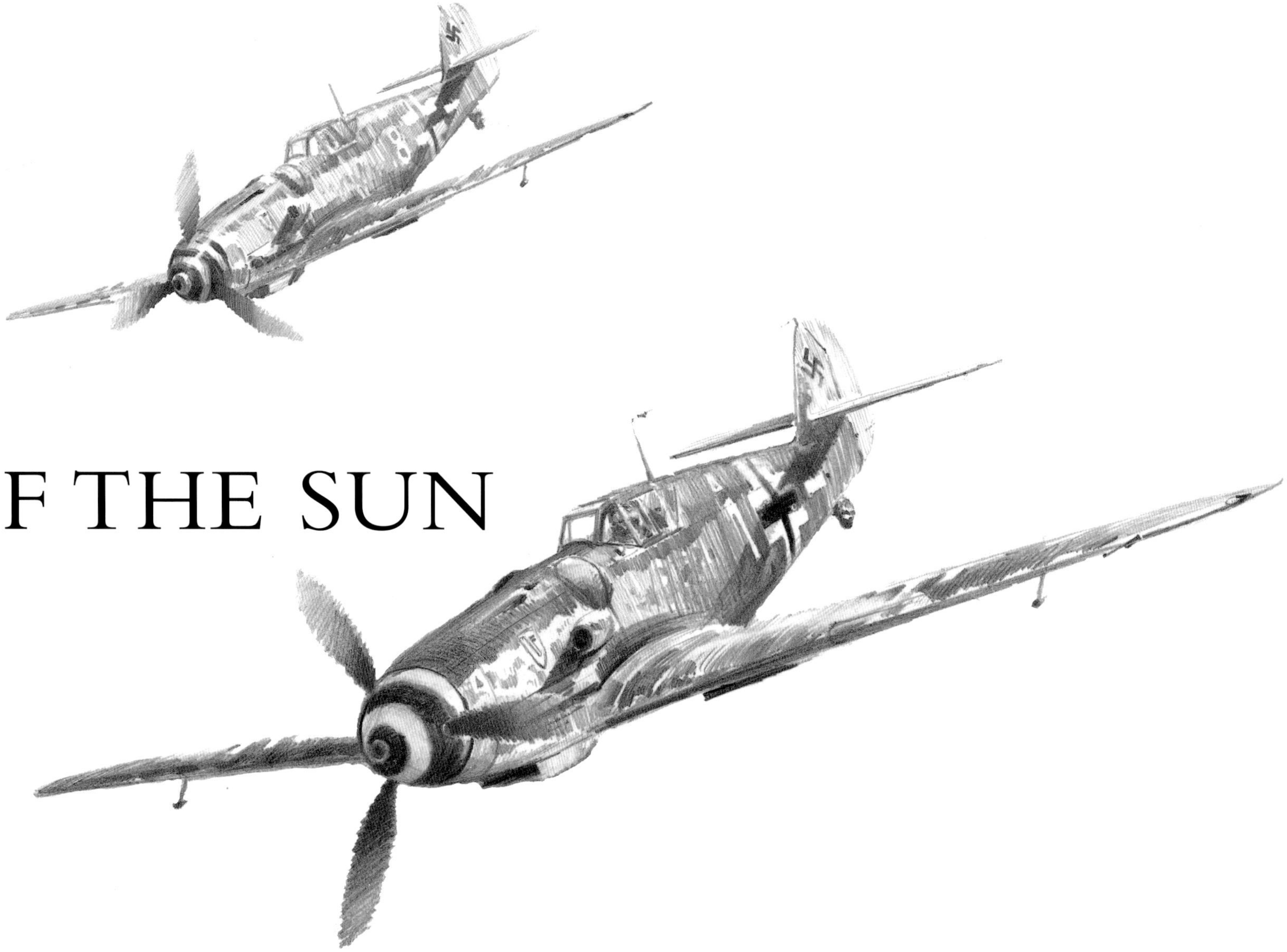

EAGLES OUT OF THE SUN

Since the early aerial contests of the First World War it became the fighter pilot's first rule of combat to make his attack, whenever possible, diving out of the sun. With blinding light behind him he greatly reduced his chances of detection and substantially increased the difficulty for opposing gunners. While circumstances often dictated a different approach, and some of the great aces perfected their own individual tactics, no other form of attack guaranteed a greater degree of that all-important element: surprise.

Eagles Out Of The Sun depicts a Staffel of Messerschmitt Me109s diving out of the evening sun to make a classic fighter interception upon B-17 Fortresses returning from a raid over Germany. The Staffel commander has selected the outer box of the large formation; leading his pilots in with cannons blazing tracer, he closes on the B-17 in his sights. His wingman, concentrating on staying with and protecting his leader, holds his fire.

Planning any air combat scenario requires a good deal of thought and experimentation; there are so many factors to consider. Over the years I have spoken with scores of pilots and aircrew and listened to countless detailed accounts of aerial encounters, and have come to the conclusion that no two were ever remotely the same. Most air-to-air confrontations, as Bee Beamont states in his foreword, were over and done with in a matter of seconds, and in those few brief hectic moments there may be a dozen or more completely different aspects an artist could choose to depict.

As I see it, those of us privileged to have sat with some of the world's great combat pilots and listened as they recounted old aerial battles have a responsibility, if our paintings are to be taken seriously, to interpret those first-hand accounts as faithfully as we know how; but it is also our prerogative, indeed our job, to put our own interpretation into the work we do, and in so doing to use whatever licence is necessary to convey something of the reality of the scenes we seek to create. Such compromises are often not easily reached.

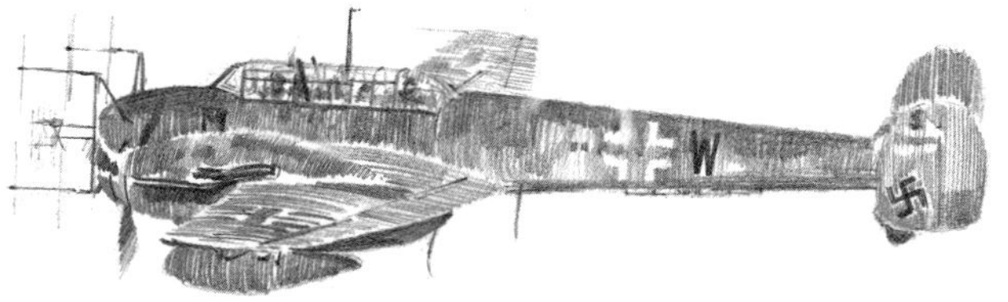

'Running the Gauntlet' – B17s Fortresses run the gauntlet of fighters on their way home. Few heavies returned without scars. Some, crippled and losing altitude, stagger back to base, but with the company of 'little friends' the tension was slighty relieved.

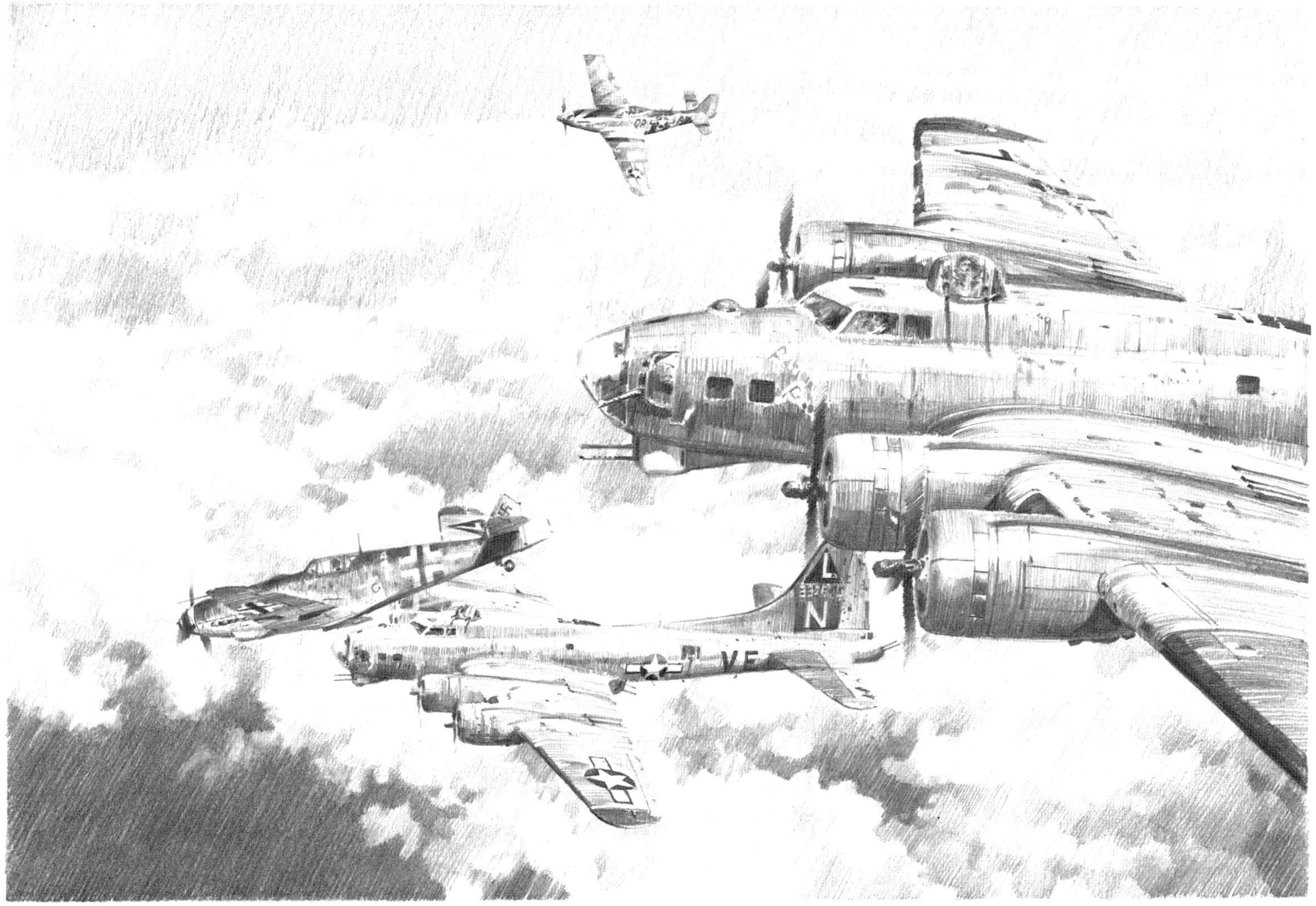

As the pilot describes a scenario, he has in his mind the unlimited space of the sky – the sky in front of him, above and below him, the sky to his sides and behind him: his recalled vision of the scene is unrestricted in its vista and surroundings. However, in providing his three-dimensional descriptions, he cannot always take into account the artist's task of converting his memories into a two-dimensional form. The artist must conjure up in his mind an accurate vision from all this information, and visualise a way to recreate it realistically within the relatively small space of perhaps six square feet of canvas.

I remember having a long discussion with Gunther Rall about the tactics employed by Luftwaffe fighter pilots attacking bomber formations. He described one ploy favoured by the experienced Me109 and Fw190 pilots. Having positioned themselves for the attack high above the bomber formation, they dived steeply at maximum speed, making a high 'g' pull-out just below the target aircraft. As they attacked they rolled to make an inverted high-speed pass underneath the target, firing into the belly of the bomber, rolling away to zoom up for another attack.

This sounded very spectacular, and when working on ideas for this painting I tried a number of sketches showing the technique – but I couldn't get it to work. Whichever way I positioned the inverted fighter in relation to the B-17 it seemed to ruin the composition. Also I noticed that I kept wanting to turn the sketches upside-down to study the fighter, and concluded that if *I* wanted to do this, then so probably would everyone else if I painted it that way! So I gave up on Gunther's idea.

The high-speed diving attack from above, particularly favoured from out of the sun, often brought the opposing aircraft very close to each other. The drawing on this page shows an Me109 making a pass right through a formation of B-17s, and was another concept I toyed with for the painting. I discarded this in favour of the final concept, however, because it had always been my aim to make the Luftwaffe fighters predominant in this painting, and I felt that in the sketch this was not the case.

Often when painting pictures of fighters high in the bright sunlight I am reminded of a conversation I once had with Group Captain Peter Townsend, during which he commented that night-fighter pilots were lamentably forgotten by us artists. I pointed out the difficulty of painting aircraft at night, but got the impression he thought it a rather weak excuse.

Immediately the Battle of Britain had been lost, the Luftwaffe turned to the night bombing of English cities, in particular London where the nightly raids were known as the Blitz. Having commanded No 85 Squadron throughout the Battle of Britain, which was fought exclusively during daylight hours, in late 1940 Peter had become one of the very first night-fighter squadron commanders. In those formative weeks and months the navigational equipment at the disposal of the night-fighter pilot was no more than he'd had to fight with in broad daylight, and with autumn turning to winter, the worsening weather made the job hazardous to say the least. Initially more losses were attributable to the weather than to the enemy.

With the RAF bombing by night, the Luftwaffe night-fighters were also having their problems; as the war progressed, however, the navigational equipment aboard the night-fighters on both sides became more and more sophisticated, and with the introduction of radar – primitive by today's standards, but nevertheless quite effective – the success ratios of the pilots who roamed the skies at night were vastly improved.

One painting I completed, although Peter Townsend would probably not have approved, featured the highly modified Me110 night-fighter. Entitled *Night Hunters,* it shows a group of Me110s, bristling with radio antennae, climbing out as dusk falls; as they break cloud they disperse, each to take up a lonely vigil as they lie in wait for the anticipated night raid by RAF heavy bombers.

The Me110 looks almost too cumbersome to be called a fighter, and of course it was no match for the Allies' single-engined fighters in daylight combat; but it excelled in the role of night-fighting. Having a good rate of climb, three-and-a-half hour endurance, reasonable manoeuvrability and good armament, it was a good 'instrument flyer' and it was when piloting this durable aircraft that most night-fighter aces scored their victories.

As I paint the various German fighters, from the racy Me109s and Fw190s to the more pedestrian types such as the Me110, I often reflect upon the astounding fact that all these Luftwaffe aircraft, both day- and night-fighters, came under the control of a general who was only twenty-nine years old. I also marvel at the fact that I have had the opportunity to spend so much time in the company of that general, and to learn at first hand something of that extraordinary period in our history: that general's name was Adolf Galland.

NIGHT HUNTERS

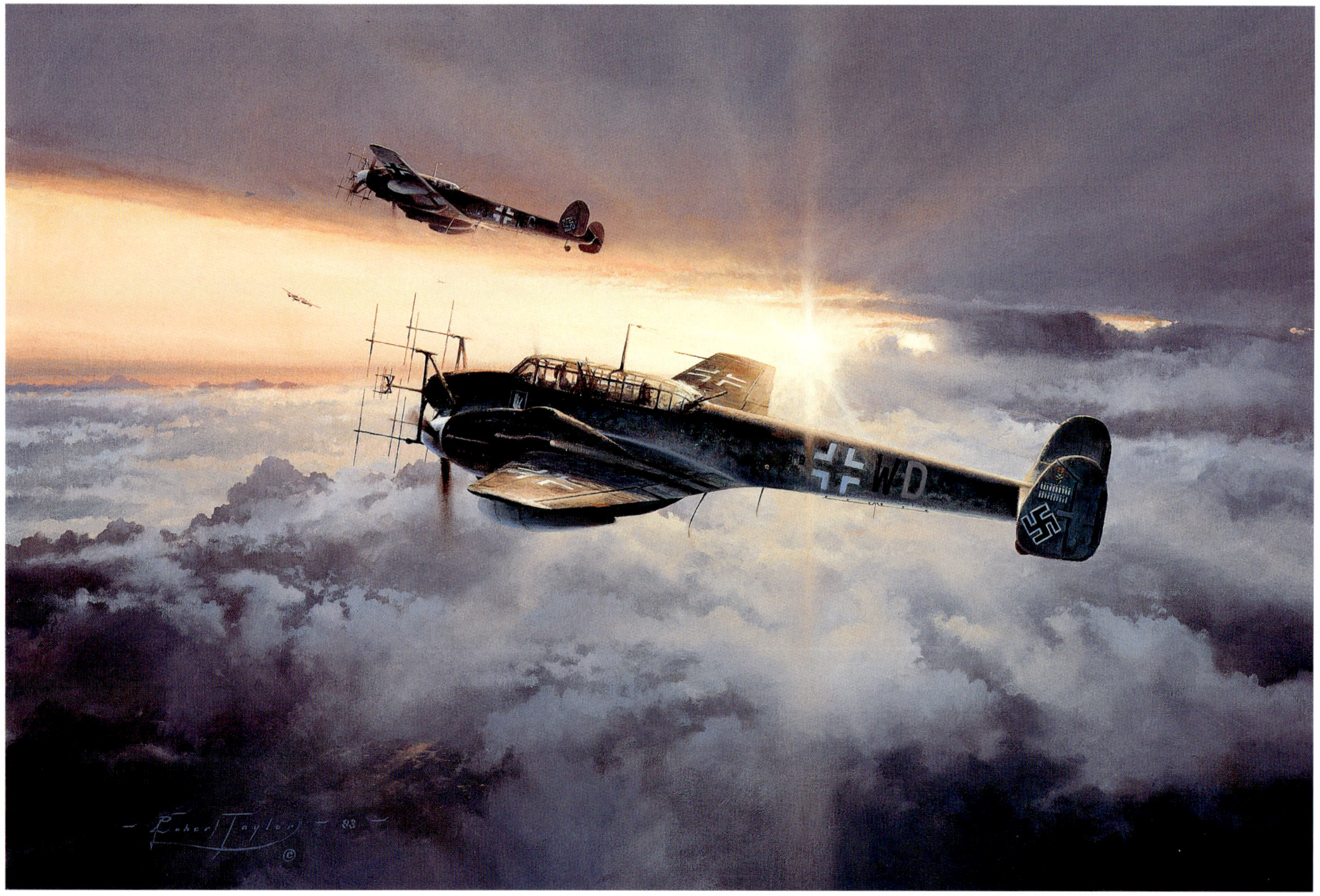

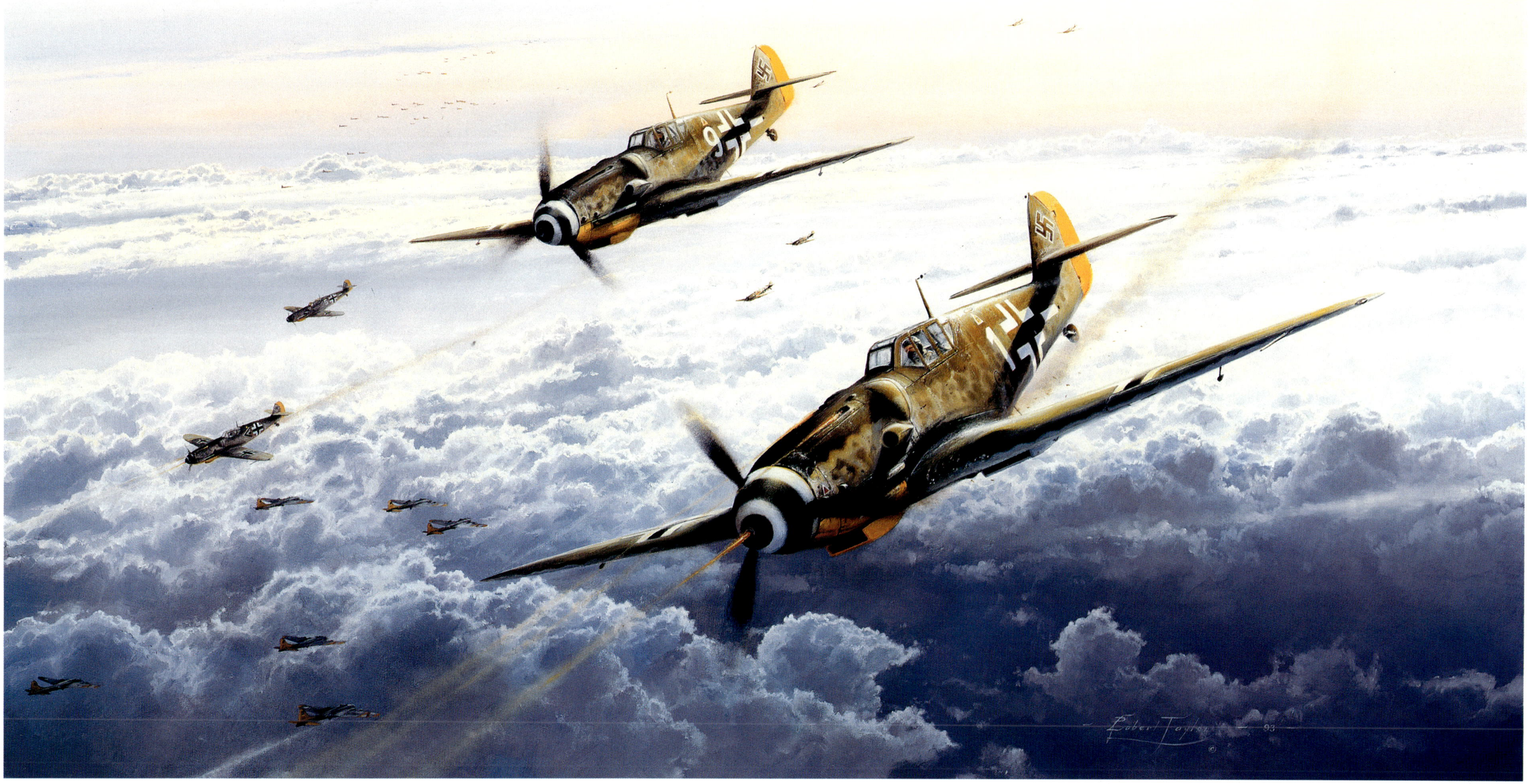

EAGLES OUT OF THE SUN

Private collection

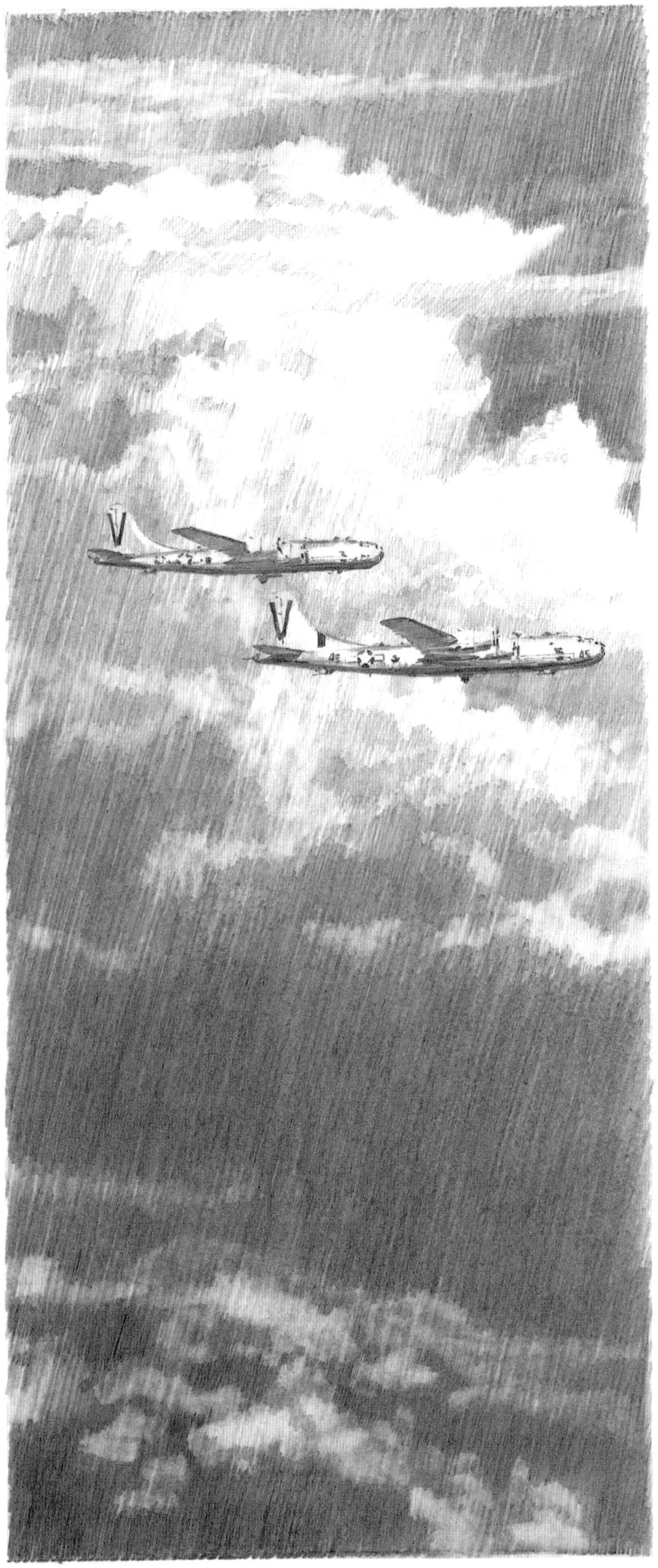

VALOR IN THE PACIFIC

I have met Bob Morgan a number of times. Bob – better known as Colonel Robert Morgan, skipper of the famous B-17 Memphis Belle – is one of those World War II pilots who just couldn't stay away from the action. After completing a full tour in Europe he returned home to take his battle-weary Flying Fortress on a morale-boosting exercise all around the United States. This was not exciting enough for Bob so he volunteered for a second tour, this time flying B-29s in the Pacific. Personally, I would have had enough!

I talked a good deal to Bob about the B-29 Superfortress and his experiences during the long over-water missions to Japan. One thing that stuck in my mind was his comment about the enormous difference in flying conditions between the two theatres of war. From a pilot's point of view, the weather in Europe can be awful for long periods in the winter; even with today's modern navigational systems, bringing a 747 into Frankfurt on a cold, foggy day in February is not every aviator's idea of fun. With the sparse equipment on board a B-17 back in the 1940s, a target such as Frankfurt often couldn't be found in the dead of winter, let alone attacked; and then, if you were one of the lucky ones to get home, the chances were that your base would have been socked-in too.

It was, I am told by Bob Morgan, different in the Pacific. Although the combat risks were ever present, generally the aircrews were not subjected to the continuous periods of appalling weather which the crews in Europe so often had to deal with. Though from time to time the Pacific region threw up massive and violent thunderstorms which earned the pilots' enduring respect, according to Bob there were often moments on the way home, if the mission had gone well, when he had time to admire the scenery.

Usually when a pilot talks about scenery, he is talking about clouds; the wonderful formations and patterns of light and shadows created by the ever-changing hues of the sun. I have flown right across the world a number of times, and when studying cloud formations from the comfort of a cabin at 35,000 feet with no danger of anybody shooting at me, I never cease to be fascinated by the ever-changing patterns of the stratosphere. I have also found it interesting to note how cloud structures in different parts of the world seem to have their own distinct characteristics.

In the days of the early great masters of landscape painting, artists noted for their magnificent cloud studies, such as John Constable, had little chance to travel beyond Europe, and understandably their powerful cloud compositions were based on those typically found in Europe. Had he and his contemporaries had the good fortune to journey to the four corners of the earth and to have viewed the world from on high, I often wonder what they would have made of it all.

My travels have taught me that clouds above the Pacific Ocean are invariably different in structure from those found above the Atlantic, or the great land mass of Europe. Remembering Bob Morgan's description of the towering cumulus clouds of the Pacific, and knowing I was to embark upon a B-29 painting when I returned, I made a special study of cloud formations on a trip to Australia in the early part of 1995. While above the Orient I was treated to some of the most beautiful aerial panoramas I have ever seen, and the basis of the cloudscape I painted for *Valor in the Pacific* came from the very part of the globe plied by those Superfortresses on their missions to Japan, half a century ago.

Digressing for a moment, in 1995 I had the honour of being asked to paint a picture of a wonderful old Avro biplane for Qantas Airways, on the occasion of their 75th anniversary. The world's second oldest airline, Qantas, flew the Avro in the remote regions of Queensland and the northern territories of Australia as long ago as 1921. It was while on the flight deck of a Qantas Boeing 747-400 that I observed and gathered authentic local cloud research material for my painting of B-29s, *Valor in the Pacific.* An interesting coincidence, I thought afterwards: two aircraft built by the same famous manufacturer half a century apart, brought together in time, so to speak, in a painting inspired by a pilot and an artist both fascinated by clouds.

On a down-to-earth note, and still digressing, while in Sydney my friends at Qantas gave me a ride in one of their 747 simulators, when I proved to all and sundry that I was never cut out to be a pilot. I made three attempts to get that big bird down cleanly on the runway 'at Hong Kong', destroying three complete sets of undercarriages and scaring myself senseless in the process. Worst of all, Channel 7 national TV network had a crew filming my awful attempts to fly the 747, and the following day my efforts went out on the popular 11am news and current affairs programme for the whole of Australia to see!

The B-29 is, frankly, an awkward and difficult plane to paint. It has a huge wingspan and a comparatively narrow fuselage which means there are certain angles, particularly those where the aircraft is coming towards you, which gives the artist very little to work with. Then there is its very distinctive greenhouse-style nose which houses the cockpit. Some say it is beautiful, some say it is ugly; I will be tactful and say it is distinctive!

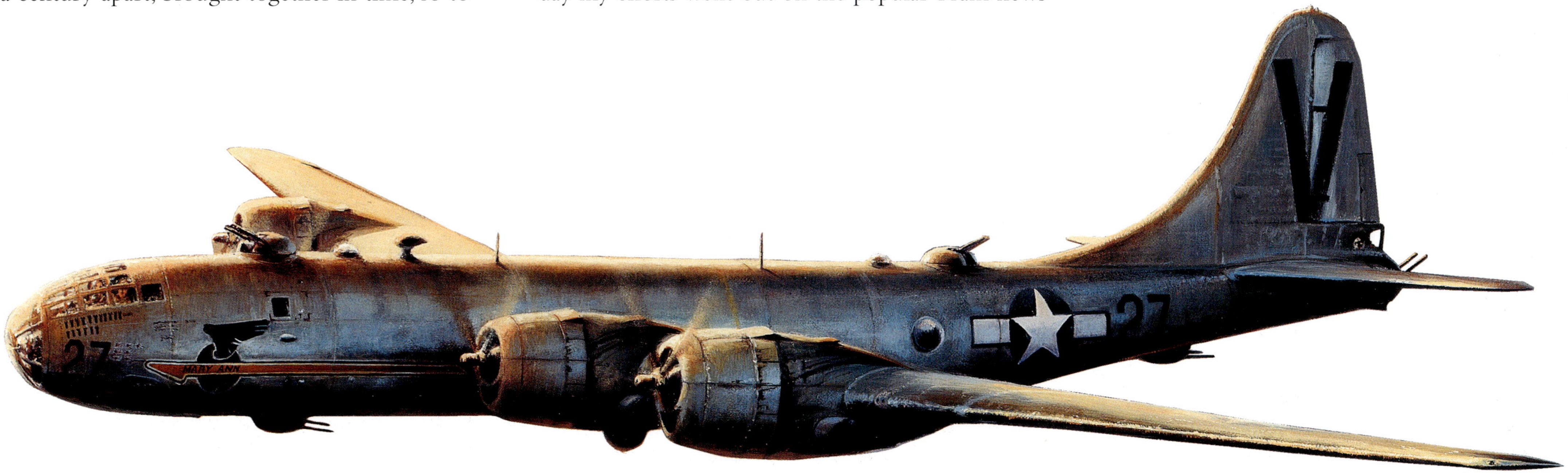

I decided to include quite a few B-29s in the painting to give the feel of a busy formation – in fact there are nine – and with the enormous wingspan of the Superfortress, it was necessary to paint the aircraft from the side; otherwise I would have ended up with a painting eight feet wide!

FORTRESS UNDER ATTACK

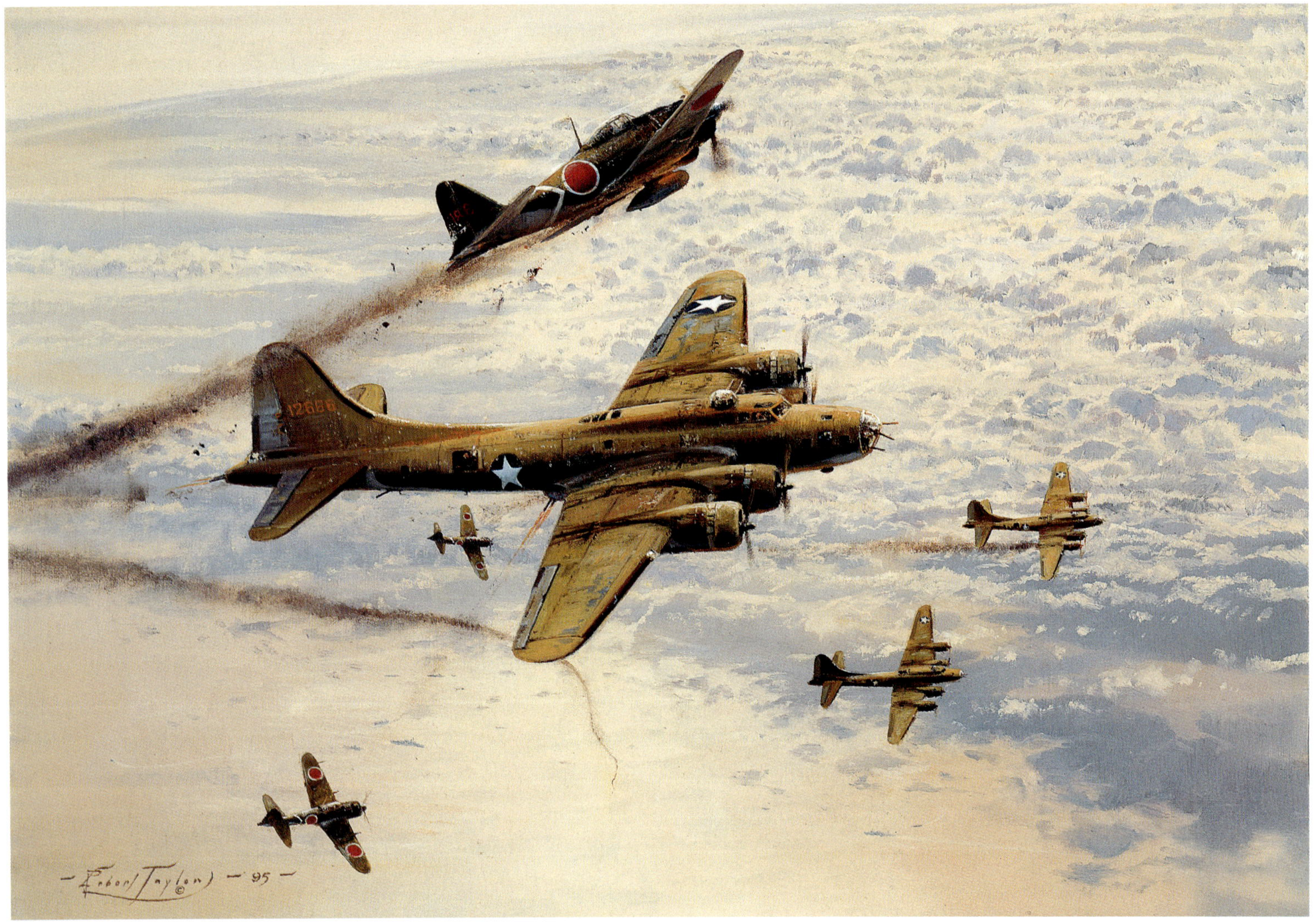

I also wanted to include some P-51 escort fighters in the painting, and yet another aim was to use warm evening light, this being much more colourful than the midday sun. But this presented another problem: most of those long missions to Japan departed in the morning, the raids taking place around midday so that the bombers could return to their distant island bases before nightfall. The escort fighters were in attendance only in the region of the target, departing soon after the bombers left the scene, their own range having limitations. Thus by the time the sun was going down they would long since have headed for home, and so on the face of it, to include P-51s and the late afternoon sun would have been inaccurate.

I called my friend Sig Unander in Washington State to find out if the 499th Bomb Group B-29s had taken part in any late afternoon raids on Japan, hoping he might find at least one or two. Sig is an aviation historian and B-29 enthusiast. After wading through the details of every raid carried out by the 499th, he was able to confirm several raids as late as 4pm, enough to satisfy me that my inclusion of evening colours and P-51s would be authentic. Thanks to Bob Morgan, Sig and my friends at Qantas Airways, this has become one of my favourite recent paintings.

The painting on the left was done as a companion piece to *Valor in the Pacific*. It shows Jay Zeamer's B-17 Fortress under attack by Japanese fighters during a typical mission in the Pacific. Jay Zeamer skippered a 43rd Bomb Group crew nicknamed 'Eager Beavers' because of its willingness to undertake any assignment. Zeamer had a .50-calibre machine gun installed just below the cockpit so he could join in the shooting while piloting the airplane. Among the many exploits of this famous crew was a mission flown on 16 June 1943 to photograph the Buka airstrip near Bougainville: set upon by around twenty Japanese Zeros, Zeamer and his crew shot down five of them; although badly injured himself, Zeamer piloted his aircraft and the vital photographs back to base. He was awarded the Congressional Medal of Honor.

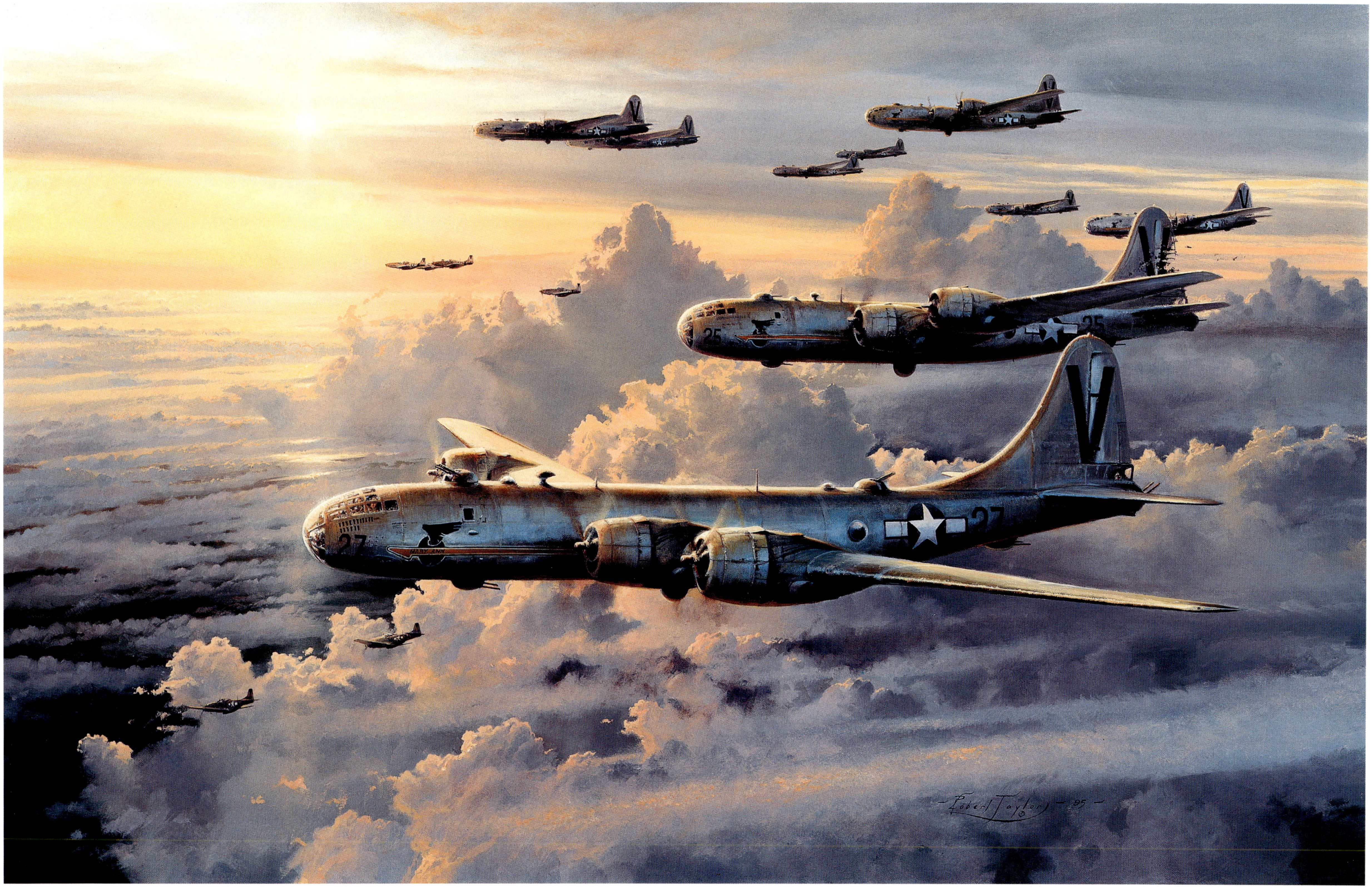

VALOR IN THE PACIFIC

In the collection of Mr Eugene Eisenberg

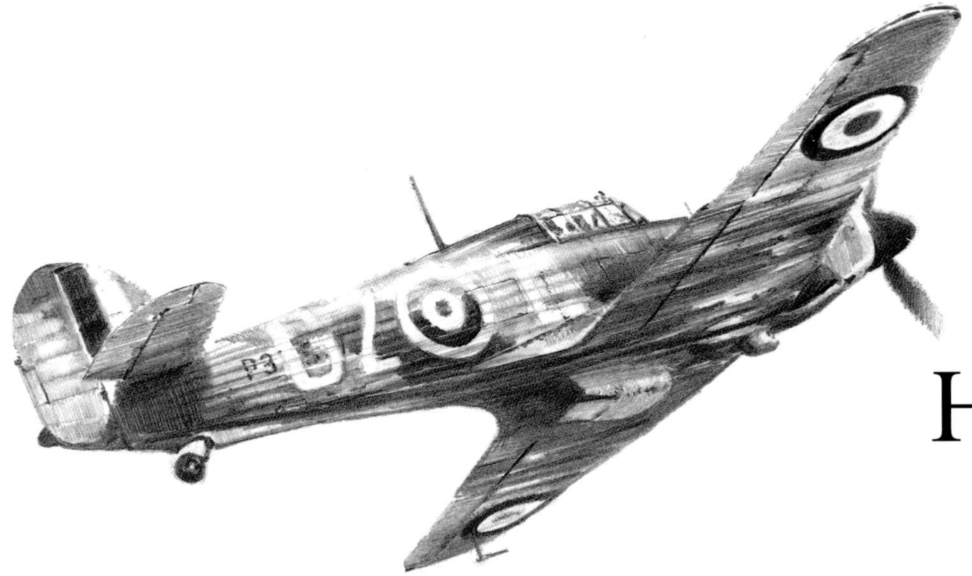

HEIGHT OF THE BATTLE

The highly spirited defence put up by the young RAF pilots during the first two weeks of September in 1940 was enough to force Hitler to call off his planned invasion of England. Goering's much vaunted Luftwaffe had failed to gain the superiority he had promised during the great aerial battles over southern England during July and August, vital if German forces were to make successful landings. Adding to the Führer's problems was the failure of his plan to destroy the British will to fight, by massed bombing of its cities. When on 11 September the RAF destroyed over one hundred of his invasion barges, he called the whole event off.

The victory won in the summer skies above Britain in 1940 gave the first glimmer of hope to a desperate nation. Hitler's planned invasion was thwarted; Goering's Luftwaffe in a few short months had lost the initiative, and their leader the respect and confidence of his pilots.

With the 60th anniversary of the first flight of the legendary Spitfire falling in March 1996, I was asked by one of my major collectors, Eugene Eisenberg, if I would paint a Battle of Britain scene as a tribute to Mitchell's supreme little fighter. Eugene's suggestion was timely because it coincided with similar requests received from at least two other long-time friends, John Rayner in Australia and Mike Johnson in Canada. Both have companies which distribute my prints in the far flung corners of the old Commonwealth, and both wanted me to paint a Spitfire picture to commemorate the anniversary, John pointing out that this happened to coincide with the 75th anniversary of the Royal Australian Air Force.

Because of the widespread interest in the project my publisher suggested I paint three smaller companion pictures to make up a 'Commonwealth' commemorative suite, one each for Britain, Australia and Canada. Originally I planned that all three companion paintings would feature the Spitfire, but as the exercise progressed it became more and more fixed in my mind as being a Battle of Britain project, and I decided that at least one of the companion paintings should therefore feature Hurricanes.

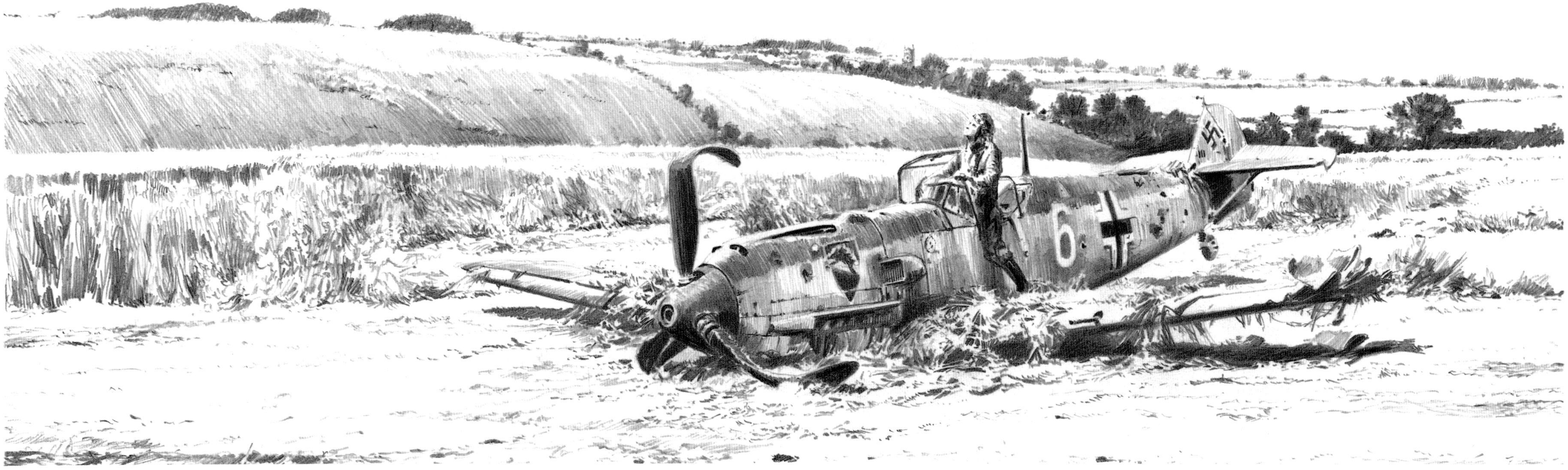

For the subject of the main painting in the suite I chose a particular day in the Battle of Britain. As dawn came up on Wednesday 11 September 1940, London was reeling from another night of bombing. Thames-side factories and warehouses had been struck, and so too had central residential areas of the city, including Buckingham Palace. But daylight brought a deterioration in the weather and some respite from enemy activity.

By mid-afternoon, however, the weather had improved and German bomber formations were detected building up over the Pas-de-Calais and Ostend; it was not long before these were plotted flying up the Thames estuary towards London, accompanied by more than two hundred fighters. Further raids were building simultaneously in the region of Seine Bay and Cherbourg, and heading toward the vital ports of Southampton and Portsmouth. Adding to the problems of RAF Fighter Command, waves of Me109 fighters were approaching the Kent coastal installations, and more were attacking a shipping convoy making its way up the Channel.

To deal with the imminent raid on London, Fighter Command had already brought nine squadrons to readiness, and as the inbound force swung in from the sea they were scrambled to make the intercept. As the Luftwaffe bombers approached the docklands area east of London, sixty Spitfires and Hurricanes fell upon them and a pitched battle ensued. Leading No 74 'Tiger' Squadron was the fearless and brilliant South African fighter leader, 'Sailor' Malan, his designated task to ignore the fighters and tackle the bombers. Flying three sections of four aircraft in line astern, Malan spearheaded the attack from 20,000 ft, their Spitfires ripping into the He111s.

I had the opportunity to discuss that particular combat in detail with Harbourne Stephen, one of the No 74 Squadron pilots who flew with Sailor Malan that September day back in 1940. He described the moments of desperate combat with great clarity, and it was with his guidance and advice that I constructed the composition for the painting *Height of the Battle*. The No 74 Squadron Spitfires are Mark Is. RAF Fighter Command flew 678 sorties on that Wednesday, and brought down twenty-five Luftwaffe aircraft, the worst hit being KG26 with eight He111s shot down.

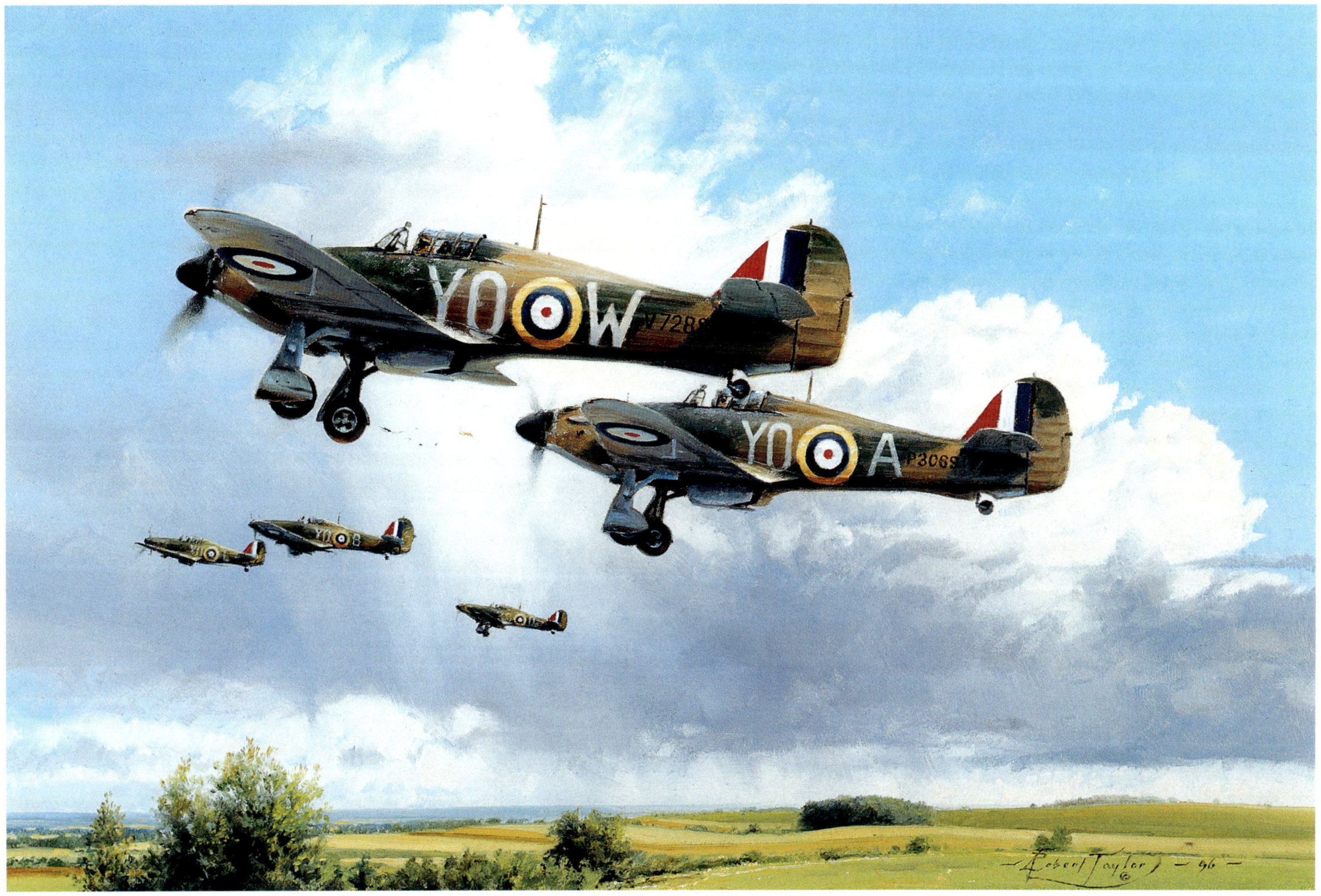

MAPLE LEAF SCRAMBLE

The companion painting above shows Hurricanes of No 1 Squadron, Royal Canadian Air Force, in a typical Battle of Britain scramble. The squadron had arrived from Canada in 1940, complete with its own Hurricanes, pilots and ground personnel, and commenced battle training virtually as the air fighting went on around it. On only its second operational patrol in mid-August, its gritty young pilots brought down three Dornier bombers and damaged three more. The squadron continued to engage the Luftwaffe formations over south London till the end of the battle when, depleted, it was amalgamated with No 401 Squadron.

Some ninety-four Canadian pilots took part in the Battle of Britain, hundreds more crossing the Atlantic to follow them into RAF Fighter Command. Later on entire wings were made up of Canadian pilots, the best known of which were commanded by Douglas Bader, and later Mike Johnson's father, Johnnie Johnson.

The painting, *Maple Leaf Scramble,* measures only 18 x 12in, which is a small canvas by my usual standards; however, even in small paintings I always aim to produce 'complete' pictures. In spite of the small area of canvas to work with, I have managed to include plenty of detail in the picture. The Hurricanes are Mark 1s.

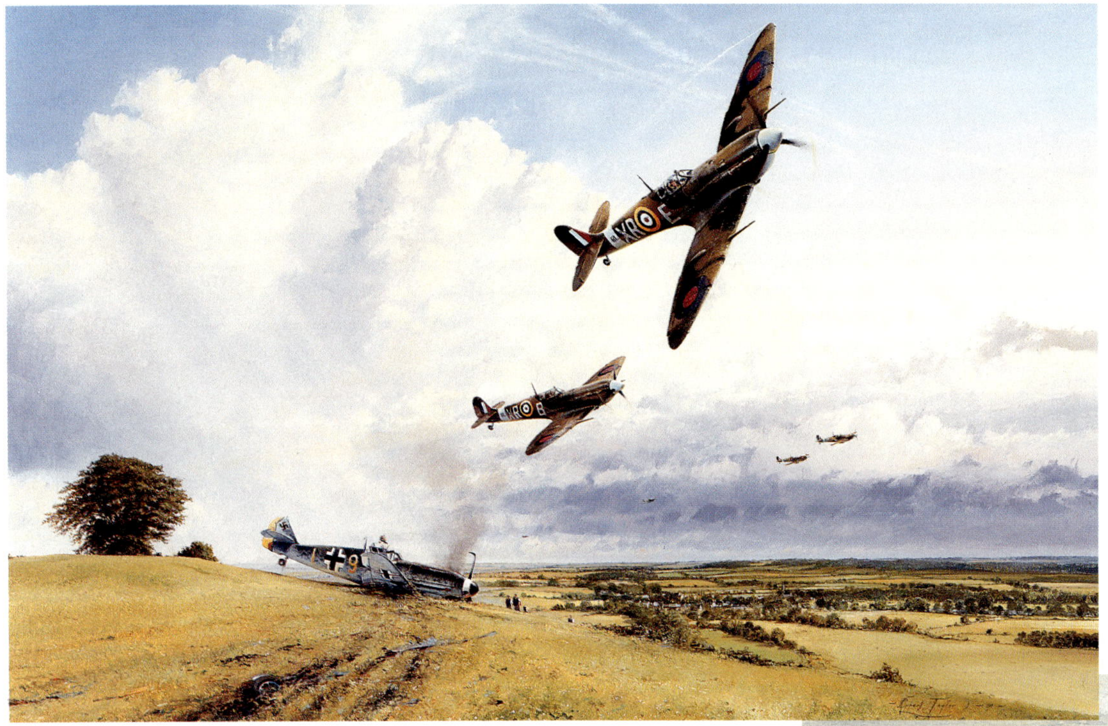

EAGLES PREY

In the months that followed Dunkirk, while Britain stood alone against the might of the massed forces of Germany, some 240 American pilots made their way across the Atlantic to join the RAF. Motivated by the urge to fight for the cause of freedom, a swashbuckling sense of adventure, and a love of flying, this happy band of warriors became known as the American Eagles. Arriving in a foreign country to fight a war not really their own, their selfless participation and sacrifice unwittingly became a symbol to the beleaguered British people. Armed with log books often wildly overstating their flying experience, they were welcomed by the over-stretched RAF, and by the spring of 1941 the American Eagles manned three Spitfire squadrons. In the month of November that year the Eagles had the distinction of being the top-scoring squadrons in the RAF.

The painting on the left, *Eagles Prey*, shows Spitfires of No 71 Squadron low over the French countryside after combat with Luftwaffe fighters above northern France during 1941. Lying prey to the Eagles is an Me109 brought down during the aerial dog-fight. The German pilot is lucky to have survived the crash-landing, and is seen climbing out of his smouldering aircraft as French farmers cautiously approach the scene. Overhead the Eagles race for home after another successful mission.

DEFENCE OF THE REALM

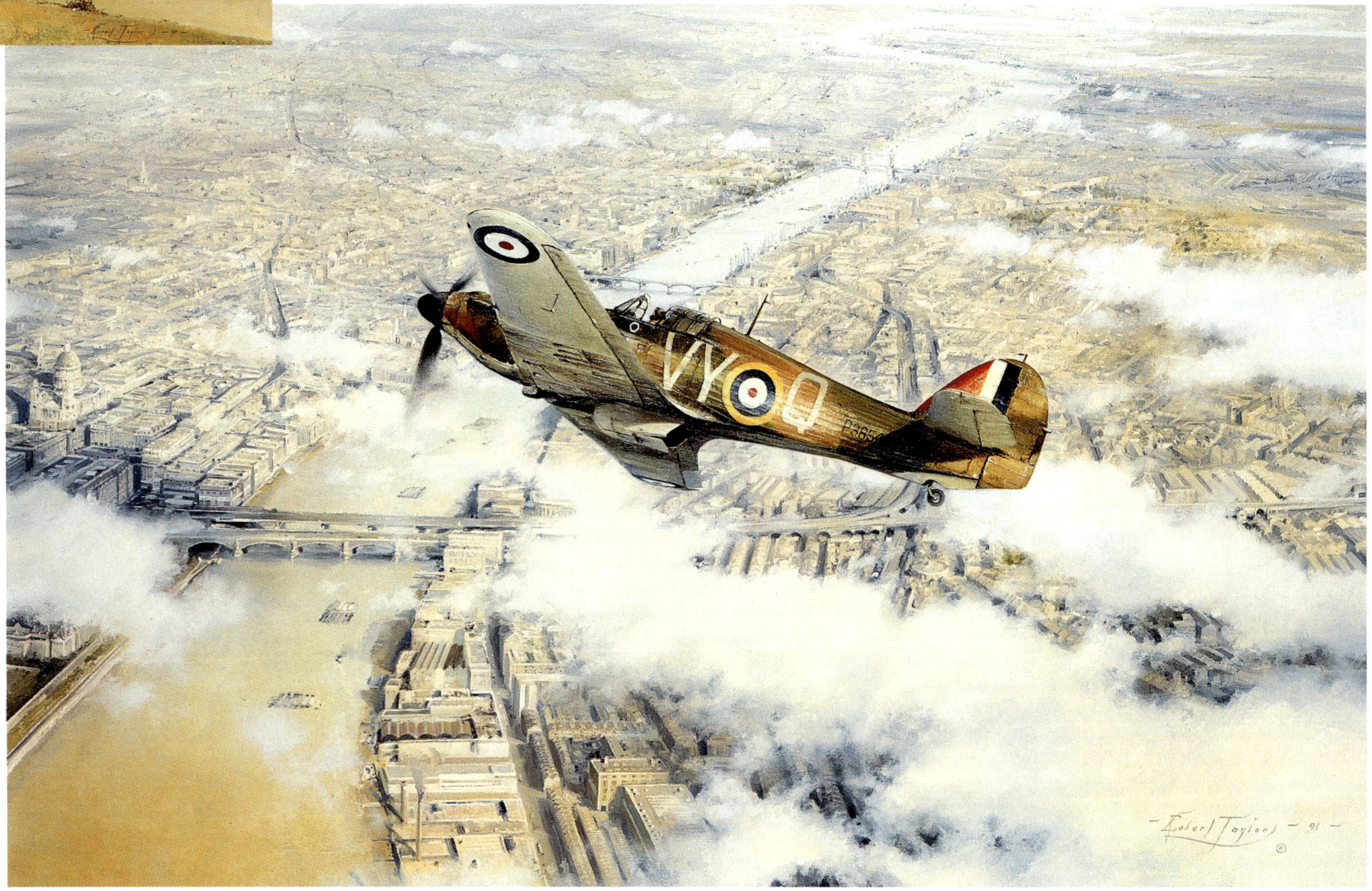

The painting to the right shows Peter Townsend's No 85 Squadron Hurricane over central London, in 1940. Peter chastised me with his usual humility and good nature when he learned the title I had given the painting: he felt that because his was the only aircraft seen in the picture, the title *Defence of the Realm* suggested that he had managed to win the Battle of Britain on his own!

I donated the original painting to the Battle of Britain Memorial and it was auctioned at a lunch at the Savoy Hotel in London attended by Queen Elizabeth the Queen Mother. I had the honour to be presented to Her Majesty during the event. The proceeds went to help fund the memorial, brainchild of Battle of Britain ace Geoffrey Page. The memorial, located high on the white cliffs of Dover, depicts a solitary fighter pilot, carved appropriately from solid granite, gazing out over the English Channel – the vital stretch of water that he so gallantly fought to protect during that historic summer half a century ago.

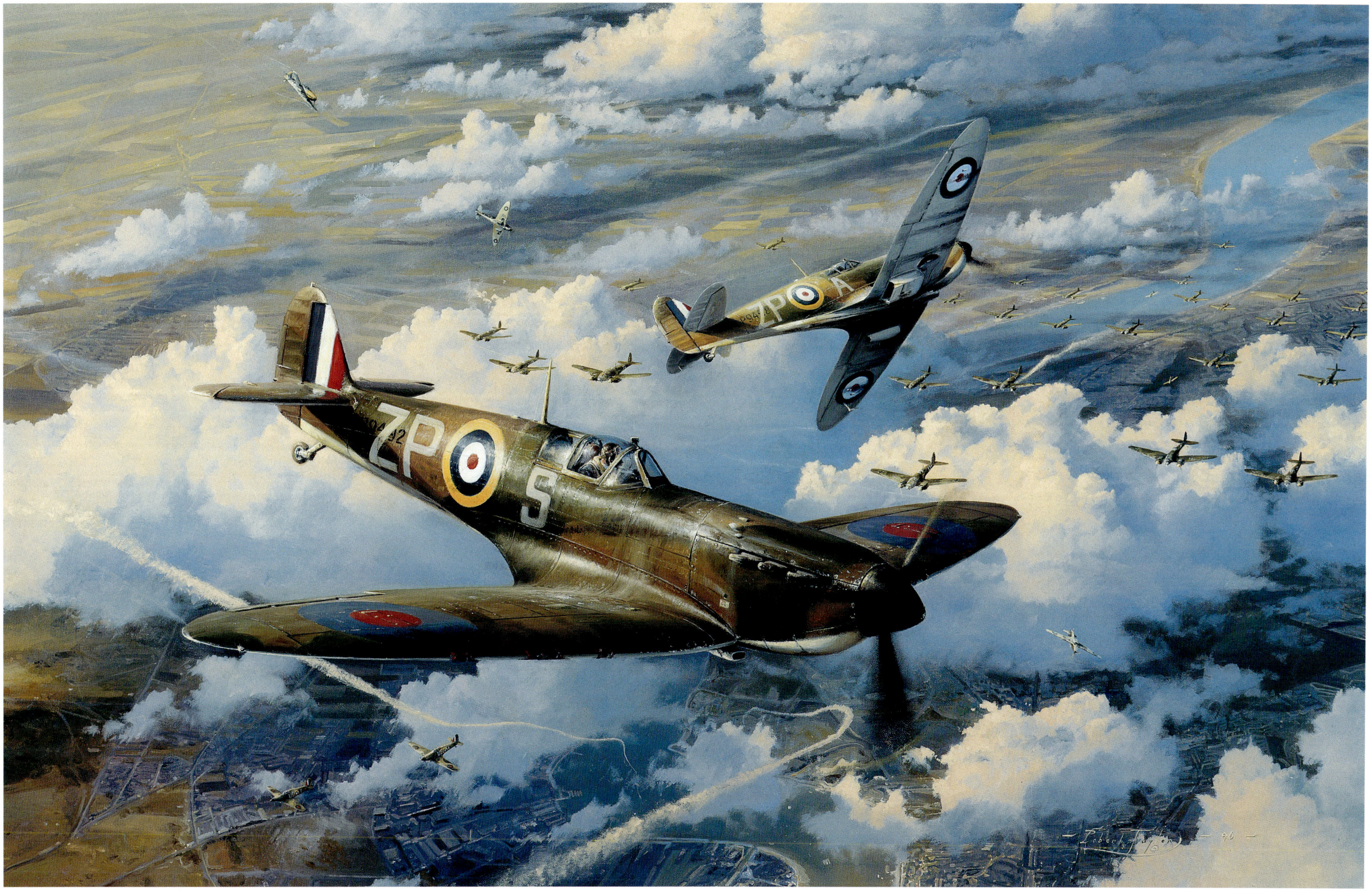

HEIGHT OF THE BATTLE

In the collection of Mr Eugene Eisenberg

MIDWAY – STRIKE AGAINST THE AKAGI

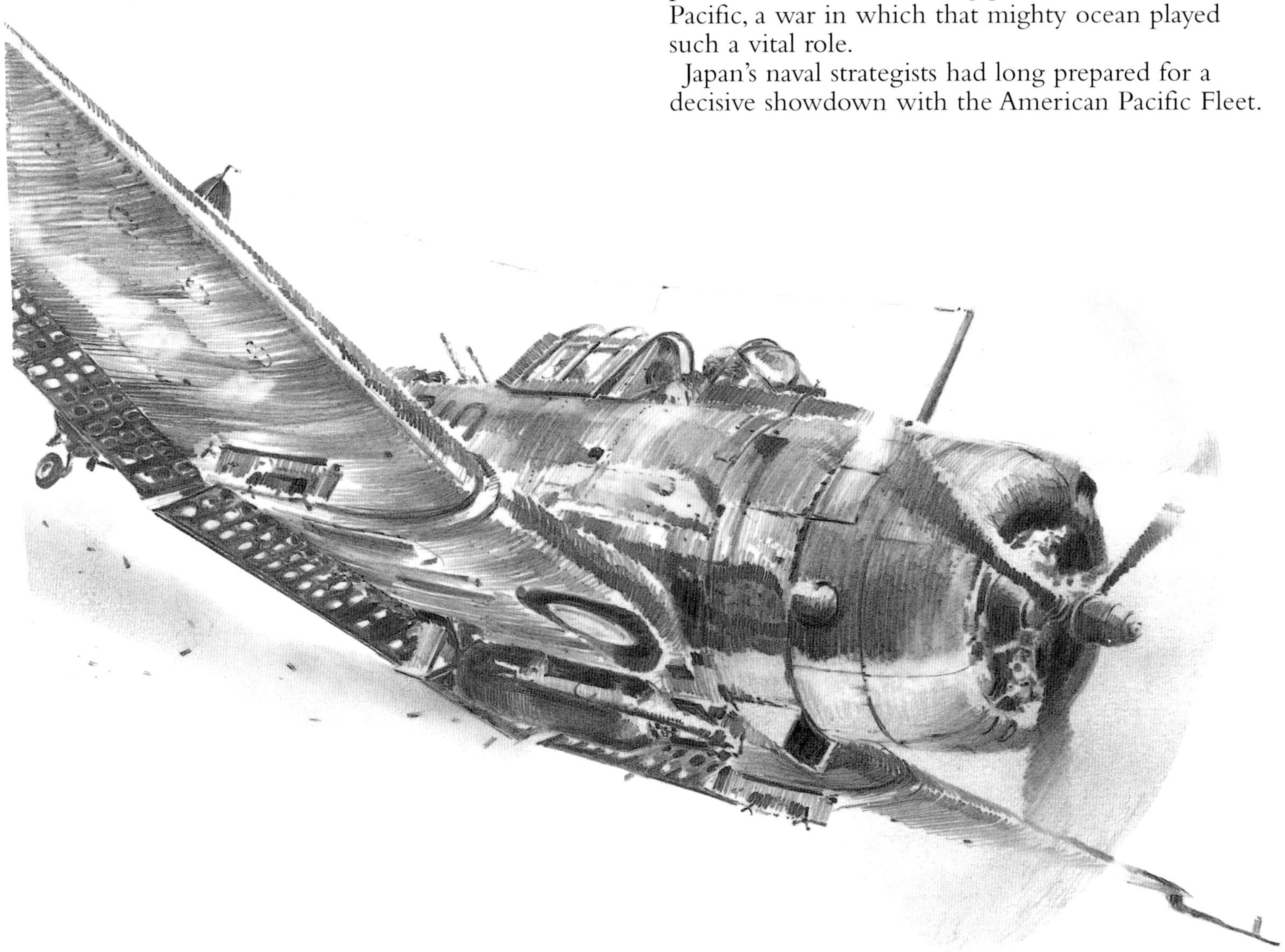

The Battle of Midway was historically significant in two ways: it demonstrated once and for all to die-hard sea captains that the era of the great fleet actions, in which ship fought ship, was a thing of the past. It was also the turning point of the war in the Pacific, a war in which that mighty ocean played such a vital role.

Japan's naval strategists had long prepared for a decisive showdown with the American Pacific Fleet. Arrogant, over-confident, and seemingly oblivious to the lessons learned from the Battle of the Coral Sea, they sailed ingloriously into the same tactical trap for a second time: at Midway they were convinced they would obliterate the American Fleet. Admiral Yamamoto, Commander-in-Chief of the Japanese Combined Fleet, was sure that a threat to Midway Island would compel Admiral Nimitz to commit his entire fleet in a massive sea engagement that he could not survive. With his superior force, Yamamoto would overwhelm the American Pacific Fleet, pounding them to destruction with the sheer weight of his firepower.

Seven Japanese battleships, 6 aircraft carriers, 63 cruisers and destroyers, together with 325 aircraft lined up against Admiral Nimitz's comparatively small sea force. This consisted of just 3 carriers, 22 cruisers and destroyers, supported by 348 sea and land-based aircraft. Confronted with such odds, in the eyes of the Japanese sea commanders it would be a walkover.

First points went to the Japanese when the heroic US Navy Devastator torpedo bombers were shot out of the sky. Only two of the aircrew who flew from the American carriers survived. Their sacrifice was not in vain, however, because gathering unseen and unmolested high overhead, and flown by battle-hardened pilots, were the SBD Dauntless dive-bombers of the US Navy. While every defending Japanese fighter was flying around low over the water enjoying the rich pickings, aboard the Japanese carriers the airborne strike force was fuelled up and ready to go. But at that crucial moment the dive-bombers struck, plummeting out of the sky like hawks swooping on their prey. Within minutes half the entire Japanese carrier force was a blazing inferno, consigned to the deep. In those few historic moments at Midway the Americans gained the initiative in the Pacific, an initiative which led to ultimate victory.

Some time ago I made a drawing showing a Navy SBD Dauntless diving in to attack the carrier *Akagi*. The pilot who led the Dauntless attack on Admiral Yamamoto's flagship, Commander Dick Best, had seen the drawing in the second of my previously published books and commented upon it, suggesting that it would make a suitable painting to record the event. Encouraged by Dick Best I completed *Midway – Strike against the Akagi*. The drawing below – *Eyes of the Pacific* – shows a PBY Catalina on patrol. The Catalinas played a vital role in many of the sea actions in the Pacific, often being the first to locate the enemy fleet positions.

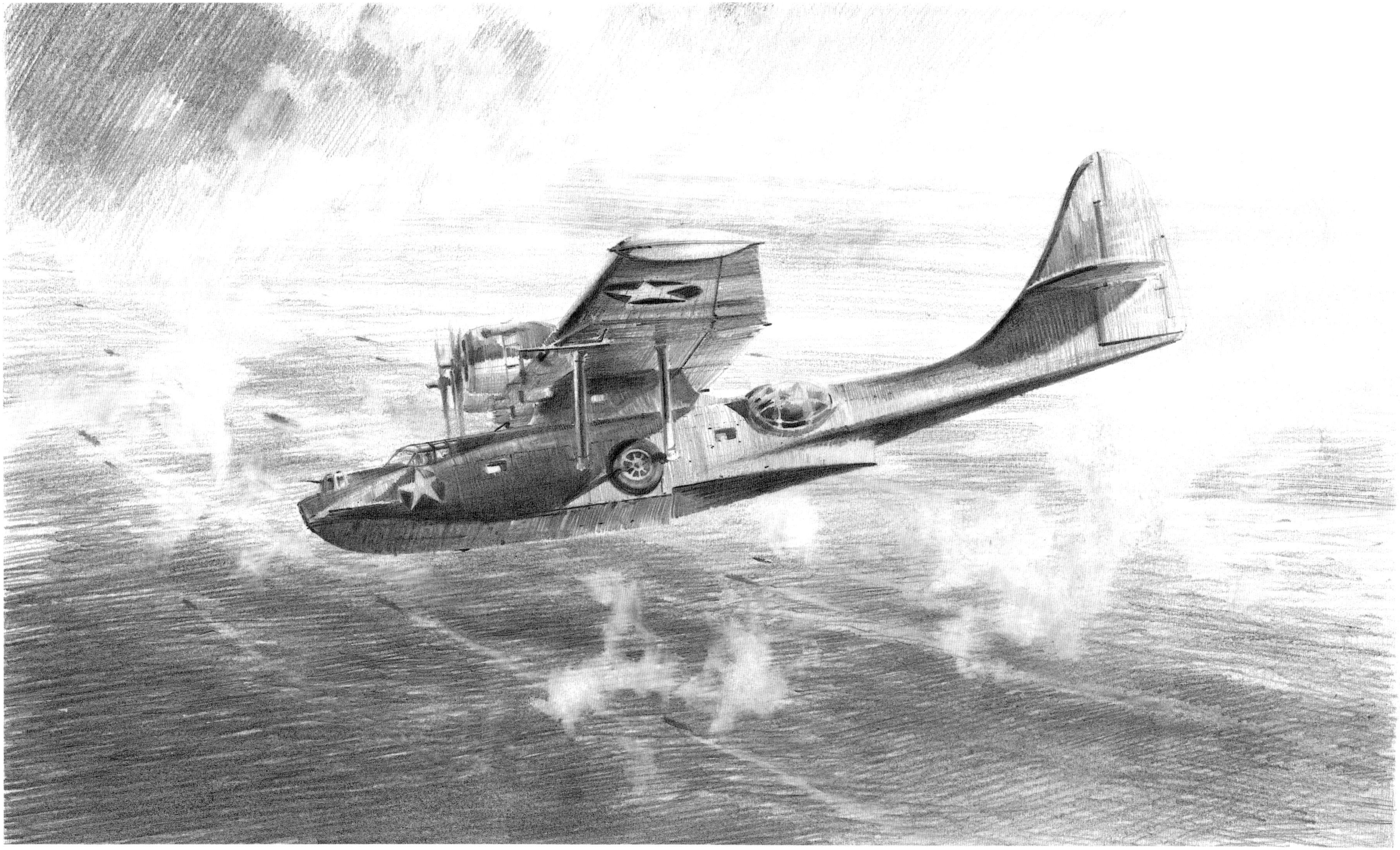

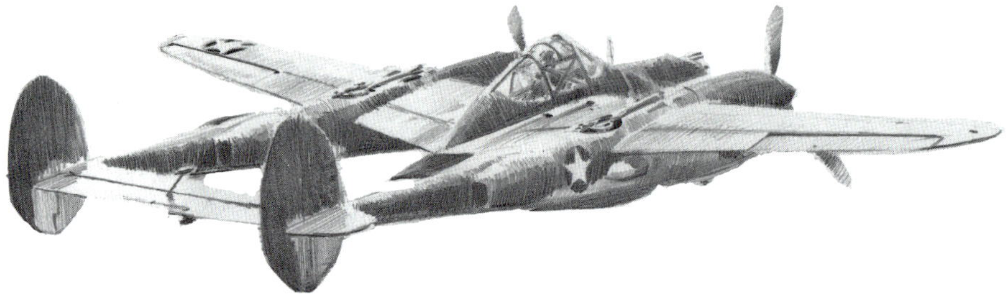

Painting water from above, particularly a large expanse of sea, is difficult. The greatest problem is perspective. Looking down on the ocean from the window of an aircraft, as many of us often get the opportunity to do, it is extremely difficult to judge the height accurately unless there is some definite focal point such as a ship or a coastline. In a painting such as *Midway – Strike against the Akagi* the perspective is taken care of by the clear view of the aircraft carrier below; but in a painting where there is nothing but water below, one has to find a way of defining the perspective.

I had been commissioned to paint a picture relating to the event which led to the downfall of Admiral Yamamoto. Because so many artists before me had portrayed this notable action, but virtually all showing the moment of his demise, I looked to do something different. Admiral Yamamoto had master-minded the infamous attack on Pearl Harbor, and a plan to secure his elimination became reality when the enemy codes were broken. Details of an imminent morale-boosting tour of the Solomons by the Admiral became known, and this gave Admiral Nimitz the opportunity to lay an ambush.

Utilising the long-range capability of the P-38 Lightning, a plan was hurriedly hatched to intercept and shoot down the aircraft carrying the Commander-in-Chief of the Japanese Fleet. Under the command of Major John Mitchell, sixteen pilots of the USAAF's 339th Squadron were to make a 420-mile flight to intercept the Japanese planes, taking a circuitous, low-level over-water route in radio silence to avoid detection. As they approached the coast of Bougainville, the two-hour radio silence was broken by one of the pilots, Doug Canning, with the urgent call 'Bogeys! Eleven o'clock high!'. And the rest is history: in a short, well planned engagement Yamamoto's aircraft was shot down, crashing into the jungle in a pall of smoke.

I was aware that there was controversy over which pilot had dealt the *coup de grâce*, and felt that in some way this detracted from the brilliant navigation, timing and leadership of the mission; I decided that however I went about portraying the Yamamoto exercise, I would include John Mitchell's aircraft. The moment I chose was that immediately following Doug Canning's yell over the radio announcing enemy aircraft ahead, his words giving me the title for the painting featured on this page: *Bogeys! Eleven O'Clock High!* Leading the formation, Mitchell has yanked the stick back, and the P-38s are about to make their attack.

In this painting the main problem was again that of the huge expanse of ocean below the aircraft, the area of water occupying almost a third of the canvas. To convey the low altitude of the aircraft it was necessary to achieve some definition into the surface of the water, but without painting more detail than was necessary to convey the right perspective. I was tempted to include a small boat which would have done the trick, but was concerned that this would affect the authenticity, since I could find no reference to any craft in the area at the time.

In the *Akagi* painting displayed on the facing page, my main difficulty was with the bottom right-hand corner of the picture, where there was a large and rather uninteresting stretch of water. To deal with this I painted the wake of one of the *Akagi's* escort ships, running just ahead of the carrier.

BOGEYS! ELEVEN O'CLOCK HIGH!

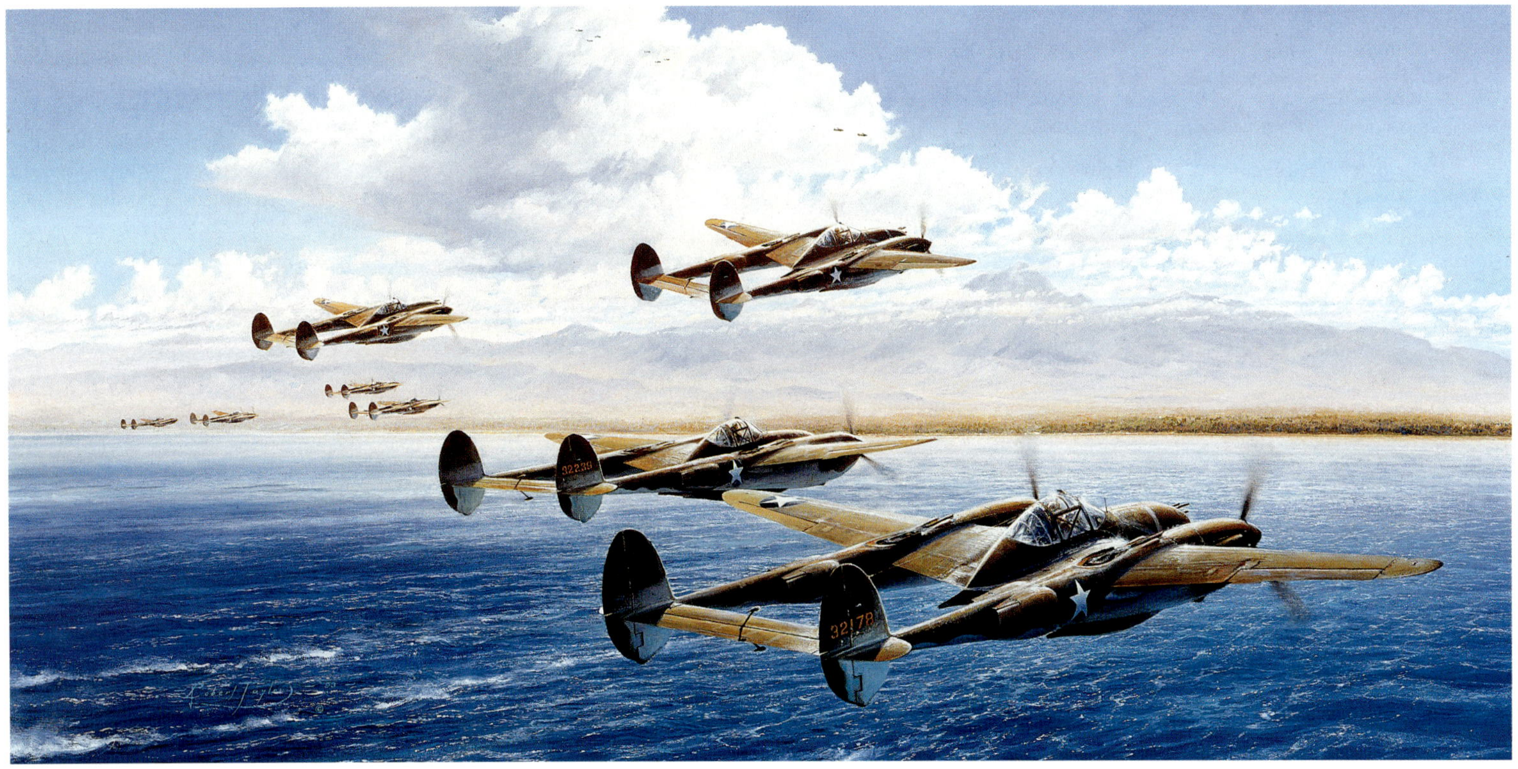

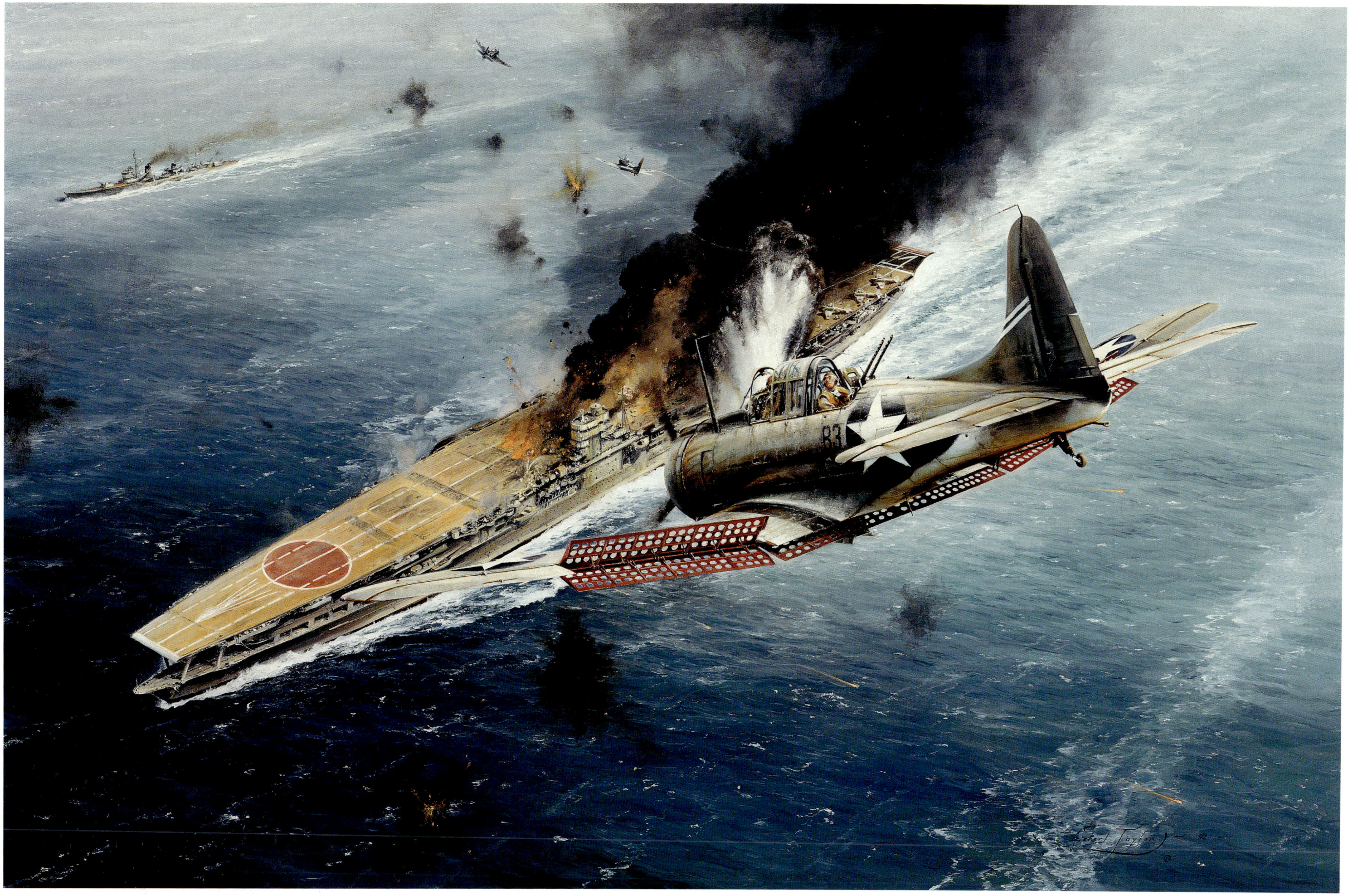

MIDWAY – STRIKE AGAINST THE AKAGI

In the collection of Mr Eugene Eisenberg

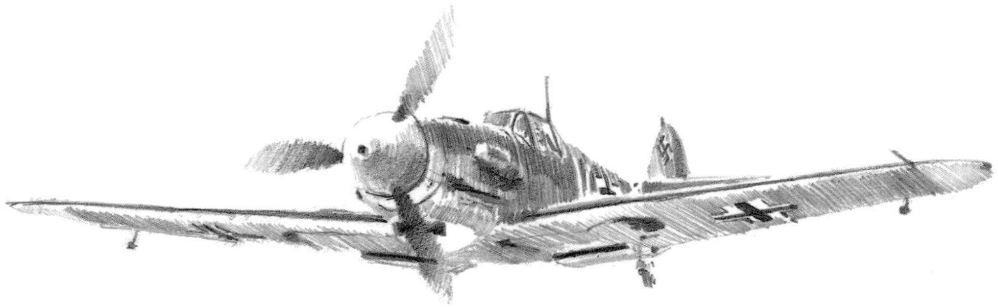

HUNTERS IN THE DESERT

Following the publication of each of my previous aviation art books I received many letters from people saying how much they enjoyed looking at the magnified 'details' of the paintings, where these were included. With close examination it is possible to detect the brush strokes in these enlarged sections, providing an interesting insight into my methods of applying paint, and giving clues as to how different effects are achieved with the brush.

The methods and techniques employed by artists are of interest to many people who love paintings, no matter what medium is used, and I am questioned constantly on the subject when I meet collectors at gallery receptions. This keen interest among art enthusiasts never fails to impress me, and personally I find it inspiring to know that people are curious to learn more about what it takes to paint a picture.

I discussed this topic with my publisher, and we agreed that in this volume we should again include a few close-up views of some of the paintings; I also suggested that we might try illustrating at least a couple of pictures as large as possible. The detail shown on the double page spread in this chapter is about as enlarged as was practical, and is from *Hunters in the Desert*, at about 60 per cent of the actual size I painted the original canvas. The complete painting is shown on the opposite page.

Generally speaking, the more impressionistic an artist's technique the thicker the paint is applied, some artists preferring to do away with the brush altogether and administering great dollops of colour with a palette knife. At the other end of the scale is the painter of photo-realism who likes to show every blade of grass, or in the case of aviation art, every single rivet. This artist is more likely to apply the bare minimum of paint required to achieve the

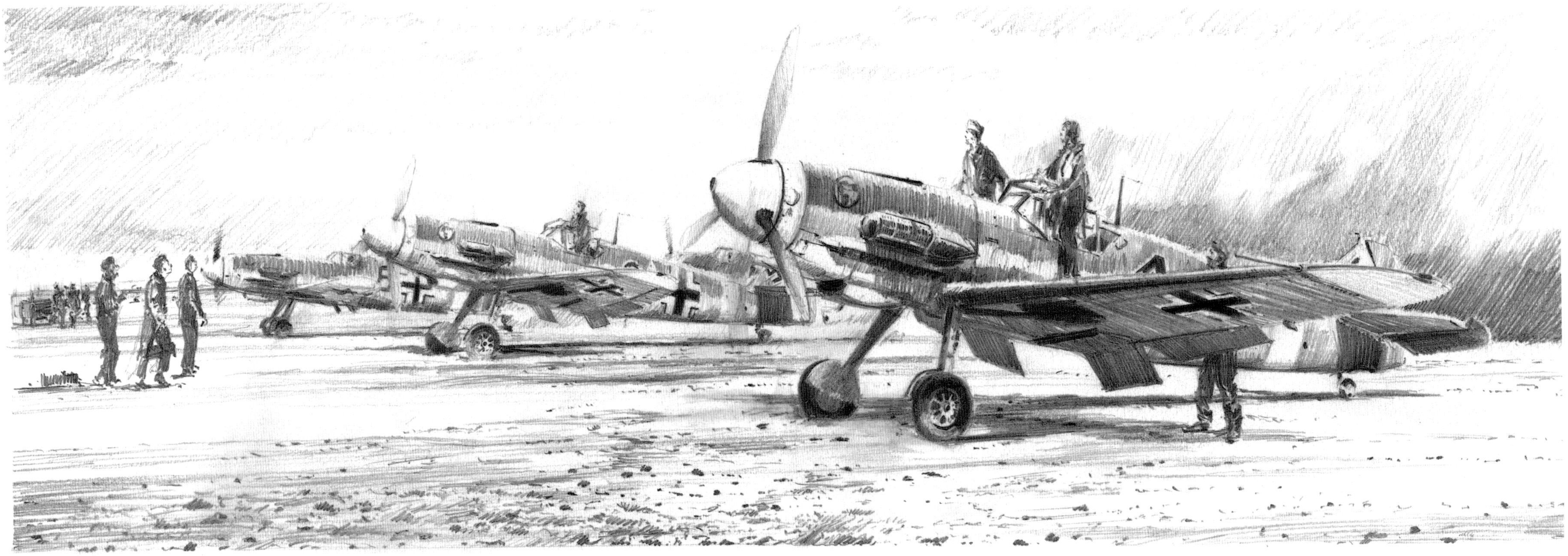

desired effect. Most photo-realist artists use water-based paints, oils being too difficult to manage in their quest for ultra-fine detail.

One of the great things about art and painting is that among the millions of people who take an interest, there is such a wide range of tastes. A basic ingredient governing individual taste, and a quality which has great bearing on what it is that attracts a collector to any one artist, is the latter's particular technique and style. Most seasoned artists have developed their own painting style, and among the better known it is this unique, instantly recognisable 'image signature' that attracts both critics and collectors alike.

In the case of oil painters, some put layer after layer of oil on the canvas, building up a sumptuous impasto; while others using the same medium prefer to apply only a thin layer, allowing the 'tooth' of the canvas to show through.

My personal preference for painting style is somewhere midway between the intense detail of photo-realism and the freedom of impressionism. Situated in this middle ground, where the detailed work is achieved with simple brush strokes, my aim is to *suggest* the finer points, rather than to labour them with obsessive accuracy.

When painting *Hunters in the Desert* I was confronted with the problem of trying to make something interesting out of a large area of rather featureless, desert terrain. Adding to the challenge was the need to inject some feeling of the oppressive heat and the dusty environment that pervaded a desert airstrip, while at the same time painting a good view of the aircraft in the picture.

It is difficult to demonstrate visually on the two-dimensional page of a book just how one goes about the three-dimensional act of applying oil paint to canvas in order to obtain the desired effect. The magnified section of *Hunters in the Desert*, seen on the next two pages overleaf, will perhaps go some way towards this, giving those interested in this aspect a chance to understand something of the technique employed.

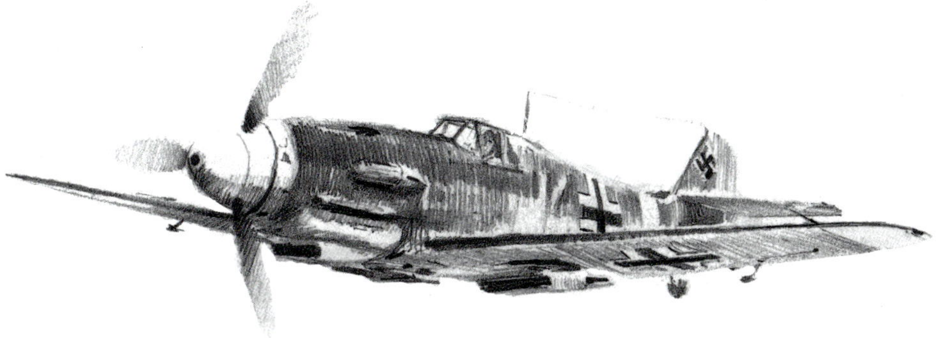

Below is the entire image of *Hunters in the Desert*. The picture depicts Hans-Joachim Marseille, who was Germany's top ace in the Western Desert, returning from the mission in which he scored his 100th victory. The Me109s are from JG-27, the first Luftwaffe unit to arrive in North Africa.

HUNTERS IN THE DESERT

In the collection of Mr Edgar Leicher

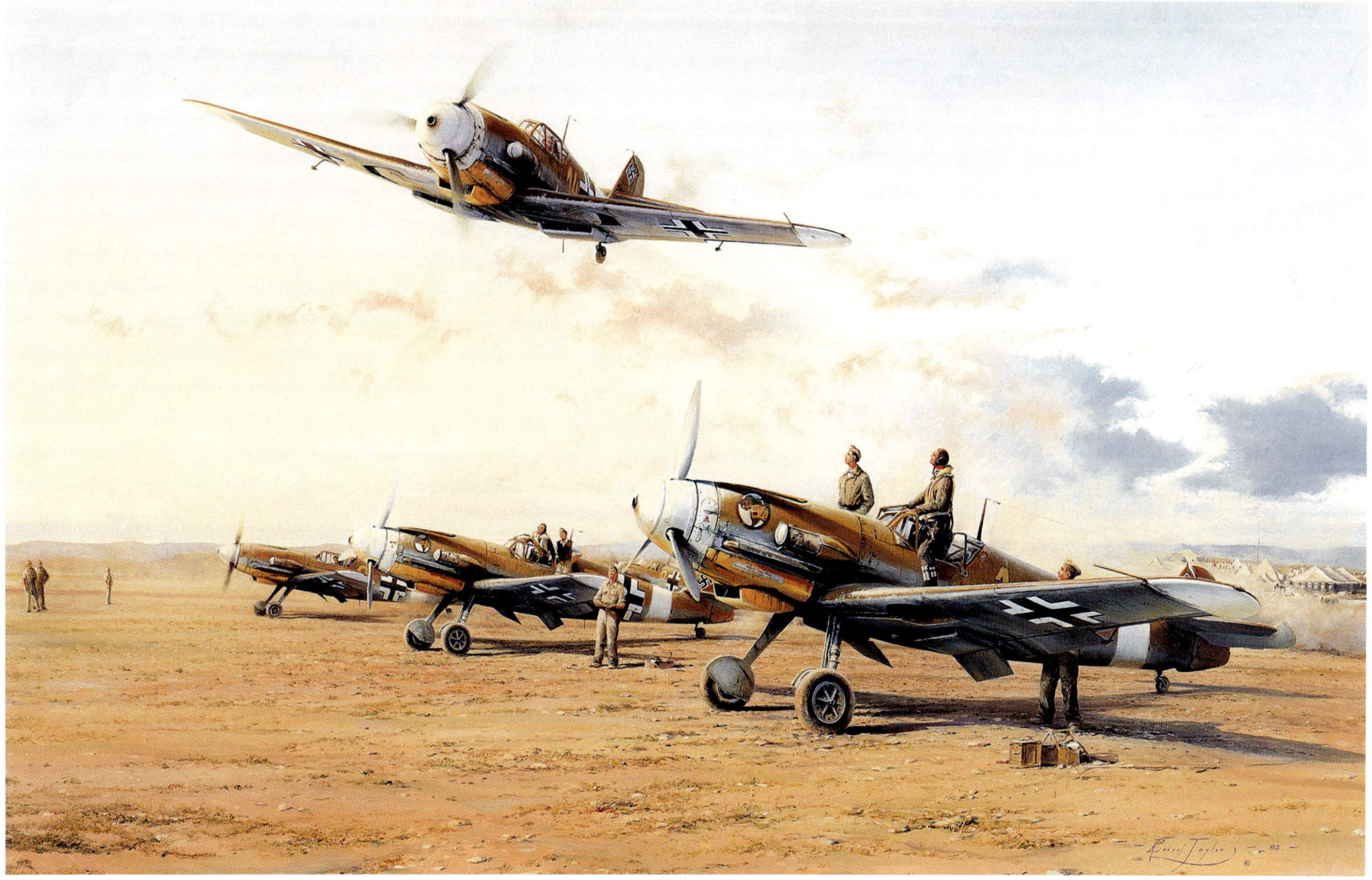

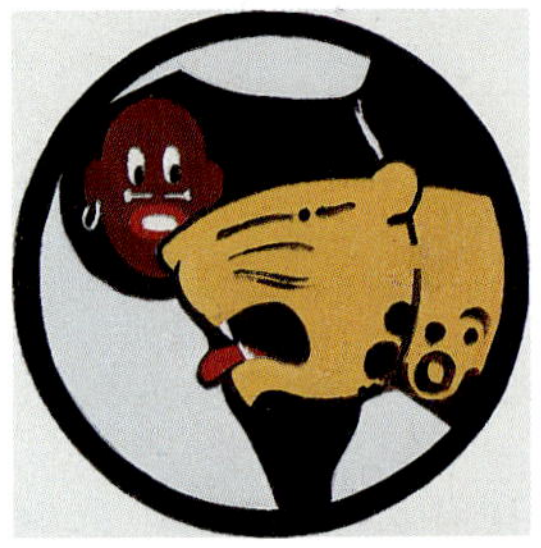

The first Luftwaffe unit to arrive in North Africa in April 1941 was to become one of its most famous. Activated during the first weeks of the war, JG-27 had already fought in the Battle of France and of Britain, and its arrival in the Western Desert presented fierce opposition to the RAF fighter pilots. Its Me109Es were superior to all other fighters in the desert at that time, and in the hands of seasoned combat pilots they were formidable competition for the Allied Hurricane and P-40 pilots.

Led by the brilliant Eduard Neumann, the JG-27 pilots were given a freedom in the air not permitted on the Channel Front. Flying in free-ranging pairs and fours, they roamed the North African skies, pouncing from height upon enemy formations. These tactics suited the talents of the more aggressive pilots, and stars quickly emerged, none more prominently than Hans-Joachim Marseille. During a short but mercurial career in the desert, Marseille claimed over 150 victories, more than any other Luftwaffe ace against the RAF pilots during World War II.

Statistics demonstrate that the great fighter battles fought over the Western Desert of North Africa were amongst the most intensely contested of World War II. From the spring of 1941 until their retreat from El Alamein at the end of 1942, the Me109-equipped Luftwaffe units claimed over 1,400 fighters shot down. In return, their opposing RAF pilots claimed over 1,200 air victories, in addition to the numerous aircraft they destroyed on the ground.

Fought above the wastelands of the desert and witnessed only by those who took part, it was a private war offering little chance of survival for a pilot forced down amongst the undulating sand, rock and scrub. The intensity of the air combat, added to these hostile conditions, brought about a special camaraderie amongst the pilots of both sides which lasts to this day.

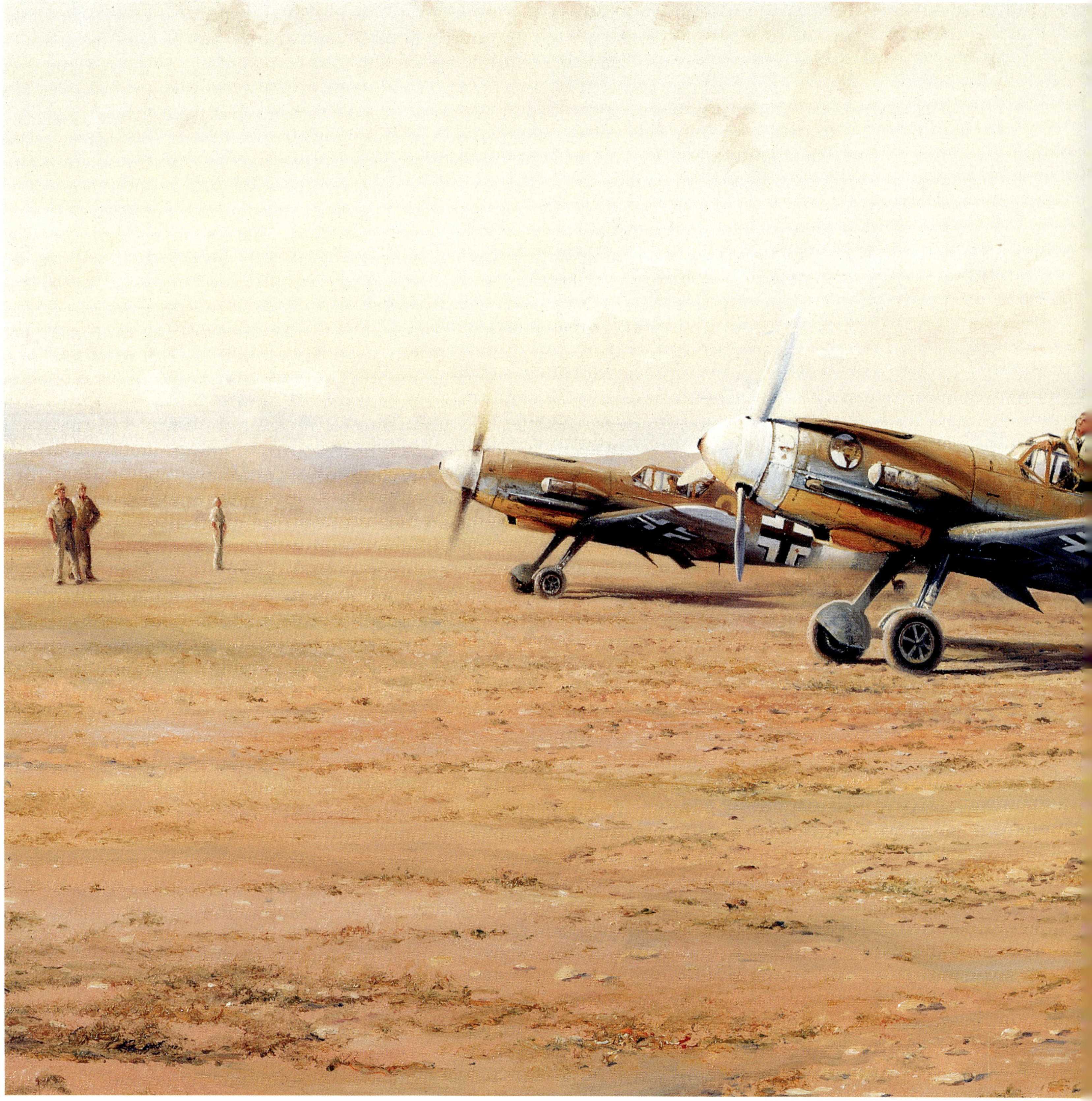

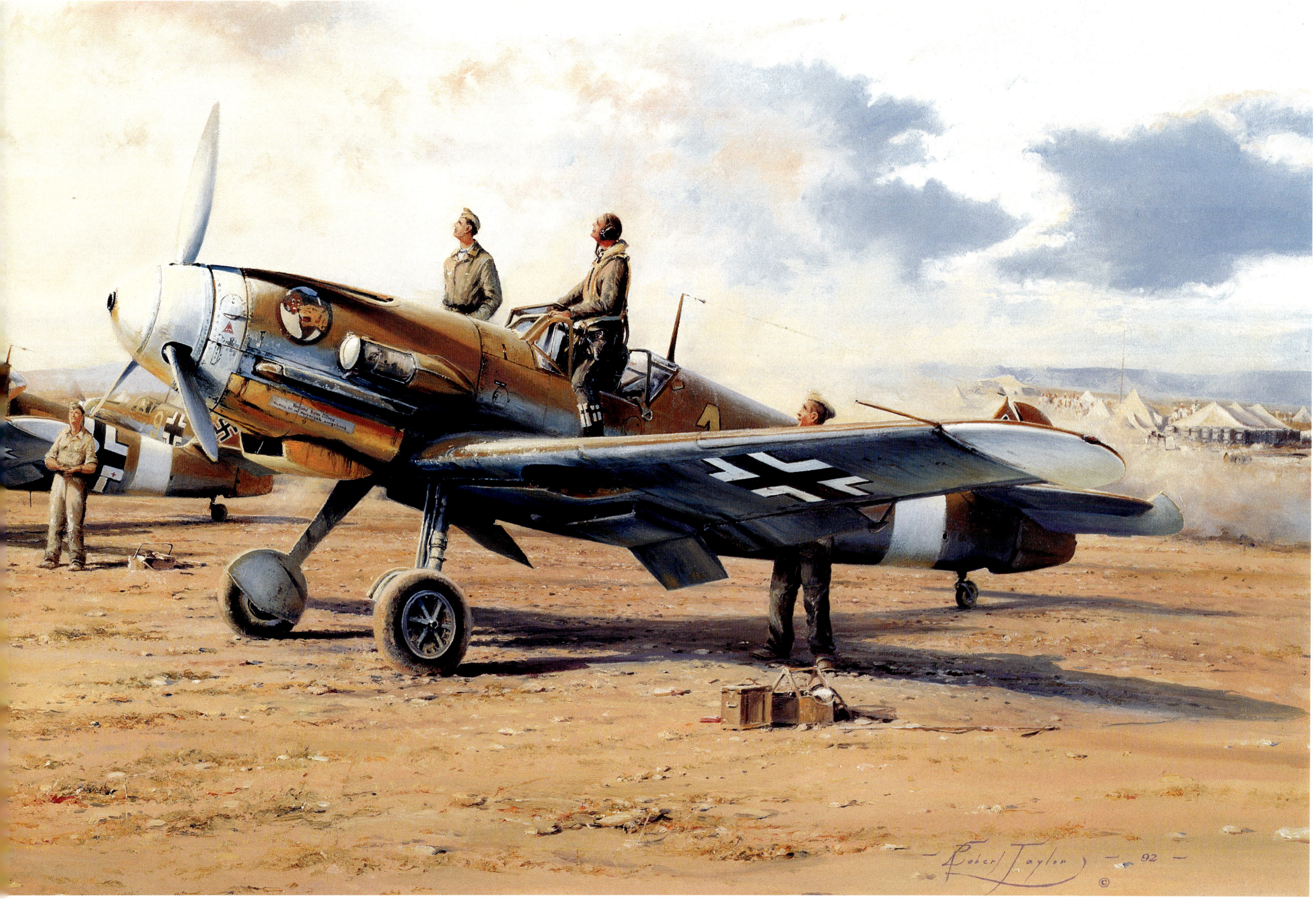

HUNTERS IN THE DESERT

(detail)

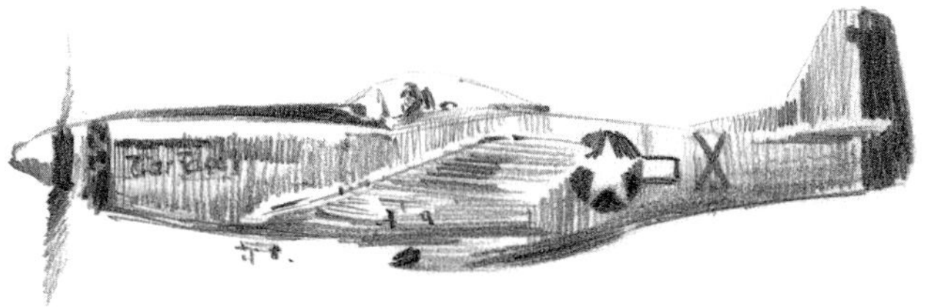

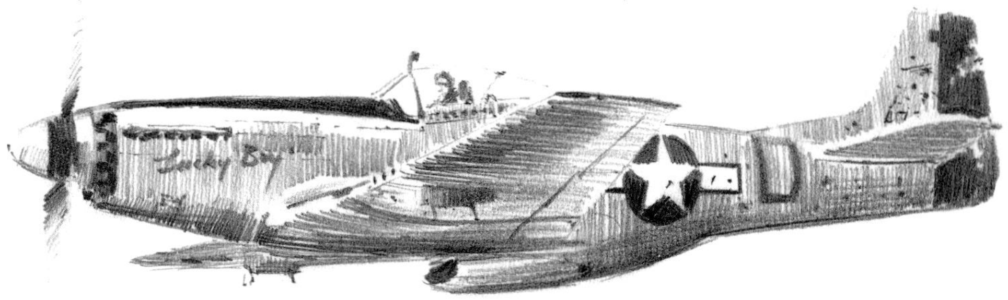

HOME AT DUSK

Most representational artists, particularly in Europe, have at some time in their careers been influenced by the works of the eighteenth-century landscape artists, the greatest of which to my mind was John Constable. Although Constable painted many large imposing canvases, he had a simple approach to art, shunning the formality of the grand and detailed designs which had become the accepted art form of the day. Looking at a Constable landscape painting today it is difficult to comprehend that his style was considered by the art establishment to be so uninhibited and radical that the Royal Academy refused, initially anyway, to hang his paintings.

Although I am not a countryman in the literal sense, I love the peace and the pace of the countryside, and can see paintings wherever I go in the country. So I suppose it is not surprising that I am an ardent admirer of the great English landscape painters, nor that I have been so deeply influenced by the great masterpieces of Constable, Gainsborough and others. I derive enormous enjoyment from travelling the rural byways absorbing the scenery, always consciously shaping what I see into possible pictures. I made the sketch below on location while on my travels. I had no specific aviation painting in mind at the time, but like many of my sketches, I knew that the scene would be useful for some future painting. In due course itformed the basis for *Home at Dusk*, a painting featuring P-51 Mustangs returning to base.

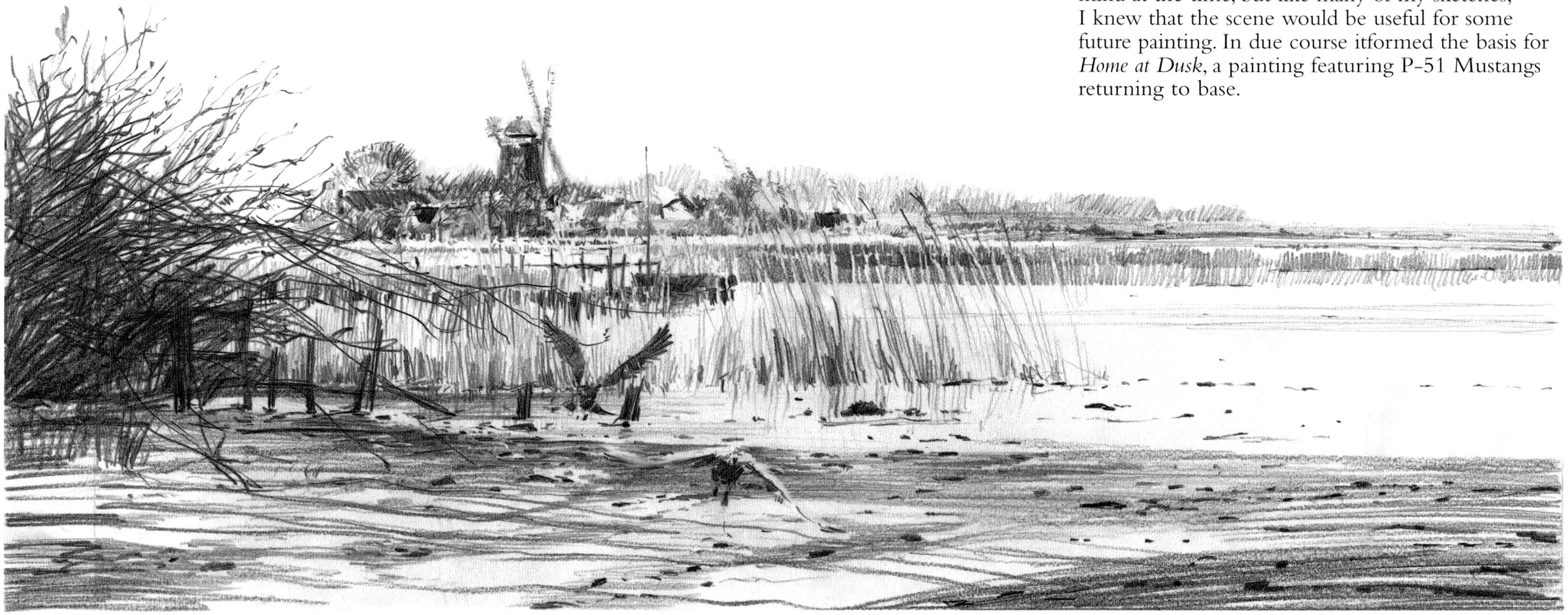

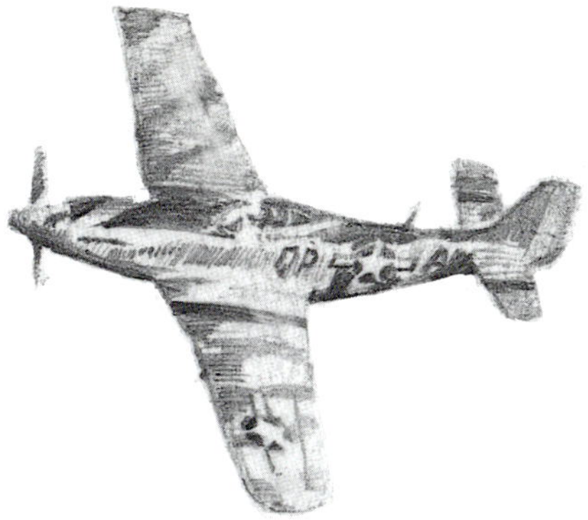

The idea of setting out to paint combat aircraft – that is, planes specifically designed and built to fight aerial battles – and then deliberately placing them in the most peaceful of surroundings, is an interesting one. When I first tried the idea many years ago I painted a Lancaster bomber coming in to land, the big aircraft descending over a summer haymaking scene. It was a departure from the normal type of aviation painting at the time, and as the genre was still very much in its infancy, I had some reservations about how it would be accepted. But my publisher liked the painting and decided to issue a limited print edition, and to my surprise – and I think his – within a few weeks everything was sold, including the painting. I was delighted because it allowed me to go forwards with other paintings containing landscape scenes, and to this day I try to do at least two 'landscape' aviation paintings each year.

There is a wonderful freedom about painting the landscape which contrasts sharply with the accuracy and detailed work required when painting aircraft and wartime airfields. While obviously a painter of realism goes to pains to ensure his work looks realistic, there is much more latitude in the way landscapes are composed. A sketch made on location usually provides only a basis for the eventual composition, and if the actual scene observed can be improved with the addition of a church or a few more cottages, I paint them in. If a hedge needs to be moved a bit to the left, or some additional trees would improve the composition, I don't hesitate to make the necessary adjustments on the canvas.

People I meet often tell me they will spend time studying different areas of a painting closely and in turn, letting their imagination take them, metaphorically speaking, right into the picture. I find this interesting, and also very gratifying, because much of the time spent on a painting involves the background material. One collector of my original paintings told me recently that he will often gaze for an hour or more at a specific area of a work, 'getting to know the painting' as he put it.

Much of the time I spend painting each aviation picture is concerned with the background areas of the canvas, often more time than is necessary for the aircraft in the picture. As the painting evolves I, too, am continually studying, evaluating, and tinkering with the areas of secondary interest. As part of this process I will often mask off most of the canvas, leaving visible only the small section that I am working on, thereby creating a small cameo of its own. In this way I satisfy myself that each section of the painting 'works' on its own, and find the routine invaluable in my efforts to paint what I describe as 'complete' pictures. An example cameo from *Home at Dusk* appears on this page; it makes quite a nice little picture on its own.

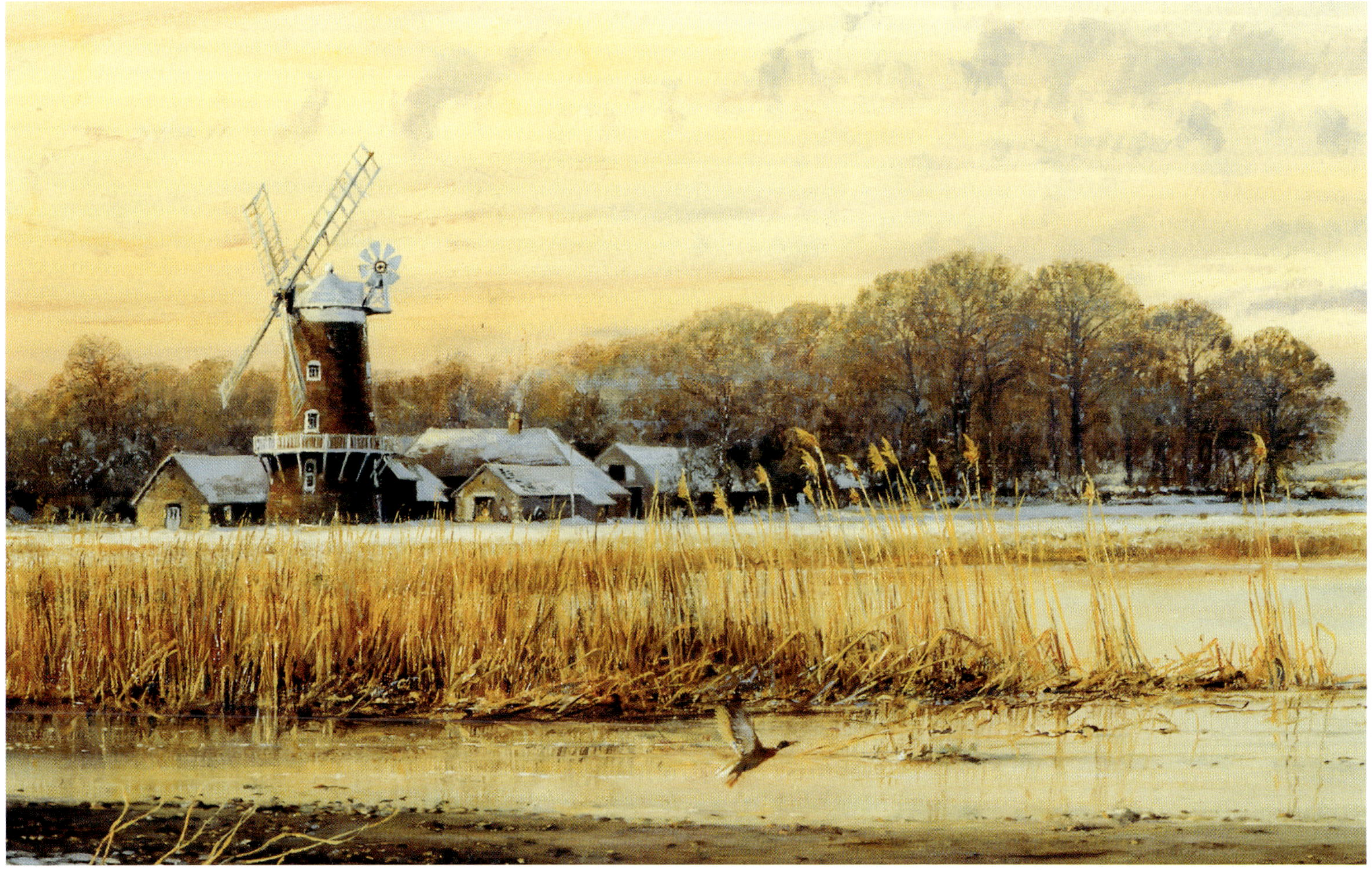

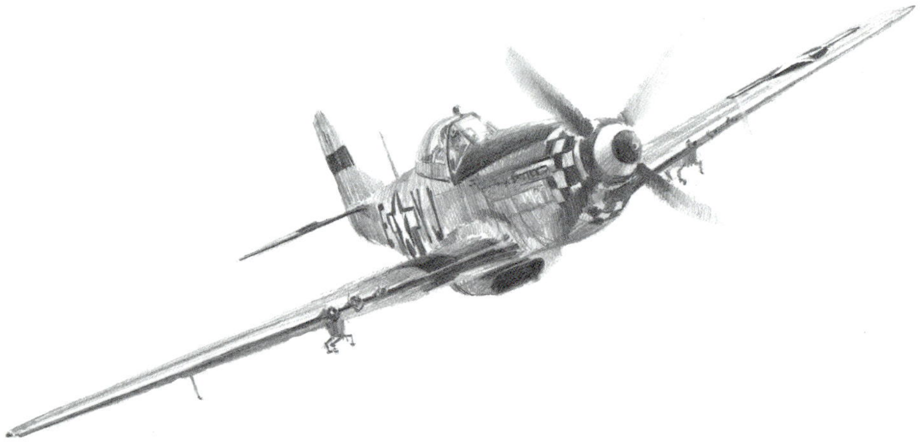

Another P-51 picture I completed recently is illustrated on this page. This was painted as one of a pair to commemorate the Air Victory in Europe (the second featured the B-17 and is shown on page 22). My aim with this P-51 painting was to create an image with a celebratory air about it, and to this end I elected to show a gaggle of these beautiful fighters making a low-level run over towns and villages along the Rhine; this famous river seems to have featured constantly in European warfare over the centuries. The aircraft in the picture are from the 353rd Fighter Group, and the lead aircraft is appropriately named 'Dove of Peace'. Below, the ancient town of Kaub, south of Remagen, appears untouched by the traumatic events of the previous years.

I decided to tilt the buildings a little off the perpendicular to give the painting a better shape, and to avoid too much of a contrived look. I have used this technique before, and each time have sworn I'll never do it again because it complicates and slows down the painting process so much. To make things easier while painting the town of Kaub, I set the canvas up on the easel at the slightly lopsided angle required so I could paint the buildings vertically. I then repeatedly levelled the canvas, standing back to check that the buildings were all leaning at the correct angle. It took ages. When I eventually finished I was quite pleased with the result – but I've again sworn I'll never paint another town off the rectilinear. Standing back to view the painting for the final time it occurred to me that I had painted the town in italics!

The two main aircraft are tilted at opposing angles partly to give movement to the picture, but also to frame the castle in the centre of the river. It was here that Blucher camped after pursuing Napoleon as far as the Rhine in 1813, before crossing the river with 100,000 Prussian soldiers.

EAGLES OVER THE RHINE

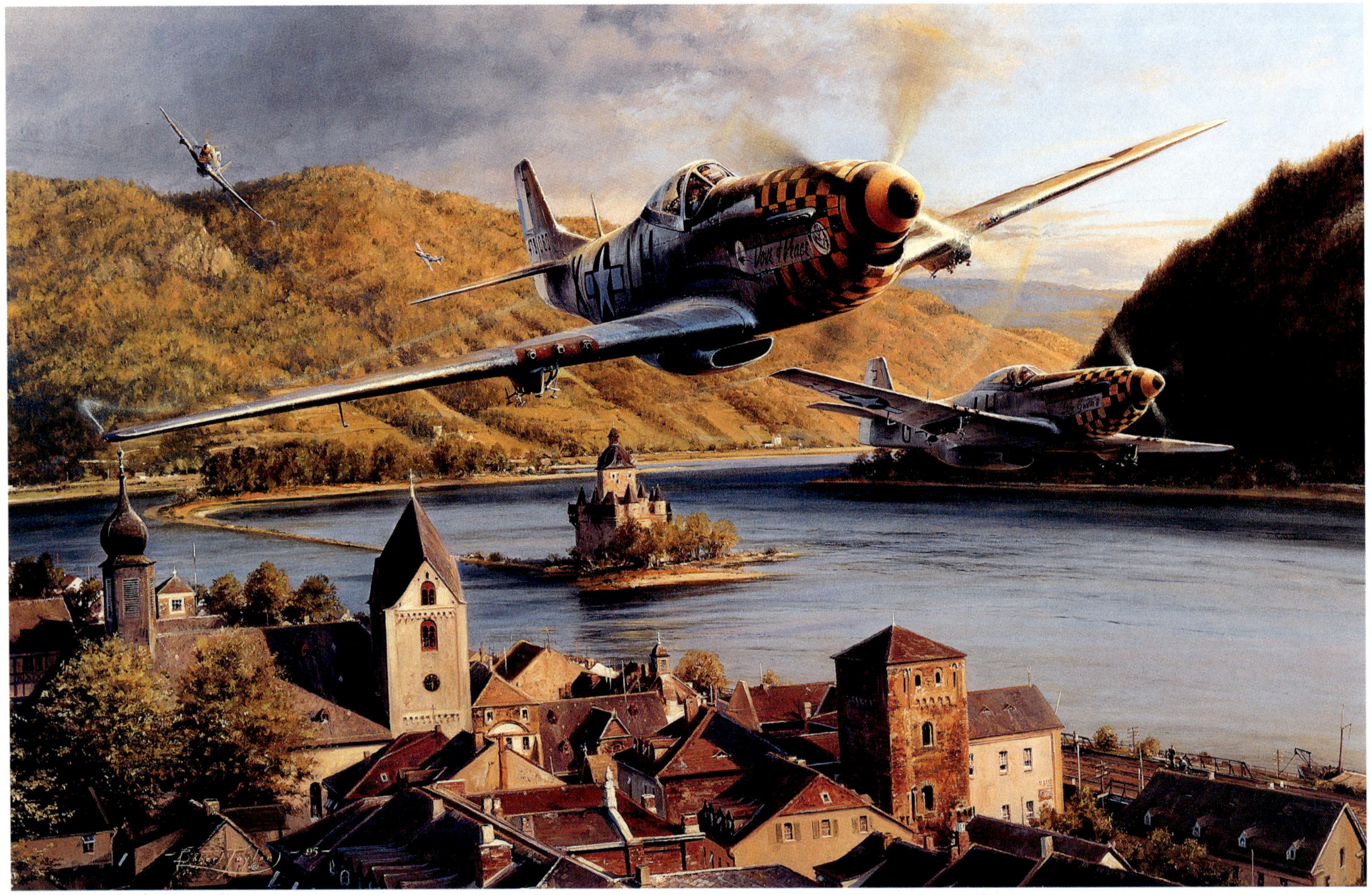

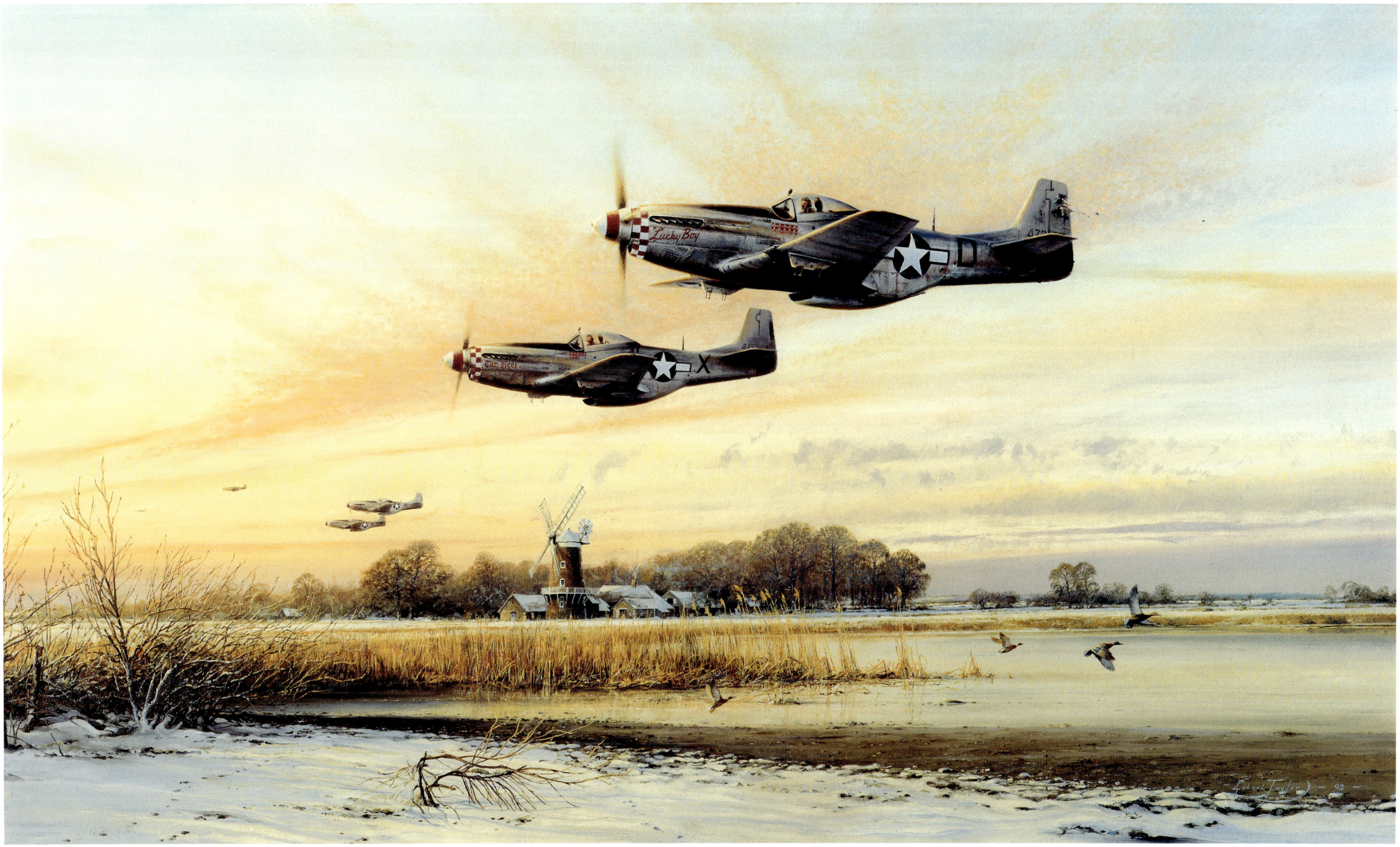

HOME AT DUSK

In the collection of Mr Eugene Eisenberg

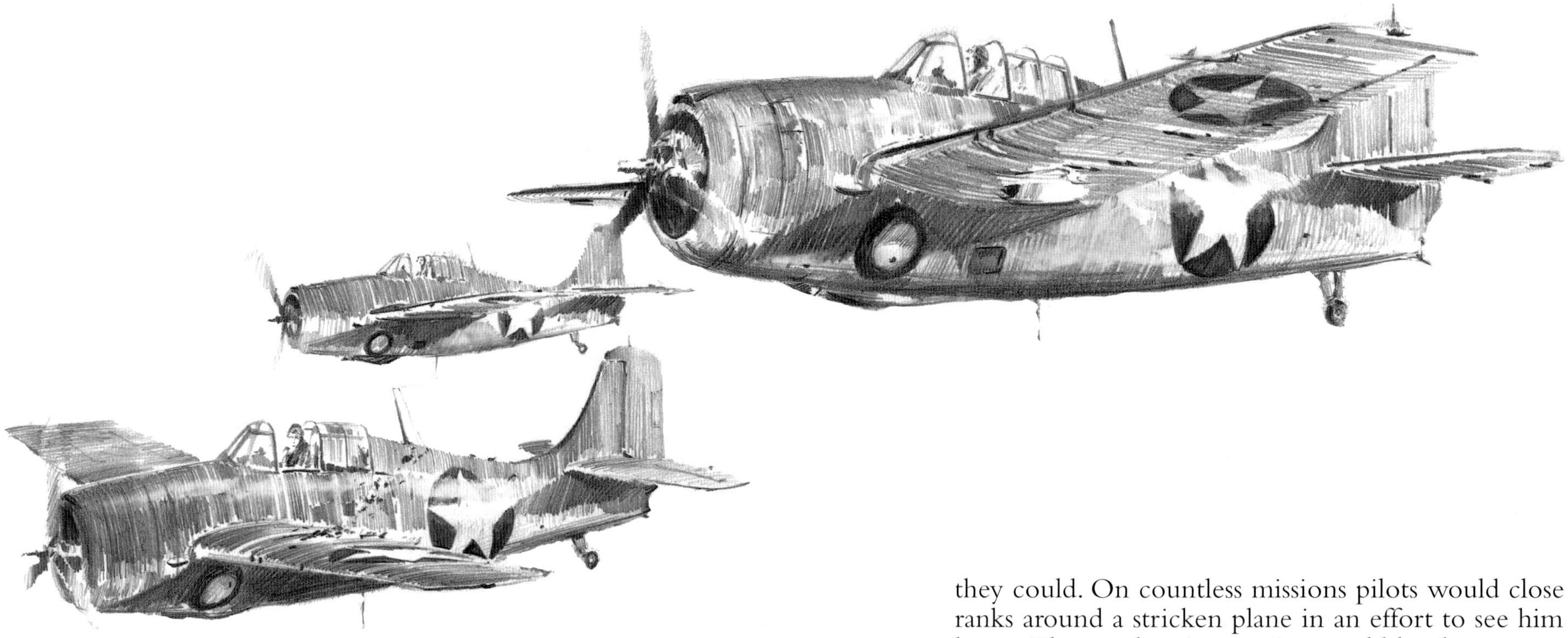

IN GALLANT COMPANY

My feeling is that an aviation painting does not always need to show fire and brimstone in order to convey the atmosphere of war; in fact a carefully designed painting can often create a feeling of high drama more poignantly where the action is suggested in some subtle way, rather than actually portrayed. Perhaps the image implies that some action is either about to happen or has just taken place, deliberately constructed to tell only part of the story, pushing the viewer to use his or her imagination to complete the scenario. Such a painting requires audience participation in order to get the most out of it, and to appreciate fully what the artist is trying to state. *In Gallant Company* is intended to be such a painting.

When flying hazardous over-water missions, a pilot's worst nightmare was having to parachute or to ditch into the vast expanse of the Pacific, where there was little chance of ever being picked up. Yet it was a concern every fighter pilot had to live with on almost every mission flown in the Pacific. Exhausted from the exertions of combat, perhaps wounded, a pilot might have to nurse home a damaged aircraft over hundreds of miles of sea. A slip in concentration or even consciousness could bring a fighter pilot's career to an abrupt and watery end. Coaxing along a badly damaged plane on a long journey home could, I am told, be more harrowing than combat itself.

All pilots in the Pacific had to contend with this ever-present fear, and they readily identified with the anxieties of another flyer in trouble, quickly rallying round to provide what support and encouragement they could. On countless missions pilots would close ranks around a stricken plane in an effort to see him home. The overbearing tension could be drawn out for over an hour or more.

My painting *In Gallant Company* endeavours to portray such an episode, and depicts a nail-biting drama in the Solomons during the great struggle for air supremacy in 1943. Marine Corps F4F Wildcats have fought a bitter air battle. Weary from the contest but flushed with success the F4F pilots head for base; they are joined by three F4U Corsairs, newly arrived in the Pacific, on the journey home. But one of the F4Fs is in trouble: it has been raked across the fuselage by gunfire, crazing the canopy, taking out the radio equipment and puncturing an oil pipe. The pilot is injured but in control and has thus far managed to maintain speed. His CO and wingman have closed in to give support; but with land in sight the F4F has started to trail smoke.

As we view the drama we are uncertain whether the islands looming up are friendly or in enemy hands. How much longer will this F4F's engine continue to run? Can the pilot hang on? Will he make it back to base today? These are the questions which might be asked, and these are the tensions I have tried to create in the painting.

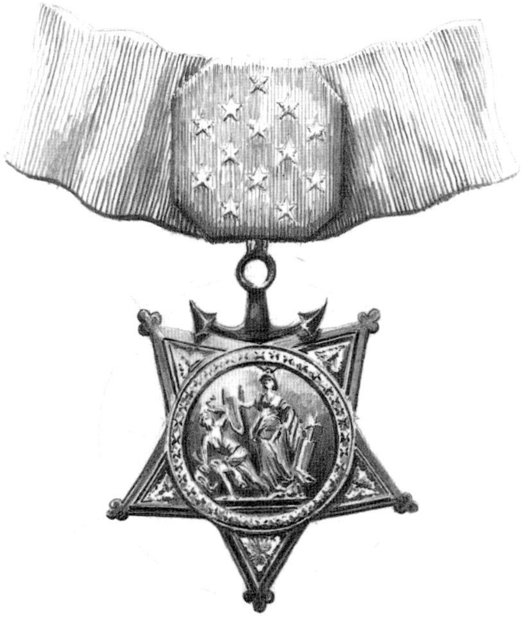

THE CONGRESSIONAL MEDAL OF HONOR

First authorised by Abraham Lincoln in December 1861, the Medal of Honor was awarded only to petty officers, seamen and marines for gallantry in action; officers were not eligible until 1915. The award was made for distinguished gallantry at risk of life, beyond the call of duty, and while in conflict with the enemy. At the outbreak of war in 1942 the Medal of Honor was established by Act of Congress, and again it was confined to those displaying extraordinary gallantry in action in the face of the enemy. It was America's highest award for gallantry, and was bestowed on eleven US Marine Corps pilots during World War II, four of whom received the award posthumously.

In Gallant Company was reproduced as a limited print edition, as are many of my paintings. After it was reproduced, five recipients of the Congressional Medal of Honor did me the honour of signing all prints in the edition. I had the pleasure of meeting and talking to these famous pilots at Virginia Bader's well-known gallery in California soon after the prints were published. All US Marine Corps pilots, they were the élite among hundreds of fighter aces who flew and fought in the Pacific theatre.

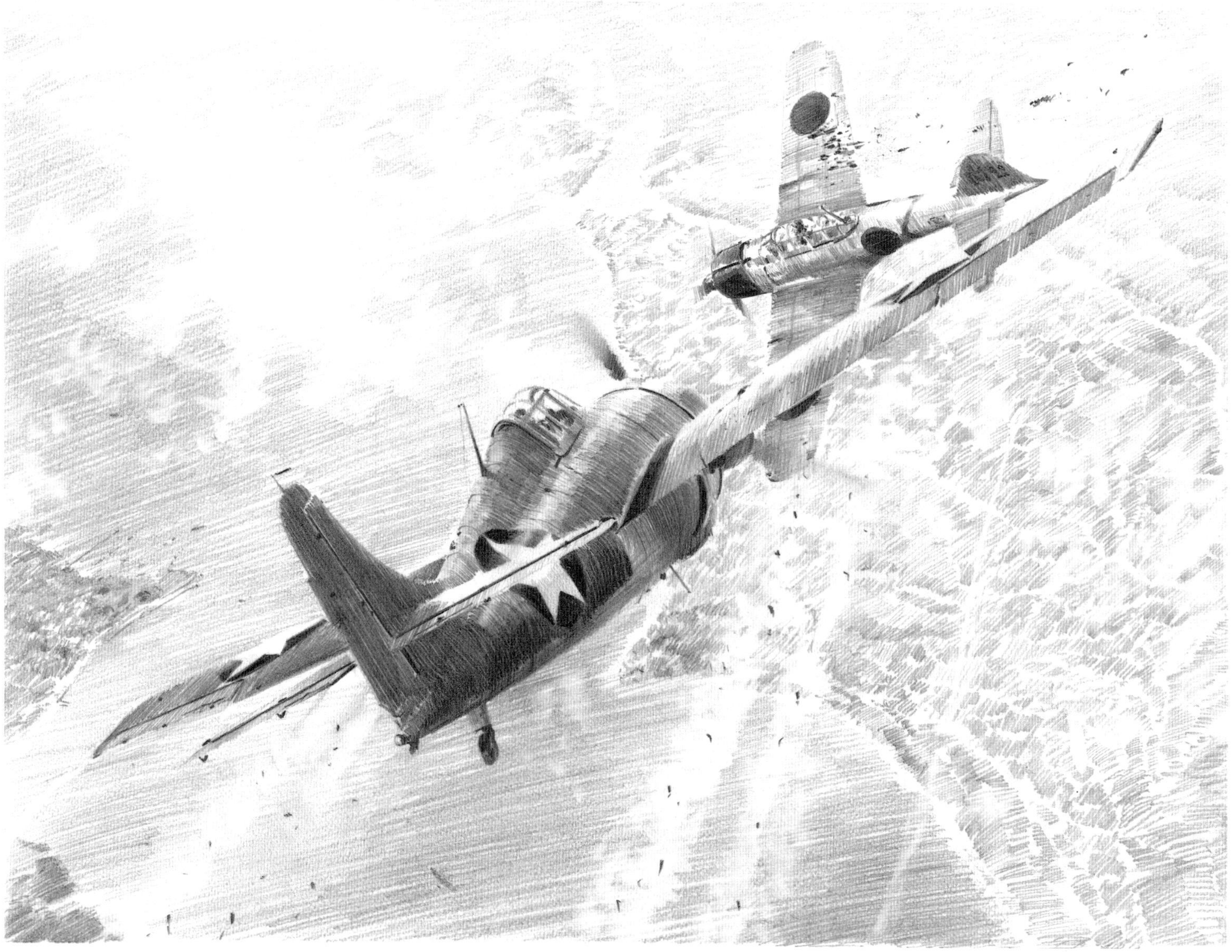

In this drawing a Grumman F4F Wildcat is seen in combat with a Japanese Zero during an action in the Solomons in 1942. The Wildcat fought from beginning to end of the war in the Pacific and was the front-line fighter of the Navy and Marine Corps from the gallant defence of Wake Island, throughout the battles of Coral Sea and Midway, to the victory at Guadalcanal.

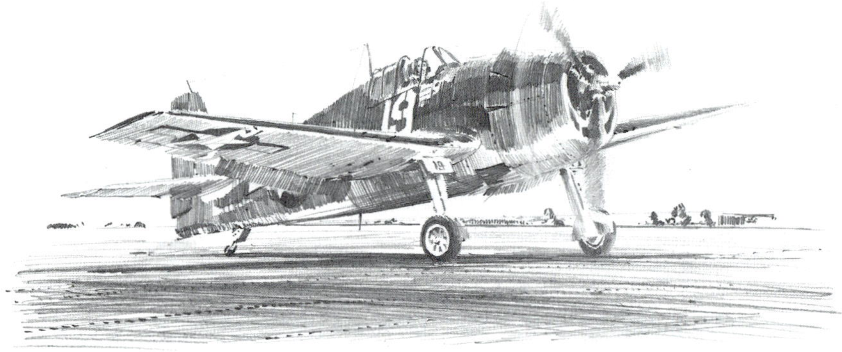

The Grumman F4F Wildcat was at the cutting edge of the American air-fighting force during all the early campaigns in the Pacific. Flying this tubby, highly manoeuvrable little fighter, the Navy and marine pilots put up heroic resistance to the Japanese onslaught until the arrival of the F4U Corsair and the F6F Hellcat in 1943.

I made the small sketch above at an airshow at Duxford during a recent World War II warbirds display. Watching and listening to these veteran aircraft performing their vigorous aerobatics is always an exciting experience. That we can see them still flying half a century after they made history is an amazing fact, and a great credit to the devoted people who restore them and keep them flying. I take my hat off to these enthusiasts, and dedicate this painting to them.

The detail on this page shows the main subject of the painting *In Gallant Company*, the impaired F4F. Before deciding which part of the aircraft to 'damage', I thought carefully about what story I wanted to tell. The principal aim was to convey something of the desperate urgency there was to bring pilots home. When trying to decide how to raise the tempo I thought it would add tension to the situation if the pilots were unable to communicate with each other over the radio; for this reason I concentrated the damage mainly just behind the cockpit, where the radio equipment is located.

I also wanted to create doubts as to whether the pilot flying the mutilated F4F was injured or not. By sliding the canopy back – which pilots often did on the way home – this gave a clearer view of the three pilots who feature in the drama. The CO, flying the nearest aircraft, is obviously trying to communicate something to the pilot in the stricken F4F, and I have turned his head to face the CO's aircraft to demonstrate that even though possibly injured, he is still alert. To keep up the tension I decided to add traces of smoke, introducing some doubts as to how much longer the big Pratt & Whitney radial engine was going to run: clearly a smoking engine is not going to go much further.

Although there are plenty of unanswered questions in this tiny cameo of the Pacific air war, I nevertheless wanted to transmit a hint that everything would turn out all right for this particular F4F pilot. To give him a good chance of survival I did this by painting the islands just coming into view – even though we cannot be sure that these are not in enemy hands.

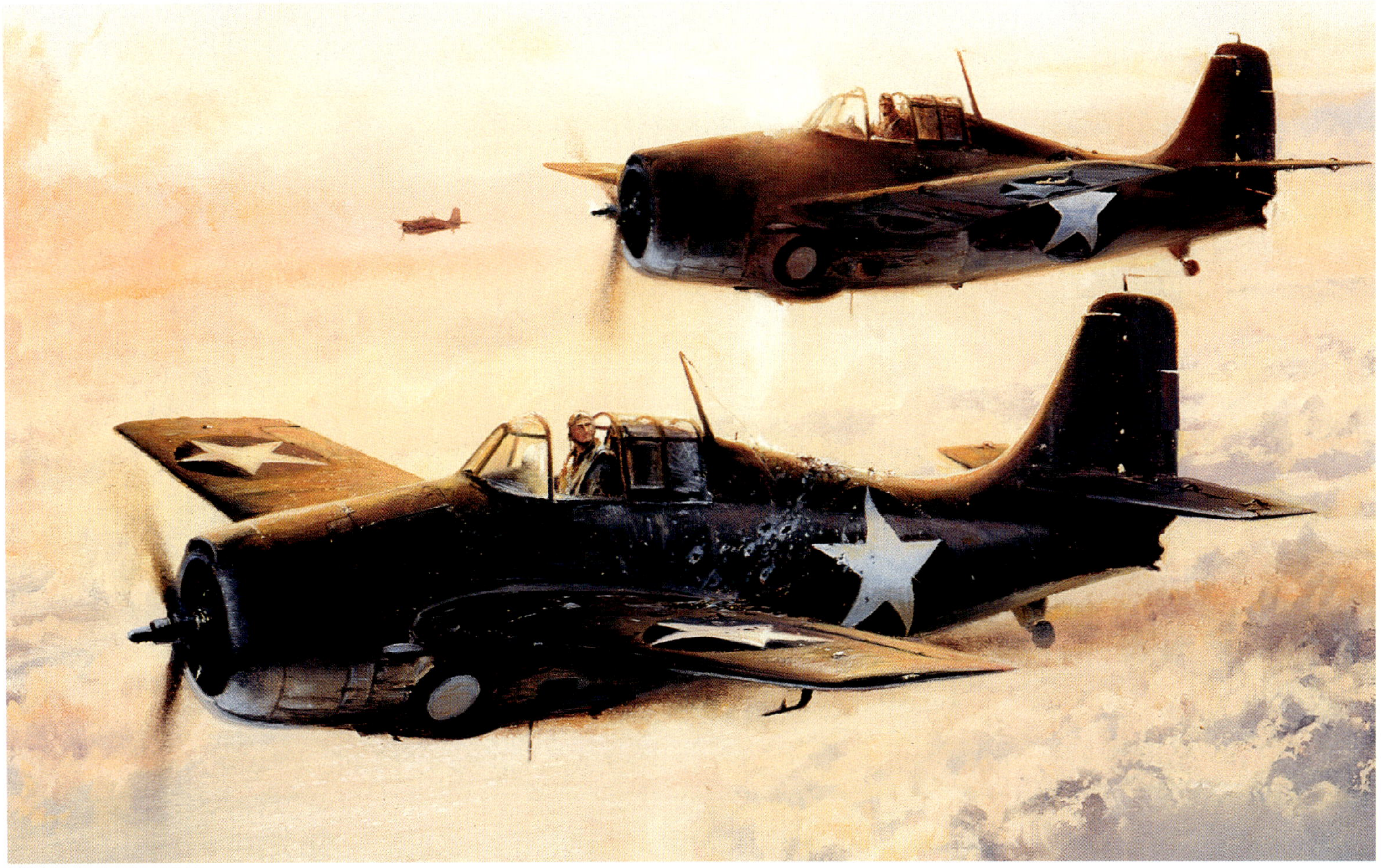

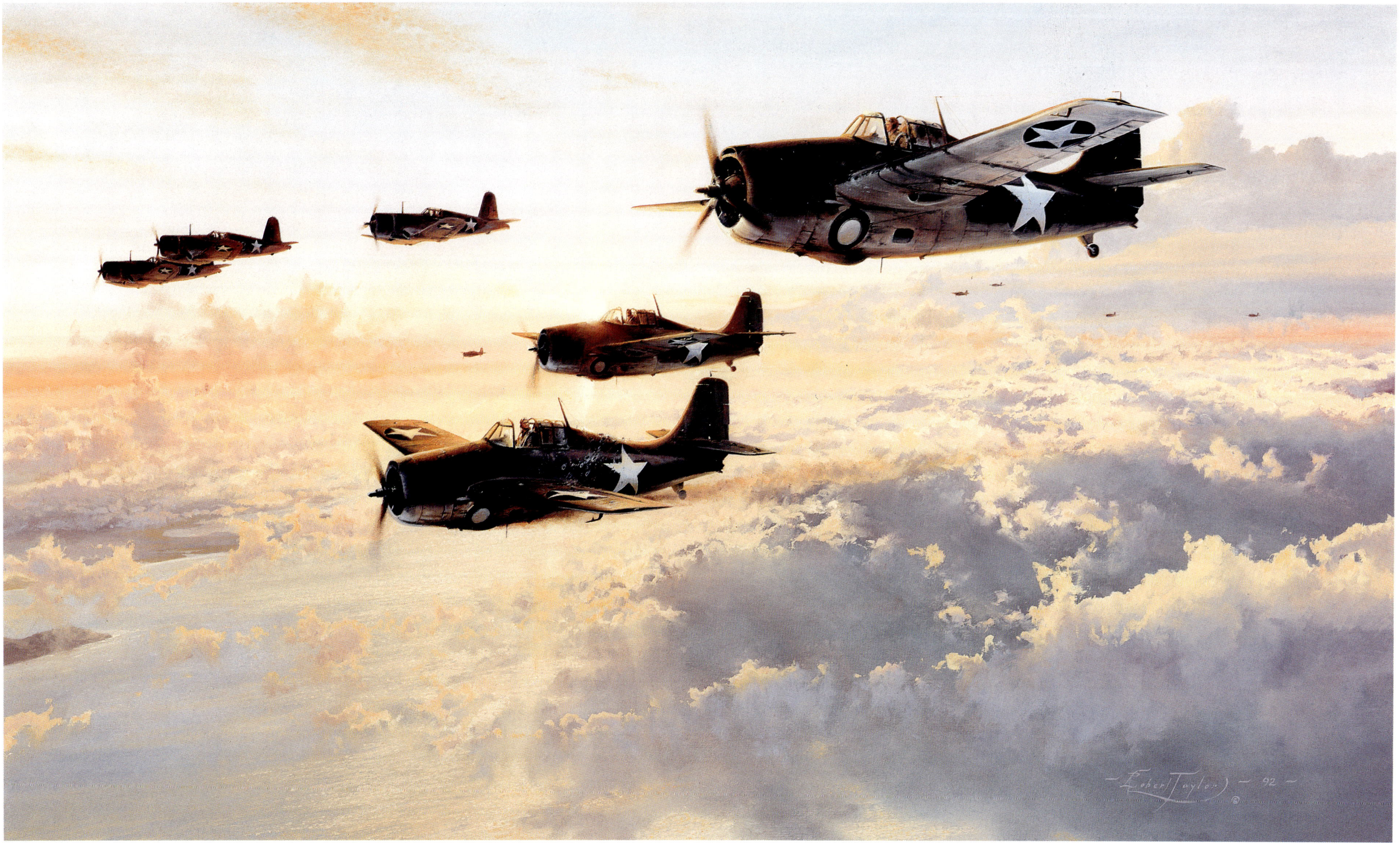

IN GALLANT COMPANY

In the collection of Mr Eugene Eisenberg

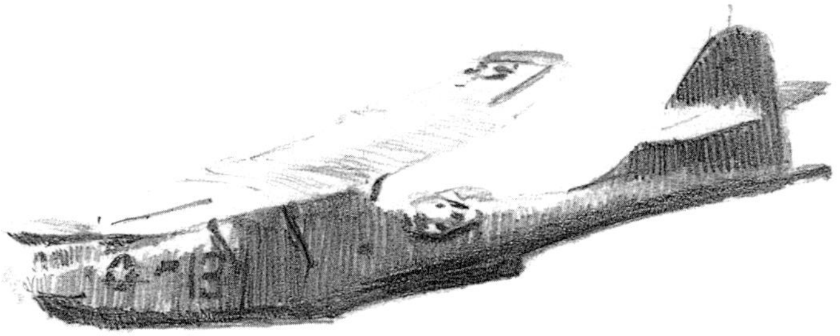

AGAINST ALL ODDS

I have been lucky enough to have spent many hours on the flight deck of modern jetliners. Looking out of the cockpit at 35,000ft the view is immense, and the curvature of the earth clearly definable. On an oceanic crossing when gazing down on what I suppose amounts to tens of thousands of square miles of sea, it has often occurred to me just how monumental the task of maritime air reconnaissance must have been back in the 1940s. Even today when overflying the busy shipping lanes of the high seas, such is the vastness of the great oceans that it is almost impossible to sight a ship in any direction. How difficult that task must have been for the reconnaissance crews under conditions of war, when ships were deliberately going out of their way to conceal themselves!

Throughout World War II, maritime reconnaissance crews spent endless hours, usually cramped in uncomfortable, extremely noisy aircraft, scanning the horizons for signs of enemy shipping, their prime task being to locate and report anything sighted as early as possible. The importance of their task seems often overlooked: more often than not the lives of thousands of sailors depended on the vigilance of the 'eyes in the sky', and of course many a decisive sea battle was won as a result of that first contact made by some lone reconnaissance patrol crew which had its wits about it.

Although not all maritime reconnaissance aircraft were amphibian or seaplanes, the best were, and two became legends of the era: the consolidated PBY Catalina, and the Short Sunderland, both of which achieved distinguished wartime careers operating in a variety of maritime roles. Both these wonderful-looking aircraft recorded historic sightings which led to decisive sea engagements, both were involved in countless heroic air-sea rescues, and both were credited with many remarkable sinkings of enemy shipping, submarines being a favourite target. My painting *Against all Odds* shows a moment during a typical encounter between a PBY Catalina and a German U-boat caught on the surface during the Battle of the Atlantic.

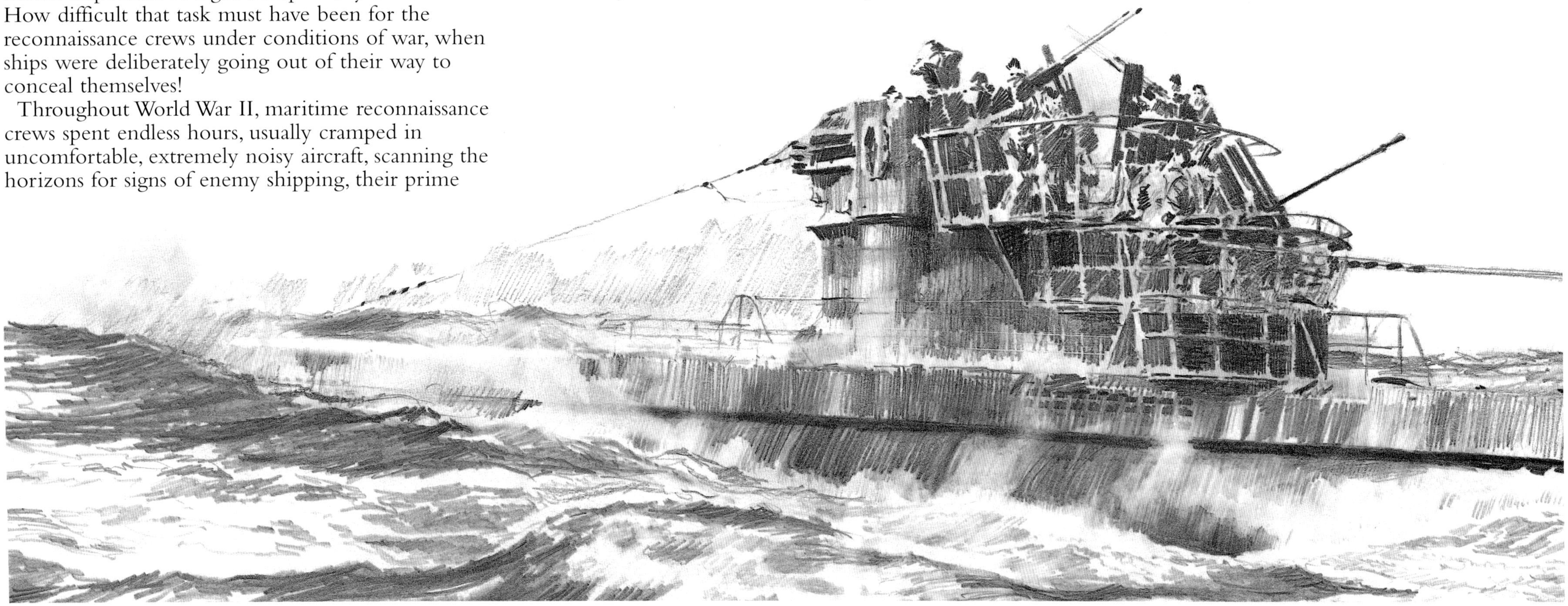

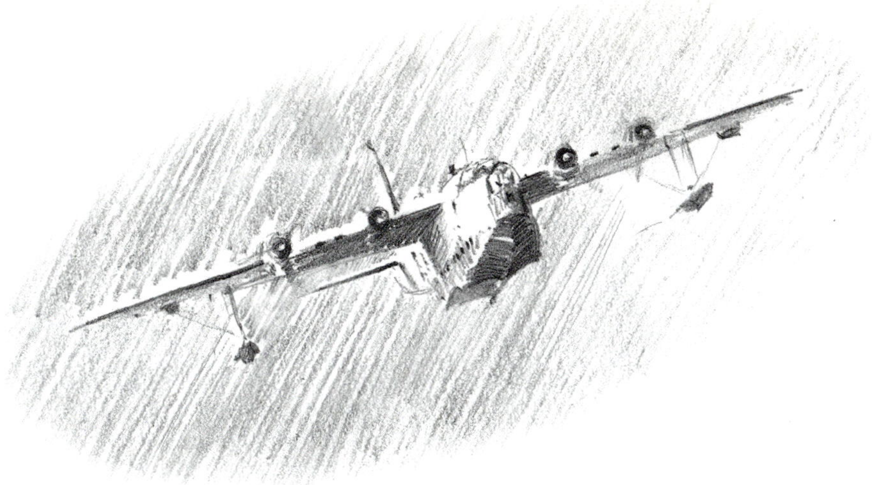

Many of the seaplanes and amphibians of the period had their origins in peacetime passenger and cargo requirements, the Sunderland being a development of the pre-war 'C' class flying boats which carried passengers on the foreign routes to Africa, the Middle East and the Orient.

Somewhat cumbersome-looking at their moorings, many seaplanes looked as if they might find it difficult ever to take off from water; but as they built up speed and rose up 'on the plane', these great aircraft took on a different personality. Streaming a wake of white foam they would lift gracefully into the air, carrying their passengers away to distant exotic destinations.

One mighty aircraft developed for the US Navy in the heyday of the great seaplanes before the outbreak of World War II was the PB2Y Coronado – a typical aircraft of the genre. Commissioned as a reconnaissance aircraft, this characterful flying boat saw service in both Atlantic and Pacific theatres, including a brief stint with RAF Coastal Command. Known affectionately as the 'Sky Giant', the Coronado was a familiar sight at the many wartime island bases in the Pacific, and had the distinction of being the first Allied aircraft to land on Tokyo Bay after the Japanese surrender.

The illustration below is a detail from a painting I was commissioned to paint for Pan American World Airways in 1990. Pan Am civilian crews operated about a quarter of the Coronados in service during World War II.

The painting shows a 'Sky Giant' at its mooring at New York's La Guardia airport in 1943. The marine terminal, seen in the background, is still in use.

SKY GIANT (detail)

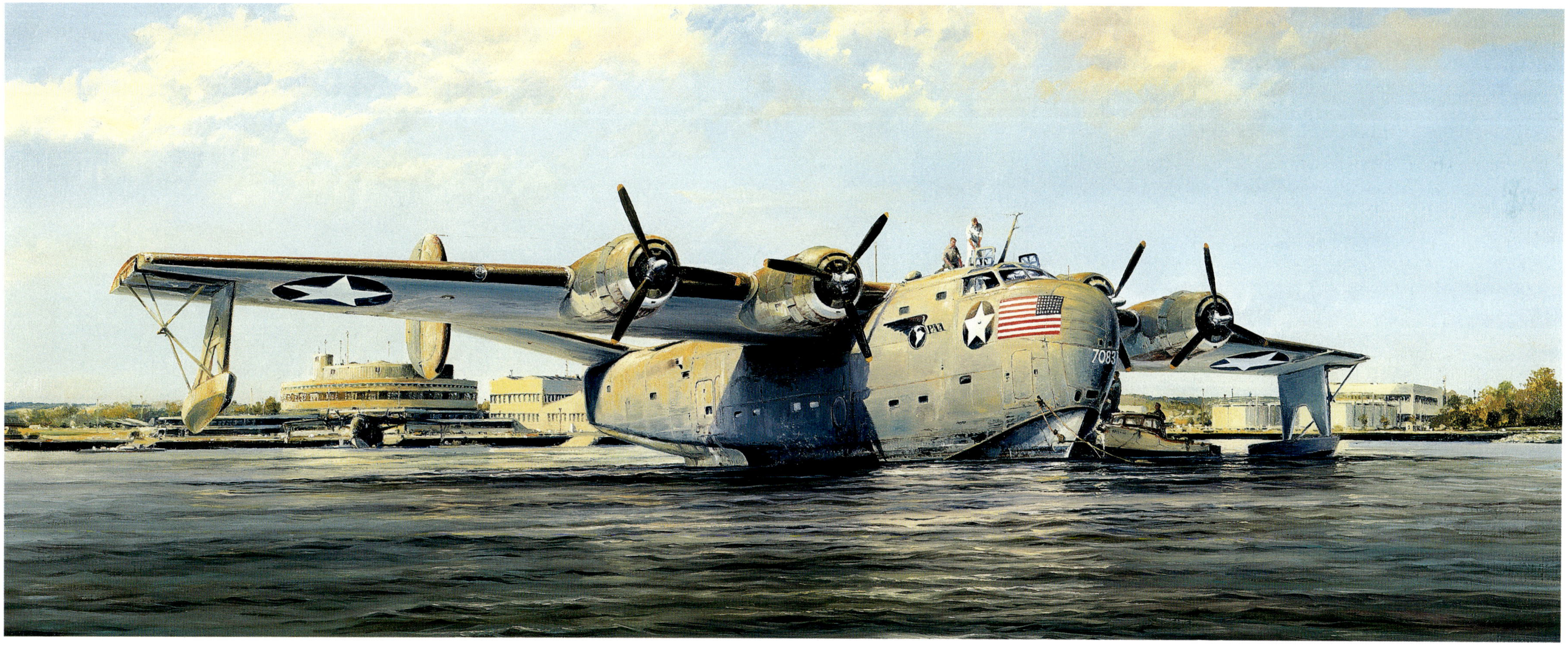

Arado 196A-3 reconnaissance floatplane.

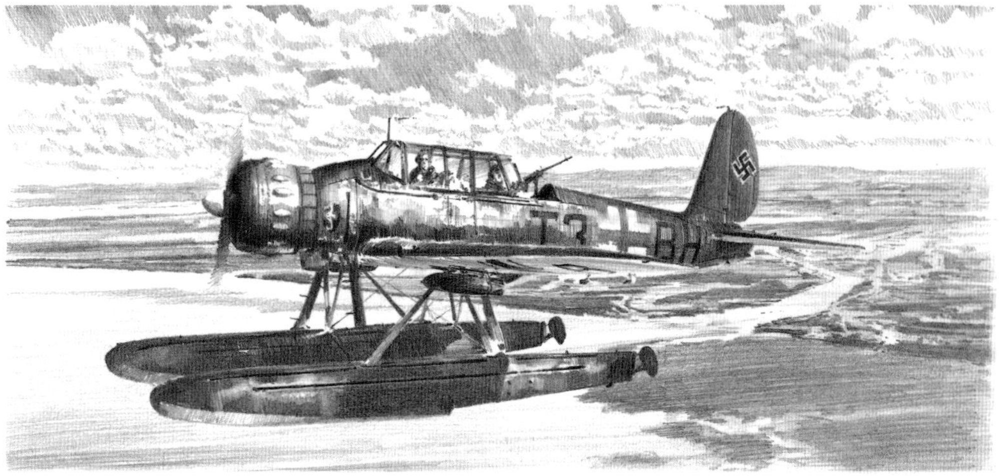

For some time I had wanted to paint a picture showing one of those famous wartime encounters between aircraft and submarine, my initial idea being to depict the scene looking down from the air. I made a number of drawings, but kept coming up with the same problem: the submarine always appeared so small in the picture. Because so little of a submarine actually appears above the surface, there wasn't much I could do about this problem – so I reversed the view, getting right down into the water alongside it.

The first drawing looking at the scenario from water level seemed to work well – a detail from that drawing appears on the previous spread – and although the aircraft seems at first glance to play second fiddle to the submarine, it is in fact the aircraft which tells the 'story' of the painting: a German U-boat, probably recharging her batteries, has been caught on the surface by a patrolling PBY Catalina; her gun crews are quickly into action and the survival of the ship now rests largely in their hands. The 3.7cm anti-aircraft gun is being hurriedly reloaded, while on the upper platform the two 2cm anti-aircraft twins take chunks out of the Catalina's tail, possibly inflicting enough damage to secure a respite from the attack. But have they gained enough time to batten down and dive to a safe depth below the waves? Will the PBY pilot risk another attack in a further bid to sink the U-boat? Those are questions I have left to the imagination of others.

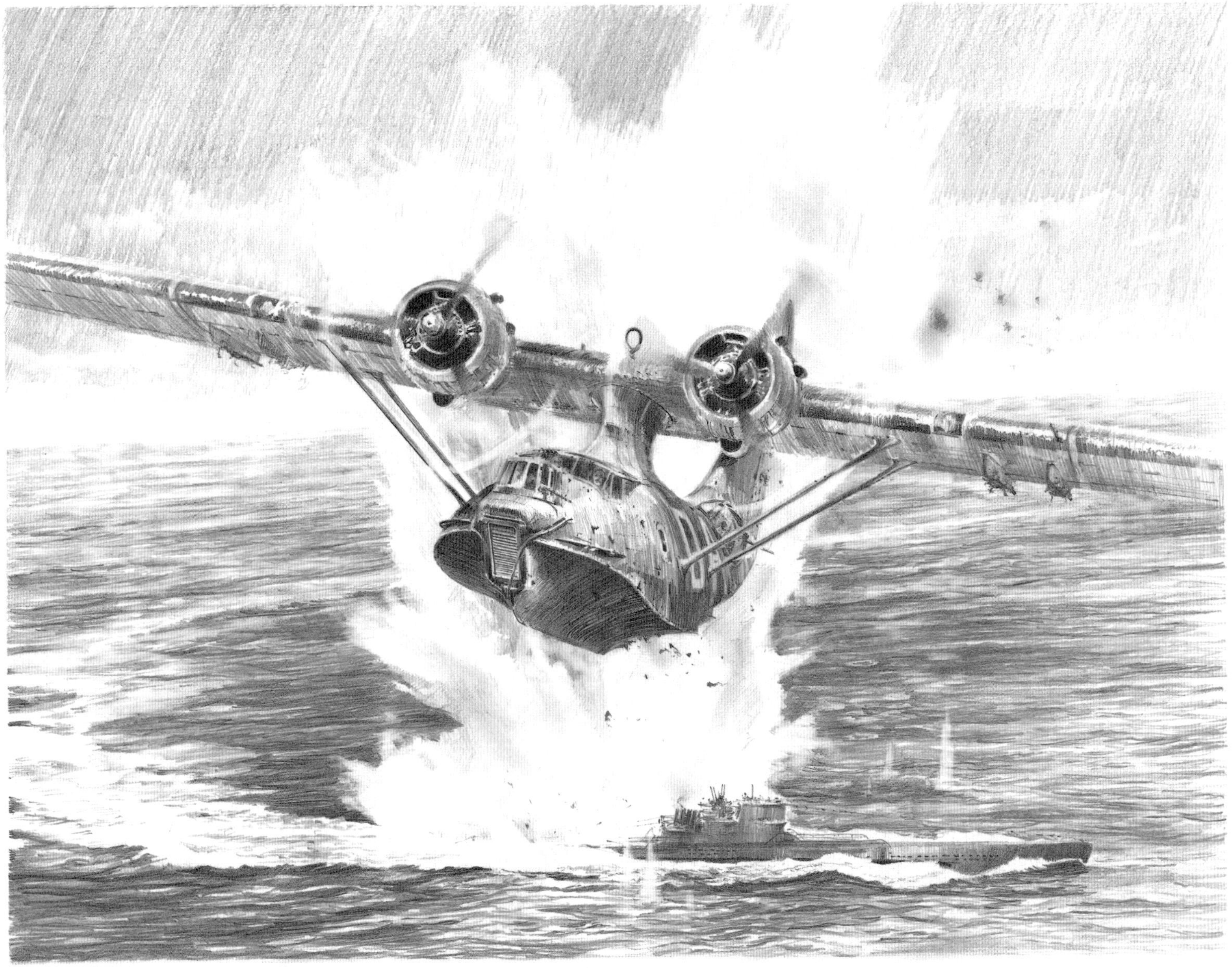

The U-boat is a type VIIc; she is on station in the eastern Atlantic just off the Straits of Gibraltar with orders to intercept and sink vital supply convoys heading into the Mediterranean. The PBY Catalina is from the Fleet Air Wing based at Port Lyautey in French Morocco. In common with the fighter pilots of the Luftwaffe, the German U-boat crews, particularly their captains, had the dubious honour of being expected to continue to serve their country without respite: they either continued to fight, or perished. Of the 1,150 U-boats placed in service, over half were lost during the 1939–45 conflict; but the measure of the fighting quality of the German submarine crews can be judged from Winston Churchill's immortal words : *'The only thing that ever really frightened me during the war was the U-boat peril.'*

As a marine craft, the submarine presents a unique aura that is fascinating and interesting to paint. Like the shark, it is the underwater hunter of the deep, evil in concept, deadly, frightening, yet in its own way both mysterious and beautiful.

The drawing at left shows the RAF Coastal Command Catalina flown by John Cruickshank sinking German U-boat U347 on 17 July 1944. Badly injured by gunfire, he nevertheless pressed home the attack, and for this act of bravery was awarded the VC.

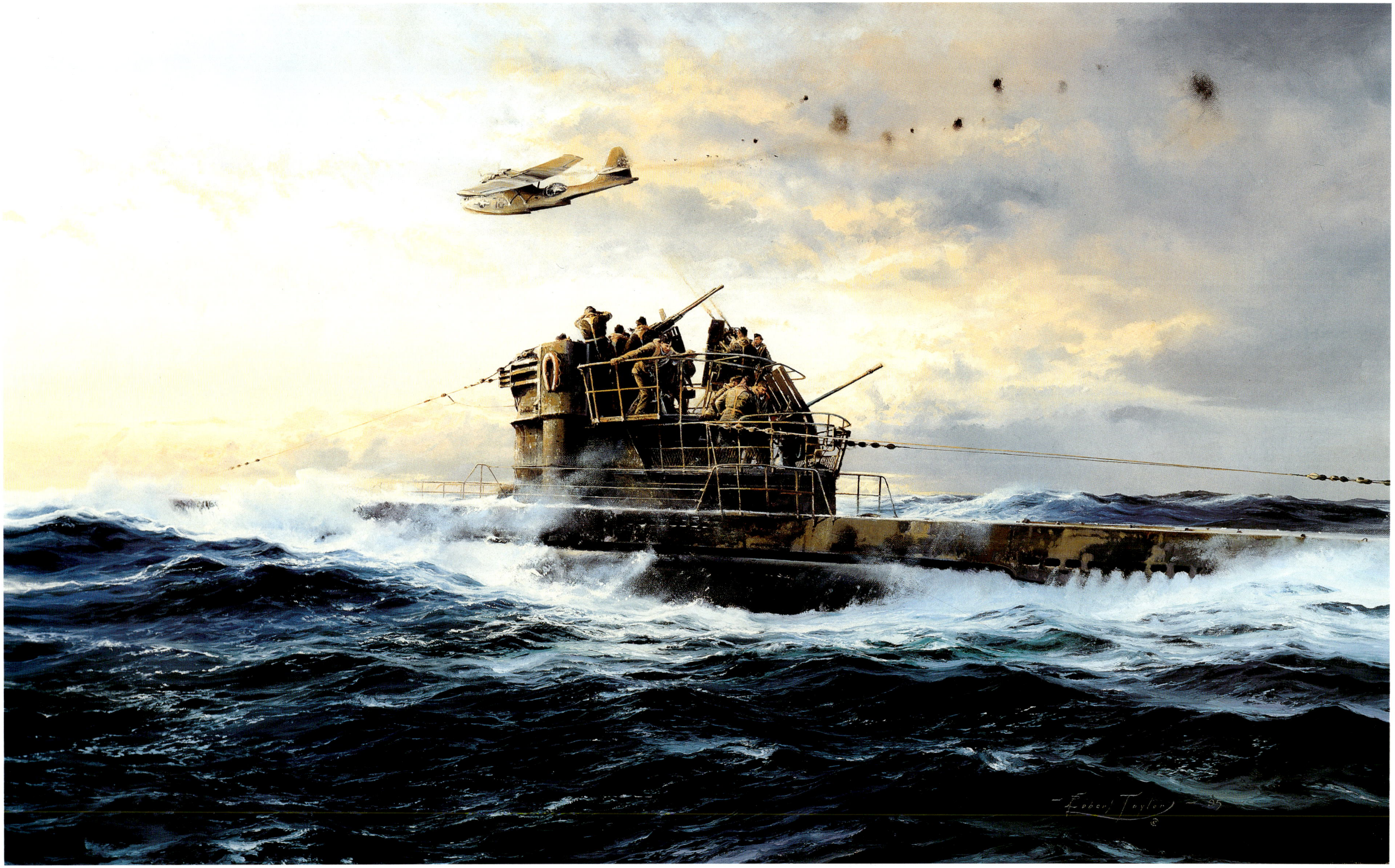

AGAINST ALL ODDS

In the collection of Mr Edgar Leicher

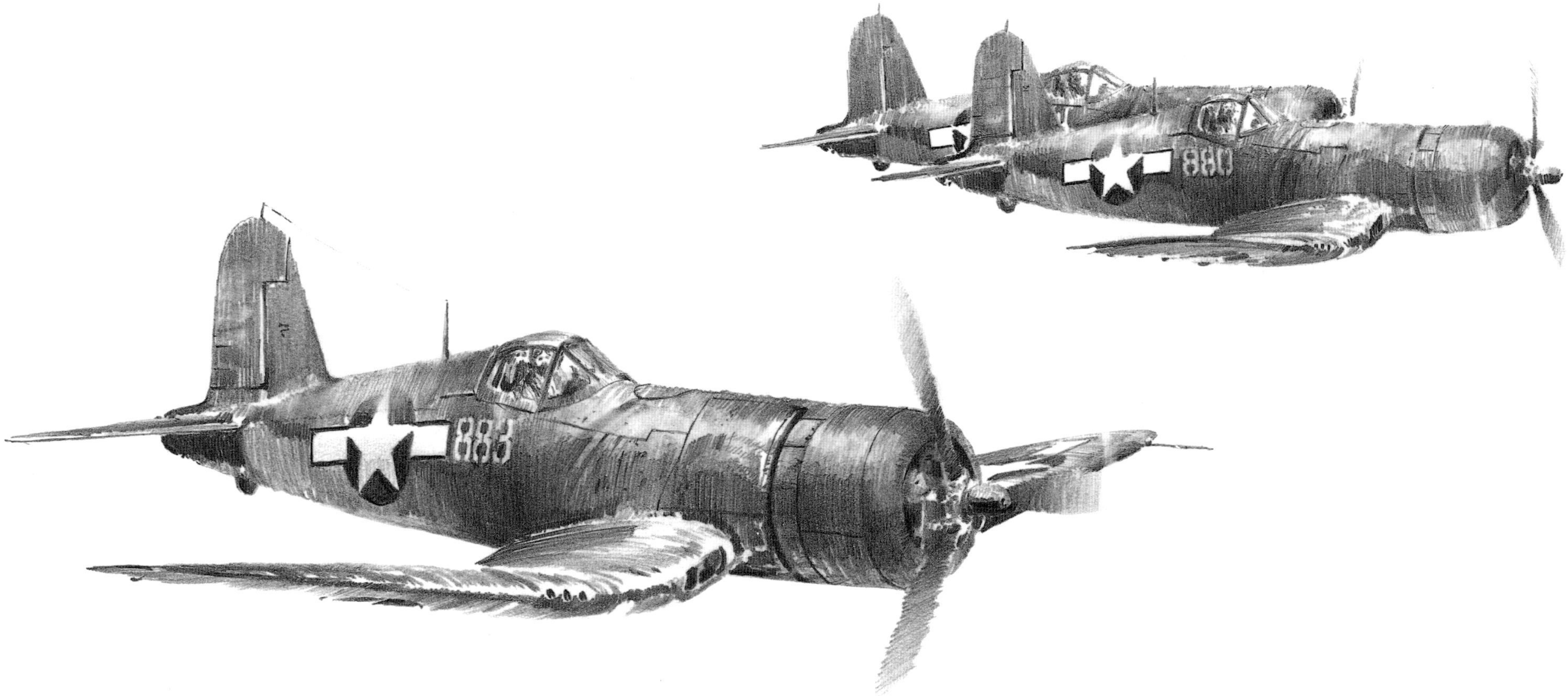

BEACH HEAD STRIKE FORCE

Some years ago a good friend of mine, Edgar Leicher, commissioned me to paint a maritime picture featuring Admiral Graf Spee's East Asia squadron. It depicted the German capital ships *Gneisenau, Scharnhorst, Dresden* and *Nurnberg* lying at anchor in a tropical bay off a Pacific island, the ships viewed from the beach. This painting became one of my favourite marine pictures, and when sketching ideas for *Beach Head Strike Force*, I came up with the idea of portraying a similar Pacific island bay as I imagined it may have appeared some forty years later.

For the scenario I chose to show F4U 1A Corsairs on a low-level strafing run during the Allied landings in the Marshall Islands in 1944. The island scene is largely accurate, although I added a few of my own touches to suit the composition; but whatever I changed can't have been of consequence because a US marine came up to me at a reception at Tamsen Munger's gallery in Fresno, California and said: 'Robert, I landed on that very beach. You've painted the island just as I remember it, except I think you've put in too many palm trees!' He then presented me with a piece of coral from the island which he'd picked up all those years ago.

Speaking of US marines, a Navy pilot once told me that the Corsair was so named with the marines in mind, the aircraft taking its name from a bunch of south sea pirates of an earlier era. He said he was certain that the manufacturers would not have had the Navy in mind when they came up with the name! The F4U was, of course, flown by both marine and Navy pilots. The Vought F4U Corsair was considered one of the best American fighters of World War II, and was generally accepted to have been the best carrier-borne fighter of the war. Although it did not enter service until early 1943, its pilots destroyed well over 2,000 enemy aircraft, achieving an astonishing 11–1 victory ratio.

The first carrier-borne Corsairs were operated by the British Royal Navy's Fleet Air Arm where they saw service with nineteen FAA squadrons, mostly in the Far East. But it was in the hands of the US Navy and marine pilots in the Pacific that this outstanding fighter made its greatest contribution to the Allied war effort. Having a maximum speed in excess of 400mph, a service ceiling of 37,000ft and armed with six machine guns, this fast, manoeuvrable single-seat fighter was a formidable opponent in any role its pilots chose.

For all its impressive performance record, however, it is an unusually shaped aircraft, and from the artist's point of view quite difficult to paint accurately from any angle where its distinctive gull-shaped wings show. But to my thinking, the more distinctive the shape of an aircraft the more it seems to take on a character of its own, and thus becomes more interesting to paint. So for me the Corsair is a great plane!

The drawing below shows the Royal Navy carrier HMS *Formidable* recovering Corsairs of 1841 Squadron following an attack against Japanese airfields and coastal shipping in July, 1945. HMS *Formidable* formed part of Admiral Halsey's 3rd Fleet which suffered so badly at the hands of the Kamikaze attacks, *Formidable* having to retire to Sydney, Australia for repairs. The main Corsair in the drawing is that of Lt Gray who later sank the 1000-ton Japanese destroyer *Amalasa* and was posthumously awarded the Victoria Cross.

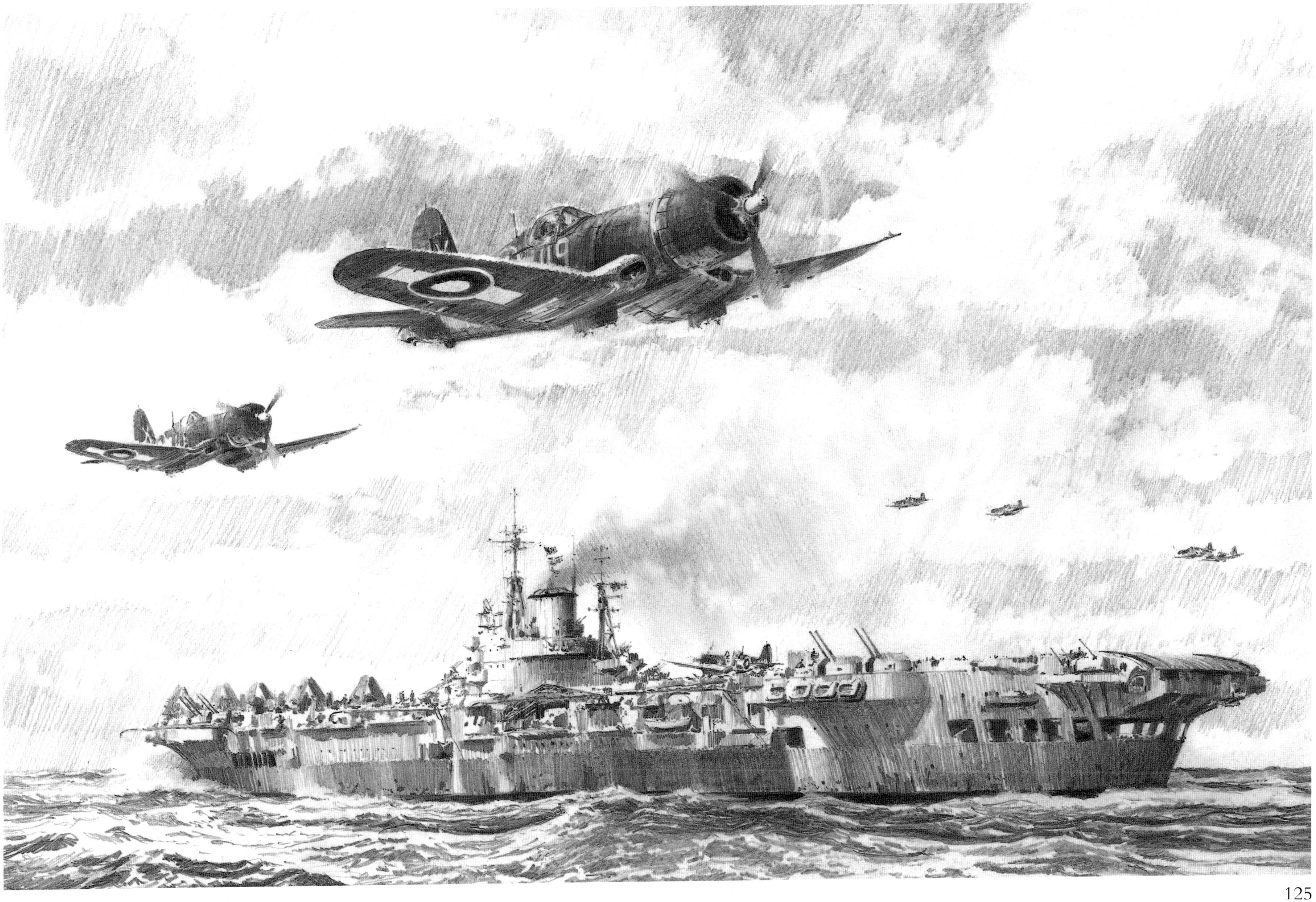

Painting any aircraft in flight viewed from ground level always presents the artist with an inordinate challenge, especially if that aircraft is to be depicted in decent size on the canvas. Although it is often difficult to find angles that show the aircraft to good advantage, the resulting composition offers more scope for secondary interest in the painting than a view high in the air. Furthermore, since most of us are not pilots, this aspect presents a view that most of us are familiar with: that is, looking up at an aircraft from beneath. The biggest challenge is to get the perspective right. It is all too easy to paint a landscape, then choose a nice angle for the airplane, then put the two together. But it cannot be done that way. If the height and size of the aircraft, and the angles and perspective are not exactly co-ordinated with the perspective of the landscape setting, the faults become apparent immediately, even to the uneducated eye.

Like all paintings of this ilk, I had my problems with the positioning of the aircraft in *Beach Head Strike Force*. To complicate the work even more I had selected the F4U Corsair: with its somewhat awkward gull-winged configuration never the easiest of aircraft to paint. It was my intention to feature the main F4U as low over the water as would be realistic, but I also wanted to show as much of the cockpit area and fuselage of the plane as was possible. Ideally I should have liked the main aircraft somewhat larger than it appears on the canvas, but the perspective dictated that this was not technically possible without showing too much of its underneath; I therefore had to keep pushing the F4U further and further back in the picture until the attitude was correct.

It was much easier to paint a nice view of the second F4U, since that extra distance, together with a tilt of the wings, allowed much more of the top of the plane to show. The steeply angled palm tree was added after both the main aircraft were completed in order to add more weight to the right side of the painting, and this was the last part of the painting to be completed.

I had toyed with several ideas about what to put on the beach as foreground interest. My initial thoughts were to show landing craft with troops coming ashore; I then tried some drawings of abandoned Japanese vehicles and equipment, but all of these had the effect of dominating the picture. I decided eventually to paint a crash-landed AM6 Zero, a victim of an earlier aerial contest, and this fell into the composition perfectly without detracting anything from the F4Us, being the main subject of the painting. I deliberately painted the Zero in a decaying state to indicate that its demise had come about some weeks, even months earlier; I felt this would be more interesting than to show a freshly downed fighter, besides which it was great fun to paint.

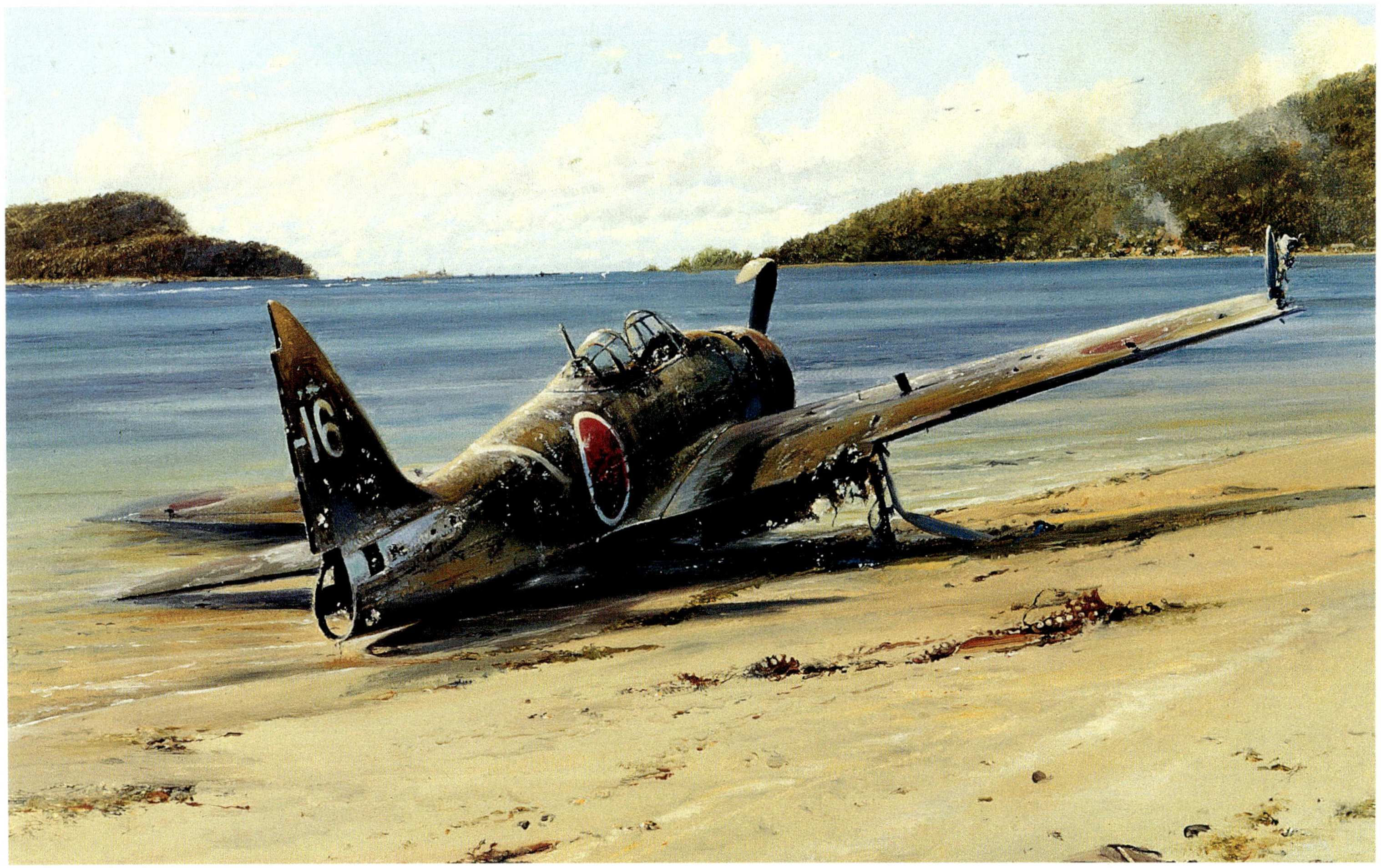

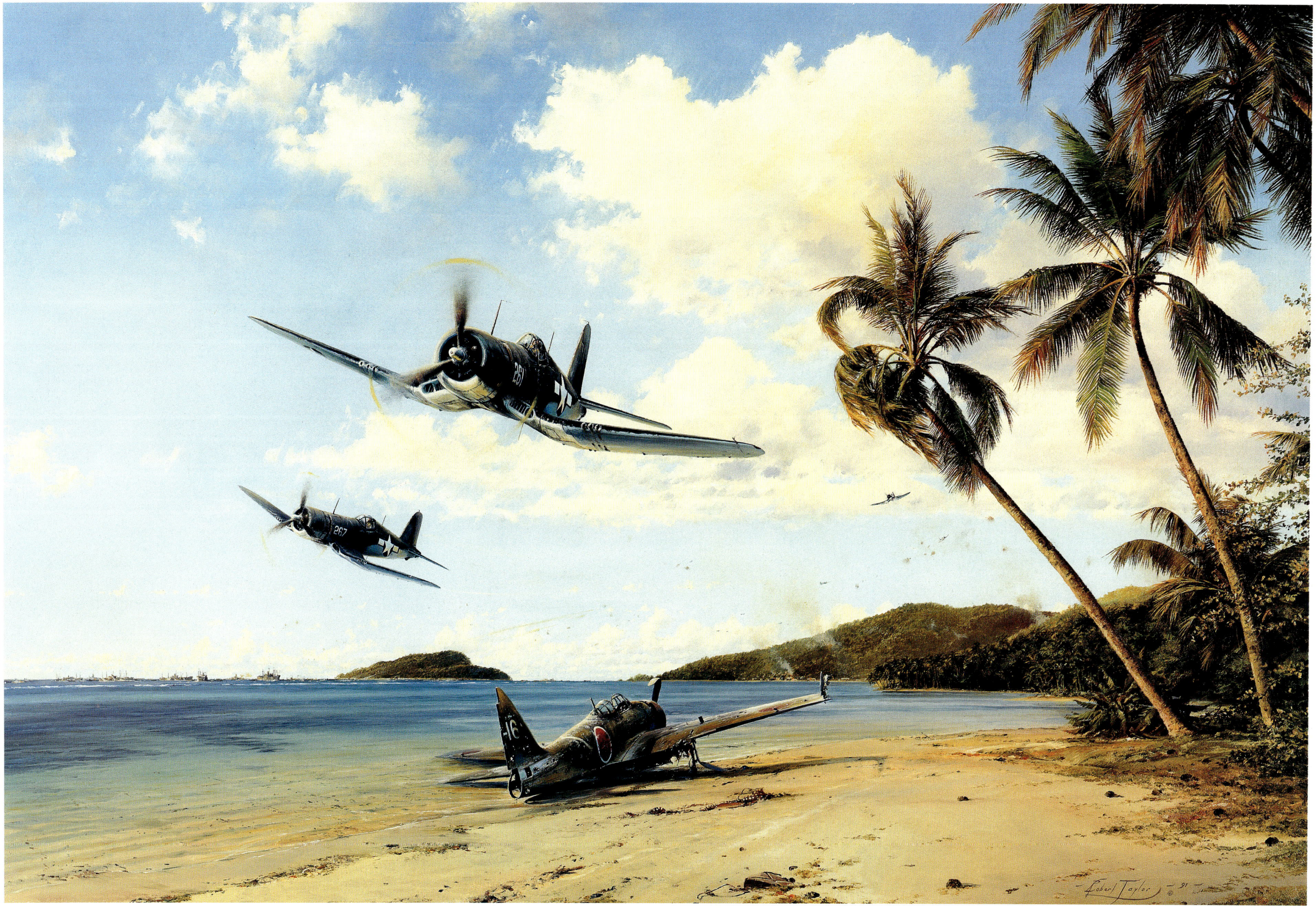

BEACH HEAD STRIKE FORCE

In the collection of Mr Eugene Eisenberg

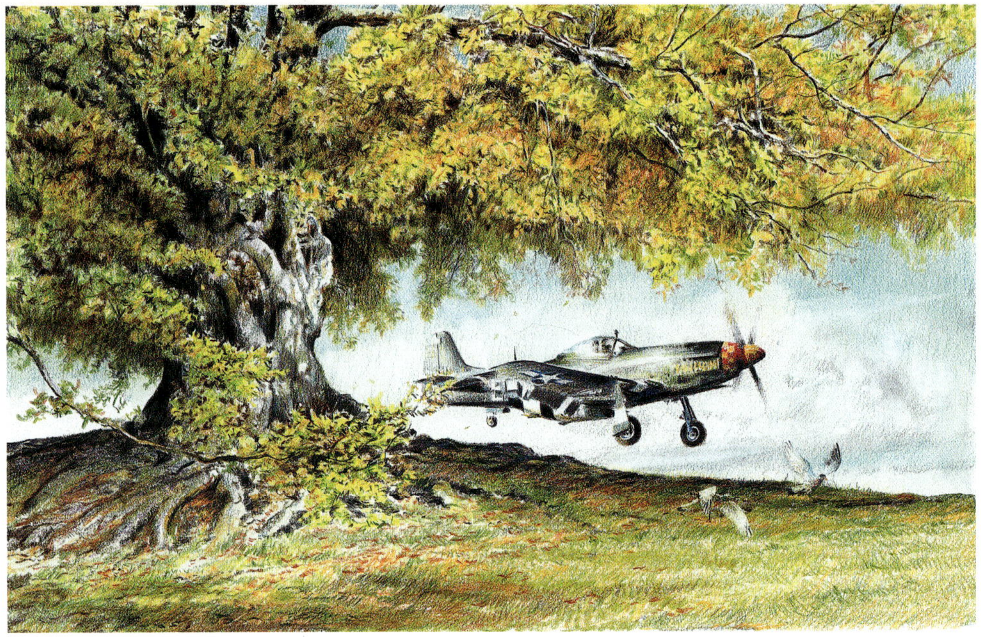

ACKNOWLEDGEMENTS

Until my first book of paintings was published back in 1987 I had no idea of the amount of work or the number of people it involved to produce such a volume. This is my third book of air combat paintings, and I am indeed fortunate that much the same team has helped me with its preparation as with previous volumes.

I am greatly honoured that Wing Commander Roland Beamont has written the foreword to this book. 'Bee' is one of the great aviators of our time. After flying combat throughout World War II, he became a household name as a test pilot, first flying such classics as the Canberra, the Lightning and the revolutionary but ill-fated TSR2. More recently he has made a name for himself as a writer on aeronautical subjects. I am proud to have known Bee for many years, and deeply appreciate his kind contribution to my book.

I am grateful to Charles Walker who has again written kind words about me, and I am indebted to him for his assistance in the writing of this book. Without his patience and guidance I would never have completed it.

My sincere thanks go also to Michael Craig who so skilfully designed the layout of the pages and positioned all the drawings and text to give the book such a pleasing appearance – so vital in an art book. I am very grateful also to Rosie Craig, who understands English better than most of us, and who proof-read all the text.

My thanks to Pat Barnard for overseeing the entire production, including editing the text, and also to Stephanie Roberts-Morgan for her skilful work on the computer. I would also like to take the opportunity to thank all the staff at my publishers, The Military Gallery, for their continuing support and effort on my behalf. One couldn't wish to work with a nicer, more friendly group of people, and it is largely due to their enthusiasm and encouragement that this book has come together.

I am grateful to John King, who photographs all my paintings in his studio in Bristol, for the fine quality of his work and for providing all the colour transparencies for this book.

It goes without saying that I am deeply appreciative of the continuing support of David & Charles, who have published all three of my books. Of particular value was their latitude in allowing me and others working on the design to have our way on so many issues concerning presentation. I want also to acknowledge the valuable contribution of David Porteous who co-ordinated all the production work with the same skill as he demonstrated with my previous books. He is a real professional.

I must express my sincere gratitude to the many people who so generously give me their time seeking out vital research material. My particular thanks in this respect go to Colonel Don Lopez, Helen McDonald at the Nimitz Museum, Major Jonathan Bywater, Colin Smith, Mike Sweet, Virginia Bader, Mike Shipperly, author Roger Freeman, internationally-known model-maker Peter Cook, defence consultant Paul Beaver, and the many others who have provided invaluable information for the paintings in this book.

Last, and perhaps most important of all, I want to acknowledge and thank all those wonderful people who have collected my paintings and prints over so many years, without whose support neither this, nor either of my previous books would ever have been published.

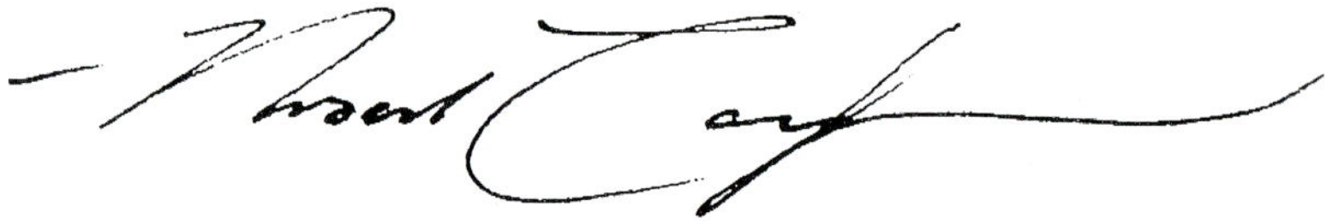

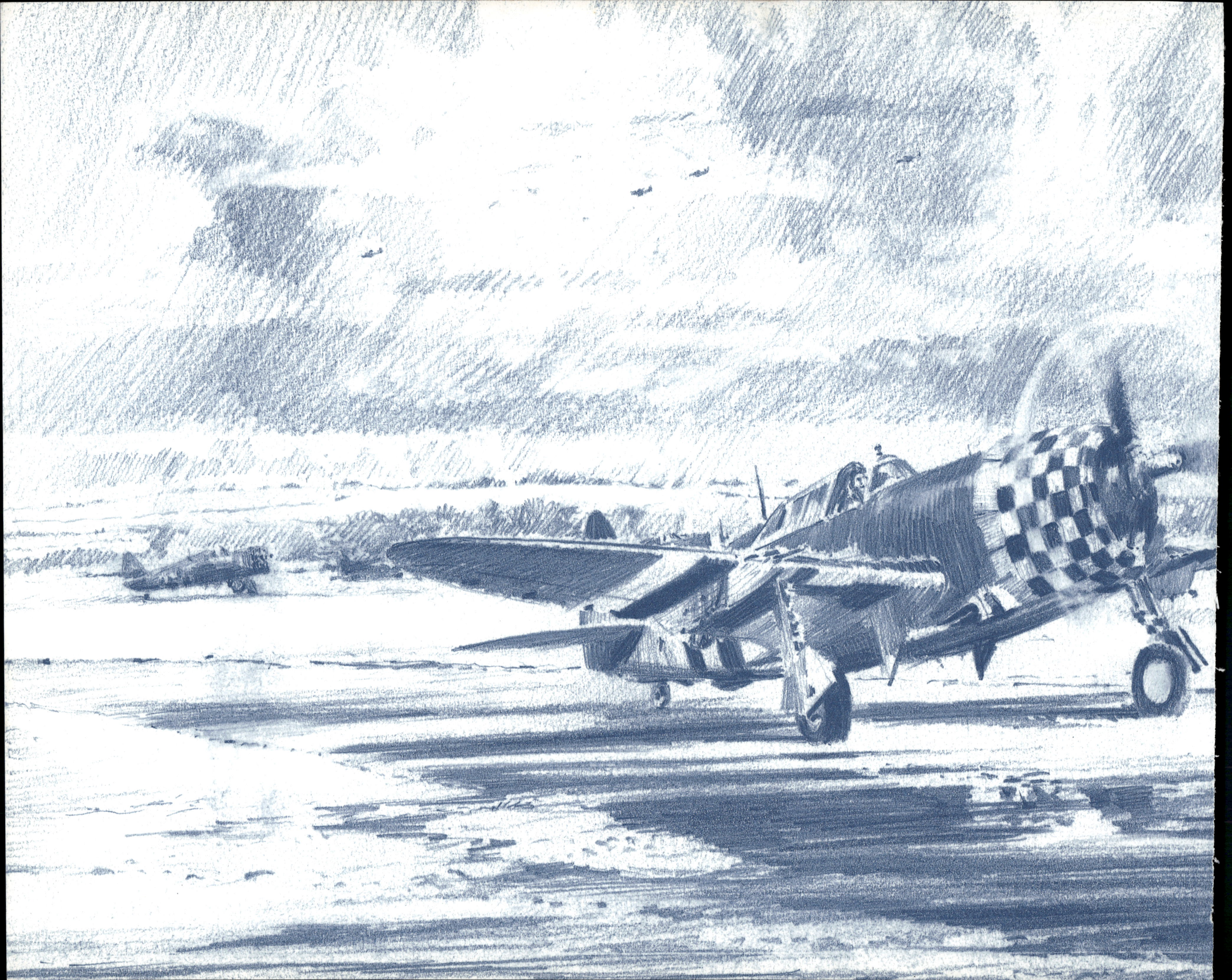